THE SCOTTISH MOUNTAINEERING CLUB JOURNAL

Vol. XLIII	2014	No. 205

EDITORIAL

THE TIME HAS COME for me to step down as Editor of the *Journal*. As is customary, this event allows me the opportunity to pen a few words before vacating the chair. When the late lamented Bill Brooker stood down in 1986 he remarked that, 'The pace of change seems to be increasing.' This continues to be the case today. Although Bill was largely referring to the changes that took place in the climbing world during his tenure, for me perhaps the most noticeable change in the last seven years has been in the way we communicate. Although one handwritten submission was made this year, the vast majority of material was sent by e-mail. Most of us now get our club newsletters by e-mail too. Digital images have largely replaced film, and many people use smart phones to take photographs now rather than purpose-built cameras.

There have been some significant changes to the appearance of the *Journal* as well. It was with some trepidation that I decided to change the font used for headings in the *Journal*. This seems to have been favourably received on the whole, though I have to say that one of my predecessors detests sans serif fonts and will never forgive me. The most noticeable change in the last few years, however, has been the use of integrated colour. This was resisted for a while, because of the extra expense, but the economics of printing have been changing too. Using colour in this way significantly increases the demands on the Editor's time, but the overall result seems worthwhile.

Another change that has been introduced has been in the date of the *Journal's* appearance. Trying to get the *Journal* out in the summer meant that the Editor was kept indoors in the springtime, which is often the best time of year in the Highlands. A later appearance allows the New Climbs Editor time to collect details of all the new routes of the previous winter as well as most of the early summer rock routes. Again this seems to have been favourably received on the whole. The target date is now for the *Journal* to appear in mid November. Unfortunately on a number of occasions during my watch the *Journal* has appeared much later than planned. This has usually been due to circumstances beyond my control, but I do plead guilty to being a 'just-in-timer' and when there have been problems in production there was no leeway.

Prior to my tenure the *Journal* had always been printed in Scotland. In my inaugral editorial I stated that 'It is not my intention to break with this tradition.' However, it eventually became apparent that we could no longer ignore the large cost savings we could make by having the *Journal* printed and bound abroad. The production of the *Journal* is by far the biggest item in our annual accounts. Last year we were able get the *Journal* printed in India for less than one third of the price at home. This experiment was not without its problems. We had been warned about the late appearance of the *Alpine Journal* and then suffered the same fate, due to a dock strike in Mumbai.

The Club guidebooks have been printed abroad for many years now. Despite the hiccups, it looks like the *Journal* will follow suit. The savings we will make by doing this mean that our subscriptions will not have to be increased for quite some time.

Is printing becoming old technology? It could be that in the not too distant future, the *Journal* will be sent to members in electronic form, maybe even direct to their interactive glasses!

The *Journal* is only as good as its contributors, and I thank everyone who has submitted material. I realise some find it rather intimidating to write for the *Journal*, but I would encourage you to be brazen. The more articles the Editor has to choose from the better.

A lot of people help the Editor behind the scenes and I thank them all for their invaluable assistance. The New Routes Editor, Photo Editor, Clerk of the List and several other regular contributors, bring together a lot of material in a well organised manner. The Editor could not function without them.

I do not wish to pre-empt the AGM decision, but I am sure the Committee's proposed successor will be a safe pair of hands. He has contributed articles to the *Journal* over many years and has done a sterling job of organising the book reviews. I wish him well. Who knows what changes he will oversee?

CUILLIN RIDGE TRAVERSE RECORD

By Finlay Wild

ON SATURDAY 12 OCTOBER 2013 I had one of the most memorable runs of my life to set a new Cuillin Ridge Traverse record of 2hrs 59mins 22secs. This traverse, in perfect running conditions, was my fourth of the year. I took in the 11 Munro summits, plus Sgùrr Theàrlaich and Bidein Druim nan Ràmh, and the four main 'climbing' sections (the T–D Gap; King's Chimney on Sgùrr MhicCoinnich; the Inaccessible Pinnacle; and Naismith's Route on the Basteir Tooth) as originally stipulated by Andy Hyslop in 1984. I started on Gars-bheinn at 12 noon and finished on Sgùrr nan Gillean at 2.59.22 p.m.

The first full traverse was completed by L.G. Shadbolt and A.C. McLaren in 1911 in 12hrs and 20mins, a respectable time that many would be happy with today. Dan Stewart recorded a time of 6hrs 45mins in 1950 and Eric Beard bettered this with 4hrs 9mins in the 1960s. These early traverses probably did not include Sgùrr Dubh Mòr and Eric Beard is not thought to have included the In Pinn. When Andy Hyslop set a new record of 4hrs 4mins in 1984 he stated exactly which tops he visited and ever since this has become the standard runners' traverse. In 1986 Stott and Davies were the first to go under four hours with 3hrs 49mins, and in 1990 Martin Moran bettered their time with 3hrs 33mins. In 1994 Andy Hyslop twice reclaimed the record with 3:32:50 and 3:32:15. Es Tresidder took a chunk off in 2007 with 3:17:28 where it stood until last year. The ridge is intricate and involves a large amount of exposed scrambling, and some short but crucial rock climbing sections (up to 'Severe' standard downclimbing). This, combined with the length and complexity of the terrain, means that a significant amount of prior reccying is normally desirable, and of course the weather has to be good too.

I first started 'Cuillin dreaming' eleven years ago when I completed my first full traverse. Apart from acknowledging the existing record as 'seriously fast' I didn't think much about it myself until I got into mountain running six years ago. In April 2012 I did my first solo traverse in interesting conditions (wind and horizontally blown snow going up the In Pinn!) in 5.5hrs which is when I first started to dare to think about how fast I could go. Between then and now I've also had many days of reccying various sections of the ridge, especially the middle section where there is lots of traversing just west of the crest where it really helps to know where you are aiming for. In May 2013 I was back and managed a little under 4hrs, the weather having deteriorated after the In Pinn. I wrote in my logbook at that time 'realisation traverse' – which as it turned out was correct as I was back in June with 3:10:30. As I've mentioned elsewhere, I decided it couldn't count as a new record due to a minor but important error where I summited Sgùrr MhicCoinnich but neglected to touch the cairn! As it turned out, this was ultimately a good mistake as it gave me the impetus to go back for my 3:14:58 record in damp misty conditions. I was fairly sure I could go at least ten minutes faster than this in good weather and living not far from Skye enabled me to take advantage of a perfect weather window for 2:59:22 in October last year. Records aside, these days exploring the Cuillin and running the ridge have been some of my best hill days ever.

The following account was written a few days after my fastest traverse on 12/10/13:

Last week I was chatting with friends and psych reached boiling point as we realised that conditions for the weekend were looking good. Very good. My dad, Roger Wild, was more than happy to accompany me for an attempt during this October weather window so we headed up to Glen Brittle on Friday. My previous fast traverses have started very early in the morning from a summit bivvy (Gars-bheinn or Sgùrr nan Eag) and this seemed a good strategy in summer to avoid both crowding and the full heat of the day. It also gave the legs a rest after the walk in. With much longer and colder nights in October this didn't seem the best strategy and we debated what to do – it was fair to assume that it wouldn't get too hot or too busy, and in fact a cold, long bivvy might not be the best preparation. I therefore opted to run in the middle of the day after a slow approach, and hoped I didn't run into snags at the T–D gap.

Saturday morning was clear and dry, with just a weak easterly wind. We walked up leisurely to Gars-bheinn and I got sorted out. Looking along the ridge it was clear this was going to be a brilliant day. Stags were roaring down in the glens. It was bone dry with perfect conditions and I was feeling fit. The view from that end of the ridge is one of my all time favourites – looking to the main Black Cuillin ridge, the lost brother Blàbheinn, the Red Cuillin, Loch Coruisk, Rum, Trotternish, Ben Nevis and beyond. I took it all in as once I started running there wouldn't be time for views.

Setting off I felt great. My last traverse (the 3:14:58 record) was done in the mist with quite a bit of damp rock. Today felt totally different, and quite a bit safer. I was four minutes ahead by Sgùrr Dubh Mòr, and headed to the T–D gap feeling good. I met some good friends who I knew were doing the ridge just before they started the abseil – good timing as it meant they weren't in the way! A quick hello and I was down and then up – I enjoyed the dry climbing. By Sgùrr MhicCoinnich I was over nine minutes ahead and knew it was going very well. I made a very deliberate effort to keep focussing on the next summit, and continually consulted the map in my head. Meanwhile I was picking up the familiar lines and shortcuts I have come to know well. As much as I could, I stuck to my previous fastest route. There were a few minor deviations – some

The author on Gars-bheinn, preparing to start, 12 October 2013. Photo: Roger Wild.

faster, some slower – but I think that is inevitable on a route this complex. I had my split times from my earlier 3:10:30 attempt (where in the heat of the moment I stupidly forgot that Sgùrr MhicCoinnich was a Munro summit and ran half a dozen metres from the cairn, so didn't count the record) and by the time 75mins had gone by (downclimbing the In Pinn) I was already ten minutes ahead of the 3:10:30 run split times. From here on, the chances of congestion problems were much less, and I knew that if I kept at it, the fabled 3-hour barrier could be in sight. But I had to focus, I had to keep the concentration and not make any mistakes. Somewhere on the traversing ground before Sgùrr a' Ghreadaidh the hip pocket zip broke on my light sac and my jelly babies were trapped – I fiddled while running for a while, then decided to break it for access. Chain eating of jelly babies continued. Some gels and water. I was running in a light baselayer and shorts, with a barely noticeable sac. It felt free and flowing. I knew the way so didn't have that jolting feeling of split second route choice decision making – but I had to focus. I couldn't make mistakes. Even after coming off Bidein Druim nan Ràmh onto easier ground there are many places where the terrain is still serious. For at least the last hour I was definitely chasing the sub-3, not in a crazed sprint but a persistent push. I had learnt this over many hill races and thought I had enough fuel in the tank. At Bruach na Frìthe things seemed a wee bit harder, maybe because I had pushed faster earlier on. I made a slight route error before Naismith's on the Basteir Tooth and went a bit low on the scree. Naismith's Route was and is my favourite part of the whole ridge. I got to the top of Am Basteir and had just over ten minutes to do it. I could get there. Push. More jelly babies. My route up Sgùrr nan Gillean could have been ten seconds shorter but it was OK, keep pushing. I was breathing hard and my knees were aching from all the high stepping. It didn't matter. The Window with a minute – keep going up the final small slab and there, to the summit, elated.

This time I knew I had done it. No doubts about summits touched, or route taken. I surveyed the ridge, counting off each top in the sunshine. I did some shouting. Some Fort William friends coincidentally arrived via the south east ridge and had to listen to my ecstatic chat. After I had taken it all in for half an hour, enjoying the view and sensation, I headed down to Glen Brittle. I found a better line for the descent to the Fairy Pools – you never stop learning in the Cuillin. I relaxed with a cup of tea. I relived a thousand memories of different handholds, technical sections, snatched views, and different weather conditions on this and previous traverses. I'm still Cuillin dreaming.

The author in Glen Brittle after the run. Photo:Roger Wild.

THE PATEY EXAM

By Henning Wackerhage

Part 1. The Patey exam

Tom Patey is a figurehead for Aberdeen-based climbers and needs no introduction in this journal. Once you break into the grade Vs you will sooner or later climb a long winter route by Tom Patey. Of the many Patey routes the long, remote grade V and VI Cairngorms routes stand out. At the time when I was getting used to grade Vs I became intrigued by the idea of trying three of the above Patey routes within one winter season: *Scorpion* V,5, *Eagle Ridge* VI,6 and *Mitre Ridge* V,6. Over time I increasingly saw these three routes as the Patey exam, set by him to test the new generation of Scottish winter climbers.

We started in 2009 when Ryan Slater and I, after much pre-season fitness training, climbed *Scorpion* on 3 January 2009. The late season névé was missing at the bottom and thus many sections required surprisingly hard mixed climbing. But the conditions higher up were favourable and we escaped without having one of the Scorpion top out epics that circulate among Scottish winter climbers. A good first exam answer although we topped out in the dark due to a late start and due to the length of the route.

Next was *Eagle Ridge*. Ryan could not make the day I had in mind but

Trias on Eagle Ridge. Photo: Henning Wackerhage.

luckily Trias, the finest winter climber from the Greek isle of Rhodes, had sent an e-mail earlier in the week looking for a partner for the first winter climb of the season. Trias hadn't heard of *Eagle Ridge* but after a drink or two in the DCA in Dundee we decided to attempt the ridge on 1 February 2009. We left Dundee early but still arrived behind two other teams. The ridge was caked in sometimes good, sometimes sugary névé. After waiting for the teams ahead we climbed the exposed tower but when I climbed the summer crux (the knife edge with the steep drop into Douglas Gibson gully) the light started to fade. By the time I had set belay and shouted 'climb when ready' it was dark. Unfortunately the batteries of Trias's headtorch were empty and so he had to 'work' the crux in the dark. After several attempts the rope went slack and Trias appeared at the belay. A last, easier pitch and we topped out into the cold night. The not quite full moon lightened up the scene for our long descent.

Time was running out for the last climb of the exam which was Mitre Ridge. However, wild and cold-enough conditions were forecast for the last weekend of March. Ryan, who had an excellent winter climbing season, was available. Because of the poor forecast we got up just after midnight on 28 March 2009 and started to cycle towards the Fairy Glen at 2 a.m. But it was snowing already and since we could not identify the path we were drifting through a snowy darkness for five long hours before dawn broke at 7 a.m. We ascended the Sneck where we were

Ryan during the failed attempt on Mitre Ridge. Photo: Henning Wackerhage.

greeted by an icy northerly. We reached the bottom of *Mitre Ridge* at 9 a.m. after a seven hour walk in. Unfortunately the northerly was of gale force and blowing up the ridge and we reluctantly decided not to start the climb. During the long walk out we went into vegetative mode and thought and spoke little. At times blizzards caused whiteouts which were particularly bad in the Fairy Glen. I remember falling down a powdery slope as I could not see any features. It was all soft but took some effort to plod back up the slope. When we left the Fairy Glen the situation suddenly changed and soon we rolled down the track in sunshine. A resit was needed.

In the following summer I met Robbie Miller and we climbed *Minus One Direct* on the Ben together. I soon talked Robbie into trying some winter climbing. He bought some ice axes and second hand crampons and quickly learned mixed techniques by drytooling at Newtyle. On 28 November 2009 the forecast suggested snow and sufficiently low temperatures for winter climbing and so we decided to try *Mitre Ridge* as Robbie's first winter climb. The early morning was frosty but there was no snow on the path and thus we could cycle all the way to the point where the path ascends to the Sneck. The snowline was just above and Garbh Choire was under deep powder with hardly any wind and temperatures around zero. Some of the climbing was quite hard due to the thick layer of powder but we climbed the chimney on the west flank, the crest of the ridge, splintered chimney and finally the two towers to the plateau before dusk. Both Robbie and I were elated since it was the best possible start for Robbie's winter climbing career and since the Patey exam was finally passed.

Part 2. Labyrinth Direct and More Vertigo

What next? Of the many quality Cairngorm routes *Labyrinth Direct* VII,6 and *Vertigo Wall* VII,7 stand out. *Labyrinth Direct* is the obvious gully and ice line on Creagh an Dubh Loch and was an early front pointing tour de force by Jim Bolton and Paul Arnold. In contrast, *Vertigo Wall* is Andy Nisbet's and Alfie Robertson's 1977 mixed climbing masterpiece, first climbed with a bivy and some aid. Andy Nisbet also freed the route with Andy Cunningham in 1985. And we were lucky: the best winter in recent years brought the Dubh Loch into condition in 2010. On 10 February 2010 Ross Hewitt and all climbed *Hanging Garden Route* V,4 followed by *Funeral Fall* IV,4 and we knew that the conditions were excellent.

The conditions remained good and ten days later I persuaded Dundee-based 'curly' Stevo Holmes and Robbie Miller to try *Labyrinth Direct*. I was sure that other Aberdonians would also go for it and so we kept quiet and got up at 4 a.m. and raced from Glen Clova over Broad Cairn to the bottom of the route. Soon after Ross Hewitt, Sandy Simpson and Neil Morrison arrived sans ice screws at the bottom of the Dubh Loch. 'Oh, hi

The author on Labyrinth Direct. Photo: Stevo Holmes.

Ross in the Hanging Garden. Photo: Henning Wackerhage.

Henning, what are you climbing?' 'Labyrinth Direct'. Robbie quickly climbed past the Hanging Garden to the start of the Labyrinth proper. First a tech 5 pitch to reach the cul de sac. All three of us spent some time to excavate some gear placements. Whilst it took a while it was worth it because we ended up with a belay made from many half decent to poor pieces of gear. Something would hold. And then the crux: step out onto the thin path of ice that bypasses the large ice umbrella and seems to end in the sky. I nervously placed my axes and front points and managed to place short ice screws on the 15m to the ice umbrella. There was a gap between the wall and the umbrella and I used it to lean against the ice for a nervous hands-free rest whilst trying not to move my front points. A few more moves and then some less steep ice to the semi-consolidated snow slopes below the cornice. Just when I managed to lean onto the cornice the rope went tight and I down climbed gingerly to the only piece of gear above the ice which I now used for the belay. First Robbie, then Stevo and finally I topped out being greeted by Ross who was very keen to borrow our ice screws for their successful attempt the next day.

When Ross and I climbed *Hanging Garden Route*, we first had a look at *Vertigo Wall* but the ice on the third pitch was not in condition. However, on 11 March 2011 Robbie Miller, Andrew Melvin and I saw plenty of ice on the crucial ice pitch and decided to attempt the route. *Vertigo Wall* is described as 'an outstanding mixed route with turf, rock and ice, near the summer line' in the SMC guide and this is what it looked. It was a wild day with constant snowfall and wind. Robbie quickly climbed the first pitch to a belay next to the large block which marks the belay. Pitch 2 is more turfy mixed climbing with some hard moves to a belay next to the ice. As Andrew Melvin had climbed ice routes such as *Astral Highway* on the Ben he was chosen as our man to open up the door to the upper wall via the third ice pitch.

He did well and since we had climbed the first three pitches quickly as a team of three we were optimistic. However, we then misread the guidebook: instead of climbing up and traversing right we thought we had to traverse left on ledges through an overhanging wall to climb up behind the prominent icicles. The new pitch started on thin ice without protection and it took some time until I reached thicker ice where I could place an ice screw. Some full body contact climbing to get established on the ledge and then finally good gear at the flake. The ledge became narrower and started to slope away but I managed to cam my right ice axe and got a good placement with the left and swung to just under that big ice fang. I chopped off some icicles so that they would not get in the way for the climb up to the belay. The icicles fell a long way.

Thankfully the turf was good and thus climbing up was easier than it looked. I climbed up to a good, exposed belay still more or less thinking that we were on route. Andrew and Robbie arrived wide eyed but when Robbie retreated from the 'easier but still steep' last pitch it dawned on us that we were on ground that had never been touched by an ice axe before. To our left was easier, turfier ground and we hoped that this would lead to *Sabretooth* without too much difficulty. Robbie climbed out of sight and quickly at first, but then the rope came back. When we arrived at the belay we saw that a left-slanting off-width had stopped his progress. The offwidth was hard to start as it was teflon-smooth inside and as there were only tiny edges for crampon placements on the outside. I managed an au cheval move but there was nothing to hook inside the chimney and after a lot of trying I cammed my lower leg into the off-width, andleant out wide to the left to gain a good hook in a crack near the arête on the left. I took a deep breath, uncammed my foot and swung left. Luckily there were another good hook and gear above. Some more tricky climbing to a spike and it all seemed to end maybe 10m below the plateau with a steep slab above an overhang. I managed to fix a peg and nut below the slab and got higher up on an arête to start the slab.

The slab was the scariest climbing I have ever done: thin hooks out of balance with no gear and the Central Gully Wall exposure below. Somehow I managed to inch up the slab to a position where a big tuft of

The author on the False Traverse of More Vertigo. Photo: Robbie Miller.

turf and safety were near but yet so far. Some moss did not even yield a marginal placement but finally I excavated a poor side pull, kept the axe steady, placed my front point out of balance high up and with a lot of stretch just about managed to whack the axe into the turf. The left axe followed and I made the sweetest pull-up of my life, scraped my feet up, ran a few steps, fell mentally and physically exhausted into the snow and shouted 'safe' into the void below. This last move was the psychological crux of the entire route and the last pitch was the hardest pitch that I have ever climbed. Robbie and Andrew topped out just before 7 p.m. We stayed roped up in Central Gully which we descended on the side to avoid windslab and after a long, long slog through deep snow we reached the cars at 11 p.m. And whilst this variation does not have the pure line that marks most Patey routes we found it to be a thorough exam of the Cairngorms winter climbing style.

[This article was submitted in 2011. The Hon. Ed. apologises for its late appearance.]

OPENING THE CHURCH DOOR

By Ian Taylor

OF ALL THE GREAT CRAGS of Glen Coe, Church Door Buttress is arguably the most enigmatic. Somehow even in this age when everything is known, it exudes an air of mystery. No one seems to have climbed there. Driving back to the Central Belt from the Clachaig with a car of inebriated passengers, you get the briefest longing glimpse up to the high crag. This is often followed by some slurred interest in a route called *Kingpin*, but somehow plans never come to sober fruition, for the crag is particularly slow to dry and the window of opportunity is very narrow.

Naturally the no-nonsense pioneering climbers didn't bother to wait for good summer conditions; indeed they didn't even wait for summer. The buttress was first considered worthy of attention by the Victorian climbers in the late 1800s and quickly became the original Last Great Problem.

The first attempt to climb the unnamed western buttress of Bidean nam Bian was by de facto Scot Norman Collie, along with guests from the English North, Godfrey Solly and Joseph Collier. During their spring 1894 campaign they poked around at the foot of the cliff and although unsuccessful they climbed *Collie's Pinnacle* as a consolation prize. They also had a good attempt at *Clachaig Gully*, getting over halfway, forty years before it was finally climbed. Training climbs done, the trio moved base camp round to Fort William, pointed their alpenstocks at Ben Nevis and made the first winter ascent of *Tower Ridge*. Collie was so impressed with *Tower Ridge* that he even repeated it the following day with his alpine partner Geoffrey Hastings.

The next reconnaissance was in July 1895 by SMC East Coast stalwarts, William Brown and William Tough. Even with the second ascent of *North-East Buttress* and the first of *North Buttress* on Buachaille Etive Mòr under their belts, they made little headway. Changing tack they inspected the buttress from above and, descending some distance from the top, they spotted a grass ledge that might be the key to reaching the top. At least now the buttress had a name:

> The buttress was christened the "Church-Door" by Mr Tough, from its appearance when seen end on, though it should be said that some think the resemblance fanciful.[1]

Eight months later a crack English team of Alpine Club members descended on Glen Coe. Walter Parry Haskett Smith, Geoffrey Hastings

---

1 J.H. Bell, 'The "Church-Door" buttress on Bidean nam Bian', *SMCJ*, 5/27 (1898), 135–40.

Opposite: Church Door Buttress and Collie's Pinnacle. Photo: Hon. Ed.

and Hubert Bowen perhaps hoped to pluck the plum from under the Scots' noses, but their attempt failed. Haskett Smith was an interesting character. He once held an unofficial world record for the long jump of 25.2 feet and was one of the first British climbers to pursue rock climbing for its own sake, rather than as training for the Alps. In his early days he eschewed ropes, considering them as aids required by inferior climbers. According to the visitors' book from the Clachaig Hotel they were sanguine that the climb would go in the best weather.[2]

There's nothing like a series of failed attempts to spark interest and Church Door Buttress became a subject much discussed in the Victorian smoke rooms.

> ...two monster buttresses... form the crown of Bidean's highest peak. There the possible climbs are likely to be few in number, and probably very difficult, especially on the right hand one, which, when scaled and written up, will be one of the finest things in first ascents that this Journal has chronicled.[3]

The SMC were back to the fore in September 1896. John Hart Bell was a keen prospector of new routes and had heard about the buttress from Tough. Bell with John Napier, Robert Napier and Edward Green made excellent progress. In fact on their first day, whilst shrouded in thick mist, they thought they had been successful and it was only on their descent as the clag lifted that they realised that they had actually climbed Stob Coire nam Beith by mistake. The following morning despite a snowstorm, peer pressure made them rope up with Green in the lead. Green, a sturdy Glasgow engineer, cracked the lower section, squeezing up cracks and awkward corners to gain the jumbled mass of huge boulders that form the Arch of the buttress. Here the party tried several alternatives, but were eventually beaten by snow-covered moss, slabs and chimneys.

The following year John Napier returned for another attempt, this time accompanied by one Harold Raeburn on his first visit to Glen Coe. After cycling all the way from Bridge of Orchy to the Clachaig into the teeth of a westerly gale, they woke up the following day to more rain, sleet and hail. Even with Napier's knowledge of the route, they were quickly defeated and had to be content with an ascent of the Victorian classic *Ossian's Cave*.[4]

A further Bell and Raeburn probe took place at Easter 1898 in the now ubiquitous bad weather. Due to the route being snow-plastered they concentrated their efforts on more inspection from above. Aided by a rope, Bell managed to make his way down to the grass ledge that Tough

2   Visitors' Book Clachaig Hotel (Aug 30 1889–May 7 1904). Transcribed by Stuart Pedlar.

3   William Brown, 'Climbing in Glencoe', *SMCJ,* 4/19 (1896), 48–51.

4   H. Raeburn, 'A Wet Day in Glencoe', *SMCJ,* 5/25 (1898), 24–8.

*Robbie Miller wades
up deep snow to the
start of Crypt Route,
November 2010.*

*Photo: Henning
Wackerhage.*

had spied three years before. A chimney below the ledge was the key to
the route, as Bell had considered it on his previous snowy attempt. Now
they had the whole climb worked out and all they needed was a day of
good conditions.

The sun came out in July the same year and a large SMC company
gathered to find the rocks nearly dry. Bell, Raeburn, Robert Napier, and
Herbert Boyd made up the summit team with William Douglas and
George Parker spectating and cheering. Bell quickly led the party to
below the crux chimney, then Raeburn took over. After a couple of false
starts, including an attempt to engineer a running belay using a ball of

string, Raeburn removed his boots and successfully ascended the exposed chimney. It wasn't long before the party reached the top and the lengthy campaign was finally over. Raeburn went on to become the finest Scottish climber of his era, adding landmark ascents all over Scotland. Bell also pioneered the classic *Great Ridge* on Garbh Bheinn and a number of routes on Ben Nevis.

The Church Door climb (later christened *Flake Route* by Murray[5]) had several repeats over the next few years, with the second ascent going to gritstone legend James Puttrell and the Abraham brothers of Keswick a couple of days after their infamous ascent of *Crowberry Ridge*. George Abraham noted that the climb should be strongly recommended and thought that 'a man who can lead safely up Moss Ghyll on Scawfell would not visit the Church Door in vain.'[6]

The First World War effectively stopped exploratory climbing in the Scottish mountains and in the period immediately after there appeared to be little desire for such risky endeavours. The English scene seemed to recover more quickly and soon there were raiders from south of the border.

In 1920 Fred Pigott, Morley Wood and John Wilding, from Manchester's Rucksack Club, made a low key ascent of *Crypt Route*, burrowing through the gloom to pop out below Raeburn's chimney. Despite a misshapen hand caused by a war wound and a temporary interest in golf, Pigott was one of the leading English climbers of the 1920s and '30s. After serving an apprenticeship on his local gritstone outcrops and usually accompanied by Wood, he progressed to adding new mountain routes from Skye to Wales, including some significant breakthroughs on Clogwyn Du'r Arddu. Pigott was described as being slim and wiry so presumably had no trouble with the *Crypt Route* squeezes, while Wood was much broader and might have struggled, as would many in the years to come.

The legendary Bill Murray led a repeat of this route in 1938, but was unaware of the early ascent. He described one of the route's dark chambers as 'not unlike the king's tomb in the heart of the Great Pyramid, but smaller'.[7] Around the same time Murray, with Kenneth Dunn and George Marskell, also added *West Face Route*, a steeper right-hand start to *Flake Route*.

In 1955 Len Lovat and Alan Dick put up *West Chimney* up the obvious vegetated line bordering the much steeper west face. It was another route that depended on tunnelling techniques and although it has probably had few summer repeats it has become a popular winter climb.

Fast forward to 1968 when local climbers John Hardie and Wull

5   W.H. Murray, *Rock Climbs: Glencoe and Ardgour*, (Edinburgh: SMC, 1949).

6   G.D. Abraham, *British Mountain Climbs*, (London: Mills & Boon, 1909).

7   W.H. Murray, *Mountaineering in Scotland*, (London: Dent, 1947).

The West Face of Church Door Buttress in evening light. Photo: Ian Taylor.

Thomson pulled out all the stops with *Kingpin* (E3,6a), the first route to tackle the futuristic west face. These two local climbers, who had worked with MacInnes in the Glencoe School of Mountaineering, were a strong team. Thomson had made an early ascent of *Shibboleth* with the *True Finish*, remarkably climbing it in big boots. Prior to *Kingpin* they had added *Crack-line*, a steep line left of *Crypt Route*, and *Inquisition*, an enigmatic route on the far right that has never been properly identified. Their inspired ascent of *Kingpin* was probably the highest major climb in the country at the time and understandably used a handful of aid pegs. A few years later Ian Nicholson and Dave Knowles managed to whittle the aid down to two points, triumphantly waving a couple of removed pegs under the noses of Thomson and Hardie in the Clachaig that evening.[8] Thomson and Hardie also attempted some of the other futuristic lines on the crag, including getting high on the line that subsequently became *Lost Arrow*.

By the mid '70s a new era had dawned. Changing attitudes to aid were backed up by better equipment, improved protection, training on indoor walls and chalk. A group of young Scottish climbers embraced the ethic and soon the 'free the Coe' campaign was in full swing. Murray Hamilton managed to free the aid on *Kingpin*, but was unlucky as bad weather prevented a complete ascent. That fell a little later to two other climbers from the new wave, Dave Cuthbertson and Dougie Mullin. However, Hamilton deserves recognition for breaking the barrier and he returned at a later date with Rab Anderson to add a better, direct finish to the route.

The '80s were the time for the big unclimbed lines on the Scottish mountains, helped by some dry summers and a more vigorous approach, including pre-cleaning on abseil. Pre-eminent in this approach was Lakeland raider Pete Whillance, who was already known for his string of bold routes all over the country. Whillance had a very friendly tit for tat rivalry going on with the Edinburgh team of Hamilton and Anderson. Freely exchanging information and often joining together, they ticked a fine series of major new routes on Creag an Dubh Loch during 1982. This informal understanding slipped briefly in 1983 when Hamilton, Anderson and Kenny Spence climbed *Flodden*, a line Whillance had been eyeing up. So two days later Whillance, with Ray Parker on board, headed up to Glen Coe, walked up to Church Door Buttress by headtorch and bivvied under the cliff. Whillance had never been to the crag before, but knew Hamilton and others had previously attempted the big groove line right of *Kingpin*, but had been stopped by a blank section of groove in the lower part. After a clean on abseil, the first ascent went smoothly, with Whillance solving the problematic section by skirting around it using the left arête. The significance of the route name clearly had as much to do with the unwritten part of the title – *(Raiders of) The Lost Ark* (E4,6a). They must have been fit, as they then hurried down to their car,

8   D.A. Knowles, 'Kingpin: A Second Ascent', *SMCJ*, 29/162 (1971), 372–3.

Tess Fryer cleans her way up Temple of Doom (E3,6a), 30 July 2011. Photo: Ian Taylor.

drove round to the Cairngorms, where they walked into Shelter Stone Crag in the afternoon and dispatched the first ascent of *The Harp*. Then if that wasn't enough Whillance teamed up with Hamilton at Creag an Dubh Loch the following morning where they put up *Masque*. Three new routes on three major cliffs in 24 hours. Not bad really!

The line right of *The Lost Ark* was next on everyone's list. First up were ex-pats Kev Howett and Mark Charlton in 1983. Howett managed to on-sight the crux first pitch, cleaning the mossy cracks as he went, whilst Charlton got very high on the second pitch before lichen and darkness ended their attempt. The following year, after a brush on abseil, Hamilton, Anderson and Graham Livingstone promptly dispatched *Temple of Doom* (E3,6a) leaving behind a brilliant classic. A few years later Anderson and Jonny May also completed *The Last Crusade* (E3,5c) over on the right side of the crag.

In the scorching summer of 1995 Gary Latter and Paul Thorburn made good use of the amazing dry conditions. That year Latter, a very enthusiastic new router, added more than fifty routes to crags all over the Highlands, culminating in the ascent of *Dalriada* on the Cobbler. At the time Thorburn had an ambition to have made the first ascent of the hardest route on all the major Scottish mountain crags. Rumour had it that he couldn't swim, ride a bike or drive a car, but could climb E7.

After a quick clean on abseil this powerful combination first climbed *The Holy Grail* (E5,6b), a direct start to *Temple of Doom* that is still one of the hardest pitches on the crag. Only two days later they returned and added *Lost Arrow* (E3,6a), the much attempted line left of *Kingpin*. The second pitch of *Lost Arrow* is particularly good on immaculate rock, but all other attempts had failed on the dirty and loose top pitch. Thorburn managed to lead this on-sight, pulling off carpets of moss and trundling loose blocks as he inched his way up the narrow chimney.

In 2002 Latter and Pete Craig climbed *Fundamentalists* (E4,6a), a route on the far left of the main face. Pete along with his brother Neil had ticked his way through many of the big Scottish rock routes with little fuss. The pair were lucky with the weather and *Fundamentalists* was climbed above a stunning cloud inversion. Unfortunately the second pitch has been reclaimed by the moss, but the testing third pitch can still be accessed via *Lost Arrow*.

Looking into a damp and murky crystal ball there are still good new challenges awaiting future generations of climbers, providing they can stomach the long approach and the fickle conditions.

Two modern climbers that fit the bill are Iain Small and Blair Fyffe. After a colossal cleaning effort by Small in July 2014, they added an impressive new route which starts up *Kingpin* before branching left and taking a subtle line up grooves and bold walls to finish spectacularly through the capping roof. *Wall of the Evening Light* (E6,6b) is yet another route to dream about while we wait for those long hot summers that are just around the corner.

Blair Fyffe nears the top of pitch 1 of Wall of the Evening Light on the first ascent. Photo: Iain Small.

Iain Small pulls through the crux roof of Wall of the Evening Light. Photo: Blair Fyffe.

JOHN MUIR AND THE SMC

By Robert Aitken

THIS YEAR HAS WITNESSED a good deal of activity across Scotland in celebration of the centenary of the death of John Muir. Born in Dunbar in 1838, Muir emigrated with his family to Wisconsin in 1849. After a harsh upbringing on the land, an eclectic education, and extensive picaresque wanderings from Canada to the Gulf of Mexico, he found his life purpose in passionate devotion to wilderness in the Sierra Nevada of California. A largely self-taught naturalist and geologist, a bold if unconventional explorer and mountaineer[1], a hugely effective writer and propagandist, Muir is credited among much else with saving Yosemite, founding the US National Parks, and establishing the Sierra Club. John Muir is a major figure in the world conservation movement, enjoying the status of something like a secular saint in the United States.[2]

Be that as it may, for at least 50 years after his death Muir's achievements – indeed his existence – went almost entirely unrecognised in Scotland. Visiting Americans were dismayed to find that Muir's birthplace in Dunbar was so little cherished that it stood at risk of becoming a chip shop. The charismatic Frank Tindall, County Planning Officer for East Lothian, did a good deal, virtually single-handed, to fan the flickering flame of interest and recognition for Muir from the 1970s on. The emergence of the John Muir Trust for the conservation of wild land in the UK, the publication in Scottish editions of Muir's writings, the restoration of his birthplace as a high-quality museum and interpretive centre, have gradually ensured a growing awareness of the significance of the man. Now in 2014 we even have a John Muir Way across Central Scotland, astonishing though that might be to 'John of the Wilderness'.[3]

1 Ted Peck offers an entertaining evaluation of Muir's climbing career in 'John Muir, Mountaineer', Section 9, pp898–907 of 'John Muir as others saw him', **in** Gifford, Terry (ed.) *John Muir: his life and letters and other writings*, London: Bâton Wicks, 1996.

2 For interested members, there is a vast biographical and critical literature on Muir, the most recent full biography being Donald Worster's *A passion for nature: the life of John Muir*, Oxford: OUP, 2008. A readable biographical summary is provided in the Rucksack Reader guide to the new John Muir Way, reviewed elsewhere in this issue of the *Journal*.
Muir's own major writings and other materials are conveniently available in the Diadem/Bâton Wicks tomes *John Muir: The Eight Wilderness Discovery Books* (1992) and *John Muir: His Life and Letters and Other Writings* (1996).

3 A helpful if not quite comprehensive account of Muir's neglect and rediscovery in his native land was compiled by Graham White in 1997: 'The rediscovery of Muir in Scotland', ppxxi–iv in Turner, Frederick *John Muir: from Scotland to the Sierra*, Edinburgh: Canongate.

John Muir, October 1913. Photo: Herbert W. Gleason, Boston Massachusetts.

But even though a high proportion of past and present SMC members may have shared the common lack of awareness of John Muir, the Club to its eternal credit was well to the fore in recognising him, by conferring Honorary Membership upon Muir during his own lifetime, in 1908. This distinction – still surprising information to many current Club members – was probably due largely if not entirely to the initiative of John Rennie, President from 1904 to 1907.[4] I suspect it was something of a crusade based on admiring personal acquaintance, since it's clear from Rennie's warm obituary for Muir in the Journal that they had met, perhaps more than once, at Muir's house in Martinez by San Francisco Bay.[5] Rennie may have used his Presidential authority to advance the nomination of his friend, a tactic reportedly not entirely unknown to some of his successors in post.

The Rennie family had been farmers on the south slope of the Kilsyth Hills before moving into coal mining, which proved sufficiently lucrative to allow John Rennie to live a life of leisure in Helensburgh with his widowed mother and two sisters. His two younger brothers, however, emigrated to California, where John visited them several times from 1888 onwards. His younger brother James became an active member of the Sierra Club when it was formed in 1892, taking part in the first ascent of several minor Sierra bumps, and earning the engaging sobriquet of 'the durable Scot'[6].

So it's not surprising that in his Journal obituary for John Muir, Rennie stresses his distinction as President of the Sierra Club, and praises his passion for the Sierra and its conservation. I suppose there may conceivably have been some concern among SMCers of the time that awarding Honorary Membership to Muir might align the Club with the

---

4   Rennie (1858–1937) was an original member of the Club. His 'retrospective' application for membership – OMs were not required to submit applications, but a number did – shows only a very thin record of Scottish hillwalking, with one tourist visit to Yosemite in 1888; and he had to be rescued by J H Gibson from an involuntary glissade on Cruachan at the Easter Meet of 1891 (*SMCJ* 1/5 (1891) p239). However, he was with Douglas and King on a traverse of the Meije in 1899 (*SMCJ* 6/32 (1900) p34) and with Raeburn and Ling on their first attempt on Observatory Buttress on Nevis in 1901 (*SMCJ* 6/36 (1901) p249), so he had evidently shifted some considerable way along the spectrum towards the Ultramontane. His obituary in the *Journal* by the usually precise Maylard (*SMCJ* 21/124 (1937) p277), strongly suggesting that Rennie was no more than one of the genial 'gentleman supporters' at the Club's foundation, and that he had gained the Presidency merely by his clubbable good nature, appears seriously to understate Rennie's climbing abilities. However Maylard was himself 82 when he wrote that obituary, so we can perhaps forgive him.

5   Rennie, J. (1915) 'In memoriam: John Muir', *SMCJ* 13/76 (February 1915) pp206–7.

6   Farquhar, Francis P. (1965) *History of the Sierra Nevada*, Berkeley: Univ. of California Press, p229.

John Muir with a Sierra Club Outing on the trail to Hetch Hetchy, 1909.
Photo: George R King, (c) Muir-Hanna Trust, University of the Pacific Library.

conservation objectives and activity of the Sierra Club, which began life as notionally a mountaineering club to promote knowledge and appreciation of the Sierra, but has metamorphosed into the world's largest conservation body. The SMC may from time to time have taken a stance against inappropriate development in the mountains, but like its counterpart clubs south of the Border it has never sought to take on a national mountain conservation role in the way that the European national alpine associations, with their broad membership, have done.

But there had been an earlier SMC connection. William Douglas, editor of the Journal, had met John Muir too, 15 years before the Club awarded him its Honorary Membership. When Muir made his one return visit to Scotland in 1893,[7] as part of a wider European tour, he carried an introduction to David Douglas the notable Edinburgh publisher, Willie Douglas' father, from Muir's own publisher and fellow conservation campaigner, Robert Underwood Johnson. David Douglas had published many American authors in Britain, including Theodore Roosevelt, John Burroughs, and Oliver Wendell Holmes.

It's clear from Muir's letters home that the encounter with Douglas was hugely positive for him:

---

7   Specific accounts of this tour are provided by Graham White (1993) 'The homecoming, John Muir's return to Scotland, July 8th to September 16th, 1893', *East Lothian Life* 13 pp16–18; and by Will Collin (2009) *A Scotchman comes home – John Muir's homecoming, 1893*, Dunbar: Friends of John Muir's Birthplace.

President Theodore Roosevelt and John Muir at Glacier Point, Yosemite 1903.

a glorious time... the most wonderful night as far as humanity is concerned I ever had in the world. ... From feeling lonely and a stranger in my own native land, he brought me back into quick and living contact with it, and now I am a Scotchman and at home again.[8]

Muir called again on David Douglas, to their evident mutual pleasure, on his return to Edinburgh after a fairly perfunctory tourist circuit of Scotland, much coloured by his lifelong enthusiasm for Walter Scott. There is rather a sense from his letters that he found it all distinctly less impressive than his cherished Sierra.

But meeting Muir was clearly a very positive experience for William Douglas too. The evidence for that comes by a quirky indirect route, via his predecessor as Journal Editor, Joseph Gibson Stott, who was by that time in New Zealand. Writing to Douglas from Dunedin on 8 February 1894, Stott comments in the midst of a letter: 'What a wonderful man your friend Muir must be. Should like to have met him'.[9] Alas, we don't have Douglas' own letter to Stott to share his enthusiasm.

---

8   As quoted in Collin, *op cit*, p.16

9   25 years ago, Robin Campbell assiduously transcribed all the Stott letters bound in the Douglas *Journals*, and circulated the full texts to a select few Club members. He then published edited extracts with a typically enjoyable commentary in the 1990 *Journal* ('My dear Douglas', *SMCJ* 34/181 pp388–99). Hardly surprisingly, Robin didn't recognise the significance of the short, obscure reference to 'your friend Muir', and omitted it from the edited transcript in his article. It required another obsessional personality to pick it up 20 years later.

Muir studied botany and geology at the University of Wisconsin. The photo shows him examining a petrified log in Arizona in 1905. At that time the fossilized logs were being dynamited by people looking for amethyst crystals inside them. There were even plans to pulverize the logs for use as industrial abrasives.

Muir alerted his friend Theodore Roosevelt to this destruction. The following year the President signed the Antiquities Act and this was used to create the Petrified Forest National Monument. A larger area eventually became a National Park in 1962.

Photo: Holt-Atherton Special Collections, University of the Pacific Library.

As an aside, it's perhaps a little surprising that David Douglas did not seize the opportunity to publish Muir's writings in Scotland. As might be expected, the firm did issue mountaineering books, including such celebrated and now much sought-after items as *The Alps in 1864* by A.W. Moore, Collie's *Climbing on the Himalaya and other Mountain ranges*, and Slingsby's *Norway: the Northern Playground*. But if that possibility were discussed during their stimulating dinners and walks together, copyright issues, or a prosaic commercial judgement on the likely sales in Britain of works on American conservation, may have prevailed against it.

It is, however, easy enough to envisage that fifteen years on Douglas would have been ready to support his friend Rennie's initiative in proposing John Muir for Honorary Membership of the Club. In doing so they showed an exceptional appreciation for the messianic Muir, who was otherwise to remain a prophet largely without honour in his native land for more than half a century. The Club can now enjoy the credit for their discernment.

Acknowledgement

I'm much indebted to the Club's indefatigable Honorary Archivist, Robin Campbell, for key items of information for this note, including his copying of historic membership application forms and his painstaking transcription of Stott's letters in the Douglas Journals.

ON THE POMMEL OF THE KNIGHT'S SADDLE

By Phil Gribbon

INDISTINCT VOICES FILTERED down from on high, and above the sheer slant of the north wall we glimpsed tiny figures outlined against a blue sky. The Swiss have got there before us. They had gone the easy way. However don't be discouraged, we'll continue to enjoy ourselves.

Weeks before we had found some neat stone wind barriers that they had constructed at one of their campsites but other than this clue the hills and the snowfields were devoid of any trace of their wanderings. They had vanished into the appropriately called Schweizerland. This name was inscribed on the official Geodetic Institute small scale map and it must have been their choice to go where their fellow countrymen had climbed before the war but they had moved further in towards the main ice sheet.

They were obviously more energetic than we were and had shunned the attractions of the readily accessible unclimbed peaks closer to the coast. We looked for the easy life so we hauled our sledges around and pitched our camps on moraines and outcrops, and then when we had scanned the heights we ran up the nearest attractive spire.

Now by chance we had chosen the same day to climb our final objective. We were two separate parties sampling the delights of one of the most spectacular peaks imaginable. Sculpted to resemble an ornate saddle fit for a medieval knight she was draped with a glistening white snow blanket tossed across her tanned flank. Rytterknaegten was her name and she dominated her surrounding lesser sisters and rose proud to claim a first rank status amongst the myriad mountains that fringe the coastal rim of Greenland.

We kept looking and listening intently but there was neither sight nor sound coming from the summit. Silence hung in the air broken only by the sibilant whispers of water drops melting off the lip of a nearby undercut snowbank. Could these figures be all in our imagination and an aberration consistent with our weeks of under nourishment, over-exertion and climbing satiation?

We agreed that those Schweizerdeutsch men had been really there but they were not going to detract from our excellent climb. We had been moving intermittently up the northwest ridge for hours, leaving our chill tented platform hewn out of the broken scree in the glimmer of early morning, then trying hard to create warmth by energetically wielding our axes, weaving up mixed ground pitch by pitch, until now we were into the glare of sunshine bouncing off the dazzling snow and with the high summit spires beckoning across the frozen sheet coating the side of the high saddle.

What you are reading had happened in the distant past. Sometimes probing a fading memory can conjure a startling fresh virtual picture. Was it really like that once upon a time?

I got out my SEGE 63 logbook diary. This was prompted by Joxer's retiral project when he had produced a scripted photo album of the expedition and this had triggered my search to see if I still remembered this significant day fifty years ago.

I had written up our climb just after we had completed the route and it now had to be reassessed and judiciously pruned. Much of the account turned out to be a tedious blow-by-blow record in detailed climbing lingo and more suitable for a guide book instruction manual. Where had the intimate sense of my emotional involvement with the pervasive personality of our mountain gone?

Let's delve into my prosaic writing efforts in the diary and see if they can help to create a picture that captures the essence of the event. Thus…

…Go across the ice band to scree blocks, loose or frozen into the ice, and clogged with powder snow. Weddeburn comes over, collects hammer and pegs, starts straight up the slope, tiptoeing on a few inches of well bound snow on hard ice…

…my turn for the traverse. What exposure as the slope slides away into the distance! The footholds give me the screamers, right foot down with 3 ins of snow for support above my left foothold and I'm soon on sideways toe holds crossing without crampons on blue ice.

Phew, this still conjures up a trembling feeling of precarious reality. My recollection is more fraught with the potential for disaster than the actual moment of carefree flitting on tiptoe above such incipient oblivion. The question now was whether it was best on the spur of the moment to put on your crampons again on a mixed but mainly rock route or take a chance on the tricky slippy traverse knowing you had a rope running horizontally across to your partner?

We relished our action shots. It was a record for our old age and impressing our pals, thus…

…Friedel follows the full runout of the rope, Wedderburn films….

Our budding movie maker assiduously ran his camera. His preference was a visual record with action; the rest of us were just Kodakchrome slide snappers. Strange how all these ancient images can be long since forgotten, stuck in personal archives, computer discs, unlabelled boxes, or dear knows where. Do we ever look at them today?

Sometimes a diary entry is backed up with Joxer's photo album picture and turning its pages you get a peaceful sense of the unspoilt serenity of a land devoid of human presence.

…We moved up towards the sun for a brewup. Again the view takes our breath away. We are looking down at the calving area of the Unter Sermiligaq Gletsher with its serried crevasses and the tranquil fjord with a city of icebergs, and beyond are low hills crossed by short cols and far away the sea pack ice jammed close and drifting slowly southwards in the sun.

We didn't need to rush to the top. It would never really get dark and we appreciated the calm and sunny days of late summer, and besides we were booked in for dinner on the summit....

...Scramble together but rope work poor as in desperate hurry to get into the sun. Set up the great wee Primus stove, snow gathered from under stones and shoved in pot, duvet on, and relax as we wait for afternoon tea. A grand brew with ginger biscuits smeared with green-flecked cheesy butter. More than an hour of idle enjoyment before tackling the final towers, tempted by the direct line...

...gain a stance under an overhanging corner, belay on rounded flake facing inwards, change a thin sling for my thick belay length. We put on double rope, give him the hammer, pegs and slings. He tries corner, comes down, and then goes up standing on my right shoulder and vanishes up the skyline. It's a staircase, he says. You could have fooled me!

...don't like it and try to lasso the top flake but sling jams and makes an admirable thing to haul on. Small gendarme circumnavigated by moving downwards jamming boots in the crack, then a laybacky move under a pink felspar nose and a belay in shelter from wind blowing up out of the southeast glacier bowl..... Without hesitation he goes up next wee gendarme... I follow, then my turn up a vertical direct crack and over a nose and at a gallop to the one and only summit of Rytterknaegten. It is 7.30 p.m. and we are 7120 ft up.

It's fabulous!

There is the Swiss cairn, a note on choc paper trusting we 'enjoyed' happily our climb, four bits of choc, a Knorr tin with the ascent book, André Roch 25.viii.38. Sigi Angerer 15.viii.63. We added our name and accepted that their choice of date was probably correct.

Far below the Sermiligaq fjord sleeps peacefully and mellow in the fading light. The valleys and other peaks we climbed are mere dwarfs around us. Our original objectives of Quervains Bjorg and Pointe de Harpon close to Mont Forel, the highest mountain in Greenland, look a mere stone's throw away and not endless miles.

The conical shadow of our mountain creeps up into the rose indigo haze of the eastern sky, and an orange sun sinks down towards the expanse of the Greenland icecap. Slowly the sun goes down, its last light spreading and shimmering across the continent. We wait without success for the green flash as it dips finally below the horizon.

Friedel produces his hip flask with its fiery contents. Our toast 'a noggin to our finest hour, this and future expeditions, the mountain and our safe return.' Yes, we were getting carried away on the strength of a mere whiff of the ould creatur.

Unanimously we decided to remain where we are. Discomfort means little now. Get in between two cracks, fill in bottom with flatish stones, scoop out food store, and ignite Primus. Iain clears space so that he can touch the summit from his pit. Snow hard to get but with ice chips we get enough. First we celebrate with rum fudge, then soup of chicken noodle plus mushroom with a corned beef chunk in it and thickened with pom, and next a main course of pom and a rich broth of meat bar, then an oatcake nibble, then double cake and hot milk. Tea to drink, expedition biscuit and cheese square with butter, ginger biscuit with butter, a banquet!

Snuggle down in my twin cracks, shift stone from under hip, feet over space, poly bags underneath to stop draughts. Crescent moon sweeps up like a thin peach slice, and the northern lights flicker in the south. Everywhere stars, the sky lives, and so do we!

Soon asleep a quarter before midnight....

Iain wakes me for the dawn; he is sitting up in bed, red balaclava on, blue padded duvet, bearded and patriarchal. Friedel asks the time, it's 4am. My stomach feels gripped with hot tar, mouth cankered, hands knotted, but sit up to pay my respects to our bivouac. Again the wonder of the sea and the icebergs, the faint colours of the hills, and the brilliance of the sky.

Go back to sleep, wonderfully...

THE EXECUTIONER

By Mike Dixon

SKYE MOUNTAIN RESCUE TEAM retrieved the body with the help of the Stornoway coastguard helicopter, about two hours after the alarm was raised. The right leg was tenuously joined to the torso, like a loose first tooth attached by a sliver of stringy fibre to the gum. The facial features were rearranged like a cubist painting. For Murdo, one of the aspirant team members, it resulted in disrupted sleep for the next two weeks.

The crematorium car park was packed. The grey sky, pregnant with rain, mirrored the mood of the occasion. The room filled up and then the family entered, clutching each other like the walking wounded from a theatre of war. You didn't have to be religious to be moved by the swelling emotion in the voices of the choir, despite it being an old recording piped over a second rate PA system.

Reminiscences and tributes were wide ranging.

'Money was really tight when they had their first mortgage and Katie was a baby. Grant even did the housework so Suzy could go out to do an evening bar job.' Laughter. A student friend said that despite the tragedy there were very few fortunate enough to end their days in a place they adored and in the company of the person they treasured and loved most of all. It was a perfect idea for the ashes to be scattered at Tarskavaig in sight of the black Cuillin. (Affirmative nods). The coffin moved on the rollers, the curtains opened and closed, people lined up to pass their respects to the family and then hurried to their cars to escape the now steady downpour.

Three months earlier Grant McKinlay had run through the arrangements for his wife's funeral. The floral display would include carnations, the music a selection from the Glasgow Orpheus choir. The eulogy would be given by a life-long friend and donations would go to a mountain rescue team. There was one problem: Suzy was still living and had no terminal illness. Her death by his hand would require rigorous planning and precise execution.

As physical intimacy lessened, insidious cracks had appeared in the relationship. He could remember the last time they'd had sex but not when they'd last made love. He was worn down by the criticism, the belittling, the glacial stares. Recently they had both been manipulating their flexi time to minimise the amount of time spent together. At weekends they escaped to different mountains. He suspected she was seeing someone else; she was visiting the hairdresser more. He was cautious about embarking on an affair which he knew he could have with a regular hill-walking companion. If Clare had been more Lady Macbeth-like he might have been planning Suzy's end much earlier. As it was, their silver wedding anniversary was fast approaching, a good smokescreen to hide his intentions. Divorce was not an attractive option for Grant. Bang goes the early retirement plan and she'd get a sizeable cut of the pension too. He imagined her gloating over the legal settlement; she'd contest everything, his mountaineering first editions, film poster originals, the lot. There would also be her interpretation of the break-up which would do the gossip rounds. Women, he'd noticed, get far more sympathy following a split. No, there was a neater alternative.

The place and method provided a challenge for Grant. With their joint interest in the hills, the setting of a mountain for her demise was not implausible. There were always suspicions following a fatality to one of a married couple together on the same mountain. But accidents do happen... a simple slip, a head smashed. He couldn't be the first to have such thoughts and others must have been successful. Police questioning would be intense but, after all, they'd kept their domestic problems private. He'd checked the insurance policy and with the pay-out he could resign his job and take on consultancy work when he chose. He needn't be lonely either... there was Clare for a start. He felt twenty years younger in an instant.

Suzy was not a climber but she was comfortable with scrambling. As well as taking pictures herself, she'd always been happy to pose for shots and it would be no problem luring her to the edge of a void. Take some general scenery shots first, get Suzy near the brink as foreground interest. There was a certain beauty in a falling body thought Grant, even the ones who'd been captured mid air in desperate leaps from the Twin Towers.

But which mountain? Suzy had been completing her Munros in friendly competition with her best friend Alison. Grant skimmed her Munro's Tables book to consider the possibilities. There were some interesting options... Liathach, An Teallach, The Saddle, Am Basteir. Choose a midweek day but not during a school or bank holiday, no prying eyes. A scrambly ridge, with a big unbroken drop below it should do just fine. Am Basteir in the Cuillin fitted the bill perfectly.

Skye held a special significance for Grant and Suzy: it was where they'd first been introduced on a student meet thirty years ago. He'd been attracted by her shyness and the fact that she didn't conceal her femininity, applying discreet make-up before any day out in the hills. A charge had coursed through his body the first time they'd held hands during a walk down Glen Sligachan, but it would take guile to coax her back there with him now.

In the subsequent weeks Grant became excited but edgy. It was the same tingling combination he usually experienced before any big climbing route. He felt he was on board a runaway train with only one outcome and alcohol had become the only reliable means of achieving a decent night's sleep.

In order to distract himself, he spent several evenings trawling through old slide boxes seeking out suitable photos for a guidebook a friend was producing on the Scottish islands. He found one of the Harris mountains from Horgabost beach: flawless vanilla sand leading into coruscating turquoise water. He remembered how on that Sunday he and Suzy had skinny-dipped in an area deliberately visible from a nearby Free Church laughing at their effrontery. Two young boys had an epiphany as they emerged from Sunday school, their squeals of delight swiftly silenced by an austere father dressed in bible black. Suzy fell pregnant during that holiday; in retrospect their relationship had already passed its zenith.

His colleagues found him unusually distant and taciturn. 'Dreaming of hills again Grant? Or perhaps the big event next Saturday night?' teased his PA Sandra.

Their anniversary party had been organised by the kids; for the parents it was another game of keeping up appearances. They had the first dance and Grant was just as inept as on their wedding day, but it didn't matter and everyone said what a great couple they still were. In Grant's speech he made reference to their first meeting on Skye and student pals from that era basked in the nostalgia. He paused several times to look directly at his wife. 'I'm looking forward to another 30 years of trips there with Suzy.' Hearty applause.

'Twenty five years!' exclaimed the taxi driver later, 'I didn't make it to five.' Grant and Suzy laughed in unison, but under the surface things were far from right and Grant felt the tension growing inside him. He began to drink more heavily.

His boss advised him to take some time off. It had got to the stage where he had to double check all Grant's decisions anyway. 'I'll oversee the Stirling job… you're worn out… take a holiday with Suzy… we'll talk about things when you get back. By the way great party the other night. You've got a great missus. And go and see your doctor. Then it doesn't have to come off your annual leave.'

'…This place isn't helping at all. Let's have a break to somewhere that holds good memories for us. Talk about things…'

She was struck by the fact that he'd taken the initiative. She'd waited a long time for this. She knew that work load wasn't the only reason for his sick leave and had noticed his drinking too.

But don't make things too easy for him she thought.

'This thing's eating into everything, isn't it?' her voice started to break up. 'I've not exactly been an angel in all of this.'

'Nor me but we can build on tonight… Let's go to Skye… We could stay at The Sligachan Hotel? No tent, no midges, no boil in the bag rice. You could finish off your Skye Munros too.' Suzy smiled, tears lurking behind her eyes.

The last time Grant had been kept so anxiously waiting for an answer was the day he'd proposed to her. When she eventually spoke, what she said surprised him.

'What does Am Basteir mean, Grant?'

No eye contact but she'd actually used his name.

'Some books say the executioner, some the baptiser.'

'Oh, I wish I'd never asked! It's not too difficult is it ? I'm alright going up but not so keen coming down. You know me.'

'But I'll be there to help you. The east ridge isn't too bad.'

Oh you'll be fine on Am Basteir, he thought. You'll be down in no time.

At the Fatal Accident Enquiry the Sheriff's dry tones rolled on and on: '… The witness who'd just arrived at the summit of Am Basteir corroborated the description of the deceased's fall. I'm recording death by misadventure,' he concluded. 'I cannot over-emphasise the danger of taking photographs near the edge of steep cliffs. I'd like to thank Mrs. McKinlay for her co-operation during this difficult time for both her and her family. I'd also like to thank Mr. Shand, the witness, who helped Mrs. McKinlay off the mountain where they were met by the Skye Mountain Rescue Team, who as usual did a magnificent job.'

Outside the hearing Suzy thanked everyone who'd attended. The rescue team leader acknowledged the generous donation from Grant's family and friends. Mr. Shand was the last person she went over to.

'Don't say too much here,' she whispered. 'We're only supposed to have met once before.'

She winked at him, before turning round to dab her eyes.

THE WILDCAT ENIGMA

By Ro Scott

OF ALL THE ANIMALS which you might encounter during a day on the hill, the wildcat is perhaps the most elusive. A fleeting shadow disappearing into the undergrowth or a pair of glowing eyes reflecting the car's headlights may be all that you see. How can you tell whether what you saw was a wildcat or not? Does it matter? Is anybody interested? These are questions which I hope to answer in this article.

Why are they rare?

The wildcat, or European wildcat to give it its full name, (*Felis silvestris*) is undoubtedly one of Scotland's most endangered mammals. Figures such as 'only 400 remaining in the wild' are bandied about in the press, but such numbers are based on extrapolation from a very small amount of data. It is a native species, having arrived in Britain while there was still a land-bridge to continental Europe just after the end of the last glaciation, about 9,000 years ago (Yalden, 1999). In prehistoric times it was widespread throughout England, Wales and Scotland, wherever there was suitable habitat. As across the rest of its European range, it was an animal of the forest edge, utilising the interface between dense woodland and open clearings, occupying the foothills and valleys rather than the high tops. A true carnivore, it would hunt for small mammals, birds and reptiles. During the ensuing millennia, as human influences over the British environment became increasingly prevalent, the wildcat, like many other native carnivores, was gradually excluded from much of its former range. Unlike our other native cat, the European lynx, it managed to survive (just about) to the present day.

This history of the wildcat in England, Wales and southern Scotland parallels that of other carnivores, such as the pine marten and polecat. The increasing intensity of human land-use brought habitat destruction and fragmentation, particularly the loss of woodland cover, as well as direct persecution. So, by 1880 the wildcat was considered extinct everywhere except in the Scottish Highlands. During late Victorian times the expansion of sporting estates in the Highlands brought even more intense persecution and, by the early 20th century, the wildcat was restricted to the extreme north-west Highlands (Langley & Yalden, 1977). This was not because the habitat there was of better quality, nor the climatic conditions more favourable, (neither of which is true), but only because these areas were less intensively keepered.

So what exactly is a wildcat?

It was at this time of extremely low wildcat population that the 'type specimen' (the original example from which the taxon was formally

A Lochaber wildcat. Photo: Donald Donnelly.

described) of what was then called the 'Scottish wildcat' was collected, from Invermoriston. It was originally given the name *Felis grampia* in 1907 because it was considered sufficiently different from the wildcat of continental Europe to be a separate species. Scottish wildcats were thought to be chunkier in shape and have darker markings than their European counterparts. Throughout the twentieth century, opinion has varied, with some experts thinking the Scottish wildcat merited only sub-specific status as *Felis silvestris grampia*.

Modern-day authorities (Randi & Ragni, 1991) now think that the European wildcat, African wildcat and domestic cat should all be regarded as one big species, *Felis silvestris*, with the different types being allowed only sub-specific rank: *Felis silvestris silvestris*; *F. s. lybica*; and *F. s. catus* respectively. The progenitor of the domestic cat was the African wildcat (*Felis lybica* or *Felis silvestris lybica*, depending on which taxonomy you follow). This is why the process of cross-breeding between a wildcat and a domestic cat, which was previously referred to as 'hybridisation' (breeding between two different species) now tends to be called 'interbreeding' (breeding between two animals of different type, but not necessarily separate species).

Recent genetic work at Oxford University (Driscoll et al., 2007) suggests that the cat was first domesticated in the 'Fertile Crescent' of the near east, rather than in Egypt as had previously been thought, and that this may have taken place with the dawn of agriculture, as long as 9,000 years ago. Some genetic markers have been discovered which are unique to either the wildcat or the domestic cat. These can be used to trace the spread of the domestic cat across Europe and to pick out cats which have a domestic cat somewhere in their ancestry. The domestic cat is thought to have been brought to Britain by the Romans. So wildcats and domestic cats could potentially have been interbreeding here for the last 2,000 years. Alternatively, this may only have started to happen relatively recently, since the early 20th century low point in the wildcat population. We just don't know. Either way, it is now certain that a major barrier to the survival of the wildcat in Scotland is inter-breeding with domestic and feral cats. Herein lies the nub of the dilemma over how best to conserve the wildcat. In order to protect something, you have to be able to define it.

Before the advent of modern genetic techniques, identifying the wildcat had to rely on those bodily characteristics which are most different from those of the domestic cat. Some of these, such as the larger brain volume and shorter gut length of the wildcat, can only be measured on a dead animal, and so are of no practical use in the field. The externally visible features thought to characterise the wildcat, such as its stripy tabby coat pattern with no white patches, and black-tipped tail with distinct separate rings around it, become increasingly blurred in an interbred population. By studying museum specimens and road casualties, the internal features have now been correlated with visible external characteristics of the cats' coat pattern, to provide a practical field identification method (Kitchener et al. 2005). This relies on seven key features of the pelage. See the diagram opposite from the 'Highland Tiger' website[1].

The most likely of these features to be seen in a casual encounter with a cat are those relating to the tail. This should be thick and bushy, with a blunt, black tip. The black rings encircling the tail should be discrete, without a black dorsal stripe joining them together. If an otherwise striped (rather than blotched or spotted) tabby cat, with no obvious 'domestic' markings such as large white patches, has this type of tail, it is likely to be a wildcat. The availability of relatively cheap 'trail cameras', known as camera traps, means that it is now much easier to obtain images of wild-living cats, which can be assessed against these pelage criteria.

Where are wildcats found now?
The two most recent surveys of wildcat distribution, carried out 20 years apart, took place in the late 1980s and in 2006–8 (before the widespread availability of camera traps). The earlier survey (Easterbee, Hepburn and

---

1 <http://www.highlandtiger.com/science_wildcatID.asp> [retrieved 8 Sept 2014].

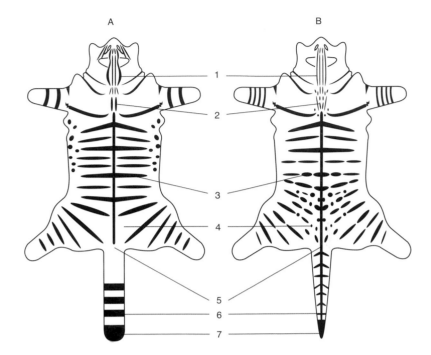

DISTINGUISHING WILDCATS

After examining more than 130 cat skins collected over the last 100 years from major UK museum collections, Andrew Kitchener (National Museums Scotland), Jennifer Ward (University of Edinburgh), and Nobuyuki Yamaguchi & David Macdonald (University of Oxford) carefully analysed the cats' coat patterns in order to work out which of 17 features could be used to distinguish between wildcats, domestic cats and their hybrids.

*This analysis revealed that there are seven coat characteristics that are useful for determining a **Scottish wildcat (A)** from a free-ranging tabby cat (B):*

    1. Four nape stripes broad, wavy and unfused.
    2. Two shoulder stripes.
    3. Unbroken flank stripes.
    4. No spots on rump; stripes may be broken, but distinct.
    5. Dorsal stripe on lower back always stops at the root of the tail.
    6. Distinct aligned tail bands.
    7. Tip of tail blunt and black.

In addition there are eight other characters of secondary importance, such as the presence of white paws, or the whiteness of the chin, which might indicate a hybrid. While these characters can easily be examined in a road casualty or a museum skin, in a field situation, this definition of a wildcat is likely to be more relaxed and would probably include some hybrids, which looked like large striped tabbies with a bushy, ringed, black-tipped tail.

Dr Andrew Kitchener, National Museums Scotland, Edinburgh <a.kitchener@nms.ac.uk>

Jefferies, 1991), found apparent wildcats to be confined to the area north of the Highland Boundary Fault, with strongholds in the Cairngorms, the Black Isle, Aberdeenshire and Ardnamurchan. This survey used interviews with land managers and other people working in the outdoors, as well as asking members of the public to submit details of their wildcat sightings. The 2006–8 survey (Davis and Gray, 2010) used similar techniques, with a view to obtaining comparable data. It found a similar distribution, but fewer records of apparent wildcats, with most being found in Aberdeenshire, Inverness-shire, Ardnamurchan and Morvern, Perthshire and the central highlands.

Compared to some other carnivore species, such as the otter, badger or fox, very little ecological research has been done on the wildcat in Scotland. Conditions here are very different from those across much of its range in Europe. What little work has been done suggests that wildcats occur at much lower densities in the west of Scotland than in the east, with each cat occupying a more extensive home range. Rabbits are an important prey item, particularly for the bigger male cats, and their absence from large parts of the west may explain this phenomenon.

Conservation measures

As well as interbreeding with domestic cats, wildcats are also susceptible to catching diseases from them. These include feline immunodeficiency virus ('cat AIDS'), feline leukaemia virus and feline calicivirus. Whilst such diseases may be treatable in domestic cats, the wildcat has no veterinary assistance, and such infections often prove fatal.

The wildcat was only legally protected in Scotland from 1988, when it was added to Schedule 5 of the Wildlife and Countryside Act 1981. Although this means that it is illegal to kill, or 'take' (i.e. live-trap) a wildcat, it was difficult to enforce this legislation before the pelage criteria were agreed in 2005. Since 1992 the wildcat has also been classified as a European Protected Species (EPS) by being listed on Annex IV of the European Habitats Directive. This gives added protection to wildcats and their dens and other places of shelter, particularly when being used for breeding. The wildcat is also, since the review of priority species and habitats in 2007, listed as a UK Biodiversity Action Plan (UKBAP) priority species, and appears on the Scottish Biodiversity List[2]. It was targeted for practical conservation action in the five-year (2007–12) Species Action Framework for Scotland drawn up by SNH[3].

Part of this initiative was a pilot project utilising a variety of approaches to promote wildcat conservation within the Cairngorms National Park.

---

2   <http://www.biodiversityscotland.gov.uk/advice-and-resources/scottish-biodiversity-list/> [retrieved 8 Sept 2014].

3   <http://www.snh.gov.uk/protecting-scotlands-nature/species-action-framework/> [retrieved 8 Sept 2014].

These included working with gamekeepers and other land managers to devise a protocol for 'wildcat friendly' predator control; setting up the 'Highland Tiger'[4] website to promote a positive image of the wildcat; working with cat welfare charities and local vets to encourage neutering and vaccination of domestic and feral cats; and collating records of wildcats and feral cats, (by public sightings or as roadkill) including monitoring with camera traps. The final report on the project can be found on the Cairngorms National Park website[5]. This project won the innovation award at the 'Nature of Scotland' awards in October 2013.

Moves are now afoot to apply for a Heritage Lottery Fund grant to extend the measures implemented in the Cairngorms Wildcat Project to several more key areas of wildcat habitat. A Wildcat Working Group, including representatives from statutory agencies, land management and cat welfare organisations and academic bodies, has been formed to take forward this proposal. A twelve page Wildcat Conservation Action Plan has been drawn up, which can be downloaded from the SNH publications website[6].

What can I do to help wildcats?

A key element of this Action Plan is to improve our knowledge of where wildcats, hybrids and populations of feral domestic cats occur. All hill-goers can contribute by being sure to send in records of any wildcats, putative wildcats or hybrids, and apparently feral domestic cats which you see. If you can get a photograph (or footage from a camera trap) that is even better. If you think you might have seen a wildcat, or indeed any type of cat apparently living in the wild, anywhere in Scotland, please do contribute your information. It is important to record what you actually saw (e.g. a tabby cat with a striped tail), rather than your interpretation of what it might have been! You can report sightings online via the Highland Tiger website[7], which includes the facility to upload photos of the cat.

If you keep one or more domestic cats, and live in an area where wildcats may be present, having your cat(s) neutered and vaccinated against contagious diseases can make a positive contribution towards safeguarding the wildcat. It will take a huge effort on the part of many different groups of people to save the Scottish wildcat. Please help if you can.

---

4   <http://www.highlandtiger.com/> [retrieved 8 Sept 2014].

5   <http://cairngorms.co.uk/resource/docs/publications/30082012/CNPA. Paper.1838.Cairngorms%20Wildcat%20Project%20-%20final%20report.pdf> [retrieved 8 Sept 2014].

6   <http://www.snh.gov.uk/publications-data-and-research/publications/search-the-catalogue/publication-detail/?id=2050> [retrieved 8 Sept 2014].

7   <http://www.highlandtiger.com/help_report.asp> [retrieved 8 Sept 2014].

References

AR Davis & D Gray, *The distribution of Scottish wildcats (Felis silvestris) in Scotland (2006–2008)* (SNH Commissioned Report No. 360, 2010).

CA Driscoll, M Menotti-Raymond, AL Roca, K Hupe, WE Johnson, E Geffen, EH Harley, M Delibes, D Pontier, AC Kitchener, N Yamaguchi, SJ O'Brien, DW Macdonald, 'The Near Eastern Origin of Cat Domestication', *Science*, 317 (2007), 519–23.

N Easterbee, LV Hepburn & DJ Jefferies, *Survey of the status and distribution of the wildcat in Scotland 1983–1987* (Edinburgh: Nature Conservancy Council for Scotland, 1991).

AC Kitchener, N Yamaguchi, JM Ward & DW Macdonald, 'A diagnosis for the Scottish wildcat (*Felis silvestris*): a tool for conservation action for a critically-endangered felid', *Animal Conservation,* 8/3 (2005), 223–37.

PJW Langley & DW Yalden, 'The decline of the rarer carnivores in Great Britain during the nineteenth century', *Mammal Review*, 7/3&4 (1977), 95–116.

E Randi & B Ragni, 'Genetic variability and biochemical systematics of domestic and wild cat populations (*Felis silvestris*: Felidae)', *Journal of Mammalogy*, 72/1 (1991), 79–88.

DW Yalden, *The History of British Mammals* (London: Poyser, 1999).

Further reading
K Kilshaw, *Naturally Scottish – Wildcats* (SNH Publications, 2011).

HOW THE DAY TURNED OUT

By David Small

EARLY ONE WEEKDAY morning in January Dave and I left Edinburgh under a starlit sky, heading for Glen Coe with the aim of climbing *Scabbard Chimney* on Stob Coire nan Lochan. There was a hard frost and the forecast was fine. The day's prospects looked good. But our optimism was tinged with just a little unease; a couple of days previously an avalanche had killed four mountaineers on Bidean nam Bian, four folk who, as far as we could make out from the reports, had just been in the wrong place at the wrong time – a very sombre case of bad luck. We would be climbing an adjacent mountain on slopes that faced the same way. If them, why not us? If not us, why them?

Leaving the car in the half light and stumbling downhill towards the River Coe, we found the path and the rocks around it treacherously covered in ice. The temperature probably hadn't been above zero for a week. As we went further and reached the snow line, there was a lot of powder snow but only the occasional patch of névé. The dawn strengthened as we sweated up the buried track and, as we came over the lip of the corrie, we saw the buttresses of Stob Coire nan Lochan in line abreast, all covered in snow and hoar frost. A few other parties were already at the base of the cliffs, beginning harder routes. The beauty of the morning and the presence of the other ropes made us confident. If these guys were tackling grade VI/7s and the like, surely our goal of a IV/6 which had first been climbed over fifty years ago couldn't detain us too long?

So we geared up and left our sacks, containing our head torches, food and water, down on the corrie floor.

The first pitch shook us up a bit. There is a big smooth slab with an off-width crack to its left. When – as on the day we tried it – neither the slab nor the crack is holding any ice they must be truly desperate, if climbable at all. After trying several alternatives, Dave forced a way of his own to the right of the slab. Faced with a choice of unpalatable options, I belatedly saw a steep little corner on the left which gave some strenuous but secure climbing and is probably the best route when the slab is bare. So the first pitch took some faffing and a fair amount of time, but at last I was taking the gear from Dave to set off up the second pitch, a fine long corner.

Soon after that, I was handing the gear back to Dave for him to set off, etc. etc. The line ahead had absolutely no ice or turf, just an unhelpful quantity of unconsolidated snow over bare rock, and I had had to admit that it was not for me. Taking over the lead, Dave made his way up for forty metres, carefully but with assurance, and belayed in an exciting position below the crux pitch. I followed carefully and with my heart,

The cliffs of Stob Coire nan Lochan, 23 January 2013. Photo: David Small.

often enough, in my mouth. Across the corrie, the sun was moving round the cliffs and the sesto/septogradists – little dots of animated colour on the whiteness of the buttresses – were leaving tracks of cleared rock behind them, apparently getting higher faster than we were.

The crux pitch was great climbing, provided you didn't want to see exactly what it was, in the hoar-filled cracks that your picks and points were resting on. It had to be climbed by the right combination of feel and trust. Hanging on the belay, I watched as Dave experimented with the placements of his crampons and axes and adjusted his weight before making each move. Seconding it was a relative formality, having seen how it should be done.

As I rejoined Dave at the belay above the crux I began to feel we could relax again; time had moved on, but one more pitch of Grade III would take us to the abseil tat and then we'd soon be back down on the floor of the corrie, without going anywhere which could avalanche, and with plenty of daylight to play with. In my more relaxed mood, as I climbed what I assumed would be our final pitch, I was able to observe the quality of the afternoon light, the views of the Mamores and the deepening shadows down in Glen Coe.

What I hadn't done, of course, before comfortably settling matters in my own mind, was to consult Dave about what we were going to do. When he came up to join me at the abseil tat, he explained that he really wanted to go to the top of the mountain, feeling that the day would not be complete without it. Some alarm bells began to ring in my mind; the normal quick descent from the summit down Broad Gully would surely be an unsafe avalanche risk, while the alternative of going round and down the ridge to the north-west would probably take too long, leaving us hunting in the dark for our elusive sacks and the head torches which we had so absurdly left behind. I had a meeting at work next morning which I simply could not miss. The car key was in the sacks. If we could not find the sacks we might painstakingly make our way down the track in the dark, no doubt with several falls on the icy bits, but the hassle and trouble which would just be beginning when, or if, we were down in the glen did not bear thinking about. However, I did not feel able to say 'no' to Dave, given that he had been mainly responsible for our getting up the climb. If we were quick, surely we should still have enough daylight to find the sacks again? So I sat down and paid out the rope as he climbed the final gully up to the ridge, which in turn would take us to the summit.

I had to move off the belay before Dave reached the ridge, about seventy metres up, and there were one or two awkward steps in the gully. It was all taking longer than I was happy with and from the top of the gully there were still at least another hundred metres of scrambling up the ridge to the summit. As I climbed I became more and more inwardly convinced that the only safe and sensible thing to do was to go down as soon as we could.

On emerging from the gully I told Dave how I felt; two quick abseils and we would be down, avoiding any risk of avalanche, stressful benightment and trouble at work. He sensed the strength of my feeling and courteously gave in. He came off his belay and, without either of us having untied from the rope, we both began looking for a suitable abseil anchor. Dave was on one side of a little bowl at the top of the gully, I was on the other, and we each adopted a rock bollard on our respective sides of the bowl as our preferred anchor. After some discussion of their individual merits, in order to demonstrate the soundness of the bollard of his choice, Dave got down below it and gave it a good shake.

The bollard came away in his arms and took him with it. He fell back down the gully.

I stood at the top thinking 'I am still tied to him and there are sixty metres of rope between us. I have to get away from the edge of the gully NOW and hope I don't get pulled after him when the rope comes tight.' Without formulating a distinct thought about it, some ridiculous part of my mind also called into consciousness the mythical Alpine advice – 'if I fall into Italy, you jump into France' – and was aware that its utility was about to be tested in a Scottish setting.

By the time my brain had come up with all that, and before I had begun to move away from the edge, Dave had stopped falling. For no apparent reason he had come to a halt, completely unscathed, in a little feature a short way down the gully. The bollard flew on out of sight. I shuddered to think what damage that plummeting lump of rock might have inflicted had we dislodged it on a weekend, when the corrie below was busy with climbers.

Dave rejoined me at the top of the gully. Both of us were shaking with relief. There was little need for further discussion; any idea of abseiling was abandoned. We would go up to the summit and descend the ridge to the north-west, in preference to the quicker option of Broad Gully, which we both thought would be avalanche prone. It would inevitably be dark before we could start looking for the sacks, but we would have to deal with that as best we could; one thing at a time.

Moving together, we scrambled up towards the summit. Near the top, we got a view across to the top of *Broad Gully*. We saw two climbers begin to descend it, apparently easily and with complete confidence. They moved quickly out of sight. Perhaps we could go down that way after all?

Being on top of Stob Coire nan Lochan late on a fine January afternoon, with the sunset colours contrasting with the darkening pit of Glen Coe, is a rare experience which one should linger and cherish to the full. On this occasion I wasn't really able to take it all in; I was too keen on keeping moving and resolving the uncertainty of what lay ahead. The re-awakening of the possibility of going down Broad Gully, which had previously been eliminated from our minds, had made the doubt feel worse rather than better.

In fact, the moment we stepped onto the snow of the gully it was obvious that it was perfectly safe – the one and only significant expanse of névé which we found all day. We cramponned down carefully and managed to find the sacks in the last of the daylight. All was well.

As we picked our way downhill back to the car we stopped now and then to switch off our torches, the better to enjoy the brightness of the stars above us. Those moments of peace spent admiring the familiar constellations were a privilege; a privilege intensely appreciated, but thoroughly undeserved.

A HEFTY DAY IN THE COE (circa 1959)

By Jimmy Marshall

ON FRIDAY I HITCHED to Glen Coe and dossed in Jacksonville, expecting owners or others to appear but only had the resident rat and discouraged him with flaming paraffin down his hideout. It was a splendid mid-summer evening, so I lit a bonfire and luxuriated in the warmth and quality of the surroundings, awaiting others to appear, but none did and eventually, I rolled out the sleeping bag and slept by the fire.

Still alone on a glorious morning, I ate and went uphill. The Buachaille was bone dry so I rambled into Crowberry Gully, which was pleasantly cool, and enjoyed a uniquely dry ascent all the way to the summit. I savoured the fine expansive views in all directions, though the sun was overly hot. I decided it had to be a day for gullies, so I descended Crowberry Ridge, then down North Face Route on Central Buttress as a convenient approach to The Chasm. The choice was made on the basis that there might still be a little water to ease the thirst. I was also being cautious as watercourse routes are serried step climbs and one wouldn't fall too far. The continuous movement in sunshine was strongly reminiscent of Chamonix climbing and, exhilarated, I sat on the summit wondering what to do next, till a group of Holiday Fellowship arrived. I grudged their intrusion but hearing they were going down for their bus back to Glencoe, became untypically sociable and was invited to rendezvous at Cameron's later.

Now I could reach the other great gully, but I climbed around some more, lunched on sandwiches, then joined the bus and was delivered right to the foot of Clachaig Gully. Feeling very smug, I sat in the afternoon sun, searched a decent drink at the river, then enjoyed a tremendous uninterrupted climb up the gully, to relax on top of Sgùrr nam Fhionnadh.

The setting sun now lit Bidean in sharp, contrasting detail, every peak, even climbs were discernible and I used this wonderful sight to enjoy a lengthy loaf. Ahead, the sun-tipped edge of Aonach Eagach beckoned like a golden bridge above the darkening glen and I traipsed along inspired at the splendour of it all. Eventually on the somewhat mundane stretch to Cameron's only thoughts of food and the horizontal took me across the final stretch to lonesome Jacksonville where a big fire, extended meal and endless drums of tea beneath a starlit sky put things to right. A perfect day!

WHY?

By Heather Morning

IT WAS DECEMBER, almost the shortest day, as I set off from the car park at the Head of Glen Clova, with Tolmount and Tom Buidhe in my sights. There is no doubt I was focused (too focused in hindsight): only 23 left to go and my completion date was planned to coincide with the Easter holidays. Work and family commitments had inevitably got in the way and the pressure was on to tick off those elusive 22 before my planned completion date.

An unexpected day off and a golden opportunity to bag a couple of roly-poly peaks in the south-east Grampians which should be a relatively short and easy day for me. I was alone, but winter conditions weren't alien to me. The harshness of high winds, snow and poor visibility were something which I had endured – and indeed enjoyed – for many winter seasons.

An unambitious route was planned: it would take me up past Davy's Bourach, over Jock's Road then north-west to Tolmount, south to Tom Buidhe then south-east, crossing the headwaters of The White Water and returning via Davy's Bourach. The drive up to the head of Glen Clova took longer than expected; driving conditions were poor, with a good deal of standing water on the road. Looking ahead, I could see the snow line around 500m and the clouds skidding across an ashen grey sky. I guess it was 10 a.m. before I left the car. The car park was deserted; not surprising really, as it was mid-week and the forecast would have driven all but the keenest hill walkers to the nearest coffee shop.

The first four kilometres up Glen Doll passed quickly, the route sheltered from wind and snow by the coniferous plantation. Only as I walked out of the forestry into the upper reaches of Glen Doll did I enter the snow line and become aware of the bitterly cold wind. It was south-easterly, blowing me up the glen. As the ground steepened, snow lay thicker; no one had travelled this way today. With the track still vaguely follow-able, I approached the first burn crossing. I reached for my axe: a slip here would have had serious consequences.

Jock's Road was a familiar route to me in summer conditions – a major thoroughfare – and familiarity breeds contempt. As the ground levelled, I spotted the door of Davy's Bourach, a corner of red paint showing in what was otherwise a monotone of black and white, snow and rock, and decided it was time for a break. The door dug out, I ventured inside. Snow had permeated every conceivable nook and cranny and the usual dark subterranean interior was transformed into a place of natural sculptured perfection, which also provided much appreciated shelter and security for food and drink. I pondered (as you do, when you have time alone) and thought of the five men who had perished near here in 1959.

Davy's Bourach, August 2008. This howff was first built in 1966. Photo: John Andrew.

It wasn't long since I'd read about their misadventure in 'The Black Cloud', and my thoughts unsettled me.

Time must have been moving on. I'm guessing it was midday as I left the relative comfort of the wee howff. The path ahead was now gone, obliterated under both old and drifting new snow. It crossed my mind to turn back, but I'd invested so much to get this far. Only another three kilometres and 220 metres of ascent to Tolmount the farthest Munro. In my mind, Tom Buidhe was just a small lump on the return journey. A bearing taken, I headed NNW to pick up the ridge heading to Crow Craigies: the ridge would be more wind-scoured and underfoot conditions would likely be less tortuous.

My pace was slow and tedious, breaking trail in a foot or more of new wind-blown snow. Looking back, my footprints were quickly covered. Wind still on my back, I didn't appreciate the severity until progress became more of a stagger than a controlled walk. Gusts would kick my normal steady gait into disarray as I moved onwards. I noted the visibility dropping; the cloud scudding across the tops was definitely building. Crow Craigies was the last feature I saw before entering that 'big white room' of white-out. There was no definition between the sky and the ground, snow cover was complete. Every vestige of rock and vegetation was blanketed in white.

A short descent dropped me to the broad bealach before the final ascent onto Tolmount. Very much in the forefront of my mind were the cornices which would likely be formed on the north side of the mountain. Overshooting on this navigation leg was not an option. The summit rocks/cairn slowly appeared as a slightly darker form in front of me and moments later I stood with some relief on the summit. Nature's beauty was again revealed in the stunning rime ice formations dressing the rocks and cairn. However, relief was brief as I turned southwards for my journey to Tom Buidhe and was hit, quite literally, by the reality of just how strong the wind had become. The snow was vicious on my face, driven by 80 kph winds. Goggles on, bearing taken, I headed south. It began to dawn on me that I'd made a very grave mistake; the following wind had lured me into a serious situation. My return journey would entail an unpleasant and serious battle into the blizzard.

Tom Buidhe was not an option. Plan B and damage limitation were now my priority. It was around 3 p.m. and would be dark at 4: what had I been thinking of? My descent line took me into the head waters of The White Water. Continuing new snow was drifting, filling any available depression. I was getting tired; the refuel of food and drink at Davy's Bourach seemed a lifetime ago. Jelly Snakes stashed in my outer chest pocket for ease of access would have to see me through, for it was too wild and cold to think of stopping. Energy was running low; that insipid damp cold that the Scottish climate is so good at was creeping in and draining my energy. I had to get to the shelter of the Howff and refuel. I knew finding it would be difficult for, from above, Davy's is almost entirely underground. With the blanket of winter it would be almost impossible to find. The light was fading, I was navigating in complete white-out still, hand-railing what I hoped was the line of the burn. Don't blow it… don't go too far down… remember the fate of James Boyle and Harry Duffin, two of the men who perished in 1959, who were found in the steep gully line below Craig Maud.

I'd timed and paced, I prayed I'd not made a mistake. My body was exhausted, my mind fuddled. One more navigation leg should get me up a couple of contours on the north-east side of the burn to Davy's haven. Would I be able to find it? What if I couldn't? The consequences didn't bear contemplating. I was staggering now, the legs had very little left. My head torch was almost useless, a pool of light illuminating wind-ragged snowflakes.

A dark form appeared ahead. I could only be a couple of hundred metres away from Davy's – perhaps other folk had headed there for shelter? The form took the shape of a human, perhaps 10 metres ahead – but there were no footprints… My exhausted frame and fuddled mind struggled to make sense of what I was seeing: definitely a figure, and right on my bearing, providing a much needed focus in the otherwise white. The figure stopped and then dropped out of sight behind what appeared to be a bank of snow. I followed and there, where the figure had been, was the red door of Davy's Bourach. Only a merest patch of red

Plaque beside Jock's Road. Photo: John Andrew.

paint was visible, with all evidence of my passage earlier in the day gone – and no sign of the figure who had guided me there or even a footprint. Could it possibly have been the shade of one of the men who sadly perished way back in 1959? That I will never know.

With a renewed sense of urgency I dug with my axe and entered the sanctuary of the Howff. Pushing the door to as best I could, I delved into the lower reaches of my sac for the emergency bivi bag and duvet. There was still some hot juice in my flask and left-over snacks. I was safe.

In those moments when the line blurred between sleep and wakefulness, there were five men around me, dressed in tweeds, capes and berets, sharing the sanctuary. Their Primus stove purred away, steam rising from the mess tin and brews handed round. Young men, with rosy, healthy, wind-scoured complexions, smiling. Robert McFaul, Frank Daly, Joseph Devlin, James Boyle and Harry Duffin.

But I, with the help of these like-minded friends, had survived, and with the light of a new day I headed down the glen to safety. I had had a very lucky escape.

Days and weeks later I reflected on the experience; time and time again I asked myself why? Why did I feel so compelled to head out onto the hill when I knew that conditions would be so challenging? Why did I continue on, when I knew the daylight hours were running short and my progress was slow? Why did I survive and the five men die? Why did they help me?

LEAVING ST KILDA

By Helen Forde

Will you share these images with me?
Standing on the edge, on the edge of the cliff on the edge of the world.
Far below the sea moves, rocking the landing boats. A sea ennobled by
title, an ocean, the Atlantic Ocean.
Unfathomably green depths constantly moving, tugging tides and
currents creating shivers of tension

The island, Hirta feels still and sheltered, the village that was the soul of
St Kilda remains but as a stone shell.
Today the sun shines but only on the unkempt native sheep and lambs,
brown tangled wool left hanging from fence wire.
No one to gather it now.
No children to take the animals up to the high summer pastures, boiled
fulmar eggs in their pockets to last all day long.

I sit down on the grass, now I feel closer to the land.
Sheep crop beside me.
I start drawing a cleit one of many scattered all over the hillside
constructed of boulders and topped by turf, vital to the St Kildans.
They have survived for centuries creating cool safe storage.
Midday approaches, sheep disappear into the dark shelter.

Time passes in glorious silence.
I squint against the white light of the sky.
Ink dries quickly on the cream paper, the only sounds are the scratching of the pen nib, the brush in the water.
Happiness is ephemeral but at this moment I feel so charmed, sharing a place where souls have lived for two thousand years.

A shadow falls across my paper.
It is time to go. Drawing unfinished but I leave, feeling the parting.

But the St Kildans were cragsmen first, crofters second.
This unique day was not over yet.
Back to the boat.
Sailing across the bay, smelling the sweet scent of fresh grass and seaweed in the air before turning into the open sea, our bows into the Atlantic swell.
Heading out towards Boreray, Stac Lee and Stac Armin.

Little can prepare you for the dramatic impact of these black monoliths of rock rising sheer seven hundred feet out of the water.
They are cruel, formidable.
Silence, the world tilts.
Pale green sea pulls away from the base then crashes back, waves hurling whitewater seeking gullies cracks and embrasures, sea pouring down from the shining cliffs.

The tiny boat cuts its engine, we drift.
Our eyes straining skywards into the arching spaces of light
at first we can make out only dark shapes above,
Then birds seabirds everywhere.
The beating of wings, white bodies flying twirling spinning diving.
Gannets yellow beaks piercing the waves their wings folding up like
jackknives, as hundreds plunge down for fish into the depths.

Surrounded by birds nesting on vertiginous ledges, endlessly calling, our
senses are filled with the sights, smells, and sounds of the largest bird
colony in North West Europe.
This was the reason for the population on St Kilda.
The survival of the Islanders depended on these birds.
Survival, an instinct that sharpens the senses
and steels the soul.

What bravery, desperation and co-operation was needed to scale
those forbidding but jealously-guarded sea stacks?
Even on a calm day the St Kildans' boat would have risen and fallen
fifteen feet at the base of the rock.
Wearing ropes around their waists made from hay and feathers, the first
man would have leap from the boat onto a wave-washed ledge.
Wait for the others to follow
then climb, often in moonlight.

First they would have killed the sentry gannet before the whole gannetry
was alerted then carefully collect their eggs.
Dead birds were flung from an overhang into the pitching boat waiting in
the darkness below.
In the early morning on St Kilda, the women would always meet the
boat, relieved at the sight of the returning men, and carry the shared
catch back to their cottages.

The bird colonies have never deserted the stacks and cliffs of the
archipelago.
But the community has long since vanished.
Leaving St Kilda forever and looking back, as the islands disappear into
the mist, is it too fanciful to hear, tangled with the seabirds' wild calls, a
hint of pibroch in the air?

SKYE'S THE LIMIT

By John Barnard, Graham Jackson & Myrddyn Phillips

I'D JUST COMPLETED my round of Munros and was standing on the summit basking in the warm glow of success, in no small part aided by the glass of Edradour in my hand. The world seemed a fine place indeed as I surveyed all those summits within my field of vision that I had climbed in order to achieve my goal. Memories of those walks and the adventures I'd had flooded back. Suddenly the bubble was burst when one of our party came up to me and said, 'Congratulations, but are you sure you have completed all the 3000ft mountains in Scotland?' He was a statistician, one of that annoying breed of people who is one step ahead of you in their thinking and to make matters worse is always right. 'What do you mean?' I asked. He went on to explain that with any measurement such as a height on a map there is an associated measurement uncertainty, so that a hill with a map height of 913m could actually be over that magic height of 914.4m or 3000ft since the measurement uncertainty of spot heights is +/-3m. With friends like that who needs enemies? But it set me thinking.

Some weeks later our walking group got together at our next meet and over several drams the subject arose again. The conversation soon expanded to encompass that irritating illusion that occurs on many hills, you know the one I mean, where you go to the 'summit' cairn only to find there is another cairn 100m away that looks higher. So you go to that and look back and the cairn you have just left looks higher. After much pontification, John Barnard volunteered to research the subject and identify methods for easily determining small height differences in the field. At the next meeting he reported on what he had found out. He described a small instrument called an Abney level that easily tucks away in a rucksack and weighs only a couple of hundred grams. For more exacting work we could buy a surveyor's level and staff which would only set us back £150. You will have noticed that alcohol is a thread in this tale so far, and since I'd had more than my share, I found myself saying what a great idea it would be to equip ourselves with this gear. Suddenly we were in business and a team of two.

Our first success came almost immediately when we surveyed a hill in the Yorkshire Dales called Birks Fell. At 609m (1998ft) it had long been suspected that it might be over 2000ft in height, in which case it would rise to the rank of Mountain in the eyes of Sassenachs. We could not measure heights directly with the equipment we had, but the hill had two trig points and these usually have recorded heights accurate to about 0.1m. After two days of hard work we located the highest point on the fell and determined the height to be 610.4m (2002.6ft). Our friends John and Anne Nuttall reported this to a contact in Ordnance Survey and it was finally confirmed that the measurement was correct and that Birks Fell was a new mountain for England.

Not long afterwards John and Anne put us in touch with another nascent surveyor, Myrddyn Phillips, a keen hillwalker who wanted to see our surveying techniques. He was even keen to carry the heaviest bits of gear, so was immediately recruited and we were now a team of three.

Despite this early success, we still couldn't measure heights without a nearby trig point to survey from. More research revealed that what we needed was a survey-grade GPS. We met up with a representative of Leica GeoSystems who showed us this shiny new toy in operation. It was indeed impressive and we were told it could measure heights to better than 10cm. Brand new these 'toys' cost £15–20k, but he just happened to have a second hand model we could have at a more modest price. He even let us borrow it for a few days and indeed it did just what he said it would. We had to have it and the rest is history!

All this happened in 2006–08 so let me fast-forward now to 2013. After many successful surveys, mainly in England and Wales, since this is where we live, we set our sights on something altogether more challenging. For a long while the question of the height of Knight's Peak had bugged us. It was made a Munro Top in the 1997 edition of *Munro's Tables* based on the best mapping information available at that time. There were lots of measurements from maps, however, which ranged from 911m to 915m, but no consensus view emerged from this wealth of data. Could we get up there to measure it carrying all our gear? Was there enough room to set the GPS receiver up on the summit? What was the best route to the top? We also knew that Knight's Peak had two summits of very similar height. Was there room to set up a surveyor's level to determine the higher of the two? If not we would either have to record GPS data from both summits or perhaps take two GPS receivers? Could we find another GPS receiver to borrow? If we took only one receiver would we have time to complete the survey in a single day? I should also add we are not rock climbers, although many years ago we had scrambled to the top of Knight's Peak from Coire a' Bhasteir and up 4/5 Gully. But we were a lot younger then and we went with just light daysacks. Clearly we needed a multi-skilled team to pull this one off! So the plan was hatched. We approached the SMC to get a view on the feasibility of the project and whether there would be interest in joining such an expedition. We were pleased to receive support and interest from Andy Nisbet and Noel Williams who said they would like to join us. Our contacts at The Munro Society (TMS) also expressed interest in the project and offered to arrange accommodation on Skye. We were also asked by TMS if we could survey the Basteir Tooth during our stay and there was the offer to help carry some of the equipment. Finally we received confirmation from a colleague, Alan Dawson, of a second GPS receiver. After many exchanges of e-mail and numerous telephone conversations it was

The Knight's Peak Survey Team.
L to R: Alan Dawson, Andy Nisbet, Iain Brown, David Batty, Iain Robertson, Colin Walter, Alan Brook, John Barnard, Graham Jackson. Photo: Myrddyn Phillips.

decided we would book the bunkhouse at Portnalong for a week in September for the attempt of both surveys. The pieces of the jigsaw had finally come together! Within the team we had the intimate knowledge of the Skye ridge, the technical skills to get us to the top and a keen band to help carry all the gear. All we needed now was favourable weather.

Wednesday 11 September dawned dark and grey with frequent showers of rain drifting across the landscape. The soft pattering of rain drops on the window pane told me all I needed to know. The forecast from the previous day was right and I tried to get back to sleep. Then a voice in the gloom declared, 'It's not too bad out there; the MWIS forecast said it will brighten up this afternoon.' Andy had been outside to inspect the weather and declared the attempt on Knight's Peak was on. I reluctantly said goodbye to a warm bunk and got dressed. After a quick breakfast we gathered all the gear together and headed down the road towards Sligachan. To everyone's amazement Andy's assessment was correct. As we approached the parking place the rain stopped and the cloud base lifted slightly. The tops were still in cloud, but at least we could see the start of the path across the road disappearing into the gloom. Crucially, there was little wind, as there is no secure anchorage for the equipment on the summit of Knight's Peak, although we did not know it at the time. We set off following the tourist path up to 550m and while the day remained dull the cloud base began to lift as we walked and we did not meet it again until we were above 600m. On leaving the tourist path we turned north-east following beneath a rocky rib for about 400 metres and gaining another 150m of height. This brought us to a boulder field whereupon we turned south-east for another 400 metres which brought

The Leica GPS receiver on the NW top of Knight's Peak. Graham Jackson is standing in shadow on the north side. Photograph taken from the SE top by Alan Dawson.

us to 4/5 Gully. At the head of this was the crux of the route, a short climb up greasy basalt to the bealach between Knight's Peak and Sgùrr nan Gillean. Here Andy set up a rope to haul up the gear (and one or two of us in the party!). The bealach gave room only for a couple of people so as we emerged on to it there was a pressing need to continue up the narrow rake to the summit. Here we inspected the challenge we had set ourselves. The first summit we scrambled up was the easier north-west summit. There was no problem getting on to it but there was very little room to set up the GPS receiver. We looked across to the south-east top, the mist clearing sufficiently to give us a view of it. It looked a harder scramble and an even less promising position for a GPS receiver. We started to set up our GPS receiver on a small tripod and then adjusted it until it was aligned with the highest point of the summit rock. Rocks placed on the base of the tripod gave some stability to the set-up and Andy then used a climbing tape to secure it further to the summit rock. In the meantime Alan managed to establish himself on the more difficult south-east top. Through the ingenious use of a woolly hat he was able to secure a stable perch for his GPS receiver right on the very summit. Both receivers were now switched on and a long two-hour wait began while data were collected. Simultaneous data collection would give the most accurate height difference between the two summits, although our small hand-held Abney level indicated that the north-west summit was about

10cm higher than the south-east one. Finally, our sojourn was complete and just as we were packing away the gear, the sun finally broke through the mist and there before us was a brocken spectre, a truly spectacular reward for those hours of gloom. Days in September are not long and darkness was upon us by the time we arrived back at the cars at 20.15hrs. But what a day!

Thursday 12 September was very wet and windy, so it was on Friday 13 September that we set out for the Basteir Tooth. The route was led by Noel who took us up the tourist path again, until at a fork we followed a less distinct track towards the start of Pinnacle Ridge. Ahead was the unpromising sight of steep scree slopes which beckoned as they loomed larger in our field of view. Then we could discern a faint path across them which turned out to be an excellent route to the Bealach a' Bhasteir. The forecast had been very promising with sunshine and the chance of a shower. The 'chance' shower foretold its impending presence as dark clouds gathered. Am Basteir was steeper than I had remembered and rain made it appear steeper still as we plodded slowly upwards into the gathering gloom. By the time we reached the 'bad step' the rain had stopped, but it had done its work, making the rock of the step as greasy as if it had been buttered. Andy set up a rope and we made our way down it one by one, some more gracefully than others. At the summit we quickly continued, descending steeply to a stance above a steep drop. Here we abseiled down to steep ground and then quickly made our way to the summit of The Tooth. 'That was quite exhilarating' I confessed and was quickly assured that the best was yet to come. There was no doubt about the location of the summit of The Tooth. The rock rose steeply to a point upon which resided a large boulder. I'm sure opinion will be divided as to whether the summit is the top of the boulder or the bedrock beneath. We set up the receiver level with the top of the boulder but also measured the height difference to the boulder's base just for good measure. We then just had to amuse ourselves for two hours while we collected enough data for OS to process. Time passed quickly from this airy perch as the views were stunning and the banter kept us on our toes. Andy and Noel also disappeared for a while to show two of the party the way down. Then another wee shower enveloped us during the last few minutes of data collection making the lower basalt section of the Tooth very slippery. Finally we packed away the equipment and made our way down to the bealach between The Tooth and Am Basteir. Noel's 'the best is yet to come' and his recent absence were now apparent. He disappeared into a hole between massive boulders and we followed like children behind the Pied Piper. This abode of troglodytes brought us to a small cavern with an awe-inspiring drop at its end. There we saw the reason for Noel's and Andy's absence. They had set up an abseil point to take us from the cave's mouth down the 24m drop to the foot of King's Cave Chimney and terra firma. The surveyors tossed a coin to decide

Andy Nisbet belays Graham Jackson down the Bad Step on the east ridge of Am Basteir with Sgùrr nan Gillean behind. Photo: Hon. Ed.

John Barnard, Andy Nisbet and Alan Brook while away the time during the two hour survey on the Basteir Tooth. Photo: Hon Ed.

who should be last. I lost and went first. Once past the overhang it was plain sailing and extremely exhilarating, although my body made as much contact with the wall as did my feet. Soon we were all down and on our way back to the car after another 11hr day.

So those were the surveys, but what about the results? The heights we obtained are tabulated below and we give both our values and the OS values calculated from the datasets we collected.

Highest point	G&J Surveys (m)	Ordnance Survey (m)
Knight's Peak NW Top	914.24	914.24
Knight's Peak SE Top	914.13	914.16
Basteir Tooth – boulder	917.14	917.16
Basteir Tooth – bedrock	916.55	N/A

Knight's Peak is less than 914.4m (3000ft) by just 16cm and subsequently has been removed from Munro's Tables by the SMC. The measurement uncertainty for the result as calculated by Ordnance Survey is +/-3cm. The Basteir Tooth is slightly higher than the height given on current maps and therefore retains its position as a Munro Top on a height criterion.

For interested readers a table of the Munros, Corbetts and Grahams that we have surveyed is given in the Appendix. Again the OS heights in this table have been calculated from our datasets.

These surveys certainly rank as the hardest we have ever attempted both in surveying difficulty and accessibility. Only with the selfless effort of every element of the combined team were we able to succeed. For the reader interested in a little more detail we describe the precision and accuracy of the techniques we use in the Appendix below along with a summary of all the Munros, Corbetts and Grahams we have measured to date.

Appendix

In this section we describe accuracy of the techniques we use, since there are some who have quite rightly questioned our claims. For summits of hills we first find the highest point using a surveyor's level and staff. This is straightforward for Munros and the uncertainty attached to this operation is of the order of 1cm or less. Flat moorland summits in the Pennines or mid-Wales can present a bigger challenge and in extreme cases we can do no better than 10cm. The GPS receiver itself records data from GPS satellites orbiting the earth at 20,000km and stores these data on an SD card every few seconds (we usually choose a time interval of 15sec). Ordnance Survey stipulates that we collect a minimum of 2hr of data if the dataset is to be processed by their geodesist and the result used for updating maps. These data are then processed in commercially

Andy Nisbet lowers Alan Brook down King's Cave Chimney. Photo: Hon. Ed.

available software along with data from the nearest (usually six to eight) Ordnance Survey Active Base Stations. These form a network of sites evenly spread across the country that have a GPS on them continuously collecting data and their positions and heights are known very accurately indeed. So we are actually measuring our position and height relative to these base stations, a technique known as differential GPS and it is a very accurate technique.

If we measure the same point twice we would expect to get agreement to within +/-6cm of the 'real' answer. This is not a figure we have made up; it is the result of taking regular measurements at a fixed point numerous times and constructing something called a Statistical Quality Control chart to check that the instrument is working properly. All the points we have ever taken (over 70) have yielded results between 136.35m and 136.45m for the fixed point we have chosen. From this work we can also calculate mathematical descriptions to define measurement uncertainty more precisely, in this case +/-0.06m to three standard deviations. Note that OS uses leading-edge software developed by the University of Berne and therefore is able to quote a smaller measurement uncertainty for our data sets usually of the order of +/-3cm. We also regularly visit an Ordnance Survey (OS) fundamental bench mark, a brass stud set in a concrete block that OS has measured by GPS numerous times and is there for surveyors to use as a check. The heights of these are quoted to 1mm. The one we use is quite close to an active base station and we have always obtained results between 73.20m and 73.24m; the quoted height is 73.24m.

Differential GPS is the most accurate technique available for measuring height and position and is used by OS and many surveying companies. Ordnance Survey is the body responsible for mapping in the UK. Nowadays its effort is mainly directed towards projects that improve the infrastructure of the UK or help generate wealth for the country. It also has a responsibility to ensure that every part of the country is mapped at least once every five years. To achieve the latter objective OS uses a technique called photogrammetry which employs aerial photography as the mapping tool. Heights calculated by this technique are accurate to +/-3m. Note that the previous technique of levelling could achieve better than 0.1m but the manpower effort involved is enormous and OS would not be able to deliver on its five year timescale if this method were still employed. Nevertheless maps are fit for purpose in that the user can navigate accurately using them. It doesn't matter whether Ben Nevis is 1341m or 1347m, you can still safely use an OS map to get to the top and down again. Of course Ordnance Survey also owns GPS receivers like our own, both in the field for specialised work and on its network of 120 base stations that we mentioned above, but once again this technique is far too slow to enable OS to meet that five year objective.

Table of Munros, Corbetts and Grahams Surveyed by G&J Surveys

Hill Name	Grid Ref	G&J Height (m)	OS Height (m)
Beinn Teallach	NN361859	914.64	914.60
Ben Vane	NN277098	915.79	915.76
Sgùrr a' Choire-beithe	NG895015	913.32	
Sgùrr nan Ceannaichean	NH087480	913.46	913.43
Geal-charn	NN596782	917.10	
Beinn a' Chleibh	NN250256	916.32	
The Fara	NN598842	911.36	
Beinn a' Chlaidheimh	NH061775	913.98	913.96
Beinn Dearg Mòr	NH032799	906.33	906.28
Ruadh Stac Mòr	NH018756	918.65	
Leathad a' Taobhain	NN821858	911.71	
Beinn Bhreac	NN868820	912.44	
Knight's Peak	NG471254	914.24	914.24
Basteir Tooth	NG465252	917.14	917.16
Sgùrr a' Bhac Chaolais	NG958110	885.21	885.21
Buidhe Bheinn	NG963090	885.51	885.50
Beinn Talaidh	NM625347	761.70	

THE UNUSUALLY SNOWY WINTER OF 2013/14

By Blair Fyffe

THE WINTER OF 2013/14 was an unusual one in terms of weather with the whole of Britain being affected by an exceptional run of winter storms. While this led to flooding and coastal erosion through much of England and Wales, it led to unusually large deposits of snow on the Scottish hills, particularly on the west coast. Although little snow fell at sea level, at higher levels it was the snowiest winter since at least 1994.

A combination of two factors produced the unusually snowy conditions. Firstly the high rates of precipitation, and secondly the consistently sub-zero temperature on the summits. This meant that at higher levels almost all the precipitation fell as snow.

The persistent storms were driven on by an unusually strong Atlantic Jet Stream which resulted in it being the wettest winter for England, Wales and Scotland, and the second wettest winter for Northern Ireland, in a series from 1910. It was also the wettest winter in the much longer-running England and Wales precipitation series which goes back to 1766. There were more days of rain during the winter than any other in a series from 1961.

The UK overall recorded 154% of December average rainfall and 151% of the January average rainfall. The wet theme continued through February, which was the 4th wettest in the series. For winter overall the UK received 161% of average rainfall.

Data more specific to the mountains comes from the Nevis Range snowsports resort which has a record of rainfall at the base station going back to January 1999. The precipitation values for the winter of 2013/14 were 471mm for December, 394mm for January and 368mm for February. These correspond to the 1st, 8th and 10th wettest months in the whole 183-month series. They are also the wettest December and February on record, and the second wettest January, only beaten by January 2005. Most of the precipitation in December, and almost all of it during the next two months would have fallen as snow on the tops.

Despite the fact that overall it was quite a mild winter, it was never really mild. There was a notable absence of frosts, and the lowest UK temperature of the winter, -7.7°C at Altnaharra, Sutherland on 17 February was the highest such winter value for at least 50 years.

Early December was quite mild, and around the middle of the month the hills were almost bare of snow. After around 20 December the summits stayed almost totally sub-zero for nearly three months. There was not a major thaw on the tops until around the 13 March. The freezing level did very briefly rise to summit level, with a 1200m temperature of 0.8°C estimated on 17 January and 0.5°C on 18 February. It is very unusual to have such a long period without a major thaw at this level.

A French guide fell several 100m (and lived) when the cornice above No. 4 Gully collapsed under him. Photo: LMRT.

The CIC Hut on Ben Nevis. Photo: sportscotland Avalanche Information Service (SAIS).

After about 13 March the winter fizzled out with a series of thaws and generally mild temperatures and no further significant snow falls.

An analysis of pressure fields by the University of East Anglia suggests this winter has had more very severe gale days than any other winter season in a series from 1871.

The result of all this was the ski areas had trouble with ski lifts being buried by the vast amounts of snow. On the west coast the Cliff-Hanger Chairlift and the Main Basin T-bar at Glen Coe ski area, and the Goose

A spectacular avalanche in Observatory Gully, Ben Nevis, 12 March 2014. Photo: SAIS.

T-Bar and Summit Button at Nevis Range regularly had to be dug out. Further east, Glen Shee and CairnGorm ski areas also had problem with tows being buried. In terms of climbing few if any routes were done high on Ben Nevis through January and February. The whole mountain was quiet with the numbers on the Allt a' Mhuilinn path being just over half what they had been the previous winter. The best climbing seemed to be in the North-West Highlands, which did not receive such unusual amounts of snow, with Beinn Eighe in particular proving popular.

A strange sight at the CIC Hut...

...and a strange man at the controls! Photos: LMRT.

THIRTY DEGREES

By John Mackenzie

IF YOU ARE LOOKING FOR a place that is remote, yet accessible for a day, far from the crowds and where mobile phones don't often work then the long Glen of Strathfarrar is just right for you. It begins as a glen on the east and ends as a strath on the west, seventeen long miles, possibly more and with a locked gate at the start. It has classical Highland scenery of Caledonian pine, deer by the hundreds, hills and mountains and bags for baggers to collect both Corbett and Munro. So far so good save for the tiny problem of the gate. The gate is open in the spring to autumn months with restricted hours and closed in the winter unless you phone the MCofS office first who will give you a combination number to let yourself in and out via the lock. Naturally the combination number changes frequently.

Apart from bagging and low level walking, what else is there to do? Lots of medium grade winter climbing for a start and a modicum of relatively high up mountain routes in summer. What are the advantages? Well, several actually. In winter it's a cold place that escapes the tendrils of thaw from either side of the country. It collects snow in quantity, its crags tend to face east or north-east as well as south and not least it's unlikely that there will be a rush to get to the crag first thing or indeed there will be anyone above you at all. You may even have not just a crag but the entire mountain to yourself. Phew! That's a good start when compared to the Northern Corries for instance.

The most developed summer and winter crags are on the east-facing schist crags of Sgùrr na Muice and Sgùrr na Fearstaig. They are not monotonously regular but vary in structure, each crag and indeed each facet being unlike its neighbour. The south-east facing slabby crags of Sgùrr na Muice are better suited for rock climbing, having delicate often rather bold routes from VDiff to HVS whilst the north-east facet is riven into an extraordinary series of folds that contain a large number of parallel corners and grooves, each offering a rather different experience under winter conditions.

Sgùrr na Fearstaig's east face is more conventional in layout having gullies and steeply slabby faces with corners that offer quite juggy summer rock climbs as well as conventional and often strongly pronounced winter ones. The crags on both mountains rely quite heavily on frozen turf for upward mobility in winter but equally present cleaner faces for summer which is geologically and botanically, very convenient. An added bonus is the good track to reach them so there are no long Cairngorms style plods with nightmare navigation to contend with. The Northern Highland Central guide gives most of the routes with the added fun of a mixed up topo for the north-east face of Sgùrr na Muice where

The North-East Face of Sgùrr na Muice. Photo: John Mackenzie.

after route No. 14, things get out of sequence by one, so route No. 19 on the topo for instance should in fact correspond to No. 20 in the text; all good fun in mist.

Apart from these two well-developed crags, there are others, more shyly hiding away in less accessible places. The splendid mountain of Sgùrr na Lapaich is the highest in the area and dominates the west end of the glen. It has many interesting nooks and crannies plus a fine ridge scramble up its East Ridge from the (very) aptly named Garbh-choire. The guide book describes several remote crags, some best approached from Loch Mullardoch and some from the far west end of Strathfarrar. Topographically, this whole area is an interesting, remote and well-contoured riot of shapely mountains in mid-Ross where any hillgoer worthy of the name will find their hill-batteries re-charged anew.

For winter climbing there are several really rather good routes, starred appropriately in the guide of which the best known – and ascended – are *Pearls Before Swine* on the north-east face of Sgùrr na Muice and *The Sorcerer* on the east face of Sgùrr na Fearstaig. Both require ice as well as frozen turf and the former is generally easier than the latter.

Having given a rather dry introduction to what is quite a big area in practice I thought a description of two outings in winter 2013, in what may be exceptional conditions, could be more interesting. The first is on Sgùrr na Muice's north-east face and the second on Creag Garbh-choire.

Sgùrr na Muice means 'rock of the pig' so almost every route name has piggy-based connections, some stretching to verbal puns such as *Pigmalion* or *Left Pork*, which is the route finally climbed in 2013. I and several patient friends, undoubtedly lulled into acquiescence into indulging me, have several times plodded up either in hopelessly snowy conditions or else in equally hopelessly bare ones. However this winter, as in so many other areas of Scotland, things were different.

The friends in this instance were Mike Cocker and Colin Wells, both SMC and FRCC Members and Dave Broadhead and I, so it was a sort of unofficial Club Meet with both clubs represented. Having just, but only just, recovered from the adult version of whooping cough, I was feeling pretty wabbit but determined to make the most of both conditions and forecast. The day dawned brilliant, clear, cold and surely ambition and patience would be rewarded. The line in question was the left fork of *Pearls Before Swine* which despite a spirited effort by Simon Nadin the previous winter was foiled by wafer-thin ice.

With hardly a breath of wind stirring on the 24 February we rounded the nose of the mountain and through binoculars saw that the line in question was white top to bottom. Pulses quickened with the thoughts of a quick nip up and a straightforward doddle; well, sort of. How many times have you stood at the foot of this easy looking ice pitch only to have the angle sweep up through 30°, the thickly rimed buttress that turns out to be a nightmarish scrabble, the well frozen turf that pulls through at every other strike of the axe. We've all been there lots of times, and no doubt will continue to do so, buoyed up by the thought 'it will be better this time!' The trouble is, it might be and so it's worth 'a look'…

The steep Grade I approach to the crags was on excellent névé which unfortunately was in better condition than I was. The 'hundred-day cough' was exacting vengeance for my as usual over-optimism and the slope seemed endless. It is hard to deeply breathe whilst trying to cough at the same time, an inconvenient marriage of opposites. Nevertheless with Dave up in front and the other pair gaining ground below our sporting instincts were insisting that we should ideally remain in pole position. Fortunately I knew exactly where the peg belay should be when we arrived below the lower tier (on the left for future reference). Sometimes a fine steep icefall flows over this tier, as on the first ascent of *Pearls Before Swine,* but now it was a barrier of rock, brown stained where the ice flowed. Fortunately this was not the end of the attempt as a hidden narrow gully runs left parallel to the barrier where a right-facing corner allows access to the main crag higher up.

Meanwhile the other pair were setting up their belays to our right and so without further delay Dave set off up the gully to then head up towards the hidden corner further up. The remains of the icefall lay close to the corner and with Dave belayed near its exit; I had the definite pleasure of climbing rather thin but quality ice to his stance.

Above lies a snow terrace that cuts across the face like a white cravat with the various routes reached by traversing left or right. The entrance to *Pearls Before Swine* lies to the right from where we were so, feeling slightly more recovered, I headed up towards the most obvious entrance on the entire face, a steep gully entered by a pair – the choice is yours – of two short ice funnels. I took the right one and headed further on up this enclosed avenue sealed in by rock walls and blocked ahead by a wall where the original route takes the more obvious right fork and bounds up a narrow gully over turfy bulges and icy excitements to the top.

My 60m of rope ran sadly short of the blockage but a fine wee pedestal with generous belays lay on the right, a good vantage point to see what was going to happen above and indeed what was currently happening below. Dave was soon moving past me and heading towards the much less optimistic-looking left fork whilst Mike and Colin were heading our way too. From here the left fork was a vee-shaped slit with a vertical right wall and a steeply sloping slabby left one. A small patch of snow lay under a roof where the right wall curved leftwards to meet a narrow icefall that disappeared above. To reach the hoped-for haven of the snow, Dave would have to somehow climb very thin ice indeed; the point where Simon had to turn back last year.

A couple of solid-looking runners at the commencement of the ice at least ensured a backup to the belay. Strange contorted shufflings ensued. The ice was barely a half inch thick at most and so to ensure upward progress Dave had his back to the right wall. This looked most precarious but interestingly, the higher he got, the more determined he came. He reached the snow patch but it must have been the only area of snow on the entire face which was soft powder and not névé. It was sugar lying atop smooth crackless rock, a continuation of the slabby left wall, offering no help. So sheltered is this spot, this hoped for cosy nook, that any snow lies protected from much of the weather and fails to metamorphose into something more usable.

Now began a fascinating sequence of slipping feet and wild torques in the fortunately cracked right wall. It was either good for the feet or good for the axes but never both together. By now the other pair were also watching Dave with interest, aware of their own vulnerable position if he should become seriously unstuck. He was well above the last runner and needed to gain just a little more height to where a bar of rock, a stone sausage, jutted out almost horizontally below the curving overhang. This, with effort, he reached and a really solid nut was his reward. However to reach the icefall to his left would mean standing on the 'sausage'. A left heel hook – most unusual for Dave – led the attack and by cramped torques he gained a simian crouch atop this feature. Because it sloped down to the left his position was untenable unless quick action was taken. A long stride out left just so happened to coincide with the only tuft of turf on the entire pitch and once clear of the overhang he could stand in balance and hook the ice. This was done splendidly well

Dave Broadhead on the crux of Left Pork (24 February 2013). Photo: John Mackenzie.

and before long he had found himself a most scenic perch on the right wall.

Now it was my turn. Just in case the lurgy would return at an inopportune moment, I swallowed some energy gel out of a squidgy tube that didn't want to easily open. This is not always a good idea. Once, just before a particularly steep ice pitch on Nevis, I ate half a packet of glucose tablets. Apparently I went 'like six men' before the effect rapidly wore off and was left, a mere human again, to finish the pitch up which I wobbled.

Up at the base of the blockage it all seemed strangely familiar, after all I had been here before. The difference was that the angle had shot up 30 degrees and the ice was thin. The boy had done good as they say. So I backed and I footed, just, and scrabbled and reached the snow only to find that like Dave the axes just scraped uselessly. However cracks there were on the right but awkward to use and once in use, lo and behold, feet simply shot off leaving a series of, effectively, pull ups to reach the stone sausage. His runner – my biggest nut – was totally bomb-proof unlike the flimsy one below which only deserved the name runner because it had slid down the rope very rapidly.

Standing on the sausage was a horribly cramped, part western roll and part twisting of axe picks in order to stand, upon which victory the inevitable slide off into the abyss was only halted by a rapid bridge out to the lonely tuft. Well done Dave! The ice was reached and soon attained by all fours, it was all over, at least for this pitch. Strangely all lurgy was quite gone, banished to lower levels.

Now it was my turn to enjoy a lovely run of ice, plastic in consistency, up the narrow chimney above. This too had a blockage which was another possible mystery but when approached suddenly revealed a tight way through and up onto more open and easier ground. I took a scenic stance overlooking the original line and had the opportunity of watching and talking to Colin Wells as he hunted around for a belay, a great spot to give others unnecessary advice!

Our route finished with another long but easier pitch up a natural groove, a pleasant but un-taxing finale to end not far from the summit cairn. We then were treated to a fine show of atmospherics with clouds dropping below us and then clearing to give panoramas down the glen in one direction and out to the West in another. Mike and Colin had enjoyed the original line greatly and the only pity was that the lower icefall had melted away. Dave came up with the totally appropriate name of *Left Pork*; very punny indeed.

Winter continued and ice began to reform and thicken at medium altitudes, together with more settled weather at the end of March. The 30th dawned clear and Spring-like but I had this hunch that a tucked in nook like the Garbh-choire at the far end of the glen might offer a sporting chance of cold and shade. This time Neil Wilson and Simon Nadin had 'volunteered' and as we drove up the long windy road, the car thermometer never registered above freezing. The far end overlooks Loch Monar and two dams are driven over to reach the narrow tail-end of Strathfarrar, Gleann Innis an Loichel. Caledonian pine stud the south side and amidst this picture-postcard scenery, our car was parked near the power station sluice, a slightly unusual piece of 'industrialisation', impressively jetting water into the Uisge Misgeach. In colder conditions it turns the bridge and surroundings into a fairy-tale grotto of ice grapes but I have never known it to freeze up entirely.

Crawling under the pipeline starts a rather brutal walk, a 160m ascent from the flat where the angle sometimes requires a quick grab of the fence or a duck under the low-lying birches. This then leads to the open wastes of the Garbh-choire, a big wide undulating peat-bogged slope that drains the northern slopes of Sgùrr na Lapaich and Càrn nan Gobhar. Neil and I had floundered up this earlier in the season through/in soft snow and found all the major bogs en route. We had succeeded in climbing a distinctly out-of-condition buttress so hoped for better things all round today.

As luck and timing would have it, the ground was frozen hard and once at the snow line the crust though breakable was bearable, especially with Neil breaking trail which allowed Simon and I to follow in his slipstream. By keeping to the left away from Sgùrr na Lapaich's north ridge, the ground was easier and the gradient moderate so we arrived at the big flats just before the crag in reasonable fettle with Neil about 300m in front.

Brilliant sun, warm and with no wind to dissipate the heat, greeted us. An anxious look up at the crag showed all the narrow gully lines runs of ice. I had never seen it look so icy before. We retired to a gearing up boulder, now a snowy ridge, to hold the traditional council of war, as one does. The obvious, the most sought after and the most visited line, all previously to no avail, now looked to be possible. The steep narrow deep-set gully on the left of the crag usually sports a series of chockstones or barrier walls with thin vertical ice curtains, possibly too fragile to climb, cascading over. Now all signs of rock save for the retaining walls had gone. For a moment it looked a doddle but I knew how steep these lines really were though optimism kept creeping in segment by segment. Before long, we were off, with Neil ploughing up the softish apron snows, trying to avoid falling through holes between boulders.

I found a good spike belay on the left of the gully entrance and with Simon self-appointed cameraman, Neil set off immediately, announcing perfect ice. In the sun it was definitely warm with dripping ice but step into the shade and the drips stopped. Here we were in Alpine conditions in the north of Scotland about to get a suntan, most unusual. An echoing voice from above announced a request for us to follow and this we did. A most pleasing warm-up on plastic ice at a civilised angle, though of course 30° steeper than it looked from below, saw us at Neil's cramped stance, huddled into the left wall.

Above looked steep, quite seriously steep and I hadn't as yet added the 30°. Strangely there was a marked reticence for up and coming leaders with Simon fixed determinedly on camera work and Neil hunched for action at his belay. I was handed the three ice screws and a load of rock gear and found myself in the front with much expected of me.

The gully had narrow walls that had squeezed a tube of ice more-or-less vertically down the slot where the summer chockstones would be. The side walls were austerely bare of cracks and so my rack of gear would inevitably hang albatross-like, weighty but useless, unless lucky. A few steps up soft ice led to the expected 30° increase in angle, any more and it would have overhung. Now, as ice goes, this was stratigraphically interesting. Bone hard on the left and soft on the right with just little bits of perfect in isolated spots; I tried the first of Neil's long, reassuring ice screws. Strangely it didn't, despite the adverts to the contrary, whizz on in. It went in a few centimetres and then stopped and simply kept turning without any gain in depth. A little judicious force and it entered a hollow. Not very good at all, rather like some of my early

The author on the crux pitch of Hollow Heart. Photo: Simon Nadin.

school reports that read 'Needs to Try Harder'. The saving grace was that if strategically placed, axe picks went in rather well unlike crampon points that often bounced off the ice despite being sharp.

Now there is only so much one can say about ice but this really was a melange of incompatible crystals vying to be the least helpful. I battered in another of Neil's screws somewhat higher as the angle approached the truly plumb but it too entered a void and woggled about. Probably best not to fall off in these circumstances and be thoroughly old fashioned. The pitch lengthened considerably and the angle kept a hearty inclination but the picks still picked and the crampons, if used with vigour, stuck long enough for another pick to take over the strain. Unfortunately, the walls either side remained quite bare until just before the final bulge, where I managed to get an upside-down 3 Friend in a flared hole. Even Simon laughed at this one. The final bulge, the third vertical section suddenly fell back to reveal nicely frozen turf, rather on the lean side but very welcome. Still no further protection but it now felt like home with a final turfy wall to end the difficulties. The angle fell back, the retaining walls opened and a most secure thread belay was attained from the left walls higher up. Neil's' third ice screw was still firmly attached to me as was the rest of the gear, still determined to be an albatross. Due to the rather hollow nature of the ice and the fact that it felt, for me at least, a bit of a heart-stopper, the name *Hollow Heart* seemed adequate.

The others came up in due course having exercised manfully en-route. Perhaps they found it not quite a doddle after all, which was pleasing to see, so it was quite relaxing to plod up the pleasant exit gully to the top and to descend, rather circuitously, to the bottom from the right-hand side. At our gearing-up 'boulder' we had lunch and realised there was quite sufficient time for another 'doddle' up the left-hand corner of the crag which was a short distance from the previous line. This looked somewhat easier and had a tree low down on the left for an initial belay.

Once up to the foot, almost immediate comedy ensued. Neil would romp up to the tree and get a sling around it and bring us up. The romp, as always steepened through 30° and included a turfy bulge which neither I, stuck below the said bulge, or Simon sensibly still at the start, refused to leave without being firmly attached to the rope, one of which fortunately was with Neil. The tree then showed who was boss by retreating up the side wall out of reach but a fine deep crack more than sufficed for a belay.

Once up and untangled, Simon was elected to be in the van, which he did with relief to get away from the excessive amount of rope and gear and the fact that any debris from above would inevitably land on me. Of course the narrow chute above was superb ice which did, typically, take screws. It was however as Simon had realised, a 'shoot' as well as a chute and the bombardment of lumps of ice had Neil and I truly 'in the line of fire'. Above, Simon seemed to have run into an entertaining final shield of ice that from here merely looked steep but foreshortened. However, once it was our turn to follow, the pitch was both long and most pleasant on thick ice until of course that final shield. This was just off vertical but made up for it by being rippled and not very thick. Axes pecked at this like woodpeckers in a flourish but only really produced starred holes before striking rock if over-zealous. It was a good, steady lead by Simon who then belayed way off to the right. This added a little frisson to seconding because, if either Neil or I had come off, we would have had an unenviable swing. (*Heart of Glass* IV,5.)

Descending to the left was both quicker and easier and being the oldest I was down to the sacs last. However, on the walk out Neil was once again in front, despite our best efforts to catch up, but he waited for us before the final decent. This can be a tricksy place, full of steepness, branches, fences and other hazards to trip and take a headlong dive into something painful at the end of a busy day. We didn't, however, fall into this trap but grovelled under the pipe at the base again and relished the luxury of a soft seat in the car at the end of a satisfying day.

So, three more routes finally climbed but I have this funny feeling that the straight gully we called *Hollow Heart* will be entirely different under a 'normal' winter, probably better protected but more athletic. We will see.

SEANA BHRAIGH – REMOTE OR WHAT?

By Smiler Cuthbertson

WITH ONLY THIRTY DAYS left before my Outdoor Odyssey to Peru and Alpamayo, I felt it was time to do some training. Seana Bhraigh (927metres) was described as occupying a remote situation and vying for the title of 'the most distant Munro'. It had been on my mind for a fair while, since tagging on to Mark and doing Ben Hope and that strenuous (full) traverse of Ben More Assynt.

Seana Bhraigh was one of Mark's few remaining Munros and it sounded tough. We were going to do it after our Ben More Assynt day but the weather clagged in and spoilt the plan. The plan was shelved until further notice.

I suspect I should have told Mark I was going, but with the brilliant forecast for Wednesday, my mind focused on the plan and I completely ignored looking for my usual walking partner.

I did appreciate the only photos I'd get would be of the route, the surrounding hills, and with no partner along, no shots of me on route? Oh well, the training was more important.

This good, long hike with a rucksack was called for. I left Loch Ness around 5.45 a.m. and sped along the A835 towards Ullapool. Turning off at the Beinn Dearg car park, I parked up, removed the mountain bike from the rack behind the car, had a last check of my belongings and mounted up.

It only takes about 15 to 20 minutes to reach the end of the forest track, where I locked the bike to the fence post, and set off up the steep track.

I had done the first section on a previous reconnaissance trip. That day I'd only started from the locked bike around 2 p.m., also on a very nice day, but it soon became apparent that no matter how swiftly I went, I wouldn't be able to reach the summit and get back home in time for dinner. As a result of this recce trip I had improved my knowledge of which path to take from the end of the forest. I quickly pulled up the steep incline and soon got pretty warm. I was carrying two separate litres of cool orange juice and a flask of tea, so there was little reason to get dehydrated. After reaching the easier-angled slopes, I stopped on the good path and had a swig of juice. It was a chance to look around.

An Teallach stood out proudly to the west, and in various other directions many more Munros poked their heads out of the haar. This would soon lift and it would turn into the forecasted clear and sunny day. After my break I continued across the ridge and dropped down into the glen leading up to Lochan Sgeireach. I then kept on the fairly good path to the right of this lochan in the corrie of the same name. I'd been this way before and the path was reasonable initially, but then I encountered some rocky ground which was awkward and time-consuming to cross.

The first lochan in Coire an Lochain Sgeirich.

This steeper terrain eventually lead up to easier ground on the plateau above.

I had anticipated that the ground would soon drop down again after reaching the col, so I was surprised to see I was in for quite a hike before reaching the succession of small lochans under Meall a' Choire Ghlais. This was new ground now and my adrenalin was rising. I knew I'd crack this beast today, hook or by crook.

That's one mistake I always make when solo hiking. I tend to go a little too fast. With no one to chat to, there seems no point in stopping for rests or other reasons. Why not crack on and get the job done? Today was no exception, and it was with some slight urgency that I tracked across the rough and then very wet ground towards where I knew the way should lead down into the wide area containing Loch a' Chadha Dheirg. Unfortunately I'd long since lost any real path, and was heading in the general direction of Gate of Ca'-derg. This was a slight mistake. As I dropped diagonally down some steeper, rocky ground between Meall a' Choire Ghlais and the rocky buttress to the east, I ended up on very nice flat terrain, but it was dreadfully wet. Melting snows had saturated large areas and I soon realised I should have held the higher ground to the north. There seemed no point in retracing my steps and I continued across what was very swampy ground. At one stage I stepped into what looked like a 25cm pool of murky water and suddenly I was up to my thighs in what can only be described as quicksand! It gave me quite a

The view west from the southern flank of Meall Glac an Ruighe.

scare, but refusing to go backwards, and with no solid ground anywhere around me, I waded forwards, lurching for protrusions of tufted grass. These appeared every four or five metres and offered islands of safety from where I could calculate my next few moves. Of course, everything below my thighs was now completely covered in slime and mud, but luckily the temperature of both the air and the water wasn't too off-putting. I was still heading in the right direction, with firmer, drier ground clearly ahead.

In a few more metres, the disaster was over, and I took stock of my grim lower half, shrugging my shoulders to the unpleasant mess I'd got myself into. With the forecast as it was, there seemed little point in changing my plans, and soon I was climbing more steeply through the Gate of Ca'-derg.

I stopped after a while to look around me, and was pleasantly surprised to see I had passed my dog-leg left point and was heading for the ring contour at 905m, before the final section to the summit. I was delighted. I switched up a gear and although there was now plenty of wet snow all around, I could usually find ways which mostly avoided me getting any wetter and possibly colder.

A quite proud Smiler reached the ring contour and without pausing, I broke a trail through the now deeper but not too offensive snow and down to the col on the summit ridge at 844m. I paused for a quick drink

Looking west to An Teallach from the summit plateau.

from my bottle and then headed slowly up towards the summit. What with the long approach, and the debacle of the swamp, I was now pretty tired. However, I was spurred on by the ever closer summit and at 11.20 a.m., just under four hours from leaving the mountain bike, I flopped against the outside of the summit shelter. The inside was full of snow, but I had no need of shelter in the beautiful weather. It was time for food and tea.

While taking the refreshments, I gazed around in a full 360° curve, and felt pretty good about my day and my surroundings. Many peaks still had snow on them. To the north there was a cluster of big peaks, which included Ben More Assynt and other great peaks beyond Ullapool, as well as Ben Hope even further north.

The tranquillity of the lunch hour was broken by the arrival of a couple all the way from London. They were on a camping trip and had done part of the ridge above Toman Còinich the previous day. They'd had a shorter climb from their tent to Seana Bhraigh's summit than I'd had. They pointed to where they said they'd left their rucksacks, but I couldn't really see anything. After a few more minutes of chatting, with my solo spell broken, I bade them farewell and headed back. Choosing to avoid the ring contour this time, I made good progress diagonally down and towards the Gate of Ca'-derg, having to re-adjust my line at one point, as I was getting a bit close to some very steep ground above Cadha Dearg.

The impressive face of Cadha Dearg where there are a number of winter climbs.

Very steep indeed, I pondered, as I looked down a huge cleft dropping vertically down to the Cadha Dearg, which I later worked out to be around 500 metres deep. The traversing ground was steeply inclined and covered alternatively in either wet snow or soaking wet grass, and I realised I'd have to re-ascend to avoid sliding into oblivion if I wasn't very careful. Completely soaked and without any stiff sole, my lovely trekking shoes were little help going sideways, so I gained height until some pressure lifted from my mind. I contoured on less steep ground now and dropping down I picked up a faint track, and soon reached the level area of the Gate of Ca'-derg. I was now on a roll and staying easily on the path, I moved rapidly towards my new goal, the flatter ground to the west of Meall a' Choire Ghlais.

Before reaching this easier section, there had been a moment when I'd thought about by-passing the steeper cliffs to the south, where it did look even easier ground, but now I was heading for home, I decided to re-trace my steps. Most of the time I was on a decent, though narrow path. I lost the path when going through the rocky section under the cliff, but I was saying to myself at regular intervals – déjà vu, I've been this way before.

There was still a small section of steep scrambling before I reached the level ground leading back over to Coire an Lochain Sgeirich, but it was easy enough and I emerged from the shadows, and headed across in a westerly direction on what was the best quality of path I'd seen for a while.

Of course, it was now clear the mistake I'd made coming up from Lochan Sgeireach. I had been on the wrong side of the glen. There were no rocks, and pretty-well dry ground, all the way across and down to the flat blocks of stone fording the outlet of the Allt an Lochain Sgeirich. I cursed silently, thinking how much easier it would have been if I'd come up the northern side of the glen. Still, no real harm done, although I did have to take a shot of my trekking trousers and boots. What a mess. At least now it was just dried, caked mud.

Reaching the ford crossing the stream, I ignored my annoyance and soon was contouring back up over the ridge into Coir a' Mhadaidh where at long last, the forestry plantations were in full view. It didn't seem long before I reached the mountain bike and was soon speeding down the track, clutching my peaked cap in fear of losing it, such was the downhill speed. The only interruptions were the gates, where I had to dismount and pass through on foot. The spare flask of tea in my car was a welcome ending to a great seven hours on the hill.

Some top tips?

Be sure to keep to the left (north) when reaching the first lochan, then the path is good and there are few rocks to scramble through. Using this northern side of the glen all the way across and below Meall a' Choire Ghlais, avoids almost all of the unpleasant swampy ground.

Take a mountain bike, in twenty fairly slow but easy minutes, to the forest end. The descent back to the A835 is sheer bliss.

FOGIES UNLIT

By John Spencer

IAN THREW ANOTHER log on the fire, sparking the embers into flame. 'Amazingly we haven't had an epic this trip' he mused, a hint of disappointment in his voice. 'So far...' I responded, 'although there's still time.' A meteor cut through the canopy of stars – an omen, perhaps? We'd been camping in the Valhalla Range in the Selkirks, British Columbia, for a week, with both families, children and all, plus some friends. Hiking through pristine backcountry, the kids rattling Coke cans full of pebbles to scare away the grizzlies. Climbing on the gnarly granite peaks, no guidebook or topos, just following our noses. Skinny dipping in the clear lakes to cool off. Sitting round the camp fire, passing the kouchie and fighting off the mosquitoes. Earlier in the holiday we'd enjoyed kayaking around the Broken Isles off Vancouver Island and some muscular cragging at Squamish, with lots of highway miles between. Plenty of opportunities for an epic, then. But nothing. So far.

A few days later we found ourselves in swirls of dust motoring up the long logging road out of Brisco, heading for the Bugaboos. I was due to fly home in three days' time so there was a window of opportunity for a final fling. Our target was the West Buttress of the South Howser Tower, known as the 'Beckey-Chouinard'. This iconic route, one of Roper and Steck's 'Fifty Classic Climbs' (1), was climbed by the legendary duo in 1961 and follows an elegant line up the remote pillar. For many years it was considered one of the more challenging Canadian Alpine rock routes, likened to the Bonatti Pillar on the Dru. For the first ascentionists it was a two-day tour-de-force, with 10 of the 20 pitches requiring aid, a total of around 130 pegs, bongs and the like (although apparently 'not a single bolt'!), with a given grade of 5.8, A2. Without aid it goes at 5.10a, albeit most of the climbing is considerably easier. Although obviously no longer considered an especially hard route, it has retained its classic status.

The Bugaboos, a.k.a. 'the Bugs', comprise a collection of granite spires and interconnecting glaciers located within the Bugaboo Provincial Park. Although easily reached from Highway 95 in the Columbia River valley, the main hazard being giant logging trucks trundling up and down the road, they really do keep themselves to themselves remaining '... hidden from view, tucked neatly away in the rugged Purcell wilderness until that final turn of the road up to the trailhead parking area.' (2) There are two explanations of the name: an old goldminer's term for a dead-end seam; and a monster frightening to little children (more recently, it was also adopted as the trade name for a line of gargantuan high-tech prams and pushchairs).

The range is surprisingly compact (136 sq km in area, compared to,

The West Face of Howser Spire
The Beckey-Chouinard Route takes the obvious arête leading to the South Tower, the highest peak on the right-hand part of the face. Photo: D. L. Ashliman.

say, Loch Lomond and the Trossachs at 1965 sq km) and there are only 20 or so distinct tops, the highest of which is Howser Spire at 3412m (11,194ft). However, it pulls no punches, indeed Fred Beckey's first reaction on seeing the western side of the Howser spires was apparently 'Patagonia'![1]

The climbing has a particularly remote feel to it – 'an encapsulated granite paradise shut off from the rest of the world.'[2] Alpine in scale, the routes range from a few hundred to a few thousand feet in length, and offer everything from ridge scrambling to multi-day big walls on crystalline grey granite. The main drawback is the weather. Violent electric storms are stock-in-trade. To quote the 1990 guide 'Nature cuts loose here with unbridled enthusiasm and total disregard for the recreationalist.' No worries for us, though the forecast was good for the next 36 hours.

The walk up from the trailhead car park to the Conrad Kain Hut, named after the Bugaboos pioneer, was a sweaty slog on this warm and

1   Steve Roper & Allen Steck, *Fifty Classic Climbs of North America* (San Francisco: Sierra Club, 1979).

2   Randall Green & Joe Bensen, *Bugaboo Rock. A Climber's Guide* (Seattle: The Mountaineers, 1990).

humid afternoon, the grind ameliorated somewhat by spectacular views across the Bugaboo Glacier as the jagged peaks revealed themselves one by one. The hut was packed to the gunwales, full of bustle and chat. Two possible consequences: we might not get much sleep; and we might have company on the hill.

And indeed we didn't get much sleep. Quite apart from the noise, there was the customary gut-churning restlessness in anticipation of a 'big day out', not helped by reading the most recent entry about the route in the hut logbook which talked of a huge cornice overhanging the descent route off South Howser Tower.

So some time in the gruesome small hours we staggered into the pitch darkness and stumbled our way up the moraine to the first steepening of snow on the Crescent Glacier. Dawn was breaking as we crunched our way onto the higher Vowell Glacier, the surrounding peaks – Snowpatch, Bugaboo, Pigeon – looming majestically above and around us. And what a glorious morning it was, very still with a bright blue, cloudless sky. In due course the Howser peaks – South, North and, the highest, Central – hove into view. We paused for a quick reconnaissance of the descent line off the South Tower, which follows a system of grooves on the north east face. It looked wet, and we noted the large bergschrund at its base.

We chose the wrong, lower, gully system to abseil from the Pigeon-Howser col into the East Creek Basin, but no matter, we were making good time and going strong, and all it meant was a slightly longer shuffle across the snow to the toe of the West Buttress, the very toe, no less, where, for the purist (or masochist?) the route started. We had a map, but no topo – Ian had done the route a dozen or so years previously, and it follows a natural line. What could possibly go wrong?

We scrambled the first couple of hundred metres, but eventually the ridge steepened, and out came the ropes and rack. Sometime previously, Ian had had to lop a few metres off the end of his rope on account of some rockfall damage but we hoped that wouldn't be a problem.

Oh boy, what fabulous climbing followed: jamming, laybacking, bridging up a series of cracks, flakes, grooves, and corners, on the very best granite, with ample gear and good stances when you needed them. The first crux came after several enjoyable pitches, a short 5.9 section through a roof, the kind of gymnastic sequence that looks daunting but is over and done with before you know it, and makes you laugh out loud. Delightful climbing up a long left-facing dihedral (the Great Dihedral) followed, then at long last, after 10 pitches – or was it a dozen? – we arrived at the big sandy ledge, visible from below. A splendid place for a bivouac, as on the first ascent, but not for us today. However, Ian needed his afternoon snooze, so we lunched then settled down for a power nap,

Top Left: The author on the first laugh-out-loud crux (5.9)
Top Right: Ian on the Great Dihedral.
Bottom Left: Ian has a nap on the bivouac ledge.
Bottom Right: The author on the Great White Headwall.

although not for long. Whilst the sun still beamed down, clouds were gathering to the west. Don't want to get caught in one of those storms – time to get moving again.

Just before the holiday I'd bought some new rock boots, 5.10 rubber and all that, but had not had the time to fully break them in. By now, in the heat of the midday sun, my right foot, larger than the left, was really rather painful, indeed throbbing, especially when jamming. So, off with the right shoe and on with a mountain boot. Asymmetrical but mighty relieved.

The next section comprises a wall of paler granite known as the Great White Headwall. Fred Beckey described it thus: 'The exposure and the starkness of the route at this point become unique, as one is climbing on the narrow headwall between the terrible drop to the north couloir and the sweep of the great south face.' Hot work, too, in the glare of those reflected rays.

The first pitch off the ledge was a strenuous corner leading up to a wide, almost off-width crack, followed by another corner which took us into the upper crack system. Here again, pitch followed pitch of joyful climbing. Finger locks, layways, bridging on crystals, jugs when they were needed. There was no distinct second crux, but the climbing was generally more sustained than below the sandy ledge, and the occasional 5.10 section was, shall we say, 'interesting' in one mountain boot and one rock shoe. On two pitches our ropes were too short to reach the next belay so we simul-climbed. Another off-width was easier to bridge than squeeze or thrutch. On we climbed as the afternoon drew on and the summit beckoned. The climbing eventually gave way to an abseil into a notch, then a couple of hundred metres of scrambling to the top. Big grins, a handshake, refreshments, enjoy the view – mountains in every direction. However there was a vaguely menacing heaviness and just the hint of a crackle in the air. Guidebooks advise aiming to finish your route in the early afternoon because of the propensity for the weather to 'cut loose' later. In September 1994 American Jerry Gore and Canadian Warren Hollinger were bivouacking below the summit having completed a new line on the Southwest Buttress of North Tower, when they were caught in a ferocious storm. They both took direct lightning hits, and clothes and bodies were badly burned, particularly Hollinger's, who was also knocked unconscious. Further storms swept through but using the only intact rope, the burned areas repaired with duct tape, they were able to retreat to safety and survived. They named the 5.11 A4 route *Young Men on Fire*.[3] No desire to become old men on fire. My hair was standing on end, and not from the shock of the climbing. Time to go.

3   Jerry Gore, 'North Howser Tower, Southwest Buttress, "Young Men on Fire," Bugaboos', *AAJ*, *69/37 (1995), 178*, and <http://aac-publications.s3. amazonaws.com/documents/aaj/1995/PDF/AAJ_1995_69_37_178a.pdf> [retrieved 8 Sept 2014].

Ian high up on the route.

On the summit in hair-raising conditions.

We scrambled down to the start of the descent line where, thankfully, there was no cornice. At the top abseil station, just before we started to head down, I decided to change the film in my camera. I opened the back and out flipped the rewound film, spinning into space and bouncing down the 300m-high north-east face.....Bugger.....there goes the record. Ah well, we still have the memory.

So off we set on what we anticipated, correctly as it turned out, would be a hassle on account of our shortened double rope. Each abseil station was at around 50 metres, as you would expect, so the first person down had to find an anchor a few metres short of the bundle of tat and pegs; number two then joined them, the rope was pulled, someone abbed or down-climbed to the station proper, set up a belay, brought down the other person, and so and so on. We were tired, we were wet, we were getting cold, the day was drawing out, we needed to keep focussed. I picked the short straw for the final abseil across the 'schrund. Off I went, inevitably straight into the yawning crevasse, coming to a halt on a snow bridge a few metres down. I contemplated the situation. Damn. This is going to be a pain. Concentrate. I had not long since read *Touching the Void*. Was something similar going to be my fate, too? Did Ian have a knife in his sac? When might he use it? I spent a couple of minutes catastrophising and attempting to communicate my predicament to Ian in his hanging belay 45 metres above (he got the gist, but couldn't do much to help). Then suddenly I noticed, some 3-4 metres away, on another snow bridge.....my film! I penduled over, grabbed the somewhat battered looking film canister, the familiar Kodachrome yellow standing out against the dirty white of the snow, and, given a considerable psychological boost by this unlikely turn of events, launched myself out of the chasm, part prusik, part hand-over-hand, kicking steps in the thankfully softish snow on the outer lip of the 'schrund. Safe again. Whoops of relief.

Ian joined me, we packed the gear and rope, and headed across the Vowell Glacier with a spring in our step, down into the Crescent Basin and back to base. We had not seen, or even heard, another party all day, let alone shared the route. Surprising in light of the crowds at the Kain Hut last night. We reached the hut in darkness to find it now quiet and empty except for a family of three, a middle aged couple and their teenage son. They were up for a few days of low-grade mountaineering. The boy seemed somewhat awe-struck at meeting this pair of wild-eyed alpinist dudes, beards, headbands, bleeding knuckles and all, just down off the – gasp – Beckey-Chouinard. We shamelessly wallowed in the adulation and milked the occasion with our tale of derring-do. A cup of tea and snack later, and we hit the trail. We still had a long way to go. The descent was uneventful and passed quickly. An occasional pair of eyes peered out of the darkness, caught in the beams of our headtorches. Is that a bear? No, 'just' a porcupine. Don't underestimate these critters.

You should know that, apart from the weather, the other main hazard of a visit to the Bugaboos is the tyre and brakepipe-munching porcupine – guidebooks strongly advise you to protect the perimeter of your vehicle with chicken wire to deter them. Of course we hadn't done this. So it was with some relief we arrived at the car park to find the car unblemished, tyres, hoses and all other rubber appendages still in situ. Ian had hidden a couple of beers in a nearby stream. We drank a toast to the day. We'd been on the go for 21 hours. The drive home was probably the most dangerous bit of the expedition, a great effort from Ian who, at his ripe age, should really have been tucked up in bed by now. We reached Golden 36 hours door-to-door, slid straight into bed and into the deepest of sleeps.

The next day we swam with the kids in the local municipal pool. It was hot and humid and the atmosphere was, well, electric, the sky dark and malevolent. That night a farewell gathering and BBQ was held at Ian's house; we were heading back down to Vancouver and home the next day after a fabulous three weeks. As we feasted on baked salmon and drank cold beer, an electric storm exploded to the south providing us with a couple of hours of entertainment – unbridled enthusiasm for sure. Just glad we weren't up there in the clouds. On fire.

So, we got our epic, thankfully not one of the 'if-I-get-out-of-this-alive-I'll-never-take-anything-for-granted-again' variety, but a big day out for sure, a fabulous, committing route in an amazing setting, particularly memorable because we'd managed to pull it in a small window without mishap, not least avoiding conflagration! Amazingly, the film survived its tumble, and although the quality of the images was affected a little by light leakage, we retained a record of events.

HALFWAY HOUSE
(a literary history of the Raeburn Hut)

By Robin Forrest

THE RAEBURN HUT, sheltering in a stand of scots pine alongside the lonely A889 road between Dalwhinnie and Laggan, has been providing a convenient base for mountaineers from the SMC and kindred clubs since the late 1980s. Climbers set off from the front door seeking adventure on the crags of Creag Dubh in summer or the gullies of Coire Ardair in winter. Mountain walkers value its proximity to the high tops of the northern Cairngorms and the lesser hills of Drumochter. Yet I wonder how many of those who cross the threshold are aware that by doing so they are – quite literally – following in the footsteps of one of Scotland's most accomplished yet unknown and underrated literary figures, the novelist Ian MacPherson, best known today as the author of *Wild Harbour*, much of which is set in the hill country around the Raeburn (or 'Halfway House' as it was once known).

Ian MacPherson was born in Forres, Moray in 1905 to a staunchly Presbyterian mother and a sheep dealer (or so he was described on Ian's birth certificate) father who hailed from Garvamore on the upper Spey, only a few miles from the Raeburn. It seems that MacPherson senior's business acumen did not match his practical knowledge of sheep – after his business in Moray failed he tried his hand at farming at Biallid (at the foot of Creag Dubh just outside Newtonmore), but this failed too and he eventually moved himself and his family to Glensaugh in present day Aberdeenshire where he managed to obtain farm work.

Ian won a bursary to Mackie Academy in Stonehaven, where he narrowly missed being a contemporary of fellow novelist Ian Leslie Mitchell, better known as Lewis Grassic Gibbon of *A Scots Quair* fame, leaving as Dux in 1924 to study English at Aberdeen University. At Aberdeen he became something of an academic star, and on graduating with 1st Class Honours he was offered a post as assistant to the head of department, Professor A. A. Jack. This he accepted, planning to spend two more years teaching at Aberdeen before moving to Cambridge to do postgraduate work and then embark upon a permanent career in academia.

Things didn't go quite according to plan however. It wasn't long before university teaching began to pall, and MacPherson started to hanker after the outdoor life, perhaps partly because by this time his parents had moved back to Newtonmore, where he himself had been spending the university holidays working as a ghillie. He had also met his future wife, Elizabeth Cameron, daughter of a free kirk minister in Sutherland whose own mother, Isabel Cameron, was also a popular novelist of the time, with over forty published books – intriguingly described as 'chaste romances' – to her credit. Elizabeth's parents disapproved of her relationship with MacPherson but, undeterred, the pair ran off together in 1930 to get married.

Having turned their backs on the respectable world of teaching – Ian having resigned from his university post and Elizabeth from hers in an Aberdeenshire school – they used what little money they had to buy a caravan and a large but ancient car of uncertain reliability, and set off to live an itinerant life in and around Ian's ancestral home of Badenoch. Their main source of income was hawking fresh fruit and vegetables (which they ordered from markets in Glasgow to be delivered by train to Dalwhinnie or Newtonmore) to hotels, guest houses and private homes in and around Strathspey. This episode in their lives is entertainingly described in the autobiographical *Happy Hawkers*, published in 1937 (authorship being jointly attributed to both of them). Other sources of income were exploited as and when the opportunity arose. MacPherson offered his services to a number of newspapers as a local reporter, an offer that was accepted by one or two who were after news on how the grouse season was doing. He tutored a local Newtonmore lad who was preparing for the Cambridge entrance exam. A somewhat bizarre source of extra cash was using the increasingly unreliable car as an unofficial taxi service for the navvies working on the Loch Ericht hydro scheme, ferrying them along the lochside track to the Hotel in Dalwhinnie where they could get drunk and carouse the night away.

As winter approached, and with the car and caravan on their last legs, the MacPhersons began thinking about more substantial accommodation, which is when they first came across what is now the Raeburn Hut, a discovery graphically described by Elizabeth in *The Happy Hawkers*:

> … three miles from Laggan and quite out of sight of every other house in the country, we saw an empty cottage by the roadside. … set so lonely by itself in a great empty circle of moor with hills beyond. The door was locked but we found an unsnibbed window and crept through it, going from room to room in astonishment that it should lie desolate and be so well preserved. It had five rooms, three downstairs and two up. … The walls of the downstairs rooms were all lined with new unstained tongued and grooved boarding which made them light and pleasant … . We rushed to Newtonmore to find who owned the place, and if it was to let. In a few days it was ours for a year at a rent of a pound a month. … The Halfway House. That was the name of our new home.

Halfway House had had an eventful history before the MacPhersons appeared on the scene. So named because it stood halfway between the Dalwhinnie Hotel and the Drumgask Inn, in the days of the drovers it had been a resting place for both men and beasts, where the drovers ate, drank and slept while the livestock fended for themselves on the moor outside. Subsequently it had enjoyed some notoriety as a shebeen, or unlicensed drinking den. Some of Macpherson's older shepherding relatives from Badenoch could remember 'wild times' in the house. Less happily local lore darkly suggested that a suicide had once taken place there.

Locals also warned that the road was often blocked by snow in winter, and that they might find themselves cut off for days on end, but the MacPhersons would brook no discouragement. Unfortunately the locals were to be proved right, as Elizabeth ruefully described:

> The road was blocked for twelve weeks, when not a car or even cart came through.
> The frost was like iron. We broke ice on our burn with our axe before we could draw drinking and washing water. We spent five hours walking the three miles from Laggan Bridge in a storm ... laden with provisions because the storm came on us suddenly when we were unprepared and had no food in the house. I trudged at Ian's heels, waist deep in snow, seeing nothing but his back and the howling drift. I had a bag of eggs in my hand which I carried safely all the way until I fell and broke them at the door ... .

The MacPhersons were made of stern stuff however:

> So our first winter went past, and when it was done we took a lease of the house for another five years at a rent of three pounds a year. That first winter was the hardest we have felt since we came to Halfway House.

The years that followed proved to be the most productive of MacPherson's literary career. He had begun writing his first novel, *Shepherd's Calendar* (published 1931) while still leading the academic life in Aberdeen, but all three of his other published novels – *Land of Our Fathers* (1933), *Pride in the Valley* (1936) and his masterwork *Wild Harbour* (also 1936) were written at Halfway House. All are connected through location with the life of Badenoch, but it is *Wild Harbour* which is the most enduring, and also the one most likely to appeal to the hillwalker or mountaineer.

Wild Harbour is set in 1944, less than ten years into the future from when it was first published. A pan-European war has broken out, and though it is never explicitly stated, southern Britain is assumed to have fallen to the unnamed invaders, which has precipitated widespread societal collapse. The protagonist Hugh, along with his wife Terry, abandon their remote little house in the wilds of Badenoch and take to the hills with a stalking rifle and some basic supplies, hoping to live off the land until such time as order and civilization – a better, more moral civilization than that which the distant war has destroyed – is restored. The genesis of the scenario, conceived at a time when a resurgent and rearming Nazi Germany was beginning to cast its long shadow over Europe, is all too obvious, as are the similarities between Ian and Elizabeth MacPherson and the fictional 'Hugh' and 'Terry'. For a while all goes well: the fleeing couple discover a cave which, with a little modification, they turn into a tolerably comfortable howff; Hugh stalks and kills deer using the rifle, the accurate descriptions of which owe a great deal to Macpherson's familiarity with hunting thanks to his personal experiences as a ghillie. It doesn't last, of course – they are not the only ones seeking refuge from the breakdown of civil society, and conflict is inevitable, culminating in an undeniably tragic but ultimately optimistic conclusion.

Wild Harbour has been favourably compared to other Scottish novels of adventure in wild countryside – Robert Louis Stevenson's *Kidnapped* for example, or the thrillers of John Buchan, but MacPherson, as well as being able to spin a good yarn was also a very literary writer, and manages to achieve a depth in his writing that lesser talents might struggle to attain.

Though the locations in *Wild Harbour* are nominally as fictional as the events which take place within its pages, it isn't difficult for the reader to work things out as the descriptions in the book are in fact very precise, to the extent you can with the book in one hand and an OS map in the other work out exactly where the action takes place. The Fara, for example, appears in the book as 'The Farrow'; the nearby Graham Meall nan Eagan is fictionalised as 'Meall nan Eacan'; and the striking crags of the Dirc Mor between the two as 'Craig nan Adhaircean', wild places that MacPherson must have come to know well during his tenancy of Halfway House. The cave where 'Hugh' and 'Terry' take refuge is on Creag Doire na h'Achlaise overlooking Loch Caoldair – 'Loch Coulter' in the book (now sadly disfigured by the construction of the Beauly-Denny powerline) – which he must have been almost able to see from his writing desk.

Ian and Elizabeth MacPherson left Halfway House in 1938 and assumed the tenancy of Tombain, a hill farm below the Knock of Braemoray on the edge of Dava Moor not far from where Ian was born in Forres. They lived and farmed there until Ian, returning from an errand to a neighbouring farm on his motorbike, collided with a timber lorry and was killed outright. It was summer 1944, exactly the time of the tragic denouement of Wild Harbour conceived less than ten years previously.

Wild Harbour is, unfortunately, currently out of print although Canongate publishing have an e-book available, and paperback copies are still to be found secondhand and in some libraries. So, if you are staying at 'Halfway House' sometime and the weather isn't conducive to climbing, or if you just want to do something a little different, take a copy of the book in one hand and a map in the other, cross the road and take the path to 'Loch Coulter' and beyond, and contemplate how much has changed (and how much has stayed the same) since the author last walked that way.

Honorary Vice-President Jim Donaldson addresses the gathering at the opening of the Raeburn Hut, 1 October 1988. Photo: Hon. Ed.

> ... our windows looked north, into that airt's steady light, upon a magnificent scene of wild hills and country where no house and scarcely a trace of men's handiwork was visible. The distant soaring Monadliaths with their peaks in cloud or snow gave the view a satisfyingness and one could see it daily without growing weary or ever finding it the same ... this country which surrounds us is never the same ... even when all circumstances that affect it seem constant. A trick of the light in this high land makes every moment alter and each hour show something new.

Ian & Elizabeth MacPherson, *The Happy Hawkers* (Methuen, 1937).

Author's Note:

Robin Forrest is a member of (and former President and Secretary of) the Inverness Mountaineering Club. He is also the Reference Librarian at Inverness Library.

Editor's Note:

The Raeburn Hut is in a fitting location to commemorate one of our most distinguished members. On his first visit to climb in Coire Ardair Raeburn walked there over the hills from Dalwhinnie Station. (W. Tough, 'Corrie Arder', *SMCJ*, 4/21 (1896), 141–8.) On a subsequent visit he cycled from Dalwhinnie Station past the Halfway House to Aberarder. (H. Raeburn, 'The Cliffs of Corrie Arder', *SMCJ*, 8/43 (1904), 4–11.)

IN SEARCH OF JENNY STORIE

By Ian Crofton

AN EXPLANATION MIGHT be in order. Over ten days in May, July and November 2013 I beat the Club's southern bounds for a book I was commissioned to write by the Edinburgh publisher, Birlinn. It is entitled *Walking the Border: A Journey Between Scotland and England*, and came out in the summer of 2014.

Here is an edited version of the fourth day, when, in wind and rain, I walked from a wild camp in a high wood on the flanks of Peel Fell above Deadwater, near Kielder, along the western Cheviots to Carter Bar, where the A68 crosses the Border. It was the toughest day of the trip. In the course of it I encountered two small but perfectly formed crags that are shared (or disputed?) between Scotland and England, and which would be worth revisiting in more clement conditions, if only for the sheer perversity of it.

***

> ... the North [Tyne] is out of Wheel Fell sprung
> Amongst these English Alps which as they run along
> England and Scotland here impartially divide.
> — Michael Drayton, *Poly-Olbion* (1612, 1622)

Today we call it Peel Fell. Michael Drayton called it 'Wheel Fell', while on an 1837 map of the Deadwater District it is marked as 'Pearl Fell'. I was to find that Peel Fell was no pearl – more like the swine one should not cast pearls before. And I suspect that Michael Drayton had neither visited the Cheviot Hills nor the Alps, as the former are as rounded as the latter are spiky. But they do have this is common: uncompromising wildness.

> On Kielder-side the wind blaws wide;
> There sounds nae hunting horn
> That rings sae sweet as the winds that beat
> Round banks where Tyne is born.
> — A.C. Swinburne, 'A Jacobite's Exile'

The wind was blawing wide when I poked my head out of the tent, and the clouds were shutting down the sky, though the tops stayed clear. The promised front had come. The wind was from the southwest, but it was distinctly chilly. I was in shelter on my greensward in the wood, but there was commotion in the tops of the trees. I breakfasted shrouded in sleeping bag and hat.

My breakfast (left), and someone else's (right).

I was hoping I might race the rain eastward. But I knew there wasn't going to be much racing today.

Though rain was promised, I still needed water, so stumbled down below the wood where the map marks four thin blue fingers that merge to form a little stream. The ground was covered in reeds, and the patches in between had been trodden by cows. Out of the shelter of the wood I could feel the bite of the wind, and wished I hadn't left my gloves back in the tent. Even the celandines had closed up against the cold. It was 27 May, Bank Holiday Monday.

I couldn't find any sign of running water, just a patch or two of oily looking drip and drool. I looked further down, where the little fingers were supposed to join to form a head of water. I found the confluence, but it was no more than a bog that cows had shat in.

At least it wasn't a hot, sweaty day. I would have to make it waterless over to the far side of Pcel Fell, to Kielderstone Cleugh, down which I hoped a stream would run.

By the time I'd broken camp the rain had arrived, though not much more than a drizzle. I'd put on all my waterproofs, hat, hood, gloves and over-gloves. At least the wind was behind me. 'From here to the top of Peel Fell is a long tramp over very rough ground.' So wrote James Logan Mack, an Edinburgh academic who spent many years walking the Border and who in 1924 published a book about it, entitled *The Borderline*.

'There is no pleasure to be had from it,' he continues, 'until the heavy tussocks are left behind and the higher reaches of the Fell attained.'

The Border here follows a somewhat irregular line up the hill, in a northeasterly direction. On the English side were mature conifers, while on the Scottish side was a plantation of young birches. I crossed over a barbed-wire fence and followed the Border along the mossy top of a broken-down dike. Here and there I had to divert into the bog or clear-felling either side to avoid a self-sown spruce, or a fallen fir. Some of the fallen trees had hauled up their roots as they fell. These roots were draped with mosses, giving them the look of giant, hairy spiders.

When at last I emerged onto the open hillside I was surprised to find a

The giant spiders of Deadwater Forest

path. There was a sign. 'Kielderstane Walk' it said. It was going my way. It was a good honest hill path and it gave me a good honest uphill slog.

And so I came to Jenny Storie's Stone, a cuneiform buttress of Northumberland (or Roxburghshire?) sandstone jutting out of the rim of the Peel Fell plateau. If I hadn't been alone, if it hadn't been raining, and if I'd had my rock boots with me, I would have tried a few of the tempting lines up the front face, using water-worn pockets and shapely horizontal breaks. Northumbrian sandstone is a delight to climb. But I was alone, it was raining, and I didn't have my rock boots, so I let Jenny Storie's Stone well alone.

I never did find out who Jenny Storie was. She still keeps her secret. But on a night of full moon, I can imagine you might hear her here, wailing for her demon lover ...

Jenny Storie's Stone, on the Club's southern March

Peel Fell, at just under 2000 feet, is the highest point in the western Cheviots. Just where its summit is wouldn't be easy to tell if there wasn't a cairn, as there's a flat expanse of peat hags up there. The tops of the hags are festooned with moss and heather, and here and there you find the stumps of an old Border fence. The going's by no means as easy as Logan Mack would have you believe.

Border posts on Peel Fell
The bog on the left falls under the auspices of the SMC, while that on the right is the fiefdom of the Northumbrian Mountaineering Club.

Nestled amongst the hags I came across a little lochan, its surface whipped by cat's paws in the strengthening wind. It was now blowing from the southeast, but it felt like it had whistled in from Siberia. I had heard that a cold front was going to be moving down the country. I think it had arrived.

I found my burn sooner than expected, on the near side of the Kielder Stone. There were no sheep up here amongst the heather, so I didn't bother with sterilizing tablets. A bit of grouse dropping never did anybody any harm, I told myself as I swallowed mouthful after mouthful. Go back go back go back, said the grouse.

If you're approaching via Peel Fell, you come to the Kielder Stone from above. From this viewpoint it looks like a huge table, part covered with a cloth of moss and heather. It is in fact a gigantic block of sandstone, 26 feet high, 133 feet in circumference and weighing perhaps 1400 tons (Logan Mack measured it). The sides are generally sheer or overhanging, though they are replete with all the wonderful features you get in Northumbrian (or Roxburghshire?) sandstone – little pockets, vertical cracks, nubbled walls, flakes of finely layered horizontal strata, jutting noses, water-worn grooves. Again, if the sun had been shining, and I'd had my rock boots, and didn't have ground to cover, I'd have had a happy time bouldering here. There's a soft landing in mossy bog if you fall.

'The eastern face of the rock is certainly unclimbable,' Logan Mack opines, 'and to the ordinary individual so are the other three, but to the skilled mountaineer the north-west corner presents no great difficulty.'

Logan Mack and friends on the Kielder Stone, circa 1920. The Anglo-Scottish Border runs through the middle of the crag.

As if to prove his point, he includes a photograph of himself and his friends posed half way up the Stone.

He also recounts the story of 'some foolhardy lads and lasses' who managed to make their way to the summit, but then found they could not descend. One of the more timorous members of the party, who had remained earthbound, walked several miles to raise the alarm, and returned with a group of rescuers carrying a ladder. Perhaps the stranded youngsters had tempted fate by walking round the Stone three times widdershins (contrary to the direction of the sun), which is said to bring ill fortune.

Apart from this tale, the Kielder Stone remains silent about its history, although it bears the inscribed initials of some of its more self-promoting visitors.

Such an obvious feature would have provided an important signpost in these featureless wastes, and a rallying point for countless raiding parties. As such, it will no doubt have seen its fair share of bloodshed. It certainly inspired the imagination of Dr John Leyden, whose poem 'The Cout of Keeldar', is included in Scott's *Minstrelsy of the Scottish Border*. The eponymous Cout rashly ventures on a hunting expedition into Liddesdale,

incurring the wrath of William, Lord Soulis, the vicious warlock of
Hermitage Castle (who could only be killed, Leyden tells us in another
poem, if he was wrapped in lead sheeting and boiled alive):

> And onward, onward, hound and horse
> Young Keeldar's band have gone;
> And soon they wheel, in rapid course,
> Around the Keeldar Stone.
>
> Green vervain round its base did creep,
> A powerful seed that bore;
> And oft, of yore its channels deep
> Were stain'd with human gore.
>
> And still, when blood-drops, clotted thin,
> Hang the grey moss upon,
> The spirit murmurs from within,
> And shakes the rocking-stone.

The only murmuring I could hear was the wind, while the rain had
washed all trace of blood and gore from the rock (which, *contra* Leyden,
does not in fact rock).

*The Kielder Stone: 'And oft,
of yore its channels deep /
Were stain'd with human
gore.' The day I visited its
channels deep were running
with bucketfuls of rainwater.*

The Kielder Stone is perhaps the most prominent landmark anywhere along the Border, which now runs straight through it. It wasn't always thus – these wastes were long disputed between the Earls (later Dukes) of Northumberland and the Earls of Douglas. It seems that which bits of land each of them decided pertained to their own private estate determined the territorial claims of their respective nations. It wasn't until 11 May 1778 that the lawyers put the matter to arbitration, and fixed the line of the Border between Peel Fell and Carter Fell. I was to find that this line was anything but logical. In fact it was to prove exasperating, exhausting, soul-sapping. Definitely the result of horse-trading on the part of a bunch of well-feed and unscrupulous lawyers.

I'd had my first slip of the day walking down to the Kielder Stone. After ending up on my backside I'd turned round to examine the spot, expecting to find skidmarks in a patch of peat. But there was nothing to be seen but steep grass, slippery as ice in the wet. After that I made a special effort to dig my heels in on the downhills, and the edges of my boots horizontally into the slope on the ups. But it was far from my last slip of the day.

It was just after noon when I left the Kielder Stone. According to my original schedule, I should have been at Carter Bar by now. I thought it might take me another couple of hours to reach the A68. As it turned out, I was not to reach the road till five o'clock, averaging something like one mile an hour. These Border miles are triple-strength.

After the Kielder Stone the Border jerks crazily about through a nightmare of cleughs and sikes. The heather on these fells is so dense and deep you could call it scrub. These were not the manicured heather moors of the grouse shoots. The line is marked by the rotten stubs of fence posts. First they take you across Wylie's Sike, then over Haggie Knowe, down again to the junction of the Green Needle and the Black Needle. Neither of these two feeders of the Scaup Burn reflected their names; both were peat brown, readying themselves for the spate to come.

Stumbling up the east bank of the Black Needle, I had to contour the flank of the heather-black hill called The Trouting. Despite the wind and the rain I sweated with the effort. I'd take a step up, then my foot, hidden somewhere deep in the heather, would slip sideways. Or my ankle would get caught in an unseen hole. In places it was two steps forward, one step back. Or even two steps back. It was harder than breaking trail through deep snow in the winter hills. I thought of the line in King Lear:

> The worst is not
> So long as we can say 'This is the worst.'

But I'd pretty much plumbed my own personal depths. Even a bank of primroses above the Black Needle failed to rouse my spirits.

I was not the first – nor, I suspect, the last – to curse these almost impassable fells. 'If I were further from the tempestuousness of the Cheviot Hills,' wrote Peregrine Bertie, 13th Baron Willoughby d'Eresby, 'and were once retired from this accursed country, whence the sun is so removed, I would not change my homeliest hermitage for the highest palace there.' Bertie was Warden of the English East March, clearly not a job he enjoyed. He died of a cold in 1601.

On a sunny day, with nowhere particular to go and no deadline to do it in, I would have loved to laze by these burns among the hills. As it was, I slumped briefly for a drink and a snack, conscious of the chill and the wet down my back, then plodded on.

Black Needle with the Border running bang up the middle.

I tried to raise my spirits by moaning into my Dictaphone:

Down Green Needle, up Black Needle, plunging down, then up another steep-sided cleuch. Deep heather, deep deep heather. No path. This is mad, totally illogical, this Border line marked by these rotting old posts. One I've just taken a photograph of has just, appropriately, been shat on by a moorland bird. Well done, it.

Who on earth designed this Border? There's a far better route up there, you know, along the watershed, without all this dropping down.

The Border here kinked north, then southeast. Any fool could see that this was an entirely unnecessary deviation from the general northeasterly drift of the Border line. I was exasperated, so angry with the Border-makers that, to spite them, I cut the corner and slogged up deep heather onto Knox Knowe. So I missed out the source of the Black Needle and the stretch of featureless nothing called Duntae Edge – which Logan Mack describes as 'the most evil piece of ground which I encountered on the Border from sea to sea'. I saved myself maybe four hundred yards, and in the process, by walking this new bound, annexed an insignificant triangle of worthless land for Scotland.

The view south-west from Knox Knowe.

On Knox Knowe there were cloudberries in flower, a rare treat. At one point a snipe burst out of the ground beneath my feet, zigzagging away from any merlin that might be on its tail.

Despite the wind and the rain, the cloud was still above the tops. Behind me dark grey ridges gave way to paler and paler grey shoulders, fading into the distance towards Deadwater Fell. To the north, peaking over the horizon, I could just make out the tops of the highest band of conifers in Wauchope Forest. Ahead of me I made out the mobile mast on the side of Carter Fell. It still looked like a long long way away. But I got a signal, phoned my sister, told her how very very late I was going to be getting to Carter Bar, where she awaited me with provisions. I was apologetic. She was sympathetic. 'Poor you,' she said. Poor fool, more like, I thought. 'No, no,' I said. 'Don't worry, I'm fine.' Well, I was. Just cold and wet and late. But still able to put one foot in front of the other.

Which is what I did, one foot in Scotland, the other in England, one foot among blaeberries, the other treading on bilberries – the same plant, with the same delicate pink bell-like flowers, but with different names on either side of the Border. If it had been August I would have hunkered down and stuffed my face with the tart purple fruit.

I was ridiculously happy to find, at last, one of the Border Stones that had been marked on the map as 'BSs' for some miles, but which had remained hidden in the heather. Here was a fine specimen of grey sandstone, part covered in white lichen. It had N on the English side, for Northumberland (the Duke that is), and D on the other, for Douglas. Except that the D was reversed. Either the mason who'd carved it was illiterate, or he'd had an inbuilt anti-Caledonian bias, and thus saw fit to upend the dignity of the Scottish Earl by bouleversing his D.

A Border Stone
– marked with N for (Duke or Earl of) Northumberland on one side,

– and a mirror-image D for (Earl of) Douglas on the other.

And so I made my way across Carter Fell. The going was certainly better than it had been down in the cleuchs (as they're spelt in Scotland; in England they're cleughs), but there were still plenty of traps for the unwary – not only shake holes and old mineshafts, but also mosses, morasses, quagmires, all ready to suck you in and swallow you. If you'd put a foot wrong by one of these wobbling green horrors, you'd sink and sink and never be seen again.

I shuddered. The bogs juddered, quaking with silent boggy laughter.

I came at last to the trig point on Carter Fell, the first trig point on my Border walk so far. After that it was downhill, and the going got considerably better. In fact there was a grassy path, and as I strode down it towards Carter Bar and the A68, I could make out two blue saltires fluttering vigorously in the strong southerly wind. Beyond them, far away in the distance through the rain, at the other end of a long snaking line of hills, I could just make out The Cheviot. It still wore a big patch of snow on its southwestern flank.

The car park when I got there was virtually empty. No one with any sense was going to stop here today to admire the view. But as I passed one solitary vehicle, a man stepped out into the wind and the rain. He was Chinese, and his car had diplomatic plates. Inside I could make out a woman and a baby. I asked him if this was his first time in Scotland. 'Ya,' he said. 'What do you think of it?' I asked inanely. 'Really lovely. Fantastic.' Clearly a diplomat. 'You?' he asked. I told him I came from Scotland, that I was walking the Border from the west coast to the east coast. 'Alone?' he said, with some concern in his voice – for both my safety and my sanity, perhaps. 'Yes,' I said. 'Very good,' he said encouragingly. He probably thought it best not to upset this maniac. Then he returned to the warm interior of his car.

Then I saw my sister's car. Inside were not only my sister Tricia but my brother-in-law Jem, and also my daughter Claire and son Archie, with whom I was to continue my walk over the Cheviot proper.

That had been the plan. But I was half a day late, and the forecast for the two to three days it would take us to traverse the high Cheviot was not good. There was going to have to be some kind of rethink. That night we should have been camped at the Roman fort at Chew Green, several miles east along the main Cheviot ridge. We examined our alternative options. After we'd spoken on the phone, Claire and Archie had reconnoitred a private hostel a few miles south into England. But it turned out the proprietor there had made an error when he'd opted for a career in hospitality. There were some possible places to pitch a tent on the edges of the woodland on the Scottish side of the Border pass. I mulled over the prospect. I was wet and cold, it was still wet and cold and windy outside, and the following days were also supposed to be wet and cold and windy, at least up high where we would be.

And then I remembered the words of Jean-Luc Godard. 'A film should have a beginning, a middle and an end,' he said. 'But not necessarily in that order.'

If that was true of a film, I thought, it could also be true of a walk...

***

WHITE LINES

Exploratory Ski Descents on Baffin Island

By Ross Hewitt

BAFFIN ISLAND SHOULD need little introduction to dedicated ski mountaineers nowadays as it is becoming the place in the world for those interested in skiing the aesthetic couloirs that split the biggest walls on the planet. Situated in a remote area within the Canadian Arctic Circle guarantees cold snow and the ability to ski around the clock in 24 hour daylight.

Our trip started at Clyde River by securing a skidoo ride from the Inuit hunters deep into the Fiords. Ilko and his son John agreed to take myself, Michelle and Marcus out to Scott Island on a Komatik (wooden sled) towed behind a snow machine. Ilko was a man from a bygone era for us Westerners and had lived in a tiny remote settlement to the north of Clyde River until he was 26 years old, surviving by hunting. He displayed the calm confidence of a man who knew how to take care of himself in the wilderness.

As we headed north across the mouth of Sam Ford Fiord we found a dead seal pup at a breathing hole which was still warm. The polar bear had only taken a bite and left the remainder of the kill, probably taking off after it heard the snow machine approaching. Nothing goes to waste in the Arctic and our Inuit guides quickly bagged the dead seal for their dinner.

Further on while passing the 600m high Ship's Prow and 71° North point into Scott Inlet, we caught a glimpse of some stunning ski lines and decided to stop. Ilko and John took off with a wave and gunned the skidoos out of sight. It would be a longer day for them with the return journey. Our final task before bed was to get the bear early warning system operational that consisted of a perimeter rope connected to an air horn. We hoped this would put our minds at rest and allow us to get some sleep, albeit with a gun at hand either side of the tent.

On the first morning there was wind down-fiord and I had to learn about ski kiting very quickly before the other two more experienced kiters left me behind. Over the next three days we skied five lines on Scott Island, three of which were outstandingly beautiful, varying in length from 450 to 620m vertical. Aside from the skiing we loved hanging out on the summit plateau enjoying the evening light and the relative warmth far above the sea ice with views stretching from Gibbs Fiord out into the void of Baffin Bay.

It was soon time to move camp and as luck would have it the wind was blowing inland so we caught a 35km ride into Gibbs Fiord to our second base camp. These cliffs had caught my eye from Scott Island and camped

in the middle of the Gibbs Fjord was quite an amazing arena. The change in height of the mountains had been so gradual on our journey from Scott Island that we hadn't appreciated the size of these lines. The following day we set off on a south-facing line on Sillem Island that looked about 700m high. After 500m we reckoned 350m remained. After another 300m it looked like it was about 150m to the top. We finally topped out at 1300m! Down below gorgeous red minarets lined the sides of our couloir, reminiscent of the Y couloir on Aiguille d'Argentière.

One day we woke up to low cloud and some fresh snow and decided to skin up fiord as far as possible to explore and look for the 'big line'. With the cloud base at 600m we passed a buttress more akin to a fairy tale fortress with some of the biggest walls we had seen. The fortress is an incredibly impressive mountain feature, immense acres of impeccable vertical rock soaring upwards with no hint of relief. A couloir split the buttress but looked like it hit a cul-de-sac at 600m so we continued on and as the weather cleared we found another good line to ski. At the top we enjoyed a five minute sunbath before putting the multitude of layers back on in preparation for descending into the cold locker. The fresh powder had accumulated in the couloir and effortless big turns took us back to the ice in a few minutes. It was 6 p.m. and the 650m line felt like a half day so we decided to go ski the cul-de-sac line at the fortress.

The climbing was quick and an hour later we found the couloir curved to the right where we thought it stopped. We continued on with little doubt that the couloir would stop round the corner, such was the scale of the walls soaring up around us. I had mixed emotions; I knew Michelle was tired and part of me hoped we would find a cul-de-sac, but if the line went to the summit it would be a once-in-a-lifetime opportunity. I slowed down slightly so Michelle didn't get demotivated and we continued upwards around another corner. The couloir narrowed from 100m wide to near 10m. At 900m we rounded the next twist on the spiral, the couloir narrowed further down to 3–4 m. I could see light at the end of the tunnel, it went the distance.

We finally topped out on the plateau at 11 p.m. just as the sun dipped below the horizon and we quickly swapped crampons for skis. Initially the couloir was 3m wide and required precision turns but incredible sluffy powder had accumulated after the night's snowfall and even on the steeper rolls the skiing was just unadulterated fun. Occasionally we stopped to film and take some photos but as the couloir opened up at the 600m point I just wanted get into the flow mode and sent the remainder of the couloir in one shot with legs on fire. At the 'shrund we all celebrated together after an amazing line that had us in doubt until the last moment and knowing that was one of those precious moments in a lifetime.

Michelle Blaydon & Marcus Waring skinning past the south-facing walls of Scott Island, Scott Inlet. Photo: Ross Hewitt.

Ross Hewitt & Marcus Waring at Base Camp 1, Scott Inlet. Photo: Michelle Blaydon.

It was time for us to move camp again and once more the wind Gods favoured us with wind down Gibbs Fiord and into Refuge harbour. I launched my kite in gusty 40 kph with a lot of apprehension and the acceleration was incredible even with two sleds in tow weighing 100kgs. With 20km behind us, we finally put the kites down at Refuge Harbour and ate a big meal in preparation for the 40km of sled hauling through Stewart Valley. As we hauled over the water ice of Stewart Lake our minds were distracted by the magical big walls of Great Sail Peak and its neighbours. Below Great Sail Peak we stopped for lunch and celebrated Marcus's birthday with some hot soup. The wind continued to blow savagely giving Michelle frostnip on her nose so we kept our heads down and got on with hauling. On the third day only 5km of moraine separated us from the Walker Arm but after fighting a battle all day we had only covered one kilometre by 6 p.m. We decided to go for a night ski in the worthy Crosshairs Couloir and raced up the couloir trying to stay in last rays of sunshine as they crept up the mountainside. At the top we soaked up mindblowing views into Stewart Valley and down the rose tinted Walker Arm to the hanging line of Northwest Passage. 1000m of creamy powder in Crosshairs was a great end to the day as we skied back to camp in the dreaded moraines. The next day we finished our work in the moraines and arrived under the Walker Citadel.

Now we were in the established skiing zone with all the classics, it was more relaxed and easier to plan the days according to the time we wanted to ski. Simply knowing the height of the lines accurately gave us a huge advantage in planning our days. Marcus and myself started off by skiing

L-R: Marcus Waring, Tom Grant & Michelle Blaydon in Broken Dreams on the Walker Citadel. Photo: Ross Hewitt.

Debris Couloir which is the left branch of the converging couloirs on the North Side of Walker Citadel. The other branch has a large hanging serac barring the way that drops all the ice debris onto the fiord. At the 900m mark there is 50–75m of rock barring access to the plateau and we skied from the cul-de-sac. Boot-deep blower pow provided very sensual turns and we skied fast and effortlessly down the first 500 m. Below this the snow turned to firmer chalk which was still fun flowy skiing.

Our base camp was only 200m away and as we rounded a spur we saw that Ilko and John had arrived bringing out our fourth team member Tom. We had all been debating whether the 'kid' would actually make it out to Baffin without responsible adult supervision. We quickly learnt it was a close run thing after missing his flight at Philadelphia because he was napping and having to hire a car and manically drive to Ottawa to catch his connecting flights to Baffin! After a long skidoo ride Ilko was starving and knelt on the ice and got stuck into a frozen Arctic Char that he brought with him.

Ilko and John headed off to Sam Ford Fiord for an overnight caribou hunting trip and we decided to spend the afternoon skiing the 600m Broken Dreams couloir on the Walker Citadel that gets evening sun. In the couloir we found the wind had scoured the snow but the notch had an amazing view of Northwest Passage, which looks insanely steep and hangs ominously over the Walker Arm. We started off down the couloir as the sun set fire to the massive west wall of the Walker Citadel.

Ilko and John returned from their hunting trip empty-handed but with tales of an all-time caribou that was too big for them to take on. We

hitched a ride 10km down-fiord to possibly the most hyped couloir in the World, Polar Star Couloir on the Beluga. I got a good view as we approached on snow machine and it's every bit as stunning in reality as the photos. Near the top we encountered a ribbon of snow with glacial ice either side. We continued up but the snow depth thinned to 7cm over death ice, good enough for one skier to pass but not the three of us. We downclimbed a little until 25cm of snow allowed us to transition to our skis. Without harnesses or ice screws there was no way to secure yourself and it was down to a balancing act. Even then my upper edge sat on the boiler plate ice and it was good to get going after the nervy transitional stress position. The snow below was powdery and some special turns with the odd face shot took us down fast. Even after three weeks of skiing there was still no way we had the legs to send a line this length in one shot and we split it into 3 or 4 pitches.

The next day we hit a 1450m south-facing line we had been spying for a couple of days. I woke up feeling nauseous with stomach cramps, suspecting the dehydrated meals had sucked too much water out of my guts. We skated over the fiord at sunrise and quickly discovered that the south faces were roasting. It was the first day without neoprene overboots and unused to the heat I stripped down to my base layers. Sweat was pouring down my face into my eyes. After being in the freezer for weeks it was a strange sensation to be overheating. As I topped out all I could think of was drinking litres of water and sleeping so I left the guys to hang out in the sun and started down the line. The velvet corn snow provided fast smooth skiing and five minutes later I was at the fiord. Skiing in the sun felt very relaxed and friendly after the more austere surroundings of Polar Star Couloir. Sitting relaxing on the beach I drained my water bottle, then proceeded to down the contents of my thermos. Back at camp I slept for the rest of the afternoon.

Our sights now moved back to the Walker Citadel and a south-facing line that Marcus had previously discovered. It seemed so unlikely that any continuous line of snow could penetrate this incredible rock bastion. We skated 5km around the east face and another 1450m torture session landed us on the summit plateau. Not many people have stood there and we enjoyed the evening light from this commanding position with stunning 360° views while eating rehydrated humus and bagels. Sitting with our legs dangling over the edge of these 1450m big walls was a trip in itself. We eventually tore ourselves away from this special place and reluctantly stripped off some layers for the skiing. The line started off with some technical turns on wind-sculpted snow before deepening into an enormous amphitheatre with views to the Stump Spire. While we

Top left: Marcus Waring in the 1200m Northwest Passage. Photo: Ross Hewitt.
Top right: Ross Hewitt skiing the NW Couloir of Stump Spire. In the background is the East Face of Walker Citadel (Mahayana Wall VII, 5.10, A4+). Photo: Marcus Waring.
Bottom left: Marcus Waring skiing on Stump Spire. Two days previously we had skied the left-hand 1450m line in the background off the Walker Citadel. Photo: Ross Hewitt.
Bottom right: Tom Grant & Marcus Waring skiing the first known descent of a 1450 m south-facing line off the Walker Citadel. Photo: Ross Hewitt.

Ross Hewitt skiing in the classics on Ford Wall, Sam Ford Fiord. Photo: Marcus Waring.

skied Marcus took photos from the plateau. We regrouped 500m from the bottom and I started to ski out the line as fast as I could, completely oblivious to the guys' shouts when a fist-sized rock came over my head missing me by 30cm. With the classic line called 'Broken Dreams' on one side of the Citadel, this line should really be called 'Wet Dreams'.

Next up on our list was the classic 1200m Northwest Passage that was a 10km skate up fiord. The meaty upper pitches hang over the Walker Arm and it sits hemmed in underneath a huge wall. After another torturous bootpack session we hung out on the plateau soaking up the warmth like lizards and entertaining ourselves with some extreme boulder trundling, trying to get something all the way to the fiord. Once again we were lucky with fantastic boot deep powder in the couloir which took the edge off the 50° turns. Lower down the line we hit the evening sun and it was possible to open up the turns and freeride down to the fiord. During another big meal we all agree on the quality of the skiing.

The next day we moved out and hauled to the bay on the NE corner of the Walker Citadel. Leaving our kit there we went to the climbers' NW Couloir right of the Stump Spire. From the summit of the Citadel we had looked down on this 1100m line. Initially the line took a ribbon of snow underneath a sea of slabs before blasting up the couloir. We found the col to have a grandstand view of Citadel's Wet Dreams and the vast East Face. The lower half of the run was bathed in milky evening sunshine and we paused for a moment taking it all in before following the ribbon back to the ice.

Tom Grant climbing a 1000m south-facing line, Sam Ford Fiord. Photo: Ross Hewitt.

After skating back to our sleds and consuming another big meal, we psyched up for the sled hauling to Sam Ford Fiord by drinking our remaining freeze-dried coffee for the caffeine hit. Setting off around 9 p.m. we were treated to moonrise between the Beluga Spire and the Polar Sun Spire. Here we encountered a lead in the ice running the width of the fiord, the first sign of break-up and a reminder that the trip was coming to an end. At midnight we were under the cross on Great Cross Peak, a natural mark that has served as a landmark to the Inuit for generations. Some fresh bear tracks put us off camping there so we continued onwards across Sam Ford Fiord in order to get a camp location in the sun that served both sides of the fiord. The polar frost had descended and it was cold and damp but by 2 a.m. the frost had lifted and the temperature had risen slightly even though sunrise was still a couple of hours away. At 3 a.m. I crawled into my bed at Camp 7, glad to be lying down and quickly passed out after our longest day yet.

This thankfully marked the end to any sled hauling and we had a lot of fun skiing all the classics on Ford Wall. One afternoon found us hanging out on top of one of the big walls on Ford Wall entertaining ourselves trundling rocks. The fall line took rocks straight into the gully system that acted as a natural amplifier as our rocks exploded on impact, 9.5 seconds later. After each explosion we would burst into fits of giggles and do it again and again.

The team also repeated Inquisition on Great Cross Peak and kited down to the 1500m buttress to the north of Great Cross and skied a fantastic spiralling east-facing line that hit a step at 1000m. Near the

Tom Grant skiing the first known descent of a 1000m south-facing line, Sam Ford Fiord.
Photo: Marcus Waring.

bottom of the couloir we found a table top rock perch and sat and shared the last of our day food. The real bonus was finding the wind was now up-fiord which enabled us to kite home in style.

With 20,220m of skiing and 26 lines behind us, our rationed meals dwindling fast and signs of the ice break-up starting, we made the call to our Inuit friends to come pick us up. This marked the end of an incredible trip which would not have been possible without all the sponsors and supporters who we would like to thank.

CAIRNGORM MOUNTAIN RUNNING

By Paul Raistrick

ANYONE WHO HAS browsed the walls in Glenmore Lodge's bar has come across a hand drawn picture of a runner, mountains and times and statistics. The face belonged to Eric Beard – he set the early standard for running mountain rounds. Later Eric's times would be surpassed by one of Scotland's most prolific long distance runners Mel Edwards. But in the late 1990s the names, like the routes, meant nothing to such a naïve mountain head. In fact to be quite honest long distance running did not rank particularly highly on my list of must do sports. Why would it?

Ten years and many thousand miles later the names and routes were much more familiar. Years of soul-destroying treadmill sessions laced with long mountain runs had done their job. Pain and boredom could now be managed in equal portion.

Fortunately running in the 'Gorms was never boring – otherwise why not live in London if all you ever do is look at the digits on a treadmill?

By 2007 running was moving from a passion to an obsession. Running the annual 28-mile Lairig Ghru Race in 03:04:25 on a dreich June day was a gauge of non-treadmill speed over ground, thus setting up an October Cairn Gorm–Ben Macdui–Cairn Gorm 'run' and a 1:23 Macdui marker for 4000s pacing. Taking 10 minutes off Mel's 1980 time inspired huge confidence.

No autumn snow was a blessing and a window was now sought for a genuine attempt before winter set in.

The ten-mile journey up to Glenmore is as nerve wracking as any big race – manifesting in some pig headed words to Eilidh regarding her parents' desire to help my round. But it's got to be a clean round so no physical support, OK you can shout … What an arse she must have been thinking.

A ten-minute warm-up and a recce of the relatively unknown final section from the access road to the biathlon range gate took me to the start point. Stop watch synced to real time as back up, it was time to leave the west end of the Lodge trying not to look at what lay ahead. There was no wind and no cloud – conditions were perfect.

Allt Mòr, White Lady tow, 00:49 Cairn Gorm was good – hi to Eilidh and Isobel passing 1141m – then 01:22 Macdui; this was spot on. Then it gets 'technical' – Taillear's burn is too far off route hence going directly off the summit and down the bouldered east face is the 'racing line'; twice or three times boulders are met with knees and before heather talus slopes a small cliff is dropped off ungracefully. But none of this matters, the descent is super-fast and soon it's up the damp grassy drainage line that falls directly off Cairn Toul. Up, up, remember to drink on the way and a gell through the easy scrambly summit boulders, 02:19 Cairn

Cairn Lochan, 30 April 2013.

Toul…it's on. All you have to do now is stay on your feet. Although Sgòr an Lochain Uaine 02:29 is not part of the old route it technically should be and is more hassle to skirt round. The summit comes up really fast and then it's tricky footing until the gravelly sands of Braeriach plateau are met. And with the plateau comes a layer of cloud. If you close your eyes you know that Garbh Choire rim is not the direct line to the Wells but through fear of 'losing' time to navigation it's followed, then the mistake is obvious and a poor running correction brings you down to the Dee from where the final blind dash to the summit is cleaner 02:56 Braeriach. No West Gully November 'training' epics tonight. In the past it had taken 90 minutes to get back to the Lodge so there's no hanging about – but who's this runner? It's Ewan (my father-in-law) sorry no time to chat positive words in my head then 90 seconds later poor footing leaves hands and knees eating gravel: again; bloody again. Shaken and shaking a thinning cloud-base gives confidence and before long the old Sinclair is passed. Then a last climb through the Chalamain Gap and its man-eating boulders where there's history with my forehead and darkness…and then freedom down past the reindeer enclosures and along the Allt Mòr faster and faster with gravity pulling you to the Lodge. A short dash on the ski road and then through and round pine scrub and over the Allt Mòr over the stile and back across the biathlon range (looking daft) to any onlookers and a last sprint round the banana building extension across the lawn to an abrupt stop at the wall 04:00:16. Exchange acknowledging glances with Blyth but it's not the time to talk.

Time to examine how badly damaged my knees are and, unsurprisingly, it's all superficial gravel burn. It's done.

2011 and running has got much more serious and much less 'fun' – assuming it once was. Selection and accompanying representation at the World and Commonwealth Championship had taken priority over the backyard games over the last four years. Like with snowboarding recognition was what it was all about. Next up The Big Six...

It's late in the season with racing out of the way and a lean early winter leaving inviting black and dry mountains (thankfully for my now chosen 'winter' sport). Again chasing an Alec Keith record from the Lodge it's up and over Cairn Gorm 01:03 and then down to Loch Avon Refuge down towards Faindouran then break right and up onto the heathery Beinn a' Bhuird, skirt the north top then head for the biggest tor you can see – unfortunately if there is suddenly a massive drop in front of you – you are way too far north and you have missed the saddle...idiot. Route recovered the saddle passed and an icy Ben Avon Tor ascended 03:29. The route is retraced over now clear tops. North Top 04:06 passed then a bit of luck as a clean route over the hags and into the Lairig Laoigh across to and up past the Etchachan Hut and then a stiff climb to Macdui 05:51. Then let history repeat itself and stumble and stutter your way across to Carn Toul 07:19 via Macdui's boulders and the Lairig. Clear skies, make the Big Six into Seven with Sgòr an Lochain Uaine 07:34 and then Braeriach 08:15 and another even tireder dash back to the Lodge 09:45:50. Much less skin removed this time.

OK so now there is a home-baked set of Cairngorm records with one big hole in it – unfortunately it is also the biggest, longest hole. The Cairngorm Munros aka The (Mark) Rigby Round are the East's answer to the Ramsay Round. Their scale can be surmised by their statistics, 73 miles 6947m (give or take), the idea being to do it in under 24 hours.

The alarm comes as a surprise; it implies that there has been some sleep. It also means that it is 0255hrs. Suntan lotion and Vaseline is applied. Cereal and banana are consumed. Compression and Nike Lunaracers (road racing flats) are donned. It feels like a very early race morning. Unfortunately in spite of the nerves domestic duties are on hold for now. Time will have to be sacrificed later especially as time is already pushing on... The head torch is removed for the rest of the day.

Standing at the entrance to the Youth Hostel the sky is clear and there is good natural light. Earlier worries of 'night naving' off the back of Cairn Gorm were misplaced. Mobile and stop watch are synced and started. 0349hrs.

Ski road is easy, two days off running have aided freshness to a degree. The Allt Mòr trail is pleasant and eminently runnable, car park. Then it's daylodge, access road, White Lady tow, up the roped access path into the unscheduled cloud base and to the summit. Cairn Gorm 01:16 (1min behind schedule). Firing a hopeful line to the tor and a bit below, the cloud base is left for the first and last time till Braeriach. The choice of racing flat Lunaracers over studded X-talons is immediately regretted upon literally hitting the wet grass down to the Saddle. This footwear decision will loom ominously from now till the Càrn a' Mhaim–Lairig descent 'crux'.

From the Saddle a second tent is passed and Bynack More 02:18 is reached. Staying high along the ridge gives a strong sense of free running over fast gravelly ground passed the fantastic Bynack Tors. The Eastern Cairngorms provide faultless granite plateau rock architecture. Staying on Bynack for too long leads to a steep heathery descent into the Lairig an Laoigh. Drumlin and hag navigation to the refurbished Fords of Avon refuge over the stepping stones and then the drag up Beinn a' Chaorainn 03:18.

Forgetting about any pre-calculated efficient lines to Beinn a' Bhuird the running takes a snaky route through light boulders and hag trying to minimise disturbance to two large herds of deer. Missing the Aghaidh lochans is a bit confusing but the summit of Beinn a' Bhuird 04:17 comes quickly.

Having messed up this next section in cloud during the November round of the Seven Tops the clear air over to Ben Avon is a welcome sight. This section provides the best running ground of the day and following a (luxurious) pause to remove stones following a scree run down to the saddle it's up and over to the Ben Avon Tor 04:54. A fine dry scramble to the tor summit far more pleasant than November's hoar frost. In theory straight back via Beinn a' Bhuird but as ever the corrie's edge seems to suck you in and you end up rimming it.

The run over it Moine Bhealaidh is initially great, then boggy, then good as the walkers' path to the rolling lowly top of Beinn Bhreac 06:31 is reached ultimately much faster than you would think.

Again a theoretical re-trace of steps and then more Moine bog action over to the descent into the Lairig an Laoigh again. First luck of the day as a faint but genuine path is located thus avoiding further bum sliding action. A steep heathery line to the left of the main burn flowing off Beinn Mheadhoin's eastern slopes. Then a traverse over to the scrabbly grand summit tor of Beinn Mheadhoin 07:55 and the first humans of the day (from earlier Saddle tent?). More fine running over a sausage in a roll to a Loch Etchachan descent.

A brief climb then the Macdui path is left for the col over to Derry. Boulder fields are mixed with handfuls of trail mix. A busy summit at Derry Cairngorm 08:51 then back over boulders to the Macdui path. Suddenly the mental state changes; thoughts of bailing at Macdui which have been slowly hatching over the preceding hours begin to fade as thoughts of cross-Lairig life come to the fore. Timing is crucial; the

Cairn Gorm Summit, 14 February 2014.

1345hrs cut off (based on a 0300hrs start) now seems extremely conservative. It would be crazy to bail now carrying a potential 1hr of bonus time over onto the western tops. Arriving Ben Macdui 09:36 summit at 1325hrs the call is made to Eilidh to tell her: 'Going for it, Ben Macdui…it's 1325hrs…all's going well…hoping to be back before midnight…started late.' That's it, decision made. Leaving at 09:42, 1331hrs; shit six minutes for a phone call, some pasta and peanuts, cursing the inefficient use of time – the race against the sun is truly on. Never will such a long stop be taken again.

Why would you look at a map when you can see the ridge of Càrn a' Mhaim straight ahead? Because if you did it would stop you trying to run down the Taillear Burn. A bit more rimming action leads to the boulder ridge that drops 500m down to the main ridge. More new ground. 30 minutes were allocated for this entire leg in my head but it drags and drags. Càrn a' Mhaim 10:29 feeling the pressure again and knowing the grip 'crux' is approaching. Returning back along the ridge to the first low section the gentle entry slopes of the top of the gully are located. Some loose ground action and memories of Castlegates stone falls abound. Terrain like this is much better descended solo. Keeping (descender's) left seems to work then breaking out further left onto more open ground avoids the steepening / seepage point at the 'narrows'. Stay focussed to the Lairig track and then over the bridge past the Corrour hut and up an excellent new track to water. Kind walkers politely step aside and pass comments about knacked knees (during previous encounters the path had been left to avoid such communication but now efficiency is best). Stop thinking about the Ramsay – you have not even finished this you fool! Devil's Point 11:21 and then the grassier track up to Cairn Toul's boulder ring. Lots of walkers and boulders, Cairn Toul 12:12. More boulders and slight drop and fast climb back to Sgòr an Lochain Uaine 12:29. For the first time the one top per hour barrier is broken. The Lunaracers have come into their own through the boulders and will continue to repay the faith placed in them over the forthcoming hours. Let's just hope they don't disintegrate (this is their third ever outing and they have just doubled their mileage).

A fast line down to the col at Loch nan Stuirteag. And it is necessary to drop further height to a boggy spring. The last of the pasta is now gone, Lucozade powder is taken. Monadh Mòr 13:17; reminisce about a fox spotted in snow-free March, thin grass provides fantastic fast running on tiring legs. A short drop to the Bhrotain col and then lots of fine flat stable boulders to the summit Beinn Bhrotain 13:46. Back over via the subtle col on Monadh Mòr, mental tiredness shows its first signs with a lost path. Sorted the days first bearing takes you west but quite frankly it's not apparent where or what the next new top is from here.

The Moines unsightly landrover track is a very welcome sight! During the run out to the Mullach Clach a' Bhlair rounded top, plans can now be hatched for the route back to Sgor Gaoith and thoughts can drift. To the trip with my father in late 1996 with old October snow patches, Sportivas and para boots. This is going to happen. 3km up the track to Mullach a glider is seen banking on a thermal over the top of Càrn Ban Mòr. Deciding not to take the high hagged but direct route on my way back, instead foolishly a last shot at hag bashing is pursued in a direct line to the top of Mullach Clach a' Bhlair 15:13. A lone figure is spotted descending east off the summit.

The track is used for the return leg to Sgor Gaoith as far as possible then more hag before fine grassy slopes and the eerie Sgòr Gaoith 16:10 summit. Another message is left on Eilidh's phone. These hills will always feel like home to us. Literally as the crow flies, home is 9km away fortunately this thought does not enter my head. Instead my daughter Sky's songs are in my head now. Try to eat the last sausage in a roll but fail after two bites.

The moraines at the head of Glen Einich are normally a nightmare but for some reason tonight they give easy passage. Digestion of crisps also fail at this stage but a Snickers works before all food is abandoned. The grassy slopes up to the Braeriach plateau and Wells of Dee are very friendly. But just as you believe you can drop your guard cloud rolls in from behind and suddenly the Wells and plateau disappear. This same weather hit me during the 4000s round (and the 4hr barrier was missed). Fortunately tonight Braeriach is kind and as quick as it came it goes, though this descending cloud sheet has brought on dusk sooner than anticipated.

As ever West Gully is reached (but not investigated tonight) just prior to the summit of Braeriach 17:38, 2127hrs. The last call is made and a short but failed phone video made. Bizarrely a tent and group of mountain bikers are pitched 10m from the summit. You are real aren't you? Do you want my food? But it's too late, the darkness is pushing me down.

The descent along the Sròn na Lairig is pushed hard in fading light. By the time the old Sinclair hut path is located light-headedness is setting in. Water at the Lairig spring and eating two dextrose tablets improves matters. The new section of the Lairig path helps to avoid trips (where my 'undercarriage' was part removed during 2007's race). Locating the Rothiemurchus Lodge track before all light is lost brings more positive thoughts. Path, water drinking, a frustrating mini-detour on the lower path to the Lodge and then relief as the main track is reached 19:01.

Panicking that the 20hr barrier is slipping the pace is pushed for the next 3km downhill, then as it flattens the pace slackens. The road thoughts of seven-minute-mile pace are long gone. It's OK, it's going to happen; cramp, disintegrating Lunaracers, getting lost, only becoming road kill can stop it now. At 2322hrs the front door of the Youth Hostel is reached. The watch is stopped for the first time in 19hrs 33mins and 50secs, it's over. You never need to run again. Till tomorrow.

Mike Stroud's book *Survival of the Fittest* strongly advocates that the average human is designed to cover such distances. In the past and in some parts of the world today it's not done for 'pleasure'. We in the West are just fortunate that we can pursue such activities through choice.

Summary:

Cairn Gorm & Ben Macdui (round) 18 miles 1450m
    02:20:54 (19 October 2007), winter 03:09:57 (7 January 2011).

Cairngorm 4000s (round) 25 miles 2300m
    04:00:16 (4 November 2007).

Cairngorm Seven Tops (round) 39 miles 3800m
    09:45:50 (16 November 2011).

Cairngorm Munros (aka 'Rigby Round') 73 miles 6947m
    19:33:50 (21 July 2012).

Lairig Ghru (Race) 28 miles 740m
    03:04:25 (24 June 2007).

NEW CLIMBS

The deadline for sending route descriptions to the New Routes Editor is 30 June each year.

OUTER HEBRIDES

LEWIS SEA-CLIFFS, Pabaigh Beag:

Pabaigh Beag (NB 099 389) is one of a small group of islands, lying on the sheltered southern side of Loch Roag, approx 1.0km NW of Bhaltos, guarding the southern entrance to the Loch. 22 routes were climbed in June 2013 by Keith Archer & Paul Headland and are in the new routes section on the SMC website.

GALLAN HEAD, The Truillich Headland (SMCJ 2003):

Knight's Move 40m H.Severe 4a **. Steve Lenartowicz, C.Humphry. 11 Jun 2013.
Down and right of *Thinner Better*. Ascend a scoop rightwards to a traverse line which is followed rightwards to the prominent groove. Climb this to the top.

MANGARSTADH NORTH, Eilean Geodha:

Note from Ian Taylor: *Clockwork Orange* (E2 5b, SMCJ 2013) is the same route as *Sea Pink* (E3 6a, SMCJ 1978). A recent ascent thought E3 5c **. The line shown on topo from FA in SMCJ 2013 is actually *Deep Blue*.

UIG AREA, Aurora Geo:

Should have gone to Kilnsey E6 6b **. Jacob Cook, Ralph Burden. 15 Jun 2013.
A right-hand alternative line to *Romancing the Moose*. Climb the right-hand corner of the sea cave until feet are level with the first overlap on the *Romancing the Moose* headwall. Quest off leftwards to reach a dirty looking crack and a break in the centre of the headwall (gear). Blast straight upwards, taking a line about 3m right of *Romancing the Moose*, moving slightly left into a groove at the top. Reasonably well protected.

Painted Geo:

Wireless in Wanderland 20m E4 5c **. Ian Taylor, Tess Fryer. 16 Jul 2012.
Start at *Director's Corner* and traverse hard right to a left-facing corner. Follow the corner to a roof, then make bold moves up and right to gain the right side of a pinnacle flake. From the top of the pinnacle finish steeply just left of the arete above.

LEWIS HILLS, Uig Area, Euscleit Mor:

This is point 85m on 1:50,000 map, NB 066 312, alt 40m. Cross the weir at the north end of Loch Suaineabhal to the line of west facing crags, 5mins approach, with descents down either end or the central grassy gully. The rock is of good quality gneiss with areas of coarsely crystalline red pegmatite.

Practice Rib 20m V.Diff. Eve & John Mackenzie. 21 Jun 2013.
Immediately right of the grassy gully is a rib and slab. Climb a juggy overhang, then up slabs to a ledge. Continue up a slabby arete to the top, initially delicate.

Solstice Pillar 25m H.Severe 4b **. John & Eve Mackenzie. 21 Jun 2013.
A striking red pillar is the most obvious line on the crag, well right of *Practice Rib*. It is much easier than it looks and climbs the pegmatite wall on generous holds to a scoop before continuing up the wall via a crack to a ledge at 15m. Continue up the easy rib to the top.

Suainabhal, West Face:
(NB 07096 30616) Alt 30m
Although this looks retiring from a distance, the crag forms a fine concave sweep of slabs leading to walls and a nose. It lies well left of the existing West Slabs scrambling route and is reached by a 15 to 20 minute walk after crossing the weir and following the loch side to the upper of two paths that run beneath the crag, to a small and narrow stony gully that leads to the slabs base, small cairn. A very prominent but shallow right-facing corner and wall that forms the third pitch and the deep groove right of a prow that forms the fourth is clearly visible from below both just left of the final nose.
Descent: Either via the narrow gully closest to Suainabhal (the second one) close to Creagan Gorma, which has a scrambling section (the first one requires an abseil off a block on the left), or continue right to join the West Slabs scrambling route to the top of the hill.

Arcadia 100m HVS 5a **. John & Eve Mackenzie. 26 Jun 2013.
A very enjoyable and well protected route once above the slabs, possibly even three stars for variety and position. Move right from the little gully under the undercut start and begin just left of a pair of parallel dark water streak marks.
1. 25m 4a or 4c Either take the crack on the right at 4c or the much easier shallow break just left to move up slabs to a short wall. Climb this to reach a grey slab and go up this.
2. 20m 4a/b Move up and slightly left over blocks left of a honeysuckle bush to move left onto a ledge below the steep wall and right-facing corner.
3. 20m 5a Climb the crack right of the corner to move left into it on top of a huge hollow flake and continue up to a curved overhang. Move right, then up and right to a hidden airy stance below a deep but hidden groove; a fine pitch.
4. 10m Climb the deep blocky groove to an overhanging crack and move left below this to another hidden eyrie.
5. 10m 4c Above the stance is a wall split by a right-trending flake-crack. Climb this to a ledge.
6. 15m Finish easily up the nice rib to a large grass patch.
The climb continues up by Grade 2 scrambling for a further 50m or so via a steepening rib and easy angle slab to the shoulder where the descent gully lies on the left.

NORTH HARRIS, Giolabhal Glas, Lochan Crag:
(NB 15365 02677) Alt 350m North facing
A clearer approach to this crag is as follows. Park at the car park by the new houses and cross the Ceann an Ora bridge and keep to the right-hand (south) bank of the Skeaudale River. Rough moraine hummocked ground leads up Glen Skeaudale for about a mile below steep slopes to where a left-slanting heather rake just west of a small ravine is followed up steep ground close to small outcrops until a line of crags runs west across the hillside. These crags form a

broken lower tier to the hidden Lochan Crag whose far left boundary is marked by a prominent pinnacle on the skyline. Contour under these lower crags to their end, then scramble up leftwards to the broad terrace below Lochan Crag. Allow about 1hr 30mins.

This pleasing crag is composed of the finest quality grey gneiss, often compact lower down but with better cracks for gear higher up where it steepens. It has a great outlook and dries very quickly apart from the slabby left side which appears to have a semi-permanent weep. The rock sports some great bollards for slings. On the right of the crag is a shelf that is near the level with the top of the initial pitches.

Descent: To the west (left looking out) down a stony rake that curves back right to the shelf and then across some scree to the foot of the crag.

The Lewisian Complex 75m VS 4c **. John & Eve Mackenzie. 24 Jun 2013.
A good varied climb, low in the grade, taking the rib to the right of the slab. Start right of the usually wet slab by a black undercut wall, cairn.
1. 20m 4b/c Starting from a low shelf, surmount the overhang via great jugs to gain a right-trending ramp. Follow this to a shallow corner and climb it and easier rocks above to grass.
2. 20m 4c Move left onto a rib, then up this to a grass patch just right of the wet slab. Traverse right into a stone niche, then move up left delicately to reach and climb a steep groove; a good varied pitch.
3. 20m 4a Move up the slab edge on the left, then step right above some grass to climb shelves and corners to a stance on the left.
4. 15m Climb into and up a short corner and scramble above.

To the right of the rib there is an open corner high up with a wet continuation below. Just right again is a fine hanging slab with a shallow groove on its left and a deep left-facing corner higher up that marks the right end of the crag.

Stonechat Corner 80m HVS 5a **. John & Eve Mackenzie. 24 Jun 2013.
This takes the hanging slab and the deep corner above, with very good contrasting pitches on perfect rock. Protection improves with height.
1. 25m 4c Gain the slab from the left via the shallow groove and continue up and slightly right up a rib to a small stance just above a lone spike; quite bold.
2. 20m 5a Climb up to the double corner and up this to step left to its continuation, all very well protected.
3. 15m 4a Move up left to a short broken corner of blocks and climb this to a stance.
4. 20m Scramble to the top.

Lochan Crag Climb 60m V.Diff *. Mr & Mrs Johnston. 1952.
This climb starts from the grass shelf on the right and traverses the 'interesting slabs' leftwards to reach the upper part of the central groove on the face.
The original description is as follows. 'Start on a ledge about 15m from the west edge of the buttress. Zigzag up to a rock recess surmounted by a prominent V-chimney, which slightly overhangs the recess. The traverse into the recess provides an interesting excursion on steep slabs.'

SOUTH HARRIS, Roineabhal, Coire Roineabhal Slabs:

(NG 049 862)   Alt 200m

Roineabhal is a beautiful little mountain in the southern tip of Harris, fortunately spared from being turned into a super quarry for its anorthosite. On the north side of the mountain is a well-formed corrie which sports long easy angled slabs on the east side and more broken ones further round to the west and on the back wall. Most of the eastern slabs will be Grade 2 to 3 scrambles at most but one easy route has been recorded. They are most easily reached by parking by a small track at NG 061 852 and following it and the Abhainn Collam over the shoulder of Tora-cleit to traverse onto the eastern slabs. Descent is down either side of the corrie or down one of the scree-filled gullies, 45mins to 1hr.

An Aite Boidheach   150m   Grade 2 to Diff **. John & Eve Mackenzie. 1 Jul 2013.
The route follows the steepest and most overlapped section of the east slabs starting at overlapped slabs just left of a white slab, cairn, reached by a descending traverse from the Tora-cleit. Climb the most continuous line up and slightly left taking in all the avoidable difficulties en-route on superb rough and compact rock. Only a few moves of Diff. at most but if the overlaps or smoother slabs are avoided then Grade 2. Well worth continuing to the summit where apart from the superb view the area beyond the summit has lenses of red garnet imbedded in the gneiss.

SANDRAY, Galleries:

Finbar's Rage   E4 5c. Neil McGeachy, Graeme Tyldesley (on-sight). 30 Jun 2013.
A high level traverse of The Louvre starting from a ramp dipping down from the top of the right-hand end of the crag and finishing up the crack emanating from the right end of the roof above the cormorant's nest.

The Madman & The Stone   E5 6b. Neil McGeachy, Graeme Tyldesley (on-sight). 3 Jul 2013.
Start up *Muscular Art*. Traverse the rung at the bottom of the lowest black band until it peters out. Hard moves in the orange rock below the band gain the obvious vertical crack at the left end of the crag. Finish up this.

The Killiwackle and The Whale   E4 6b. Graeme Tyldesley, Neil McGeachy. 3 Jul 2013.
Start up *Muscular Art*. Follow the high traverse line past *Physical Graffiti/ Defining Form* and under the long roof. Climb up past the left end of the roof to a quartz pocket. Finish left and up the ramp.

MINGULAY, Arnamul Wall:

Friends with the Arnamuls   85m   VS 4c *. Eamon Quinn, Danny Carden. 28 May 2013.
This climbs a crack system beginning 5m beyond a brief narrowing of the ledge at the south end of the crag, at the north end of a pool upon the ledge itself.
1. 25m 4c Climb a left-leaning crack to a roof, just to the right of a large hanging shield of rock at 15m. Swing up and left on to the shield and belay above and slightly to the right on a ledge beside a prominent hole.

2. 25m 4b Go up the juggy steep wall above and trend slightly leftwards to beneath a capped square-cut corner.

3. 35m 4b Near the roof of the corner, step right and finish direct via broken, vegetated ground. A finish trending leftwards may be more enjoyable.

The Big Arch:
Arch Deacon, Variation Start 15m E1 5b *. Jonathan de Leyser, Jamie Sparkes. 6 Jun 2013.
A direct line up the centre-right of the headwall on pitch 1 towards a pegmatite corner, through the tricky little overlap.

Arch to the East of Geirum Walls:
A large caved inlet marks the eastern end of the Geirum Walls. Beyond this lies a wave-washed platform which can be gained by an easy scramble down from above in calm seas, otherwise requiring a short abseil.

Arc Arsenal 25m E1 5b ***. Danny Carden, Neil Morbey. 31 May 2013.
A striking horizontal fist-width crack allows a leftwards traverse to be made over the entire inlet, with a crux move leaving the crack, from where easier corners lead leftwards to the top of the crag. Seconds will appreciate good gear.

Captain Redbeard 15m E3 5c *. Neil Morbey, Danny Carden. 27 May 2013.
From the right-hand (south) end of the inlet is a pedestal which allows access to a the leftward traverse of *Arc Arsenal*. From the start of the horizontal line begin to work up and leftwards with small protection. Continue until reaching better holds on the upper left of the slab.

Seal Song Geo, North-West Face, Upper Tier:
The Trusted Scallop   15m   E2 5c *. Danny Carden, Eamon Quinn. 27 May 2013.
Follow a right-facing corner midway between *Solid Dude* and *Flying Hex* for 5m to a hard but well protected move off sloping scalloped crimps up a steep wall to the rail beneath the prominent grey roof. Lurch up and left through the overhang in a very exposed position to better holds, to finish on the same ledge as *Solid Dude*.

The Monster Waves 15m   HVS 5a *. Neil Morbey, Piotr Bamberski. 27 May 2013.
Start 2m right of *Flying Hex*. Climb up to a small overhang, surmount this via small jugs heading for a rightwards diagonal line, which tops out on the arete for a lovely belay position.

SOLON MOR:
A small island to the north-east of Mingulay. This small island is accessed via a 10m wide divide, which requires a swim or boat crossing. From the south-east end of the channel a tyrolean can be set up, but gentle sea conditions are necessary. The walls are located on the north-west of the island and are easily accessible by scramble on the north edge of the cliff. The face itself is overhanging, making for a truly incredible venue. It is approximately 25m tall, perfect clean rock and has a small belay platform on its eastern edge which is available at high tide.

Sunset Walls, North-West Face:

Sunset Boulevard 30m E3 5c ***. Neil Morbey, Tim Catterall. May 2010.
Climb straight up to the end of the striking rising horizontal crack, where there is a clear cross formed. Follow this for 8m to a set of obvious jugs leading up and slightly right over steep ground for 5m. Launch up the thin headwall above for 5m, an exciting finish.
Note: An E4 has also been climbed here by Tim Catterall.

PABBAY, The Galley:

Washed out Yummicks on the Road to Transition 70m HVS 5a **. Robert Taylor, Jonathan de Leyser. 14 Jun 2013.
An adventurous, though escapable, undulating left to right traverse across the obvious fault running through almost the entirety of Galley Wall. Start on a large ledge at the left end of The Galley, near the top, below and right of (looking at the face from Poop Deck direction) a large boulder.
1. 10m 4a Step down and turn the corner to a ledge before a roof.
2. 20m 5a An excellent wild pitch. Step beneath and traverse under the big roof. Continue 8m to the hanging arete and pull up over this. Traverse across a short wall to belay in a deep blocked chimney.
3. 20m 4c Traverse across great rock (shares with *Wiggly Wall*), stepping under another roof right round the corner.
4. 15m 4c Take the good rising diagonal line on the wall above the huge roof.

Grey Wall Recess:

The Vital Spark 70m E6 6a,6b. Iain Small, Tony Stone. 10 Jun 2013.
Climb the crack right of *U-th*, then the super steep right arete of the *More Steam McPhail* wall.

Guarsay Aga:

The Ocean of Time 110m E5 6a ***. Sam Williams, Uisdean Hawthorn (on-sight). 10 Jun 2014.
1. 45m 6a Start 3m left of *Taking the Hump*. Use black jugs and make a long move to a prominent spike (good gear). Move up the obvious corner above. Step left, gain a slopey right-rising handrail, then lunge to a big pocket. Continue straight up more steadily. Follow the quartz tongue of rock to belay under the left edge of the large roof.
2. 45m 5c Step left, continue straight up, taking a hanging corner with interest.
3. 20m Scramble to glory.

The Bouldering Cliff:

This is left of the Poop Deck. The bouldering cliff is home to a house sized undercut boulder on the wave washed platform in front of the great arch. Five lines climb the seaward face of the boulder itself. If they turn out to be new, they will be on the website file.

INNER HEBRIDES AND ARRAN

RUM:

In March 1983, Iain Young & John Dalton made a winter traverse of the Rum

Cuillin taking the classic route, including the ridge up to Askival direct as the crux, Grade III. The new guide doesn't mention a winter traverse but they thought it worthy.

MULL, Calgary, Arch Wall:

No Escape 12m E2 5c *. Jamie Sparkes, Joanna Liciowicz, Claire Holland. 31 May 2014.
A direct finish to *Rescue Me*. Where it heads off rightwards, continue boldly up the thin flake (poor wires) above the left end of the handrail. Harder for the short.

Steeler Nation 9m VS 4c *. Colin Moody, Cynthia Grindley, Cynthia Chalupa. 18 Jun 2014.
Start up *Little Brown Jug*, then take a steep ramp up left.

Aird Dearg:

Red MacGregor 7m H.Severe 4b. Colin Moody, Fiona Murray. 4 Jun 2014.
Twin cracks left of *Ailsa*.

Ailsa 8m VS 4c. Colin Moody, Fiona Murray. 4 Jun 2014.
Left of *Dearg Ard* is a 3m high block forming the lower part of the crag. Climb twin cracks round left of the block.

Red Dwarf 7m E1 5b *. Colin Moody, Cynthia Grindley. 15 Jun 2014.
Between *Dearg Ard* and *Red Oak* are twin cracks; the right crack is in a dark streak. Climb these cracks.

Red Rag 10m F6b **. Colin Moody, Cynthia Grindley. 11 May 2014.
The pillar left of *The Great Purge*.

Pipit's Crack 8m Severe 4a. Colin Moody, Cynthia Grindley 15.6.14
The wide crack on the left side of the pillar left of *Restricted Access*. The lower part is guarded by brambles so start up rock just to the right.

The pillar right of *Red Cross* is a project.

Reddymix 8m F6a **. Colin Moody, Cynthia Grindley, Steve Kennedy. 20 Apr 2014.
The rib right of *Shepherd's Warning*. Gear at the start, bolts higher up.

The Killing Fields 8m H.Severe 4b. Colin Moody, Cynthia Grindley, Steve Kennedy. 13 Oct 2013.
Start right of *The Magnificent Seven*. Climb up right to the grass ledge, then climb the crack on the right.

Ginger Rodent 7m VS 4b. Colin Moody, Cynthia Grindley. 20 Oct 2013.
Start down to the right. Climb over the detached flakes, then finish up the thin crack.

Red Squirrel 8m H.Severe 4b. Colin Moody, Cynthia Grindley. 20 Oct 2013.
Start down right again. Gain a ledge, then another ledge and finish up the hand crack.

Redpoll 6m HVS 5a. Colin Moody, Cynthia Grindley, Steve Kennedy. 13 Oct 2013.
In the bay to the right is a pillar. Climb the corner-crack left of the pillar.

Red-backed Vole 6m VS 4c. Colin Moody, Cynthia Grindley, Steve Kennedy. 13 Oct 2013.
Climb the crack right of the pillar.

The short gully is easy.

Body Belay 6m Severe. Steve Kennedy Colin Moody, Cynthia Grindley. 13 Oct 2013.
An easy crack on the west facing wall left of the gully.

Field of Poppies 7m H.Severe 4c. Colin Moody, Cynthia Grindley. 10 Nov 2013.
Awkward moves gain the shelf. Move up to another ledge on the left and up to the top.

Jam Piece 7m VS 4b. Colin Moody, Cynthia Grindley, Steve Kennedy. 13 Oct 2013.
The obvious jam crack.

Red Tide 7m Severe. Steve Kennedy, Cynthia Grindley, Colin Moody. 13 Oct 2013.
Round right of *Eilat* is another bay with an hourglass chimney. Move up left of the chimney and climb the cracks on the wall.

Creag Mhor (NM 467 393):
Second Round 12m HVS 5a *. Colin Moody, Paul Gillies. 21 Apr 2014.
This route is on the cliff facing the houses. At the right side is a tree growing out of the crag. Left of this are cracks going over a bulge low down. Climb up to the cracks, then step left and continue up.

To the right is a flake; the cracks either side are both Severe.

Balmeanach:
Unnamed 20m F6a *. Cynthia Grindley, Colin Moody. 5 Apr 2013.
Climb a line at the right side of the main face between *Mur Sans Spit* and *Baby Kissing Tour*. The last bolt before the anchor is over a bulge so hidden from below.

There are a couple of projects at the crag.

Stac Liath:
Wreckers' Slab F6a+ *. Colin Moody, Cynthia Grindley. 6 Apr 2013.
Start right of *Shipwrecked*. Climb two bulges, then continue up slightly left and back right (harder if taken direct). Move left to join *Shipwrecked* and finish up that route.

Laggan, Loch Buie:

(NM 622 249)   Alt 10m   South facing

This gabbro area has been popular with boulderers for years. Midden is a short, slightly overhanging wall that overlooks the track to Laggan Farm. Grey Cave is just to the east, bigger and also overhangs. Both crags are handy for showery weather.

Midden:

Ten Green Bottles   10m   F6a+ *. Pete Whillance, Cynthia Grindley, Andy Hyslop. 28 May 2013.
The central line, up a groove.

Screwtap 7m   F6a *. Colin Moody, Cynthia Grindley. 22 Jun 2013.
The groove at the right side of the crag, climbed using holds on the right.

Grey Cave (Uamh Liath):

Drop Jaw Crack   25m   F7a+ ***. Andy Hyslop. 28 May 2013.
Climb the obvious right-slanting diagonal crack come ramp to a vicious lurch left from a painful jam into the hanging groove. 9 bolts.

A project starts left of *Drop Jaw Crack*, crossing it.

Hidden Crag:

Unnamed   12m   E2 5b **. Steve Kennedy, Cynthia Grindley, Colin Moody. 19 Apr 2014.
Start up *Ramp* and immediately traverse left to the large ledge. Go over the bulge and continue up the buttress. The best route at the crag; protection is awkward to place.

EILEAN NAM MUC, Rendezvous Wall:

(NM 282 193)   Tidal

This is on the north side of the inlet on the north-west of the island.

Early 8m   Severe *. Colin Moody, Cynthia Grindley. 17 Jun 2014.
Climb the crack at the left side of the crag, the line marked by a quartz vein.

ISLAY, North of Portnahaven, Eilean Cam:

Quick Trick 13m   VS 4c. Graham Little, Christina Woodrow. 14 Sep 2013.
Start 5m to the right of *Mr Bridge*. Climb the flaky, slightly overhanging wall to a narrow ledge, then finish up easy rock.

Hidden Geo (NR 174 513):

The next geo to the east of Geodha na Toine Moire (holding The Fan) has a slabby south-east facing side with some big roofs. There is a narrow ledge about 7m above the sea and all routes start from it after abseil access. Although well above high tide, waves can wash this ledge in rough weather.

Short Shift 10m   Severe 4b. Graham Little. 17 May 2013.
Start on a rock ledge below the right-hand end of a vegetated ledge near the left (seaward) end of the face. Climb the slabby face to the vegetated ledge and the easy rock above.

Magma Moments   15m   VS 4c *. Graham Little, Christina Woodrow. 19 Apr 2014.
The first distinctive feature in from the seaward end of the face is an open roof-capped corner. Climb the steep slab just left of the corner, move right into the corner (under the roof), then pull strenuously out right to finish straight up.

Irony Edge   13m   VS 4b **. Graham Little, Christina Woodrow. 19 Apr 2014.
Takes the left edge of the narrow slab immediately left of *Corrosion Corner*. Start below the open roof-capped corner as for *Magma Moments*. Pull out right and then climb the slabby edge and short slab above.

Corrosion Corner   18m   Severe *. Graham Little. 17 May 2013.
From a belay in a little corner below a low roof in the centre of the face, move left then take the obvious diminishing inverted stepped corner, finishing up an easy slab.

Giotto was a Slab Boy   20m   E1 5a **. Graham Little (unsec). 21 Jun 2013.
From the *Corrosion Corner* belay, move 5m right to the narrowest and highest point of the ledge, below the left-hand end of the roof capping the rust coloured slab. A sequence of exquisite moves lead straight up the slab to the junction with *Rust and Bone* which is followed easily to the top.

Rust and Bone   25m   VS 4b **. Graham Little. 17 May 2013.
This atmospheric route takes a left-diagonal line up and under the big roof from the bottom right-hand corner of the obvious rust coloured slab then goes straight up on much easier rock.

Overhanging Wall Area (NR 177 512):
This area lies immediately to the west on The Block above an enormous, gently dipping, tidal slab backed by an amphitheatre of walls. The most impressive feature is the 12m high radically overhanging south-east facing wall of greenish rock. Around from the left edge of Overhanging Wall is a narrow face, short corner and wall, whereas the right-hand side becomes an overhung recess with a black grooved wall and a series of rock steps angling away from it. The footing slab can be accessed by scrambling in from either side with the left-hand side being the easiest.

Biscuit Wall   7m   V.Diff. Graham Little. 17 May 2013.
The wall just right of the little cave.

The Flake   8m   Diff. Graham Little. 17 May 2013.
The left-facing flake, left of the obvious corner.

Cracking Corner   10m   Diff *. Graham Little. 17 May 2013.
The obvious corner.

Scarface   12m   VS 4c **. Graham Little. 17 May 2013.
This striking route lies on the narrow south-west facing wall between *Cracking Corner* and the left edge of Overhanging Wall. Move up to and climb the diagonal crack to the edge.

The Big Drip   15m   Diff. Graham Little. 21 Jun 2013.
Start in the recess at the right end of the overhanging wall – an occasional stream falls from the notch above. Climb an awkward little wall, traverse right under the drip, then follow an easy ramp up and right to finish.

Inverted Staircase   15m   V.Diff *. Graham Little. 21 Jun 2013.
To the right of *The Big Drip* and to the left of *Stepped Groove* is a steep blocky groove. Gain and climb it.

Stepped Groove   15m   V.Diff *. Graham Little. 17 May 2013.
Climb the dark groove well right of the overhung recess and just before a change of angle footed by rock steps.

Ledge Route   20m   Mod. Graham Little. 21 Jun 2013.
A low wall abuts the main face at a change of angle forming a corner. Climb it and then take a series of steps and ledges up and right.

ISLE OF JURA, Carraig Mor:
Note from Brian Davison: The route *Jurassic Nipple* described in the new guide goes up the right arete of a basalt dyke and is probably closer to 40m rather than 60m, grade probably OK. The left arete (35m H.Severe) was climbed (2 May 2014) and was a bit loose and vegetated at the top and not as good as its neighbour.

Ben Garrisdale Slabs:
(NR 634 950)   Alt 270m   South-West facing
These slabs are on the left side of a gully found on the west side of the hill north of the main summit. There are four quartz slabs sloping up the side of the gully. Four routes were recorded, *Left Route* (30m, Severe) starts from the lowest slab and climbs up to a small square slot, then follows the two slabs above. The third slab has a series of pocketed scoops in its centre with two cracks above them, both 20m V.Diff. The highest slab has a crack up its centre which was followed to the top (20m, Severe). All climbed Brian Davison, 3 May 2014.

SKYE

SGURR NAN GILLEAN, Sligachan Face of First Pinnacle:
The Curse of Global Warming   150m   III. Mike Lates, Grant Rawlinson, Simon Evans. 28 Mar 2013.
In exceptional conditions the frozen central watercourse in Coire Riabhach led to a broad, 50m high, curtain of ice that ended abruptly at a terrace. Escape was made by easily traversing right to the broad ridge above the Bhasteir gorge.

SGURR NAN GILLEAN, Second Pinnacle Basteir Face:
Original Route   170m   IV,4. Mark Francis, Matt Barratt, Gill Houlsby. 30 Jan 2014.
1. 55m A line of ice runs down just left of the toe of the buttress. Climb this, then the small snowfield to the rock band.

2. 55m   Traverse left and climb steep snow to another small snowfield, then follow the steep shallow chimney that leads to the base of an open corner.

3. 60m   Enter the corner and follow an icy groove for 40m of superb climbing.

SGURR A' BHASTEIR, South-West Face:

Cracking the Wimp   150m   II. Matt Barratt, Norman Macleod, Mark Francis. 5 Dec 2013.

The companion route to *Running on Numpty*. Start to the right of the prominent pinnacle.

1. 50m   Climb into a bay, then follow a gully line to the right. At the top, go direct through a steeper band of rock to a bay above.

2. 50m   Follow a groove line on the right.

3. 50m   A small step up is followed by easy ground to the crest of the ridge.

AN CAISTEAL:

Castle Wynd   110m   III/IV,4. Neil Urquhart, Helen Urquhart, Chris French, Richard McGuire. 30 Jan 2014.

This route lies on a slabby buttress between *North-West Chimney* and the Bairnich/An Caisteal col. Start a few metres left of a prominent dyke corner which is visible from a distance. Climb an easy shallow dyke, then a succession of steps with a 15m ice pitch at three-quarters height. Finish on the ridge. Reasonable conditions but poor belays and scant protection.

SGURR AN FHEADAIN:

Note: *Edgeway* was thought Severe by John Mackenzie & Stephen Reid (separate parties) and an improved description was provided.

SGURR A' GHREADAIDH, South Face:

Terrace Gully Direct   VS 4b. David Ritchie, Neil McGougan. 26 May 2012.

On this occasion, after a prolonged dry spell of weather, the gully was found to be almost totally dry. The chimney pitch containing the prominent arched block which was avoided on the first ascent was climbed direct. The main difficulty on the next pitch was an overhanging chockstone surmounted by wide bridging moves. Scrambling led to a further final steep chockstone pitch below the terrace.

SGURR NA BANACHDAICH:

False Gully   170m   II. Mike Lates, Ally Macaskill. 31 Jan 2014.

So named because many parties start descending this feature when heading north from the summit of Banachdaich. Grade 2 scrambling in summer (Mike Lates, 2012). From Bealach Thormaid, descend on the Coruisk side for 8m to where a ledge system breaks out horizontally across the north face of Banachdaich.

1. 30m   Traverse to a broad ledge.

2. 50m   Walk horizontally across an open bay to a wall with a short gully on the left.

3. 50m   Ascend the gully, then break up left across slabs. Bear back right above and belay centrally to blocks in the broad gully above.

4. 40m   Easy snow slopes to the top.

COIRE NA BANACHDAICH (NG 439 218):

The Bard's Gully   60m   IV,5 *. Tom Davy, Richard Hines, Tam McTavish. 25 Jan 2012.

In upper Coire Banachdaich. Skirt the Banachdaich slabs by the normal route to reach the bowl below the final cliff band. The route climbs the prominent chockstoned gully immediately above and gives an interesting and accessible mixed pitch on the way to Sgurr Dearg summit. Start below the first big chockstone which is passed on the right by a couple of thin technical moves. Continue up the narrowing gully over three more awkward chockstones (and under two huge blocks), then exit directly up the vertical and fractured back wall to easy ground.

Window Buttress:

Broken Windows   85m   VS. Mike Lates, Simon Titmuss. 28 Aug 2013.

An attempt to follow the description of *Upper Window Buttress* tackled the weakest line from the left end of the bay above *Widow's Eye* etc.

1. 30m 4a Turn the initial steep wall on the right by slabs, then a blocky chimney. Traverse left across slabs to a broad grassy ledge and belay below a clean crack-line.

2. 15m 4b Climb the crack with steep moves to reach the toe of a prominent rising slab.

3. 40m 4b Make a rising traverse right past loose rock to gain a system of vertical grooves. Ascend these until the angle eases.

Scrambling terrain leads to the top of Window Buttress in about 100m.

AN STAC, Coire Lagan Face:

The Hanging Slab   120m   E1 5a. *. Mike Lates, Paul Brunner. 28 Apr 2013.

Gains then climbs the upper of two overhung groove lines high on the face. Start immediately below the area of fresh rockfall on the An Stac bypass. Traverse easily right to gain the groove that leads vertically up to the overhangs above. Scramble easily to reach the overhangs (70m Mod). Climb carefully to a sloping ledge below the steep section (25m). Climb the shallow groove 4m left of the corner passing some thin flakes to an overlap formed by a layer of basalt. A ladder of holds gives good climbing to eventually reach easier ground (25m).

SGURR THEARLAICH:

Deliverance   50m   E2 5b *. Mike Lates, Guy Steven, Lucy Spark. 12 Jul 2013.

Follow the winter line on good rock with a fierce crux layback at half-height.

SGURR SGUMAIN, Final Tower:

Jacobite   40m   VS 4c *. Lucy Spark, Mike Lates. 11 Jul 2013.

Start 50m right of *Penitentiary Grooves* where an easy cracked slab leads to a band of overhangs at 20m. Step left and climb the fault splitting these to an easy gully. Step immediately left (crux) to gain a prominent crack in the headwall and follow this to a block.

Too Hard for the Old Man   60m   E2 **. Guy Steven, Mike Lates, Lucy Spark. 12 Jul 2013.

Tackles the nose of the Final Tower directly through the Old Man's face.

Simon Richardson leads King Cobra (E1,5b), North Face of Sgùrr MhicCoinnich, Skye.
Photo: Tom Prentice.

1. 25m 5c Climb directly to a ledge passing a prominent flake by steep moves (crux).
2. 35m 5b Make a rising rightward traverse (6m) until a break through the overhangs is possible. Continue more easily to the top.

COIRE LAGAN, China Crag:
(NG 435 197) Alt 300m
This crag lies west of Western Buttress and is probably the easiest crag to approach in Coire Lagan. It faces west and gets the afternoon sun. Take the path towards Coire a' Ghrunnda, but soon after crossing the burn coming out of Coire Lagan, leave the path and walk up left to the crag.
   Most routes stop at a grass terrace, from where descent is by scrambling down left of the top of *Aloo Gobi* on a rib, or down the right side of the crag. Above the left end of the grass terrace is a small slab containing the first two routes. They are approached by walking up the left side of the crag.

Cobra 25m VS 4b. Steve Kennedy, Cynthia Grindley, Colin Moody. 30 May 2014.
Climb the rib at the left edge of the slab to belay under an overhang. Scramble off left and down.

Balti 25m VS 4b. Cynthia Grindley, Steve Kennedy, Colin Moody. 30 May 2014.
Climb the middle of the slab until under the overhang; protection is spaced. Descent as for the previous route.

Hueco 35m Severe *. Steve Kennedy, Colin Moody, Cynthia Grindley. 19 Jun 2014.
Start about 8m left of *Aloo Gobi* at a basalt shield. Climb up, then left to the fault. Continue up the fault on huge holds to easier ground, then go left of the upper buttresses to the terrace. Poorly protected.

Aloo Gobi 35m HVS 5a *. Steve Kennedy, Cynthia Grindley, Colin Moody. 30 May 2014.
Start just left of a gully which lies left of the main slab. Climb the rib then a steepening to easier ground. Start up the right side of the buttress above, then step left onto the edge and continue to the terrace.

Puffy Eyes 45m VS 4c **. Colin Moody, Cynthia Grindley, Steve Kennedy. 31 May 2014.
At the left side of the main face is a small overhang. Climb the crack up to the overhang, continue past the overhang, then follow a left-slanting crack up the slab to the terrace.

Lightsaber 50m E1 5b **. Steve Kennedy, Cynthia Grindley, Colin Moody. 30 May 2014.
The prominent left-slanting crack line right of *Puffy Eyes*. A short ramp leads into the crack-line which is followed to a fault containing a small grass ledge. Move right along the fault for about 5m, then climb the slab above via a pale

Stephen Kennedy leads Hueco (Severe), China Crag, Coire Lagan, Skye, June 2014.
Photo: Colin Moody.

streak to reach another fault. Belay on the right (35m). Finish up the parallel cracks (15m).

Auld Chinas   45m   E3 5b ***. Kev Shields, Cynthia Grindley, Colin Moody, Steve Kennedy. 7 Jun 2014.
The moves are reasonable but this is a bold and sustained route. To the right of *Lightsaber* is a large flake before an area of steep slabs. Right of the flake is left-rising basalt dyke. Start below and left of the foot of the dyke. Climb a short crack, then slabs left of the dyke to a steepening at 8m. Move right into a scoop, then back left, following the dyke, to reach the lower fault line. Continue slightly rightwards, crossing the fault, and climb directly up slabs to the upper fault (30m – possible belay). Climb the slab above (to the right of the parallel cracks) to reach the terrace (15m).

Curver   35m   VS 4c. Colin Moody, Steve Kennedy, Cynthia Grindley. 19 Jun 2014.
The prominent crack at the right side of the main face. At the top move up left to a thread at blocks shared with the last route.

Take the Train   16m   VS 4b *. Colin Moody, Cynthia Grindley, Kev Shields, Steve Kennedy. 7 Jun 2014.
Round to the right (west) of the crag is a short slab with a prominent crack-line. Move up right to gain the crack, then follow it. There is a good belay 9m higher up. Traverse off left from the top of the climb.

COIRE A' GHRUNNDA, Sron na Ciche, North Crag:
Eyes of the Dragon   125m   VS 4b *. Steve Kennedy, Andy MacDonald. 21 Jul 2013.
The pronounced corner/chimney line below and immediately right of *Gonzo Jamming*. The route aims for two small caves (the eyes) in the upper headwall. Gradually steepening slabs just right of the corner lead into a deep groove which in turn leads to the foot of a deep chimney on the left (45m). Squeeze up the chimney, then move up rightwards and climb a short wall to reach the right-hand cave (the right eye) – 45m. Traverse hard right from the cave, beyond a steep wall, to reach a groove which leads to the top (35m).

CASTEIL A' GARBH CHOIRE:
Diamondhead   30m   V.Diff ***. Mike Lates, Lucy Spark. 11 Jul 2013.
Climbs the jigsaw SW face by a prominent right-rising crack. Pass through a small overlap before 10m of vertical climbing on large flat holds. Superb!

SGURR NAN EAG, Coire nan Laogh:
Slanting Chimney   150m   Diff. Paul Brian, Robin Campbell. 6 Jun 2013.
The route follows a distinct line of chimneys slanting slightly left from the base of the crag. Start on the bottom tier 20m left of *Central Gully*. Climb to the terrace above the tier (30m). Go left up a ramp to a corner-crack and up this to belay (30m). Continue easily by a shallow chimney (30m). Follow the chimney more steeply (30m). Continue to reach easy ground (30m).

Between *Central Gully* and *Lambda* are slabs with a centrally placed wall. The

Peter Wilson leads Shangri-La (VS,5a), Coire Lagan, Skye. Photo: Tom Prentice.

wall has a leaning left-facing corner and the route below climbs slabs to and up this corner to further slabs above. A good route that has adequate protection where needed. Allow two or three dry days for the slabs to dry. The best descent is to the right (looking up) that curves round the crag and descends broken ground in zigzags. The slabby back wall is defended by a belt of lower slabs that were climbed on the left near *Central Gully* at Moderate standard to reach a sizeable grass terrace below the main crag.

Golden Calf 170m VS 4c **. Noel Williams, John Mackenzie. 4 Jun 2014.
Start slightly left of and below the left-leaning corner at a trap dyke.
1. 55m 4a Climb straight up clean slabs left of the dyke to a block belay.
2. 25m 4b Step onto a short undercut slab to reach a grass ledge. Move right into the left-leaning corner and climb cracked shelves immediately to its left finishing up the corner. Move left to a block belay.
3. 55m 4c The smooth slab has a thin trap dyke going straight up. Climb this feature and follow it rightwards below an overhang to a ledge. A fine pitch on superb rock.
4. 35m 4c Above the ledge is a short wall with a right-trending trap dyke and an indented crescent to the left. Climb the delicate crescent to progressively easier ground. Scramble to finish.

BLABHEINN, North Face:
Black Magic 535m V,5. David Ritchie, Neil McGougan. 25 Mar 2013.
This fine route climbs the obvious left-trending fault situated between *Ledge Route* and *North Face Direct*, with a key pitch being a fine deep narrow hidden chimney running parallel to and well left of the great rift of *North Face Direct*. This intriguing route is equally as good as *North Face Direct* but with more short sections of technical interest. Highly recommended.
Start as for *North Face Direct* and *Ledge Route*.
1. and 2. 100m As for *Ledge Route*, climb the initial icy step, then follow the easy left-trending snow terrace to a fine small cave.
3. 40m Above and right is an obvious unclimbed parallel chimney capped by a large chockstone. Climb ice issuing from this chimney, traverse delicately left and climb the fault above the cave to belay at a wall on the left.
4. 50m Traverse right to gain the main fault above the unclimbed chimney. Follow this under chockstones to gain a deep cave.
5. 40m Move up left, then back right to back and foot out of the cave recess, then gain an open gully. Follow this to below the obvious curving chimney.
6. 40m Climb the initial shallow chimney above, bridge over a steep chockstone, then enter the depths of the narrow curving chimney passing under huge chockstones until progress is barred by a further jumble of chockstones.
7. 10m Climb steeply over the first chockstone, then squeeze through two through routes to emerge at a fine stance at the top of the chimney.
8. 55m Move up left into a snow bay and climb up to below a short wall left of a prominent cave.
9. 60m Climb up to below an obvious overhung chimney on the left, then move right and climb a right-slanting crack to gain easier snow. Follow this under a huge boulder and move up right to gain a notch behind the prominent pinnacle.
10. 70m As for *North Face Direct*, climb mixed grooves directly above the notch.

11. 70m Further mixed ground followed by easier climbing, a snow arete and final rocks led to a top belay round the summit trig point.

Forked Pinnacle Ridge   600m   IV,5. David Ritchie, Neil McGougan. 26 Mar 2013.
This route was found to be somewhat longer than the 350m as recorded in the current guidebook. On this ascent the initial pleasant slabby buttress was plastered in unconsolidated snow so the long corner to the right was followed as a more natural winter start. Halfway up this corner, one pitch of IV,5 was encountered up a steep icy corner. At the top of the corner, a right traverse led to several ropelengths following an easy snow gully weaving between pinnacles. A further pitch was taken over the forked pinnacle from where easier ground led to the top of *Pinnacle Gully*. This was crossed and a snow gully followed up right to gain the upper ridge which was followed with interest to the top.
Note by Hon Ed: The original ascent of *Forked Pinnacle Ridge* in April 1905 by Clarke, Goodeve and Walker was done in 'very wintery' conditions. See *SMCJ* 9/54 (1907) 362 and the account in Walker's obituary, *SMCJ* 14/79 (1916) 29–31.

CORUISK, Mad Burn Buttress:
Worsel   90m   VS 4c *. Tom Evans, Amy Till, Matt Bello. 15 Jun 2014.
Takes the direct line which *Warlse* avoids. Start at the pulpit block of *Warsle* and pitch 1 is as for that route.
1. 25m 4c Take the tough central crack of the pulpit before the easier basalt seam. Belay on a ledge beneath the crack above the seam.
2. 20m 4c *Warsle* heads left but ascend the crack with interest before reaching another spacious ledge.
3. 20m 4b Head up a groove to the right before trending left boldly aiming for a slab above with a water streak. Upon reaching a massive ledge, traverse leftwards for 5m to just right of a shiny groove.
4. 20m 4c Pad up the groove boldly before stepping right onto a vague rib containing just enough pockets to encourage upward progress. A delightful pitch. Belay below a steep looking flake-line on a big ledge.
5. 5m 4c The final short avoidable pitch takes a flake-crack before trending right to a final tough pull.

PORTREE AREA, Braes, An Aird:
Black Wall   25m   VS 4b *. Mark Hudson, Roger Brown. 6 Jul 2012.
Climbs the north facing black wall 10m north of *Feriae Paternales*. Good solid moves and fine positions on one of the longer climbs at An Aird to date. Start below a blocky corner-crack 2m right of the weeping green arete. Low tide essential. Climb the crack for 12m, then hand-traverse left across the black wall. Continue to the blunt arete and climb this delicately to blocks and ledges that lead up the final tower. Belay 5m back on the jutting horizontal arm.

CARN LIATH, The Blade Area:
The Sword of Damocles   25m   E6 6b ***. Andrew Barker. 26 May 2013.
A direct start to *The Blade*. A precarious and unrelenting sequence up the prow leads to the first ledge at 10m. Mantel as directly as possible onto the second

ledge and finish up the arete of *The Blade*. No gear until the first ledge and the landing is awful. Solo after top-rope practice.

Note: The route was repeated in 2014 and thought E7.

LITTLE KILT (NG 510 652):

This is the area to the south of Kilt Rock car park where several routes have been climbed recently, mostly after fairly extensive cleaning. The routes average around 30m and protection is good, mostly with cams. There are still plenty of good lines to climb, though most require substantial cleaning. The steeper, more futuristic lines require less cleaning.

Approach: The best approach is to park in the Kilt Rock car park, hop over the fence by the Drive on the Left sign at the south end and walk the hundred metres or so to the cliff and the top of a gully with a path (steep) that goes down to the sea. This is the same approach as for the climb *Risco Peligrosso* (p69 new guide). The first couple of routes can be accessed by descending this path, whilst others require an abseil. A 'tour' of the crag is recommended on first acquaintance to spot the existing lines and plan your new route! Go down the path, follow vegetated sheep tracks south for 200–300m under the cliff, scramble up a gully at the far end (more about this later) and wander back along the top, where there are in-situ stakes.

The climbs are described from north to south, the first two of which can be accessed by descending the grassy gully. Approximately 20m south from the bottom of the gully, three prominent cracks run the full height of the cliff. The right-hand one has not been cleaned, the left and centre have; these are the Trident Cracks.

Vanguard   40m   E1/2 5b *. Steve Abbott, Linda Taylor. 5 Jul 2012.
Takes the excellent central crack-line which is clean and well-protected, although the last few metres are still a little fragile. Belay stakes are hiding in the dwarf willow 8m back from the clifftop.

Valiant   40m   E2 5b/c. Steve Abbott, Linda Taylor. 10 Jul 2012.
The left-hand of the Trident Cracks, also clean lower down and a little fragile at the top. The top overhang is well protected. Belay stakes as for previous route.

Another 40 to 50m further on, a fabulous crack runs up the centre of a brown wall. Unfortunately the crack is very shallow and awaits an ascent by someone with short fingers! The crag falls back a little now into Hudson's Bay and a lower band of bad rock makes abseil descents the norm. A pinnacle lies against the face in the middle of Hudson's Bay and the following route climbs it on its left-hand side.

Midsummer's Men   30m   HVS 5b *. Mick Tighe, Simon Fraser. 4 Jun 2012.
Climb the crack up the left side of the pinnacle to the neck between it and the crag. Get up onto the top of the pinnacle and step across onto the upper wall. Finish by a tricky move out right. Belay stakes are in place for belay and abseil for this and the next route.

Endless Tide   30m   E1 5b ***. Mick & Kathy Tighe. 6 Jul 2012.
One of the best routes so far. The prominent crack just left of the pinnacle is the

perfect exercise in hand-jamming, and can be protected entirely with large and medium cams.

Run of the Tide 30m E2 5b *. Mick & Kathy Tighe. Jul 2012.
Left (south) for 10–15m from *Endless Tide* is a 4m pillar and a fine chimney-groove line just to the left – this gives the line of the route. The fierce 5m finger crack at the start of the route required a point of aid on FA; excellent acrobatics follow!

There are some interesting-looking crack-lines on the small north facing wall at the south end of Hudson's Bay, after which there is a section of broken rock (going south) before the high point of the crag is reached – with many interesting lines for the passing 'tyro' sitting on top of a big band of horizontal bed-rock. The next route takes the big corner at the left of the main face and is easily identified from above, finishing just in front of a clump of wind-angled birch on the high point of the crag (good anchors). There is a mini crack come crevasse at the top of the corner. Abseil approach.

Ceitidh Fiona's Watz 40m E2 5b/c ***. Mick & Kathy Tighe. 13 Jul 2012.
Fabulous climbing up the perfect hand crack in the lower half which takes as many medium friends as you can carry. A sentry box provides a rest or belay at halfway before throwing oneself at the chimney-crack which requires a large cam to protect the crux move.

There is another 20m or so of rock to the left of *Ceithidh Fiona's Waltz*, with a couple of routes that have been cleaned and top-roped but not led. The crag then recedes into another bay with two excellent routes on the edge.

Black Panther 30m E1 5b **. Steve Abbott, Linda Taylor. 6 May 2012.
The outermost/seaward crack-line, where the crag turns the corner. This and the next route can be accessed by descending *Birch Tree Gully* (see below).

Pink Panther 30m E1 5b **. Mick & Kathy Tighe. 5 May 2012.
Another fine crack/fault line 2m left leads to a joint finish through a tricky recess right at the top.

Birch Tree Gully is nestled in the back (northerly) corner of this bay and gives access to this area of the crag. A rope is in situ attached to a small birch at the top. Just left of the gully is a fine 20m buttress.

Clivvy 20m VS 4c. Mick Tighe, Simon Fraser. 19 Apr 2012.
A broken corner a few metres left of *Birch Tree Gully* still needs some cleaning.

Route 62 20m HVS 5a *. Mick Tighe, Simon Fraser. 19 Apr 2012.
A few metres left again a fine crack-line runs up the much cleaner buttress. A step right at the top is slightly easier than the direct to a stake belay.

FLODIGARRY :
Note: Paul Donnithorne & Emma Alsford thought *Hogmanay* to be E3 5c and possibly just 2 stars. They started on a small ledge just above high-tide level.

From here a slim groove leads up to the described starting point under an overhang, which is very restricted. This was thought to be more obvious and better, adding about 5m of climbing.

RUBHA HUNISH:

Four Years On   40m   V.Diff. Chester Robinson, Tom Last. 12 May 2012.
This route is found on the columnar cliffs immediately below the lookout. Looking in, there is a descent gully lying between Lookout Cliff and Meall Tuath. The left side of this gully is flanked by an obvious broken ridge. Ascend the gully for a short distance to the first rake leading up left onto the ridge. Start on the right had side of the rake on easy black stepped slabs.
1. 25m Follow these to mount the rib and follow to a steepening that is skirted back left in the rake to avoid loose ground.
2. 15m   From a pedestal, climb up behind to mount the ridge proper and immediate exposure. Follow a good crack above to climb carefully over very loose blocks to easier ground and the top.

RUBHA HUNISH, The Headland, Seal Buttress:

Seal Buttress can be found on approach to the Non-Stack. After scrambling down to the neck, where access via a scramble is gained to Non-Stack, walk down the gully southwards towards the sea. The big arch with all the nesting sea birds is in front and the black slabby wall of Seal Buttress is on the right-hand side. The cliff is comprised of generally solid black rock with grooves and thin crack-lines.
   Care is needed with anchors. It's often best to belay just before topping out but beware of loose rock. The tide affects the lower section but the following route was climbed when the tide was almost in.

Seal of Approval   18m   VS 4b *. John Lynch, Bethan Davies, Hannah Knight, James Buckley. 28 May 2014.
The central line of the buttress, following a vague crack system which starts thin and widens. Start on a flat boulder which contacts the base of the cliff and climb boldly up and left to get stood on a sloping ledge at 5m. Follow the crack above trending slightly rightwards at the top to big flat holds up the slab.

RUBHA HUNISH, Meall Tuath:

Hasbeenfeast   80m   E2 5b **. Ian Parnell, Jonathan Winter. 20 Sep 2013.
Takes the obvious weakness starting between *Opening Gambit* and *Willey's Last Stramash* before climbing a dramatically exposed diagonal line rightwards across the headwall. The rock on the first pitch is loose in places but much better on the last two pitches.
1. 40m 5a Start from the top of a rock and grass scramble 20m left of the cave of *Willey's Last Stramash*. Climb the obvious line of grooves and cracks trending slightly leftwards over a series of ledges until steep and awkward moves gain a stance level with a band of double overhangs to the right.
2. 25m 5b Climb up slightly left into a niche topped by a roof crack. Pull out rightwards from the right side of this niche to gain a horizontal break and then flake-cracks which lead diagonally rightwards across the headwall to a bridging rest beneath a roof. Rock up back left to a large comfy ledge.
3. 15m 5a The overhanging off-width corner proves an awkward finish.

NEIST UPPER CLIFFS, Seagulls Area:

Neist's dolerite offering to the limestone aspirant starts with a straight line 2m right of the vegetated crack that bounds *Gruinard Mutant* but with a more complex second half. A sustained climb. Good double rope work is essential to reduce drag and to protect the second.

The Flying Door   40m   E2 5c ***. Nicky Bassnett, Roger Brown. 26 Aug 2011.
Take the wall direct on excellent rock using a fine variety of knobbles, fins, crimps and pockets to the obvious break. Climb up and left to gain the clean corner and a possible belay. Move up to the rising seam that splits the recess and follow this. At the left end of the disjointed overhangs a flake hold leads to a short corner. Gain the crack on the right and easier ground above.

Shimmering Area:

An intricate and absorbing line weaves up the tower between *Shining Path* and *Mrs Bong* on sound rock with a variety of curiously shaped nobbles and pockets.

The Physician   40m   E2 5c ***. Nicky Bassnett, Roger Brown. 15 Aug 2012.
Belay at the top of the ramp next to the leaning needle. A discontinuous shallow right-facing corner leads to face climbing and a good ledge at a left-facing blank corner. Step left and up to gain a cluster of pockets before moving back right to gain another ledge with difficulty. Surmount the block in the big corner above before joining the left-slanting ramp of *Mrs Bong* to finish up its final diagonal crack.

Lochan Area:

This broken crag lies directly under the lochan that lies just north of Tower Gully. It is immediately right of the gully seen at the right end of the photo of Shimmering Area on p148.

Tottering-by-Gently   40m   Severe. Stephen & Sally Reid. 3 Jun 2014.
Round on the seaward face, but towards the left end of the crag is a clean buttress with twin grooves in the middle halfway up. The route was climbed on-sight; some dodgy rock remains, including some quite big bits.
1. 30m 4a From the path, scramble up from the right to gain the buttress. Climb up centrally, then rightwards into the right-hand groove but quit it for a ledge on the left. Move up the left-hand groove until it steepens, then step delicately right back into the right-hand groove and follow it to a ledge.
2. 10m Easy rock leads to the top but no rock belay.
Note: It is not known whether this climb is in the same area as *Wobble* and *Rogue Reporter* (SMC Journal 2011) but it is thought unlikely due the amount of loose rock.

Financial Sector:

Pieces of Change   25m   HVS 5a. Roger Brown, Nicky Bassnett. 10 Apr 2012.
Take the crack of *Redd Sales* direct for about 6m until a horizontal traverse enables a crack system to be gained. Move up to a protruding block and continue using sidepulls before moving leftwards to top out just left of the dominant block at the crest of the arete. It offers consistent climbing throughout.

This climb takes characteristics from both *Bridging Interest* and *Security Risk*.

Grampus   30m   HVS 5b **. Roger Brown, Nicky Bassnett. 9 Aug 2012.
Climb *Bridging Interest* until the corner closes. Step right to a crack left of the arete which is followed until a capped roof forces a move rightwards to join *Security Risk*.

Grammy's Purse – Open Air Finish   25m   E2 5c. Paul Donnithorne, Emma Alsford. 21 Jun 2014.
Follow *Grammy's Purse* (or one of its alternative starts), until in the groove at half-height. Pull left onto the narrow left edge of the face and climb on pleasant flakes to the top.

Long Day Lurcher   30m   E1 5b *. Paul Donnithorne, Emma Alsford. 21 Jun 2014.
Start 2m right of *Wall Street*. Climb a crack up and right to the dank niche on the next route. Follow the corner, going slightly left to gain the roof, pulling into the steep crack and a fine finish.

A Midsummer Night's Dream   30m   E1 5b **. Emma Alsford, Paul Donnithorne. 21 Jun 2014.
Start just right of *Long Day Lurcher* by a left-facing blocky corner left of *Pinnacle South*. Climb blocky cracks up left to a dank niche at the base of a corner. Follow this to a step up right into a steep crack to finish.

Bit-Coiner   35m   E3 5c ***. Emma Alsford, Paul Donnithorne. 22 Jun 2014.
An entertaining pitch starting 2m left of the chimney taken by *Brass Monkeys*. Climb a dog-leg crack up and right to a bridged position in the chimney. Pull up left and climb the subsidiary corner until below the large boulder capping the top of the chimney. Follow the steep crack out left, going direct up the exposed rib above to finish through the bulge, as for *Bingo Wings*.

Bingo Wings   35m   E3 ***. Paul Donnithorne, Emma Alsford. 23 Jun 2014.
A characterful climb starting as for *Cold Comfort for Change*, below the low roof right of *Brass Monkeys*.
1. 25m 5c Pull up to the roof, undercut left and pull into the fine crack. Follow this up and right, stepping right to climb a thin crack/groove to join the chimney of *The Glove* and thus the belay ledge above.
2. 10m 5c Follow the thin crack up and left to join the exposed rib and finish as for *Bit-Coiner*.

Gritstone Reminiscence Bay:
Slot Machine   25m   E3 5c **. Paul Donnithorne, Emma Alsford. 23 Jun 2014.
A fine exercise in off-width crack climbing, taking the wide crack rising above the start of *The Glove*. Requires a set of cams, up to Camalot 6. A few small wires may also be useful. Finish up pitch 2 of *Bingo Wings*.

Braveheart   30m   E5 6a ***. Emma Alsford, Paul Donnithorne. 25 Jun 2014.
An outstanding route, climbing the very obvious thin crack in the south facing

wall to the right of *Brass Monkeys*. The crack is gained from the right. A sequence of technical and dynamic laybacks provides the crux up the thinnest part of the crack, which is well-protected but pumpy placing gear. The bulging crack at the top provides a fine finish.

Daylight Robbery 30m E3 5c ***. Paul Donnithorne, Emma Alsford. 25 Jun 2014.
A superb and energetic route of great character taking the chunky crack just right of *Braveheart* and utilising its start. Holds on the right help progress low down and the climb culminates in spectacular jamming through the final bulge.

The second crack right of *The Glove* is a striking straight line.

Seven Days 30m E4 6a ***. Nicky Bassnett. 5 Aug 2012.
Excellent wall climbing followed by cruxy laybacking, and overhanging jamming to finish. Much practised; graded for on-sight.

A three-tiered slab on the right of *The Groat* has a triangulated block as its right foot.

Astute Ground 20m HVS 5b. Roger Brown, Nicky Bassnett. 29 Oct 2010.
From the block, gain the break and hand-traverse left to a horizontal slot. Move up to a second break and back to the arete. Stretch up for the crux and finish as *Veggie Rap*.

Stone Wall Buttress:
An alternative start to *Twegolapps* takes the jagged fins on the right. Above the V, a step left pulls in the best of *Steer Clear*. Roger Brown, Nicky Bassnett, 9 Apr 2011.

Wallsend 20m Severe. Roger Brown, Nicky Bassnett. 9 Apr 2011.
A leaning boulder sits 3m right of top of the wall. Climb disjointed slabs and the arete with minor juniper irritation.

NEIST SEA-CLIFFS, Poverty Point:
Fryerbility 25m E2 5c **. Tess Fryer, Ian Taylor. 24 May 2014.
A line between *Michelangelo Buonarotti* and the Prow. Start just right of the Prow at a jammed block in a big flake. Go up to stand on the block, swing right and follow the flake to a ledge. Continue up the cracks above.

Euro Zone:
Jammy Knuckles 25m E2 5c **. FFA: Tess Fryer, Ian Taylor. 24 May 2014.
Recorded in the guide as climbed with rests. Route is 25m rather than 40m.

Portrait Area:
Handyman 25m Severe *. Mark Hudson, Nicky Bassnett. 12 Aug 2013.
A fine jam crack starts up the cliff 5m left of *Portrait Gully*. Follow this to some steps leftward above a large spike, then finish direct.

Chutneyella   25m   VS 4c *. Mark Hudson, Nicky Bassnett. 16 Aug 2013.
Just right of *Golden Leaf*, a line of large steps runs rightwards across the scooped wall to a steeper corner. Layback up this to an easier finishing corner. Belay at a lower tier just below the clifftop.

The Uncommon Mole   25m   HVS 5a. Nicky Bassnett, Mark Hudson. 12 Aug 2013.
Five metres right again, and just before the cliff turns a corner into the bay holding the *Skyelarking* stack, a steep crack is followed through a gritty bulge, to an easier finish via open ribs. Belay as before.

Cumhann Geodha:

The following routes climb the cracks/grooves between *Bagpipe Deadline* and *Clam Dredger* (p208 new guide).

Orpin Rose   15m   HVS 5b **. Mick & Kathy Tighe. 30 Mar 2013.
The first major crack-line right of *Bagpipe Deadline*. Abseil to a good barnacled ledge which is clear at half-tide.

Clais Dubh   15m   E1 5b **. Mick Tighe, Simon Fraser. 17 Jun 2014.
The next recess right of *Orpin Rose* has a good ledge above the tide-line; this route takes the excellent left-hand crack which requires some large cams for protection low down.

Black Jack   15m   E2 5b *. Mick & Kathy Tighe. 30 Mar 2013.
A metre or so right of *Clais Dubh* is another black crack with a fierce well-protected start. Easier start via *Vertical Vice*.

Vertical Vice   15m   HVS 5b. Mick & Kathy Tighe, Morton Hanson. 17 May 2013.
The crack/chimney line in the right wall, starting out left from the bottom of *Clam Dredger*.

South of the Steps, Sonamara Area:

Beans   25m   HVS 5b. Roger Brown, Nicky Bassnett. 7 Jun 2012.
A variation finish for *Alias*. The well-defined, right-facing undercut corner right of the finish of *Alias* offers surprising holds and gives a good overall climb.

GLEN BRITTLE:

These two small DWS buttresses lie within a mile of the beach at Glen Brittle. Nine routes have been completed to date, although there is room for more but possibly dangerous DWS at both sectors. Together, these two sectors would provide the easy to mid-grade climber with a half-day to day's worth of good, largely safe climbing on solid rock and easily accessible from the campsite. Probably a good option when the Cuillin are in cloud. The best line of the crags is the excellent *Haul Away Joe*, which should not be missed.

Northern Sector:

The water here is too shallow to be safe at low tide, but a mid to high tide should be OK for most of the lines (although a spring high will cover the base of the routes), with the exception of *Jim'll Fix It*, which is above only three feet of water at low tide and the starting moves of *Owlman of Ponsanooth*, which cover the same ground. There are a few obvious (and perhaps some less obvious) submerged boulders along the line of *The Mayor of Praze an Beeble*, but these tend to be along very easy sections of the route. High tide can make the exits a bit tricky as the sea surges into the zawn rather violently.

From the campsite, follow the lower path on the east side of the loch past the water tanks, and for 200m south of the beach, past three vegetated bays until one obviously larger bay with steep vegetated walls is reached. *The Mayor of Praze and Beeble* starts on the buttress at the southern end of this bay.

Beyond the first buttress is a deep narrow zawn with a pebble beach and small waterfall. The next buttress accross the narrow zawn is steeper and home to *The Owl Man of Ponsanooth*.

Southern Sector:
Approach: Continue along the coastal path for about 1km mile past the Northern Sector. Once drawn level with the first low rocky outcrops above the path, head down large open-bowl slopes towards the coast to the square-cut zawn of the Southern Sector. The first three routes *Sausage*, *Row Bullies Row* and *Haul Away Joe* are all on the north wall of the zawn. *Claire's* and *Cosmopolitan* are on the southern wall, with an easy descent.

This larger area currently has five existing routes, with potential for more. The zawn is characterised by the massive patterned sea-cave at its rear, somewhat reminiscent of the Cave Hole area of Portland; all routes begin with one of two traverses from the mouth of the zawn in towards this cave, before ascending at various points. Every route is above deep clear water and all are safe with the exception of the awkward exit of *Claire's Big Day Out*, which is above boulders.

The routes should be climbable at every state of a neap tide and exits are good on both sides of the zawn. All routes climbed by Tom Last and friends in May 2010.

Sausage and the Chipolatas 15m V.Diff S0.
Traverse in along the north wall of the zawn and climb the buttress at its highest point.

Row Bullies Row 15m H.Severe 4a F4+ S0.
Traverse in along the line of *Sausage*, pass the buttress and climb diagonally upwards on large holds above the roof to finish on the dyke.

Haul Away Joe 15m HVS 5a F6a S0.
Traverse in along the line of *Sausage*, pass the buttress and haul away steeply on good holds below the roof to make a snatch for the crazy spike and finish up the dyke.

Claire's Big Day Out 20m H.Severe 4b S1.
Traverse in with some difficulty along the south wall of the zawn to finish awkwardly up the obvious diagonal ramp of the dyke.

Cosmopoliton and a Chunky KitKat   15m   H.Severe 4b S0.
Traverse in along the line of *Claire's* to finish up the obvious pillar on good holds.

FLADDA CHUAIN (MacDonald's Table), South Face:
Crumbs from the Table   25m   E3 5b. Ian Parnell, Jonathan Winter. 19 Sep 2013.
Climbs the obvious cracked grooves on the left side of the face. Varied and intersting moves with plenty of protection but unfortunately marred by dangerously loose rock. A thorough clean on an abseil rope could potentially give a pretty good route.

MINGINISH, Na Huranan:
A SW facing crag 200m on the north side of the Carbost to Talisker Bay road. Park by a big red shed on the saddle. A 15mins walk to the right end of the crag. The rock is compact and protection can be hard to find. Near the right end of the crag, just before it starts to diminish in height, is a detached pillar sitting at half-height. A block lies against the cliff base 5m to the left.

Sun and Air   20m   E1 5b. Paul Torode, Alan Hill, Brett Drinkwater. 1 Apr 2013.
Start 1m left of the block and climb a deceptive groove with short wide crack section (crux). Move up and slightly right, then back left up a final groove.

A Boy Named Sue   20m   HVS 4c. Alan Hill, Paul Torode, Brett Drinkwater. 1 Apr 2013.
Two metres left is a small block jammed at the cliff base. Climb the groove just left with a small overhang at 3m. Move right to a vague ledge and good gear in a short steep corner-crack to the right. Move back left and onto a ledge, then finish leftwards.

Uphill and some 12m to the left is a short dirty wide slot, where this section of crag is at its shortest.

Scratch Mahatch   15m   HVS 5a. Alan Hill, Paul Torode, Brett Drinkwater. 1 Apr 2013.
Two metres left of the slot is a groove leading to a prominent hand crack.

Karate Kid   20m   E2 5b *. Paul Torode, Alan Hill. 1 Apr 2013.
Four metres left is an obvious steep narrow V-groove below a large flake feature. Move up and right after the groove, finishing right of the flake. A large block at the top of the groove is balanced on a ledge.

The next route is up and left.

One Fell Swoop   12m   HVS 5a. Alan Hill, Paul Torode. 1 Apr 2013.
Start on a blocky ledge below thin parallel cracks. Finish direct or up a left-hand corner.

Note: The two routes listed in Skye Sea-Cliffs/Outcrops are perhaps further left.

RAASAY, Calum's Crag:

Beer and Ticks   8m   Severe. Jack Copland, Michael Byrne. 6 Jun 2014.
Start just to the left of *Diagonale* and climb straight up the obvious 'nut friendly' crack, staying straight all the way over the bulge at the top.

Dyke Crag:

The following route is situated on a crag situated well right (south-east) of Calum's Crag, at a slightly higher level, below One-In-Three Cliff. The crag has a dyke at the foot and contains a steep undercut wall with a slabbier section on the left.

Kids' Korner   10m   VS 5a. Steve Kennedy, Colin Moody. 24 May 2014.
On the left, near the end of the undercut section, a steep boulder problem start up a short steep crack leads to a much easier finish up a brown slab.

One-In-Three Cliff:

Zebedee   8m   Severe 4b *. Steve Kennedy, Cynthia Grindley, Colin Moody. 24 May 2014.
Takes the line of a crack up the wall left of *My Cloud*, finishing directly.

Mr McHenry   8m   V.Diff. Cynthia Grindley, Steve Kennedy, Colin Moody. 24 May 2014.
Climbs the light coloured slab and corner right of *My Cloud*. Step left at the top of the corner, then finish directly.

Brian   10m   VS 5a *. Colin Moody, Cynthia Grindley, Steve Kennedy. 24 May 2014.
Climbs the prominent crack through the roof right of *One-in-Three Gradient*. Start up a left-facing corner, follow a hairline crack to the roof, and finish strenuously up the crack.

Ermintrude   12m   Severe 4a *. Cynthia Grindley, Colin Moody, Steve Kennedy. 24 May 2014.
Right of *Low Gear* is a small roof on the lower slab. Start below the roof, climb the initial slabs, then pull directly through the roof. Continue up slabs, over a small bulge, to the upper slabs.

Dylan   12m   V.Diff *. Colin Moody, Cynthia Grindley, Steve Kennedy. 24 May 2014.
Climbs the cracked slabs immediately right of *Ermintrude*. Climb the initial slab, cross a heather break, and continue up cracked slabs. Finish up a short groove.

Florence   12m   VS 4b *. Steve Kennedy, Cynthia Grindley, Colin Moody. 24 May 2014.
Takes a fairly direct line right of *Dylan* up the smoother section of slab above the heather break, starting at the lowest point of the crag.

Time for Bed   14m   V.Diff *. Cynthia Grindley, Steve Kennedy, Colin Moody. 24 May 2014.
On the hillside immediately behind and above One-In-Three Cliff is a prominent cracked slab. Take a line more or less up the middle of the slab.

Ocean-Going Cliff:
Schapps Route   15m   E1 5b *. Heike Puchan, Brian Whitworth. 24 May 2014.
Start at the base of the central arete (right of *Fingerlicker*). Climb straight up the
arete for a few metres and then the wall immediately to the right of the arete.
Finish steeply up the left of two small corners. A later ascent thought E2 5c ***.

Beinn na h-Iolaire:
Arfender   18m   V.Diff   Roger Brown, Nicky Bassnett. 3 Jun 2011.
The left end of the buttress has a right leaning square rib with a disjointed vague
central crack. Above the crack, move right to follow the groove.

Sgurr nan Gall, South-East Wall:
Crazy-8   10m   Severe. Jack Copland, Miles McConville. 1 Jul 2013.
Start at the low overhang in-between *Sidestep* and *Walrus Wall*. Pull through
onto a small ledge, then follow the crack straight up on the left to the top.

NORTHERN HIGHLANDS NORTH

BEINN DEARG, Glen Sguaib:
Drumcree   180m   IV,4. Andy Nisbet. 16 Feb 2014.
On the steeper grooved section of buttress between *Garvachy Road* and *White
Settlers Gully*. Start up a groove with an icy step right of the icefall of *White
Settlers Gully*. Continue easily to the right-hand of three right-slanting grooves
on the steeper upper buttress. Climb this to a steepening. Step left on to a rib and
climb this to the upper groove, followed to a terrace. Take the wall above just left
of a large pinnacle-block, then move left along a ledge and make an exposed
move left on to a nose. Finish up snowy ground.

Redskin   180m   II. Andy Nisbet. 16 Feb 2014.
Start as for *Drumcree* up the icy step but then trend left to reach the left-hand of
the three grooves. Climb this to the terrace, then zigzag up the final wall to the
top.

BEINN DEARG, West Buttress:
The S Word   240m   V,5. Ian Bryant, Cat Hendrie. 7 Feb 2014.
Left of *Vanishing Shelf* are steep walls low down and cut by an icy groove.
1. 40m Climb the iced groove with a tricky move right around a roof at its top.
2. 40m Continue up to the right of the groove come gully line over icy bulges
and a vertical step. The gully looked easier.
3.etc. 160m Continue over gradually easing ground to the summit ridge.

ALLADALE SLABS:
Scorchio   180m   VS. Matt Dent, Dave Allan. 20 Jul 2013.
This climbs the right side of the crag right of *Smear Test* but left of the grassy
rake. Start at the right side of the face near the foot of the grassy rake.
1. 40m Climb two short slabs, then move left and up a first large slab initially
trending left. Belay on a grass ledge directly below a prominent left-facing
corner 20m above.

2. 30m Climb towards the corner, then traverse right up an obvious fault for about 10m before going straight up to a narrow grass ledge just below a long narrow overlap.

3. 25m Traverse right, then cross the overlap where it steps upwards. Continue up and right before moving back left to beneath a blocky overhang.

4. 45m Move left to a nose, then pull over on to a ledge. Climb a steep, blocky left-hand groove above (this is 5m right of the right-hand of the two left-facing corners described for *Smear Test*). Climb this fine long corner to the next ledge.

5. 40m Move about 10m right along the ledge and climb a big heathery left-facing corner, then twin cracks above.

ARDMAIR, Fish Farm Walls:
Dunderheid 20m E4 6a *. Ian Taylor. 12 May 2014.
An exciting right-hand finish to *Hammerhead* through the twin-cracked roof. Follow *Hammerhead* until 2m below the roof, traverse hard right, then climb up to the right-hand crack. Move left and reach blindly over the roof to huge holds. Further good holds lead to the top.

Monster Buttress:
Tubby's Terrific Trundles 30m E2 5b *. Ian Taylor, Tess Fryer. 16 Jun 2014.
Start up *Raingoose*. From the ledge after the initial wide diagonal crack, move up and right and follow flakes to the big ledge. Above is a right-trending groove. Mantel on to a ledge in the groove, then follow it until able to pull left onto another ledge. Finish up the crack above.

KEANCHULISH, Morning Wall:
Bowsprit Corner 12m VS 5a. Martin Moran, Jonathan Preston. 29 Apr 2014.
The first feasible line left of the 'continuously overhanging lower section' of the crag. Climb a jutting overhang (well left of *Steel Spider*) to a heathery ledge. Continue up the corner above.

Mustn't Grumble 12m VS 5a *. Jonathan Preston, Martin Moran. 29 Apr 2014.
The cracked wall left of *Grumbling Grooves*. Start below and left of the upper corner (which 'widens to a narrow chimney') of *Grumbling Grooves*. Climb the fine crack and wall above to the top.

BEN MOR COIGACH, Creag Garbh Choireachan:
Six-Step Corner 25m VS 4c *. John Mackenzie, Andrew McKenzie. 20 Jul 2013.
To the left of the arete of *The Strumpet* arete is a deep groove and on its left wall is a series of stepped corners finishing with a conspicuous curving flake-crack. Pleasant well protected climbing on good rock. Climb the corners direct to the curving crack (No. 4 Cam runner). Go up this to a ledge and finish up the groove above.

Cairn Conmheall, Crucifix Buttress:
This Way to Pass a Fist Crack 25m E1 5b *. Michael Barnard, Alan Hill. 23 Aug 2013.
The left-facing corner-crack immediately left of *Class War*, joining that route higher up.

Note: *Class War* would maybe be better described as 'the bulging crack immediately left of *Anarchist Crack*', as the above is a more obvious corner-crack.

Feeding Frenzy   30m   HVS 5b. Michael Barnard, Alan Hill. 23 Aug 2013.
Start as for *Dragon Rider*, up vegetated ground to the base of the diverging cracks. Climb the left-hand crack (a bit dirty).

The next two routes lie on the left side of the buttress (past where the ledge peters out), and are reached by slanting up the slope below the crag.

The Aftermath   30m   HVS 5a. Michael Barnard, Alan Hill. 23 Aug 2013.
The obvious crack-line on the left, and which becomes a chimney higher up. A bit vegetated.

Fortunes of War   30m   E3 5c **. Michael Barnard, Alan Hill. 23 Aug 2013.
The crack a few metres right of *The Aftermath* gives a fine route on good clean rock. Climb the crack, with a short thin section before a flake-crack on the right can be reached. Gain the ledge on the left, then continue directly up the cracks to the top.

REIFF, Pinnacle Area, Second Geo:
Sanderlings   15m   E6 6b **. Gary Latter. 31 May 2014.
The direct start to *Strangeways*, through the obvious break in the widest part of the roof. Climb with difficulty to a good break (often wet), then out left past a good slot to pull over the lip on huge holds. Finish up *Strangeways*.

Bouldering Cliff:
Pinky Breaker   HVS 5a *. Pete Abernethy, John Cummings. 6 Jun 2010.
Start as for the right-hand variation to *Monster Breaker*. Climb on to the right edge of the slab to a ledge with a large suspended boulder. Traverse left across the obvious break to cross *Monster Breaker*. Take thin vertical cracks direct to the top.

Camus Crag, Main Wall:
(NB 968 156)   Partially Tidal   South-West facing
Groove and Slab   10m   V.Diff. Jeanie & Stuart Macfarlane. 12 Oct 2013.
Climb the groove at the left end of the crag, then once above that climb the slab on the right to the top.

Left Edge   10m   V.Diff. Jeanie & Stuart Macfarlane. 12 Oct 2013.
Start as for *Double Bluff* to the first break, then head out left to the edge and climb the arete.

Camus Crag, Slab Wall:
This wall is just to the south of the main wall of the crag and running at almost a right angle into the crag. Much of this crag can be soloed at Mod/Diff.

Central Groove   8m   V.Diff. Jeanie & Stuart Macfarlane. 12 Oct 2013.
Start at what appears to be the most obvious shallow groove with a boulder (4a) start and follow the groove to the top.

An Stuir, Minch Wall:

Jim Nastic Direct Start 12m E1 5b *. Fergus Cuthill, Jamie Sparkes. 26 May 2014.
An excellent but optional direct start to *Jim Nastic* up the left arete of the steep wall above which the ordinary route sneaks. Dyno to the large ledge and an awkward mantel brings you onto the original line. Camalot 5 protects.

Slim Pickings 10m E2 5c **. Jamie Sparkes, Fergus Cuthill, Liyen Nhuyen. 26 May 2014.
Starting at a low groove midway between *Dunskiing* and *Athlete's Foot*, climb directly up a blunt black rib. Make balancy moves to get standing in a low break, then make an insecure rockover onto the slab above. Finish more easily.

An Stiuir, Bay of Pigs:

Grandmaster Flash 15m E6 6b. Iain Small. 29 Apr 2012.
The grossly leaning wall right of *The Thistle*. Monkey along a break, then launch up the shield of rock above to a run-out finish.

Golden Walls:

Fresh Mince 12m E1 5b *. Alan Hill, Michael Barnard. 22 Aug 2013.
The steep jamming crack in the left wall of *Klondyke*, finishing as for that route.

Rockers Cliff:

Lethe Walk 20m E3/4 6a ***. Tess Fryer, Ian Taylor. 20 Jul 2012.
Start as for *Spaced Out Rockers*. Swing left on to the front and follow the edge (as for *Aqua Rambling* SMCJ 2012) and the black streak above to a break. Go right along the break until under a corner at the left side of the big roof and gain the corner by a hard move. At the top of the corner, swing round right onto the front face and go up the wall above.

Pink Bay:

Between the two main prows (mentioned in the description for *Gabhagan*) is a smaller prow/arete. On the wall left of this is an obvious flake-crack. The routes can be accessed by an abseil down the adjacent wall. The belay anchors at the top of the route (cam placements) are difficult and best checked in advance so the cams are available.

Shape Shifter 12m HVS 5a **. Michael Barnard, Alan Hill. 20 Apr 2014.
Climb directly up the arete.

Flakey 12m VS 4c. Michael Barnard, Alan Hill. 20 Apr 2014.
The big flake-crack is a bit dirty and crumbly in places.

Leaning Block Cliffs:

Brasso 15m E3 6a **. Ian Taylor, Tess Fryer. 6 Jul 2012.
Start up *Caoraich Mhor* to the first break. Traverse left and climb the thin hanging crack.

Skeddadale 15m E3 5c **. Tess Fryer, Ian Taylor. 6 Jul 2012.
Start just left of *Maud* and climb more or less direct to the top.

Murdoch Jamieson on Warnings of Gales...Rockall, Malin, Hebrides (E6,6b), Amphitheatre Bay, Reiff.

Blair Fyffe on Spirit Air (E5,6a), Loch Maree Crag. Both photos: Iain Small.

Yonipool 15m E2/3 5c **. Ian Taylor, Tess Fryer. 20 Jul 2012.
The right-leaning corner at the left end of the *Caoraich Mhor* wall. Well worth doing if you ever find it dry.

Fulmar Juice 20m E2 5b *. Ian Taylor, Tess Fryer. 15 Jun 2014.
Start up *Goldeneye*. After 5m move onto the wall on the left and follow flared cracks to a big break. Continue up a crack and through an overhanging slot to a ledge. Finish steeply leftwards up the headwall.

Golden Plover 18m E3 5c **. Gary Latter. 30 May 2014.
The left edge of the west facing wall, 3m left of *Golden Fleece*. Pull over the roof direct to a good hold in the rightmost of the twin hairline cracks. Step left and go up to a good break, then climb the pleasant arete above, then easier past ledges.

Mumble, Mumble 12m E4 6a *. Tess Fryer, Ian Taylor. 16 Jun 2014.
An eliminate up the wall right of *Wall of Silence*. Join *Wall of Silence* for a few juggy moves at three-quarters height before heading right to gain a ledge on the right arete.

Gilt Edge, Direct Start 6m E5 6a *. Gary Latter. 29 May 2014.
Pull through the initial roof to a prominent incut hold on the left side of the arete, then up the left side of the arete to the ledge. Good small cams, but strenuous to place.

Amphitheatre Bay:
The Convolutionist 30m E5 6a ***. Ian Taylor, Tess Fryer. 30 Jun 2014.
This lies on the back wall of the amphitheatre, left of *The Furious Fifties*. In its main section it takes a line of cracks heading for the left end of the crag's capping roofs. The route is gained by a cunning traverse line, starting 10m to the right at a corner. Go up the corner to a good break and traverse left round a nose, to a good ledge. To avoid further rope drag, keep all the gear on the right-hand rope for the first section then drop a loop of the right-hand rope and get re-belayed. Climb up and left and follow the cracks past a pumpy section to a high ledge. Finish up the nose above via a wide horizontal slot. Save a Camalot 3 for the top.

Sea of Madness 25m E3 5c *. Michael Barnard, Alan Hill. 20 Apr 2014.
Start up the initial corner of *Lost at Sea*, but continue up to gain the ledge on the left. Reach up to pull over the roof using an obvious jammed block, then continue to finish up the corner above.

From Hero to Zero 30m E6 6b **. Ian Taylor, Tess Fryer. 20 Jul 2012.
Start left of *Minjeetah* at a steep groove with keyed-in blocks. Grunt up the groove to its top and move left to a big ledge. Climb direct to a hanging left-leaning crack and follow this to a huge thin hold under the roof. Traverse left with difficulty and pull round to a big jug, then go straight up with a final trying move on small holds. Good pumpy well protected climbing, but loses a star due to flaky rock.

Note from Michael Barnard: Starting up the initial crack of *Relatively Free* to join *Lost at Sea* gives an excellent E2 5b. The name *Relatively Lost* is suggested.

Warnings of Gales.....Malin, Rockall and Hebrides   25m   E6. Iain Small, Tony Stone (both led). 18 May 2013.
The flying arete right of *Hyperoceanic*.

Ampitheatre Bay, South facing cliff:
Kipper's Lament   HVS 4c. Alan Hill, Mike Barnard. 22 Aug 2013.
The next corner left of *The Shoogly Corner*. Climb the corner to a small roof, move right and gain a ledge which has a grass-capped slab of rock. Finish up crack behind this.

ACHMELVICH, Creag Rodha Mor aka Super Crag, Main Wall:
Guanissimo now graded E2 5b 5b ***. It's best to run pitches 2 and 3 together.
Pabbay Express now E4 6a and soft E5 **** if combined with *Personal Mingulay* in one long pitch.
Undertoad now E6 6b ***.
Ambassadors now E6 6b ****.

A Man in Assynt   40m   E7 6b **. Iain Small, Blair Fyffe. Oct 2012.
A direct line heading straight for the ramp of *The Ambassadors* and boldly tackling the technical headwall. Some hollow flakes on the lower section lose it a star. Start up the large flake of *Rodha Mor* to a roof. Pull out and follow a series of flakes until a tricky move out left gains a break and small ledge at the base of the ramp. Awkward moves lead to a break (gear) then a junction with *The Ambassadors* at the top of the ramp. Arrange a nest of smaller wires then make a long reach up to gain sidepulls. From a strenuous position a vital BD micro stopper 5 can be placed high in the small left-facing corner above. Either reverse for a rest or continue hard left by a series of sidepulls (crux), to gain the hanging flake and some micro cams. Sustained moves lead to a break and holds above allow a foot traverse right along the thin ledge to reach a bigger ledge. Finish up the short wall above.

TIFS   35m   E6 6b **. Ian Taylor, Tess Fryer. 2 Jun 2013.
This is the vague hanging groove line on the wall left of *Rodha Mor*. Start under a short right-curving flake. Gain and follow the flake, then continue direct, with a hard section through brown rock, to a thin break. Continue more easily to another break, move right, then up to the ramp of *Ramp It Up* and a possible belay. Finish up and left as for *Ramp It Up*. Climbed in very smeggy conditions so unsure of the grade.

Burnished Walls:
Rusty Buckets now E3 6a ***.
The Shiner now E5 6a **.

The Melting   20m   E2 5c **. Ian Taylor, Tess Fryer. 19 May 2013.
Start left of the easy ramp and go more or less directly up the wall to finish up *Small Time Girl*. The best route on this section of wall.

Mega Flake now E2 5c **.
Rolling Foam takes a hanging corner round to the RIGHT rather than LEFT.

The following two routes are on the wall right of *Rolling Foam* and are easily accessed from the grass terrace at the right end of the crag.

Foamo 20m E3 5c *. Tess Fryer, Ian Taylor. 2 Jun 2013.
Go up left-trending ramps easily to gain a right-trending crack. Follow this to a grey niche with a steep right wall. Go up rusty rock left of the niche to the top. Worthwhile, but some snappy rock.

Midget 20m E2 5c. Tess Fryer, Ian Taylor. 2 Jun 2013.
Lies right of *Foamo*. The vertical crack above the grass terrace is climbed direct.

LOCHINVER CRAGS, Creag Chlais nan Cruineachd:
NH North p205; Although the crag looks quite broken, the following two routes are on the steep, clean central tower. Further routes would need lots of cleaning.

Grin and Go 30m E4 6a ***. Tess Fryer, Ian Taylor. 12 Jul 2013.
Start up a crack-line right of an imbedded pinnacle, then move left and up to a ledge. Continue directly to gain the main left-trending crack, which is followed to a rest below the final tower. Go steeply up to, then round the right side of a roof to a strenuous finish. A classic.

Mistaken Identity 30m E5 6b **. Ian Taylor, Tess Fryer. 12 Jul 2013.
Follow *Grin and Go* to the left-trending crack, then move right to an easy corner, which leads to a steeper corner under a roof on the right edge of the tower. Make hard moves out the left end of the roof (crucial Friend 0 in a horizontal slot out left), then go straight up to finish.

OLD MAN OF STOER:
Original Diamond Link VS 5a ***. Andrew Marshall, David Docherty. 25 Aug 2013.
Harder, more direct than the original finish with the benefit of avoiding fulmars. Follow the original route to the cave belay at the chockstone. Head up and right as per the original route, but not all the way round to the landward face. Instead, head straight up as soon as possible then step left onto a thin ledge with a prominent corner-crack above (finish of *Diamond Face Route*). Go straight up this to the summit.
Note: This has been done before but seems worth recording.

Note from Ian Taylor: *North-West Corner* – the crux on the first pitch is solid 6a and not well protected at that point, so definitely E3 and perhaps E4. The bolt placed two years ago by some slackliners has now been chopped.

QUINAG, Bucket Buttress:
Pails of the Unexpected 60m IV,5. Alan Buchan, John Lyall. 24 Mar 2013.
On the north-west facing wall, starting from a second bay, to the left of *Paily Wally*.
1. 25m Climb up the left side of the bay to the terrace.
2. 35m Climb just right of the obvious left-facing corner, taking a shallow groove through a roof, then cracks to the top.

The Great Gig in the Sky   HVS 5a. Davy Moy, Dave Allan. 26 Jun 2009.
By the winter route.

Pick Nicker   Severe. Davy Moy, Dave Allan. 26 Jun 2009.
By the winter route.

Barrel Buttress:
Beefheart   60m   E2 *. Guy Robertson, Adrian Crofton. Sep 2013.
A good exposed route direct up the front face of Barrel Buttress. Start in the
centre of the face at a point roughly midway between the *Direct Route* on the left
and the big black fault on the right.
1. 30m 5a Climb into and follow a steep flake system to a good ledge below a
substantial steepening.
2. 30m 5c Climb the wall on the left to gain the little corner above, then make
hard moves to swing right beyond this into the continuation groove. Step out
right and climb directly up then back left before finishing direct.

TARBET CRAGS, Foindle Crag (NC 187 477):
These are two west facing crags of gneiss with a strongly left-slanting structure
west of and below the road to Foindle, just north of the Clar Loch and approached
in 5mins. The left-hand crag is Big D crag and the right Big M crag; for those
alphabetically challenged, look more closely. Descents either side or on the right.

Big M Crag:
Climbs are described left and right of the central rib where a left-slanting ramp-
line is very obvious.

The Drag Queen   20m   VS 4c *. Bob Brown, John Mackenzie. 9 Jun 2013.
This climbs the rib just right of the left-slanting ramp with interesting climbing at
the top. Start at a wedged block and move past some vegetation and a small tree.
Climb to the overhang, then traverse left around a nose to a scoop. Move up the
wall and step right to reach a bay, then move back left around an overlapped slab
to belay on a big block. Extensive rope drag if not carrying long slings.

Foindle Me   25m   HVS 5a **. John Mackenzie. 9 Jun 2013.
The left-slanting ramp gives some entertainment and is very well protected.
Climb the ramp to step down onto the big block, then climb the wall into the
scoop and finish as for *The Drag Queen*. The same caveat applies regarding long
slings.

LAXFORD RIVER CRAG:
(NC 247 471)   North-West facing
A small outcrop visible across the river from the road 1km east of Laxford
Bridge.
Approach: Either wade the river just west of the crag or take the foot bridge
750m to the east. The climbs are described from the left or top of the crag. Topo
provided.

Windy Arete   13m   VS 5a **. Davie Moy, Dave Allan, 19 Jun 2013.
The arete right of the holly and rowan trees. Pull over the overhang and continue

more easily up the arete. Step right at the second overhang, then go back left to finish.

Holly Tree Groove 13m Severe. Davie Moy, Dave Allan, 19 Jun 2013.
Climb the big corner right of *Windy Arete*, then the left-trending crack above.

Rowan Tree Crack 13m V.Diff. Dave Allan, Greg Humble. 8 Jun 2013.
Climb the little arete right of *Holly Tree Groove*, then the thin crack in the top wall.

Sideshow 20m V.Diff. Dave Allan, Greg Humble. 8 Jun 2013.
Start about 10m left of *Flake Crack* and trend slightly left taking the left-facing groove at the top.

Flake Crack 25m VS *. Dave Allan, Greg Humble. 8 Jun 2013.
Start below and right of the island of vegetation on the face. Cross the slanting overlap, then follow the flake-crack direct.

Gargoyle Bypass 15m Severe. Davie Moy, Dave Allan, 19 Jun 2013.
Start left of a boulder and climb up to and follow the big left-slanting crack. Step right at the gargoyle and across the overhang.

Three Tiers 25m V.Diff. Dave Allan, Greg Humble. 8 Jun 2013.
At the right end climb three tiers up a vague arete.

Serendipity Crag (Guide p253):
7-Plane 15m E2 5c *. Matthew Thompson, Steve Perry. 30 Apr 2014.
Steep varied climbing left of *Left Crack*. Climb steeply up to the reasonably solid block and make awkward manoeuvres to stand on this. Trend left beneath the overlap and pull over to finish up the clean slab, or the dirtier flake just right.

Serenity 12m E4 6a **. Matthew Thompson, Katie Long. 30 Apr 2014.
Committing climbing up the attractive clean wall right of *Left Crack*. Climb the corner and mantel on the red ledge just right of *Left Crack* (wires in low seam). Fingery moves lead up right to a hidden rail, then up the seam (blind Offset placement) to finally reach better holds.

Back Stage:
Forgotten Lines 20m H.Severe 4b. Andy Moles. May 2014.
A slim left-facing corner just right of *Back Stage*, above the lower end of the slanting shelf. Boulder onto the shelf (directly is about 5a) and straight up the corner, which merges with the right finish of *Back Stage* at the top. Either belay on the big ledge or carry on directly up the headwall to the summit of the crag.

Kinlochbervie, Barking Dog Slab (NC 223 563):
This convex grey slab provides a few pleasant short routes. From the layby at NC 224 562, walk along the road, then up a small drive to cross the fence by a telegraph pole and up to the crag, 5mins.

Bark Worse than Bite   8m   VS 5a. Michael Barnard, Alan Hill 24 May 2014.
Climbs the blankest section of the slab. Small RPs required.

Poodle   8m   V.Diff. Alan Hill, Michael Barnard. 24 May 2014.
The thin slanting crack just left of *Bark Worse than Bite*.

Red Snapper   8m   VS 4c. Alan Hill, Michael Barnard. 24 May 2014.
Climb intermittent cracks just right of *Bark Worse than Bite*.

Doodle   8m   Severe. Alan Hill, Michael Barnard. 24 May 2014.
A better defined crack further right.

Clash Bay Crag:
(NC 222 569)   West facing
This crag lies just above the road and is reached just after leaving Kinlochbervie
on the Sheigra road (though more obvious going the other way). The main left-
hand side of the crag is a bit lichenous. The following routes lie on a short clean
wall on the right. An obvious feature is a large flake-crack at the left end of the
wall.

Dandelion Crack   10m   V.Diff. Michael Barnard. 7 Jun 2014.
Climbs a thinner crack right of the large flake-crack.

Clash Bay Rocker   8m   Severe. Michael Barnard. 7 Jun 2014.
Start 2m right of the above and climb directly up the wall.

Stay Free   8m   H.Severe 4a. Michael Barnard. 7 Jun 2014.
A line 2m right again.

SHEIGRA, First Geo:
Flotsam and Jetsam   26m   E7 6c ***. Steve Crowe, Karin Magog. 28 Jun 2014.
The direct finish to *Flotsam*. Crucial gear is hard to place on sight. Continue
direct to the top where *Flotsam* escapes left along the footledge. Powerful and
long moves on small crimps and undercuts.
Note: The climb was well practised and the gear pre placed!

Second Geo:
Dreams by the Sea   30m   E2 5c ***. Gary Latter. 1 Jul 2014.
A fine direct line up the centre of the wall. Start from a belay on the shelf, at the
start of the roof, a few metres down from *May Tripper*. Pull up rightwards on
good slots to good holds (crux) at the small roof in the left-facing groove. Move
left and steeply up to good ledge, common with *May Tripper*. Climb the centre of
the orange wall above, between the twin black streaks, finishing direct.

WHITEN HEAD NORTH COAST STACKS:
Note: James Duthie & Michael Barnard climbed *Stac Thormaid* (SMCJ 2008)
by the normal route and thought Severe (given H.Severe 4b). Certainly well
worth it at the grade though – from a distance looks about E1! New tat now in
place for the abseil.

BEN LOYAL, Sgor a' Chleirich:
Note from Ian Taylor: *Milky Way* (SMCJ 2006) was repeated and thought to be very worthwhile. Grade and stars confirmed.

Mars Direct Guy Robertson, Richard Biggar. Jun 2013.
Climbed by straightening out pitch 3 (5c) and finishing direct (5b) at E4 overall.

SKERRAY SEA-CLIFFS:
Note from Ian Taylor: *Ishmael* was thought to be E3 5c **. It loses a star due to the very loose finish.

THE TIGER (NC 727 641):
Situated in the atmospheric Bay of Swordly where the ancient history of Borve Castle is intertwined with the natural history of age old rock, this incredible sweep of black and orange cliff resembles the coat on a tiger's back and climbing on it is probably just as euphoric. The platform below the cliff is non-tidal in all but rough seas. There is an abseil station situated on the hill above the crag and taking a separate abseil rope is highly recommended.

Lick from a Tiger's Tongue 45m E1 *. Steve Perry, Matthew Thompson. 29 Apr 2014.
'Refreshes the parts that honey-pots like Sheigra don't reach.' The long left-facing corner is an obvious feature.
1. 35m 5a From a ledge at the right-hand base of the face, make easy moves to enter the left-facing corner. At the roof make an awkward move out right and continue to a belay at the top of the corner on a pink spike.
2. 10m 5a Climb cracks in the steep face above and finish at a right-facing easy corner.

Who Rattled Your Cage? 45m E3 **. Matthew Thompson, Steve Perry. 2 May 2014.
Requires a non-provocative approach and a double set of cams. An intense adventure up the central black stripe with good climbing, but spaced protection and variable rock.
1. 12m 5b Start as for *Lick From a Tiger's Tongue* or on a rock left of the blowhole, depending on swell. Gain the smooth wall at the black/orange boundary, where fine bold climbing leads to a good foot ledge and large cams above. Belay here or on the ledge just right to prevent rope-drag.
2. 33m 5b Continue up the orange/black boundary to the overlap and traverse right beneath this on quartz rails. Pull over leftwards onto a block. Step left to avoid dubious blocks, then climb boldly to the final slim quartz groove. Finish delicately up this.

CAITHNESS, Mid Clyth:
Note from Ian Taylor: *The Fearful Void* was thought to be E4 6a ***.

CAITHNESS SEA-CLIFFS, Auckengill:
Bellyflop 6m HVS 5a *. Steve Perry, Katie Long. 6 Jul 2013.
The roof right of *Traction Control*.

Limpet Love   6m   VS 4b *. Steve Perry, Katie Long. 6 Jul 2013.
On the flat wall before the arete are two pin scars. Climb the undercut face through these (between *H.T. Lead* and *Big End*).

SARCLET:
On the big wall right of *Bonxies' Last Beat*, in the same bay as *Occum's Razor* and *The Haven*. There are belay stakes in-situ.

The Ugly Bug Ball   30m   E1 5a ***. Charlie Macleod, Rob Christie. 30 Jun 2013.
Follows the arete at the north end of the slab, from a good stance. For the last 10m, move left and pull through the roof on a loose hold, to finish up the right-facing corner.

Another Day at the Office   30m   HVS 5a ***. Rob Christie, Charlie Macleod. 7 Jul 2013.
The big right-facing corner in the middle of the wall. Start from a small ledge 5m above the water. Climb on big holds up and left into the corner. As the corner slants left, swing round the roof to the left on a good hold onto a small ledge. Move up under the roof and traverse right 2m to a line of weakness leading steeply up to the top.

ULBSTER, Salad Wall:
This wall is visible from the promontory which overlooks the Stack of Ulbster. Looking north from there, the pink slab of Salad Wall looks daunting but is very straightforward. No fixed abseil points are available.

Salad Wall   30m   HVS 5a **. Raymond Wallace, Rob Christie. 2008.
Follow the crack-line to the left of the slab reaching the left end of the mid ledge. A second pitch climbs directly into a square corner. Make steep moves (crux) to gain the top.

Dressing for Dinner   30m   Severe 4a **. Rob Christie, Raymond Wallace. 2008.
Easy climbing up the centre of the slab gains the middle ledge. Climb up and out onto the face to the right of the square corner and finish straight up.

Lunchtime at the Lost Sock Launderette   30m   VS 4c **. Rob Christie, Raymond Wallace, Charlie Macleod. Apr 2011.
Right of the angled slab of *Dressing for Dinner*, take a line up the middle of the vertical wall, eventually to join with it for the last 3m.

Mizuna   30m   Severe 4b. Gordon Milne, Rob Christie. Jun 2011.
The big chimney-crack to the right of *Lunchtime at the Lost Sock Launderette*. Finish at the same point.

Firing Line   30m   VS 4c *. Raymond Wallace, Charlie Macleod, Rob Christie. Apr 2011.
Starts beneath a roof to the left of *Mizuna*. Turn this to the left and climb directly up.

MID CLYTH, Stack Area:

Shelf-ish 15m E2 5c **. Rob Christie, Charlie Macleod. 25 Jun 2013.
Between the *Layback Crack* and *Silverfish* is a jutting spiky roof. Using good holds, swing onto the small ledge above the roof. Follow the crack in the slab above over the shoulder of the arete onto the steep wall. Climb directly up.

LATHERONWHEEL, Pinnacle Area:

I Claudius HVS 5a. Paul Torode, Alan Hill. 17 Jul 2011.
Start 3m left of *Slither*. Climb the steep rounded arete, then up jugs on the left side of a lichenous slab. Awkward moves gain a small ledge on the left edge of a final wall; finish up short crack in narrow corner.

Note: *Imperial Lather* was accidentally claimed as a new route at HVS 5a (not E1 5a).

Big Flat Wall:

Welzenbach variation: Steve Perry & Katie Long started as for *Welzenbach* into the alcove where that route follows a crack in the back on its left. Instead of following this crack, they moved out of the niche onto the wall on good holds, then climbed directly up the wall finishing left of the right-slanting crack at the top.

Wallace and Christie – A Grand Day Out 200m E2 ***. Raymond Wallace, Rob Christie. 8 Sep 2012.
The two-thirds height traverse of Latheronwheel, following the obvious horizontal break between *Fallout* and *Surf and Turf*.
1. 5b Descend the corner of *Fallout* for about 3m to reach a handrail on the overhanging right wall. Follow this strenuously to *Rig Raped Seascape*.
2. 5b Struggle to *Guillemot Crack*.
3. 4c Move around the arete to the ledge on *Shocket*.
4. 4b Easy ground and around an arete to the chimney of *Catching the Worm*.
5. 4a Skip across to the small high ledge of *Stepping Out*.
6. 4a Go around the arete to the large ledge of *The Lama*.
7. 4b Traverse the Little Flat Wall from the descent chimney to *Two Bit Ram*.
8. 4c Cross *Sunspot* and around the arete onto the front of the stack to the right-facing corner in the middle.
9. 4b Continue around the stack to the top of *The Beast*.
10. 4c The first half of the Big Flat Wall to *The Other Landscape*.
11. 4c Across the black streaks to the arch of *Macallan's Choice*.
12. 4c To the end corner of the Big Flat Wall and continuing to the big ledge of *Kelp Line*.
13. 4c Around the next three aretes and corners to *Border Raid*.
14. 5a Across the wall and around the steepening arete to *Pipit At the Post*.
15. 5a Around a steep wall to *Freakers Crack*.
16. 4a Across a chimney and easy wall to the large ledge above *Surf and Turf*.
17. 4b The headwall of *Surf and Turf*.

Note: The three pitches along the Big Flat Wall would make a great individual route.

SHETLAND, FOULA, Logat Stacks (Da Stacks o da Logat):
These are the excellent, wedge-shaped stacks 300m west of Gaada Stack. Access is by abseil from the summit of Da Logat (stakes) and a short swim across the channel (possible boulder-hop at low tide), followed by a gentle amble up immaculate slabs to the summit. The seaward side is an equally fine, much steeper, sweep of rock, averaging 35 to 40m in height. The following routes are on the fabulous black wall, halfway along the seaward face, which sports a large sea cave.

Peace to the World 40m   H.Severe **. Liu Yong, Simon Fraser. 28 Aug 2013.
Abseil down to a choice of small ledges at sea-level (higher if a big sea is running) and climb the fine left (eastern) edge of the wall. [See front cover.]

Fraser Ratter 40m   V.Diff ***. Mick & Kathy Tighe. 28 Aug 2013.
Abseil as for the previous route and climb back up the excellent central crackline.

Note: 13-year-old Fraser Ratter was drowned when returning from a fishing expedition on the stac in the 19th century.

Arc of the Ocean 40m   Severe **. Mick & Kathy Tighe. 28 Aug 2013.
Access as for the previous two routes, then climb back up trending right above the sea-cave.

NORTHERN HIGHLANDS CENTRAL

BEINN A' MHUINIDH, Bonaid Dhonn:
Toblerone 120m   V.Diff *. Ewan Lyons. 20 Apr 2014.
Start 20m left of the start to *Route I* and climb a triangular-shaped leaning pillar to its finish. Climb the short, steep wall above (easier for the tall, watch out for a loose block) or avoid on the right. Step left over one rib and gain another further left; follow this at an easy angle, crossing *Route II* to below the chimney. Step left to the foot of a right angled corner, climb this, then step left again into another corner that leads to a blunt arete. Easy scrambling leads to a final steep wall.

STONE VALLEY CRAGS, Stone Valley Crag:
Inside Inside Information   E1 5c. John Mackenzie, Peter Macdonald. 25 Apr 2014.
A new direct start. The normal start of *Inside Information* takes the right side of an A-shaped wall via a crack at 5a. This direct start climbs the centre of the wall to holds and a ledge, possible belay. Climb the heathery overhang above (5a) on the right side to easy ground to the foot of the second pitch of the original route.

CREAG MEALL AUNDRARY:
(NG 845 730)   Alt 230m   West to NW facing
A crag of amphibolite approached in 25 to 30mins from Loch Bad an Scalaig via Choille Aundrary and thence by the bottom of the glen that runs parallel with the

crags. The biggest crag lies at the north end and forms a distinctive peak with the top a short distance from the summit of Meall Aundrary. The climbing is harder than it looks but gives sharp edged holds and reasonable protection. There is an easy descent to the north.

The Main Crag has a steep slab as a lower tier with a broad terrace above. The Upper Crag has a narrow terrace cutting across it and can be gained by scrambling from the left via a grassy chimney.

Mumbo-Jumbo 70m VS 4c. Charles White, John Mackenzie. 21 Apr 2013.
The left end of the Upper Crag is steeply slabby and the climb starts from a small platform 3m up below a curiously shaped flake.
1. 20m 4c Climb on to the flake, then up the rib above, moving left then right to a good ledge.
2. 15m Either scramble up to the left or take a thin crack on the right (4b), to the Upper Terrace. Move left to below a slabby rib and groove, with a 'pod' belay.
3. 25m 4c Climb the groove to a heather patch and take the overhang above via a slanting crack to another heather patch. Move left and climb the rib direct to the top.
4. 10m Scramble up the final wall.

RAVEN'S CRAG:
S&S Special 50m Diff **. Stephen & Sally Reid. 8 Jun 2014.
A good and exciting climb, surprisingly consistent at the grade. Start just right of the jutting blocks (Dark Slab) at a pointed block stuck in the ground.
1. 20m Move up to a right-slanting ramp and follow it almost to its end, then go straight up the buttress above to ledges.
2. 15m From the very right side of the top belay ledge, step across into a groove and follow this as it curves leftwards and becomes a broken ledge. Traverse the ledge leftwards to a break and move up to a ledge.
3. 15m Climb easy slabs on the left to a bulge and pull over this to gain a shallow white chimney; exit this leftwards and so reach the top.

Otter Spotter 20m Severe 4a *. Stephen & Sally Reid. 8 Jun 2014.
Start as for *Jutting Blocks*. Pass the jutting blocks on the left and continue up a thin left-slanting crack, maintaining the same line directly to the top.
Note: Sections of these routes have been climbed before.

CARNMORE CRAG:
One Hundred Years of Solitude 55m E8 6c ****. Iain Small, Murdoch Jamieson (both led). 7 Jun 2014.
A great, sustained, technical and run-out route tackling the centre of the impressive orange wall right of Carnmore Corner. Belay as for the direct start to *The Orange Bow*. Move up a slab to the same recess and pull out right onto a pedestal as for that route. From a short rib above, follow an arching crack-line out left to a small ledge and then gain a larger overhung ledge. From a handrail above, move hard right to a hollow flake and climb boldly up and right to a slight crack and better holds. Pull out left to quartzy holds and a good cam in a crozzly crack on the left. Head directly up to the large triangular niche and awkwardly enter it from the right. From this haven, arrange plenty of gear in the diagonal crack and further gear out right in a short crack (strenuous to place). Pull directly

Murdoch Jamieson, One Hundered Years of Solitude (E8,6c), Carnmore Crag.
Photo: Iain Small.

out of the niche and make big moves up an incipient crack to a rough finger flake, then follow crimps out right to a slight horizontal break. Further long moves up a faint crack-line and a lunge gains the big horizontal break with a good thread, cams and a shakeout. A further hard move gains the diagonal crack and improving holds to a respite in the angle. Go up to a big diagonal crack with a spike and finish directly.

Note: *Welcome to the Terror Dome* at Gruinard was also climbed by the team and thought easier than this route. E7 6c has been agreed by the FAists.

GRUINARD CRAGS, Leg End Crag:
This buttress lies about 100m right of Bog Meadow Wall. It has a long undercut base along most of its length.

Trouser Ripper   12m   E4 6a **. Ian Taylor, Tess Fryer. 2 Jun 2013.
Go up the shallow groove at the left end of the crag. Move right and make a stretchy move up to a niche. Hand-traverse right and finish steeply up flakes. The belay is 15m back. A little pokey in the lower section, but the crux is well protected.

No Coast   15m   E4 6a **. Tess Fryer, Ian Taylor. 2 Jun 2013.
Start just right of *Trouser Ripper* and follow the obvious ramp rightwards to good holds. Take the crack above directly to a fighting finish. The belay is 15m back.

Inverianvie Crag, Optic Wall:
Half Measures   25m   VS 4c. Allen Fyffe, John Lyall. 22 Aug 2013.
A direct version of *Gill* starting about 3m right of the left-facing corner of that route. Climb the fault starting up a pale coloured rib to follow the upper crack to vegetation. Move right and climb the front of the broad rib on fine orange coloured rock.

Fibre Optic   25m   VS 4c. John Lyall, Allen Fyffe. 22 Aug 2013.
Takes a line going up to then right of the obvious roof at 10m. Start just right of the previous route and climb up to where a ledge goes right into a left-facing corner below the roof. Use the corner to exit right, then climb a fine crack in the wall above.

GRUINARD RIVER CRAGS, Goat Crag:
Homunculus   20m   E4 5c *. Tess Fryer, Ian Taylor. 24 May 2013.
Start at the steep crack between *Homosuperior* and the big block corner to its left. Climb the crack until able to bridge left onto the big block. Continue bridging up to the tree, step right and go up rough rock until able to trend right to gain the top section of *Homosuperior*, which is followed to the top.

Freak Show Direct   20m   E5 6a **. Ian Taylor, Tess Fryer. 17 May 2013.
Start right of the normal route and go straight up the cracked wall until moves diagonally rightwards lead to a loose-looking block on the right arete (keyed-in). Stand on the block and follow cracks back left to a junction with *Freak Show* just below its downward jutting spike. Finish up the original route.

Summit Fever 20m   E1 5b. Ian Taylor, Tess Fryer. 18 Jun 2013.
A second pitch above the *Freak Show/Homosuperior* abb point. Move right from the belay and follow a corner up the left side of a rib. After 10m break right onto the rib and follow a crack to ledges. Scramble for 30m to gain the top of the crag.

GRUINARD NORTH CRAGS, Carn Dearg an Droma:

Tetrus Rocket Direct 25m   VS 4c *. John Mackenzie, Eve Mackenzie. 6 Aug 2013.
From where the original route veers off rightward above the lower corners, step left and surmount the crack into the left-slanting pod, crux, and up this to the top. A bit mossy but not without interest.

Slideline 25m   H.Severe 4c. John Mackenzie, Eve Mackenzie. 6 Aug 2013.
Climb the thin crack just right of *Game Boy* to below a steep wall which is well equipped with holds, a pleasant excursion.

Let's Play Scrabble 25m   E2 5c/6a **. John Mackenzie. 6 Aug 2013.
This takes a thin right-slanting crack left of *Tetrus Rocket* up the vertical wall. Thin moves up the crack lead to a wall with a shallow groove. Climb this to a bulge and step left and up to heather. Cross this to the apex of the heather rake and climb a left-slanting thin crack to the top. A good varied and well protected route despite being a bit mossy.

AN TEALLACH, Ghlas Tholl:

Last Orders 95m   VII,8 **. Kenro Nakajima, Neil Adams. 1 Feb 2014.
A good icy mixed route taking the right side of *Major Rib* aiming for the prominent corner and chimney high on that buttress. Start about 50m up *The Alley* at an icy corner on the left where *The Alley* curves rightwards.
1. 25m Climb the icy corner direct to a niche capped by a diagonal roof. Continue up a thinly iced slab to the left, then move right to a sloping ledge below a short turfy corner.
2. 15m Climb the corner and the icy slab above, then step left onto flakes. Follow these to a good stance in a clean-cut corner below the main corner.
3. 35m Rock onto the ramp on the left and follow this to the main corner. Climb this with increasing difficulty, passing the big roof on the left (crux). Continue into the chimney above and follow this more easily to a good stance.
4. 20m Continue up the chimney to easier ground leading to the crest of *Major Rib*.
Some 120m of easy ground leads to the top of *Major Rib*.

AN RIABHACHAN (Glen Cannich):

The following routes are on the section of crag with *Spindrift Gully*. This is the section nearest the Bealach Toll an Lochain.

Bealach Gully 140m   II. Andy Nisbet, Jonathan Preston. 12 Mar 2014.
A right-slanting gully at the left end of the crag. There is one ice pitch and the gully ends in slopes below the cornice.

Gatekeeper 150m   V,5. Andy Nisbet, Jonathan Preston. 12 Mar 2014.
The steepest section of the crag lies right of *Bealach Gully* and has two steep

bands of rock. Start below a point about three-quarters of the way towards the right end of the lower band. Climb a short introductory tier to below a left-slanting ramp of intermittent turf (20m). Climb the ramp until possible to break right and reach the terrace between the steep bands. Cross the terrace slightly leftwards to reach a right-slanting groove which is immediately right of the steepest rocks of the upper tier. Go up to the base of its narrow section (60m). Climb the groove and steep turf above to reach the upper slopes (50m). The cornice was breached at the same point as *Bealach Gully* (20m).

Bazinga 180m III. Andy Nisbet, Jonathan Preston. 12 Mar 2014.
The crag has a low toe just left of the base of *Spindrift Gully*. Go up into a bay left of the toe and take the highest break out right to reach another bay. Go to its top and take an iced groove up right (the right-hand of two). Go up to a big slightly left-slanting fault-line which leads over snow with icy steps to the top.

SGURR NA MUICE, South-East Face:
Hogwarts' Express 135m IV,4 *. John Mackenzie, Andrew James. 7 Feb 2014.
A good varied route with a suitably entertaining crux. The true nose of the crag is easily reached by the steepish slope of the 'easy angled' rib well left of the normal approach up the left-hand couloir. The route takes the buttress between *Porker* on the left and *Sow's Ear* on the right, where a slabby rake hemmed in by a wall to the right lies on the left side of this buttress. The rake ends in a steep groove squeezed between the wall on the right and a drop into *Porker* on the left.
1. 55m Climb the slabby rake close to the bounding wall on the right with a little bulge and slabs above to the base of the steep groove.
2. 25m The groove has no turf higher up but a deep parallel sided crack and can be awkward, two in-situ nuts! An exposed but scenic turf ledge has an escape out on the right wall.
3. 55m Above is a broken overlapped slab. Move easily up to it and follow its right edge via a shallow gully to a steeper snow exit.

BEN WYVIS, Coire na Feola:
Risk of Ice 250m   V,4. Sandy Allan, Andy Nisbet, Jonathan Preston. 1 Mar 2014.
A line up the left-hand buttress of the main section of cliff (*Quiet and Peacefall* splits the two sections). Start at the same place as *Discovery Buttress* but traverse easily right into the centre of the buttress (20m). Continue the traverse line on a small ledge gained with a step up until a turfy groove leads back up left to a terrace and wall above (45m). Climb through the wall by a right-slanting turf line, then continue slightly right through steeper turfy ground to snow and a belay on the right (40m). Go straight up snowy ground to a right-facing corner below overhangs (40m). Break out left through the corner, then make a left-rising traverse to a break near the left end of the overhangs. Go straight up to a snowfield (45m). Joining *Discovery Buttress*, go up to rocks (10m). Go left through a break in the rocks above, then right to a break in the cornice which often forms at a change in angle of the clifftop (50m).
Note: Grade possibly IV,4 in more consolidated conditions.

NORTHERN HIGHLANDS SOUTH

SGURR NAN COIREACHAN, Sgurr a' Choire Riabhaich:
(NM 908 873) Alt 700m North-East facing
The crag has two sections, a more broken left section with several gullies and buttresses and a steep right section with an obvious right-rising ramp-line.

Towards the left of the left section is a deep narrow gully with a sharp ridge to its right. To the right of this are three gullies before the section ends with a bigger buttress. The left section is separated from the right by a Grade I snow gully which makes a convenient descent.

The right section has a right-slanting ramp near its left end and to its right a bigger ramp which starts from a ledge and curves rightwards over a steep wall.

Georgy Porgy 150m II. Dave McGimpsey, Jonathan Preston. Jan 2013.
The deep narrow gully. At its top, traverse into and finish up the left-hand groove above finishing as for *Gully 1*.

Neck Ridge 200m II. Ed Edwards, Dave McGimpsey. 8 Feb 2009.
The sharp ridge. At its top, join and finish as for *Georgy Porgy*.

Gully 1 200m II. Dave McGimpsey, Andy Nisbet, Jonathan Preston. 23 Feb 2013.
The first of the three gullies starts lower down and runs up left close to the sharp ridge. It has one definite ice pitch and may have a couple of smaller ones high up.

Gully 2 160m II. Dave McGimpsey, Andy Nisbet, Jonathan Preston. 23 Feb 2013.
A parallel left-slanting gully has one short steep ice pitch and may be Grade III in lean icy conditions.

Light Fingers 120m IV,5. Dave McGimpsey, Jonathan Preston. Jan 2013.
Climbs near the left-hand side of the buttress between gullies 2 and 3. Start up *Gully 2* but move right after the initial short step to climb short walls to below the buttress proper. Gain a ledge and belay near its left-hand end below a short steep corner (60m). Climb the short corner onto a slab, move right and up through a break in the steep wall above. Belay below a narrow ledge (30m). Traverse right along the narrow ledge, then move up to easier ground and the top (30m).

Gully 3 150m II. Dave McGimpsey, Andy Nisbet, Jonathan Preston. 23 Feb 2013.
The last gully on this section starts from just inside the previous route but slants up right to finish a wide funnel which may cornice badly. There is a tricky chimney step low down which can be avoided on the right. In the narrows above is another ice pitch and there may be a smaller ice pitch higher up.

Fat Chance 40m IV,5. Dave McGimpsey, Andy Nisbet. 29 Mar 2013.
A steep iced groove on the left wall of the narrows.

Operation Safecrack 130m V,6. Dave McGimpsey, Andy Nisbet. 29 Mar 2013.
Based on the crest of the bigger buttress. Start right of the toe of the buttress

below a slabby section of face and where there is a turf ledge just above the base.
1. 65m From the left end of the turf ledge, climb a narrow line of turf and continue trending slightly left to below a wall (possible belay). Return right and climb a steepening fault to reach the crest.
2. 35m Go right to a big pinnacle and climb a steep corner behind it. Continue up the crest to a barrier wall.
3. 30m Go left and back right to pass the wall, then finish up icy grooves.

Hit and Run 85m III,4. Dave McGimpsey, Andy Nisbet. Jan 2013.
A route on the right side of the bigger buttress, starting some 20m above the previous route. Start about 20m up the descent gully where a line of weakness leads up left on to the crest of the buttress (60m). Finish up an unusual right-slanting turfy line to the top (25m).

Next is the Grade I snow gully which separates the left and right sections.

Parson's Pleasure 120m IV,5. Dave McGimpsey, Andy Nisbet, Jonathan Preston. 23 Feb 2013.
The ramp near the left end of the right section. An ice pitch to gain the ramp is the crux by far and the grade may vary (20m). Move right and follow the ramp to the top.

MacCloak & Ben Dagger 90m VI,7. Ed Edwards, Dave McGimpsey. 10 Feb 2009.
Climbs the left to right diagonal line above the initial ledge on *Zag-Zig* to a finish up a shallow icy groove on the final tier. Follow *Zag-Zig* for 15m to the start of the left to right diagonal crack/groove.
1. 30m Climb the crack and follow the groove above to belay at the base of a pinnacle.
2. 30m Stand on the pinnacle and climb the left to right diagonal crack (as for *Tales of the Unexpected*) and the continuation crack to where this peters out. Step left and climb a turf groove to the large ramp and belay to the right of a shallow icy groove.
3. 30m Climb the groove then move left along the ledge to a pinnacle. Climb around the pinnacle and up the awkward corner above stepping left at the top on to a flaked arete.

Zag-Zig 150m III. Dave McGimpsey, Andy Nisbet, Jonathan Preston. 23 Feb 2013.
The big ramp above the ledge. Start in the centre of the cliff. Gain the right end of the ledge by a short step and traverse it to the ramp (but don't continue beyond the ramp) – 50m. Follow the ramp up and right (80m) until an icy ramp leads back left to the top (20m).

Tales of the Unexpected 90m VII,7. Ed Edwards, Dave McGimpsey. 8 Feb 2009.
Climbs the right side of the wall above the initial ledge on *Zag-Zig* before crossing the diagonal fault of *MacCloak & Ben Dagger* to a steep finish up the final tier. Start as for *Zag-Zig* below a right arching slabby corner.

1. 30m Climb the right-arching corner and continuation corner above to belay on a narrow ledge below a pinnacle.

2. 35m Climb the crack above to stand on the pinnacle and join the left to right diagonal crack of *MacCloak & Ben Dagger* for 5m to a point where moves left lead to a turf ledge. Continue to the ramp and belay at the base of a corner in the wall directly opposite.

3. 25m Climb the corner then move left onto turf ledges leading to a short steep corner. Follow this to the top.

CREAG COIRE AN T-SLUGAIN:

Argentine Lemon VI,6. Susan Jensen, Marie Leroux. 30 Jan 2014.
A combination of *Lemon Groove* linked into *Argentine Chimney*, giving a direct line. The grade reflects icy but not helpful conditions.

MORUISG, The Great Grey Slab of Coire nam Mang:

A Right Guddle 70m Severe. Peter Macdonald, John Mackenzie. 22 Jul 2013.
Takes the left arete of the steeper bounding slab to the left of the Main Slabs, starting up the bounding slab then moving up to the arete at a break before marginally better climbing up the very edge in a good position. Climbed in two pitches but would be improved by starting from its base rather than moving in from the right at one-third-height.

Blankety-Blank 135m VS 4c *. Peter Macdonald, John Mackenzie. 22 Jul 2013.
A good clean route apart from parts of the second pitch but overall some nice padding with good belays and occasional gear – take Cams 0 to 4 and some wires.

1. 40m 4c Start left of *Close to the Edge* below a big blank slab and climb straight up the middle to an overlap (4 Friend runner). Go over this to climb a slab and Friend 3 belay on the arete of *Close to the Edge.*

2. 35m 4a Follow a left-trending groove to the lower terrace and walk left to below another blank slab bounded by a corner and topped by an overlap.

3. 40m 4a Go easily up the blank slab to take the overlap at a little corner in the centre, then up steeper slabs to near *Close to the Edge.*

4. 20m 4c Climb the overlap and climb the next blank slab up and slightly left to the top.

Hybrid Combinations 95m VS 4c. *. John & Eve Mackenzie. 9 Jul 2013.
A direct line up the centre of the main slab taking in parts of *The President's Men* and *Rock Surfer* at a reasonable grade and solid Friend protection, albeit spaced.

1. 25m 4c Start roughly centrally at the right end of the higher of the two short horizontal ledges that are gained from the wet left-slanting rake. A grassy crack runs up slightly right and to the left are a pair of overlaps, (as for the start of *The President's Men*). Climb the slab right of the shallow corner and over the first overlap, then direct to the top overlap, taken near the left, to reach a left-slanting ramp which is followed more easily or more boldly direct to the terrace. This is more or less the same as the initial pitch of *The President's Men* but less direct.

2. 40m 4b Pad up the good blank slab on the left to reach a small overlap on the right, move up right towards the right-hand edge of the slab to cracked blocks.

3. 30m 4c Climb a steepening slab on the left towards the right-hand of the two

corners but keep to the right on a clean section of slab left of *Slapstick* to join the corner at around three-quarters height. Climb to the top.

SGURR NA FEARTAIG, Coire Leiridh:
Silver Lining III,4. Alan Buchan, John Lyall. 29 Mar 2013.
A continuation to the route in SMCJ 2010. Continue up the ravine for a further 100m, finding several good short ice pitches, with one on vertical ice giving the crux.

SGORR RUADH, Raeburn's Buttress:
Cupid 100m III,4 *. Ewan Lyons. 14 Feb 2014.
Start 70m left of *Narrow Gully*. Climb an icy wall, then follow icy mixed corners and steps trending right. Escapable on the left at half-height.

Stunt 120m III,4 *. Ewan Lyons. 14 Feb 2014.
Start 20m left of *Narrow Gully*. Climb the intermittent gully line split at half-height by a large ledge with a large chockstone low down and a much smaller one in the upper section. Threading the upper chockstone can be quite technical depending on conditions.

Upper Buttress:
Riotous Ramble 140m III. Ewan Lyons. 14 Feb 2014.
Start halfway between *Frivolity* and *Riotous Ridge* and climb a turfy scoop (the original start to *Riotous Ridge*). Trend left and up following turfy ramps over two steep steps alway right of *Frivolity*, to finish at same point as this route.

MEALL GORM:
Blue Lamppost Variations VII,8. Michelle Kadatz, Ian Parnell. 1 Feb 2014.
A turfier line which may be in condition more often. The start was made by scrambling along large grass ledges from the right to access the main headwall.
1. 15m Go up turfy corners to access the final grass ledge under the headwall.
2. 30m A new winter pitch up turfy grooves between *The Smooth Creep* and *Blue Lampost* (winter), in a line directly under *Blue Lampost's* final pitch and belaying at prominent horizontal break/ledge capped by steeper ground.
3. 45m Climb a steep groove (perhaps pitch 3 of *The Smooth Creep*) and the left side of a flake topped by a huge balanced block to join and climb the final pitch of *Blue Lampost* (winter). Belay at the top of the chimney below easy ground.

Cobalt Buttress Direct Start 70m IV,4. Gwilym Lynn, Felix Sattelberger. 1 Feb 2014.
A more direct start up *Cobalt Buttress*, taking in part of the lower tier of the buttress. Start about 40m up the gully on the right-hand side of the buttress.
1. 30m Climb a short corner to gain a horizontal terrace and follow this left to the crest of the buttress
2. 40m Follow grooves and corner lines trending rightwards to the join the original route at the end of the awkward traverse.

Note: Nick Bullock & partner on 1 Feb 2014 climbed a harder direct line right of *Rattlesnake* to join *Cobalt Buttress*.

APPLECROSS CRAGS, Ardheslaig:

Note: Stephen & Sally Reid on 7 Jun 2014 repeated *Fire in the Glens* (SMCJ 2011) and can confirm the star. At the top, they started up just right of the quartz vein as per the description but then traversed right to pull over a bulge – Severe 4a.

A' Bhainlir:

The following routes are on small bluffs in the vicinity of the larger cliff on A' Bhainlir (NHS p191). After crossing the bridge mentioned in the guide one can see a prominent slabby outcrop up to the left. This has an easy lower skirt of light coloured slabs on the SW face below a short steep wall with a prominent crack. Round the corner to the left is a higher slabby wall of much darker, lichen stained rock. First on the lighter coloured face.

Zigzag 15m V.Diff. Roger Robb, Peter Biggar. 8 Aug 2013.
Climb easily up the slab to the right end of a ledge. Traverse the ledge left, with an airy step. Go up and left to finish.

On the darker face.

Spider Slab 25m V.Diff. Roger Robb, Peter Biggar. 8 Aug 2013.
This takes the dark slabby face on the south aspect. Start at the lowest point and climb small stepped slabs and a thin vertical crack. Trend left after 5m. Harder than it looks.

Further up the hillside from the left of this crag, but to the right of the larger crag on A' Bhainlir, is a pleasant sunny area of mainly broken rock with some pleasant scrambling, but in the middle of the crag there is a prominent thin crack.

Good Craic 10m V.Diff. Peter Biggar, Phil Gribbon. 21 Oct 2013.
Getting established in the crack is the problem.

Continuing up the path below the first crag mentioned above, one comes to the old Applecross coastal path. A short distance along this and up to the right there is an area of crag with several possible lines flanked on the right by a slab.

Gritty Slab 20m V.Diff. Peter Biggar, Phil Gribbon. 22 Oct 2013.
The slab itself is straightforward, though not well protected, but a good steep finish can be found by traversing right on a broad heather ledge and climbing a prominent light coloured pillar with an accommodating crack.

BEINN DAMH, Little Corrie:

Far Left Gully 120m II. Peter Biggar. 30 Dec 1993.
A clearly defined snow gully with a large piece of rock in it; it would be a good ice pitch if it ever formed, but can be avoided on the left. Steep exit.

Second Left Gully 130m I. Peter Biggar. 5 Jan 2014.
The obvious gully slanting right from near the foot of the previous route. Straightforward but steep and narrow.

Laura Nicoll on Teacher's Pet (VS,4c), Discovery Rock, Loch Torridon.
Photo: Mel Nicoll.

Salt Beef Buttress:

This is the large sprawling buttress left of *Ne'erday Gully*. There are two recorded lines and scope for more.

Left-Hand   160m   II. Roger Robb, Peter Biggar. 4 Feb 2014.
A wandering line starting near the foot of *Ne'erday Gully* and trending left by grooves and snowfields to a good finish by a large pedestal block well to the left of centre in the last band of sandstone. Traversing adds to the length.

Right-Hand   130m   II. Peter Biggar, Barry Hard. 2 Jan 2000.
This goes by snow and short steep rock steps overlooking *Ne'erday Gully*. Harder moves can be found.

Creagan Dubh Toll nam Biast:

Heather Fest   350m   III,4. Pat Ingram, Andy Nisbet. 12 Feb 2014.
Start just right of Boundary Gully at a depression. This is its alternative start but leave the depression immediately on the right and climb ice, or turf if the ice isn't formed. Head left and back right up a ramp to easier ground. Follow snow or easier turf to the top.

DIABAIG, Charlie's Dome:

Ma Broon's Variations   80m   VS *. Ben Sparham, Dave Porter. 24 Aug 2013.
Right of *Charlie's Tower* is a fine slab climbed by the route *Broons' Wall* (SMCJ 2011).
1. 40m 4c Climb the left side of the slab, left of *Broons' Wall*. Start by following cracks which form a prominent right-angled arrowhead shape. Continue up the left side of the slab before moving right into *Broons' Wall* at the top of the slab.
2. 40m 4c Climb the cracked wall between pitch 2 of *Broons' Wall* and the prominent V-groove to the right, using the crack just right of the V-groove. Continue more easily to the top.

The Witch is Dead   30m   E3 6a *. Gary Latter. 12 Apr 2013.
The blunt left arete of the dome which is climbed by the second pitch of *Broons' Wall*. Move up to a ledge on the left, arrange protection, then climb the arete on its right side. Easier climbing above, then rightwards leads to an in-situ abseil point.
Note: A rope sling and maillon was left on a thread in the prominent left-slanting fault left of the top of *Boab's Corner*, facilitating a 60m abseil descent. This can be gained by easy scrambling leftwards from the top of *Boab's Corner*.

LIATHACH, Coire Dubh Mor:

Note: Martin Moran notes that a large rockfall has taken place on the left side of the classic route *George*, just before the steep section. The belay bay has disappeared. This has deposited a huge chockstone in the gully just below, creating a short additional pitch of potential difficulty. A hard pull was required early in 2014 (tech 5) although later it banked up considerably. Without ice it could be problematic.

Martin Moran reckons IV,6 for *Sinister Prong*. The two crux sections on *Sinister Prong* are really quite hard in most conditions (either of them can be 6).

Coire na Caime:

First Foot 230m IV,4. Dave McGimpsey, Andy Nisbet. 22 Jan 2014.
A route starting up the centre of the face between *No.1* and *No.2 Gullies* before finishing on its left edge. *First Face* is always well to the right of this route. Climbed entirely on snow and ice so good conditions. Start up an icefall at the right end of the short base, then climb straight up (55m). Continue up and slightly left (65m). Move right to avoid a smooth wall and climb ice up the right side of the wall (30m). Traverse a ledge left to near the left arete of the wall, then climb iced grooves to easier ground (55m). Finish just right of rock outcrops (25m).

Two Faced 170m V,4. Sandy Allan, Dave McGimpsey, Andy Nisbet. 20 Jan 2014.
An ice line up the centre of the face right of *No.2 Gully*. Start at the right side of the face and climb two icy steps before moving into the centre below the main ice line, which was followed over several steps to the top. The crux was a longer icefall at mid-height and if this was thick enough for ice screws, then the grade would be IV,4.

Strike 2 150m III,4. Sandy Allan, Dave McGimpsey, Andy Nisbet. 20 Jan 2014.
A gully which bounds the face on the right and some 20m left of *3rd Pinnacle Gully*, also slanting away from it. A short section of steep ice at 50m was the crux. Finish by a right-slanting ramp directly above the lower gully.

Strike 3 120m III. Dave McGimpsey, Andy Nisbet. 22 Jan 2014.
A parallel gully left of *3rd Pinnacle Gully*. This is the gully which *3rd Pinnacle Gully* joins high up. The gully contained three short steep ice pitches to below the junction but then finished up left on snow (so the routes didn't touch).

The James Caird 130m IV,5. Matt Green, Andy Nisbet, Ed Wardle. 8 Feb 2014.
The buttress between *4th Pinnacle Gully* and *Gully 5*. Start up *Gully 5* (25m) and take the second break (the first being a vertical groove) left to the crest. Make steep moves up the crest (crux by far), then follow the easy crest to a block below a wall (50m). Zigzag up the crest to the top (30m, 25m).

BEINN EIGHE, Far East Wall:

Root of all Evil IX,8. Murdoch Jamieson, John Orr. 18 Feb 2014.
By the summer line, except that the traverse left on pitch 3 was immediately under the main roof, not below it as in summer. Very sustained and generally well protected with a strenuous pitch 3 leading to a poor belay as for *Hydroponicum* summer (although the summer route made some moves up to improve the belay).

Crazy Eyes 110m VIII, 9 ***. Will Sim, Olov Isaksson. 30 Jan 2014.
This route starts up *Hydroponicum*, then takes up the challenge of the overhanging off width and continuation groove, following a very strong line.
1. 40m Pitch 1 of *Hydroponicum*.
2. 30m Climb a right-facing corner above the belay. Then tackle the off-width to round the lip and belay on the right.

3. 40m Continue up the off-width and steep bulges above to easier ground.

One Step Beyond   110m   IX,9 ****. Pete Macpherson, Guy Robertson. 29 Jan 2014.

Extremely strenuous, then very bold on pitch 2 with pitch 3 being extremely strenuous, technical and sustained. High in the grade!

1. 20m Start directly below the big corner of *King of the Swingers*. Climb up via grooves to the right of icy slabs. Belay on a turf ledge below a wall.

2. 30m Go to the base of *King of the Swingers* corner via turfy grooves. Place gear then step down and left round onto the face. Technical thin moves horizontally left gain a niche. Launch up the overhanging cracked groove above with difficulty (very strenuous and sustained). About 2m before the groove ends, pull out left round onto the ice on the front face in an unbelievable position and gain an icy niche. Climb the ice above (very serious) to gain a hanging belay on a left-hand crack system.

3. 20m Climb the steep wall via the left-hand crack system, making moves out to the right arete to gain the belay ledge of *King of the Swingers*. Very technical and strenuous climbing with little for the feet at times.

4. 20m As for *King of the Swingers*. Climb up to the roof, traverse right then head up groove above pulling through steep moves to gain a ledge below the final short steep corner.

5. 20m Climb the corner then move up easier ground to belay.

Central Buttress Note:

Masa Sakano, Steve Towne & Rob Goodman on 30 Jan 2014, instead of 'pull up left' and 'step left' after the crux, climbed through an overhang and wide crack on the right. VII,8.

Central Buttress:

Making the Cut   130m   VIII,8 ****. Nick Bullock, Jon Walsh, Greg Boswell. 30 Jan 2014.

The soaring crack-line left of *West Central Gully*. Start on the opposite side of the gully to *Blood, Sweat and Frozen Tears*.

1. 40m Climb a stepped roof into a bulging cracked wall. Continue upwards to gain a big snow ledge (this is the terrace below the Upper Tier of Central Buttress).

2. 25m Traverse the snow ledge easily rightwards to gain a belay in a corner to the left of a cave (probably the belay at the start of *Nunn's Route*).

3. 35m Traverse right 10m to gain a soaring crack-line/off-width in the headwall. Climb this until it is possible to step left to a bay.

4. 30m Climb up and right to gain a ledge on top of a pillar beneath a bulging wall with two thin cracks. Climb this short wall to gain easy ground and belay about 15m back.

Note: Pitches 3 and 4 climbed separately would be VII,7, high in the grade.

West Central Wall:

Crème de Violette   100m   IX,9. Nick Bullock, Tim Neill. 7 Feb 2014.

A direct on *Bruised Violet*, culminating in two new long and quite serious pitches. Super sustained and burly.

1. 30m *Chop Suey* pitch 1.

2. 40m Climb cracks up the right wall of the groove (as for *Chop Suey*) to the *Upper Girdle* ledge, then pull through the roof and follow the committing groove (past an in-situ pecker of *Bruised Violet*,) until beneath a roof. *Bruised Violet* now goes right. Carefully pull right around the roof and climb the even more committing groove above. At the top of the groove, cross *Bruised Violet* and continue direct following a wide bulging crack.

3. 30m Climb direct to beneath an overhanging corner and thin crack. Pull into the corner and climb it to the top to a rest and a wide crack. Climb a few moves right before continuing direct via small overhangs to the top.

West Buttress:
Note: Adam Booth & Martin Zumer on 30 Jan 2014 climbed a line of corners formed right of the crest of the lower section of West Buttress (quartzite) – Grade V,6. Start up a crack system about 20m right of the initial crest of *West Buttress Quartzite*, passing a small roof on its right side at about 30m. This led direct to the *Direct Finish* (part of the *Direttissima* in winter).

Fuselage Wall:
Fuselage Wall Variations 70m VI,7. Peter Flanagan, Dan Commander. 1 Mar 2014.
Start 15m in from *Fuselage Gully*, directly below a groove (small chimney) barred by a small roof. This feature has two parallel cracks running up its length.
1. 25m Climb the groove using the right wall until met by the roof, a few awkward moves over this and a step left leads to the belay.
2. 25m A step right and a direct approach up the corner, using cracks and small niches, passing a couple of small bulges leads to a belay on the left, below a roof.
3. 20m Step right and move up, tentative footwork and a hidden hook allow a move up and right and onto easier ground.

CAIRNGORMS

COIRE AN T-SNEACHDA, Fluted Buttress:
Note: Ron Walker started *Western Rib* direct up iced slabs left of the mushroom on 10 Mar 2014. The normal way starts from *Goat Track Gully*.

Fiacaill Buttress:
Note: Adam Russell, Douglas Russell & Steve Johnson climbed the first pitch of *Houdini*, then the second pitch of *Fiacaill Buttress Direct* (the wide crack), ending at the halfway terrace; V,6; 24 Nov 2013.

COIRE AN LOCHAIN, No. 3 Buttress:
The Demon IX,9 ***. Greg Boswell, Douglas Russell. 7 Dec 2013.
By the summer route.

COIRE AN LOCHAIN, No. 4 Buttress:
Snuffleupagus 65m IV,6. Lee Harrison, Michael Barnard. 23 Nov 2013.
A line between *Sarcophagus* and *Oesophagus*. Start below a less prominent groove 5m up and left of *Oesophagus*.

1. 40m   Climb the groove (bold) then go up to ascend the obvious shallow left-facing corner. Continue up more broken ground, trending left to belay on a platform.
2. 25m   Above is an obvious groove leading up to finish between two towers (*Sarcophagus*). Climb the wide crack to its right (crux, a bit artificial).

Torquing to Myself   70m   III,4 *. Simon Yearsley. 25 Nov 2013.
A good early season route at the far right end of the crag. By mid-season most of this area banks up, with the grade of the route reducing accordingly. Start at a short wide crack 8m right of the blocky fault of *Cut Adrift*.
1. 50m   Climb the short wide crack, move up and left, then up to a turfy ledge and then diagonally right up a series of short walls to a large blocky ledge below the steep wall.
2. 20m   Follow the left-trending flake system in a fine position to the top.
Note: This area of crag was popular with instructors in the past (becomes easier with more snow) but routes were not recorded.

CREAGAN COIRE A' CHA-NO, Arch Wall:
Max Encouragement   55m   VI,7. Masa Sakano, Luke Abbott. 18 Feb 2013.
1. 20m   Climb a turfy groove as for *Smooth as Silk* to a ledge.
2. 35m   Step right for some 2m, then climb the very obvious parallel cracks directly, crossing an overlap. From 2m above the overlap, follow a horizontal break to the left for 2m to join the arete of *Jenga Buttress*. Finish up it. Steep and sustained with good protection.

Once were Alpinists   60m   III,6. Gary Kinsey, James Edwards, Roger Webb. 2 Jan 2014.
Start at the toe of a slim buttress with a crack running down its middle, 70m to the right (north) of *Smooth as Silk*.
1. 40m   Climb the crack, stepping right 3m below a small roof and passing it on the right side to reach the top of the buttress. Continue through some easier ground to belay in the rocks 5m above the top of the buttress.
2. 20m   Continue up easier ground to the top.

Blood Buttress:
Giant Steps   50m   IV,6. Simon Richardson, Roger Everett. 7 Dec 2013.
The left side of the crest between *Blood Thirsty* and *True Blood* consists of a series of giant steps topped by steep twin grooves. An enjoyable climb, technical and well protected, but escapable at several points.
1. 35m   Start midway between *Blood Thirsty* and *True Blood* and climb the steep wall on the left to a ledge. Continue up four more 'giant steps' via a wall, crack, groove and wall, always to the left of the crest, to a stance below the twin corners.
2. 15m   Approach the right-hand corner from the left, and climb it to a steep exit.

True Blood Direct   50m   III,4. Simon Richardson, Roger Everett. 7 Dec 2013.
1. 20m   Start right of *True Blood* and climb mixed ground straight up into the bay overlooked by a hanging groove and icicle (*True Blood* goes left from here).
2. 30m   Pass the icicle on the left, and climb the groove to exit up the final corner of the original route.

CREAG NA H-IOLAIRE:

This south-east facing crag comprises a number of schist ribs. The quality of the climbing does not match Cairngorm granite, however the bedding plane of the schist provides helpful holds. The simplest approach is from the Coire na Ciste car park but the cliff can also be reached by walking from Glenmore Lodge in about 1hr 30mins. This provides a useful fall back when the ski road is shut. The most attractive feature is the distinctive buttress feature in the centre of the corrie. This provides two routes – Central Buttress the attractive steeper line on the left leading to a slender neck (80m III,4 – Simon Richardson & Rose Pearson, 27 Jan 2014) and the longer Central Ridge with a barrier tower at its top to the right (100m III – Andy Nisbet, 1 Jan 2013). Left of this are two steep ribs to the right of a steep wall which defines the left edge of the corrie. The left-hand rib has two routes, one up the crest (70m IV,5 – Simon Richardson & Ricardo Guerra, 1 Feb 2014), and the other taking a groove on its right flank (70m III – Paul McKenzie, Stepan Ptacek & Radoslav Savov, 1 Feb 2014). The right-hand rib is similar in character (60m III,4 – Simon Richardson, Ricardo Guerra & Radoslav Savov, 1 Feb 2014). To the right of Central Ridge is another prominent ridge that has two routes – Left Flank, Right Ridge (100m II – Andy Nisbet, Tuvshintur Ragchaa, Battulga Damiran & Undarmaa Badrakh, 1 Feb 2014) and Right Ridge (100m II – Simon Yearsley & Micha Yaniv, 1 Feb 2014).

STACAN DUBHA:

Lazy Daisy   150m   II. Andy Nisbet. 12 Jan 2014.
A gully which forms the left side of *Ribbon Ridge* and which slants up right to the upper crest of *Ribbon Ridge*. Two short ice pitches low down, then snow to gain the upper crest of *Ribbon Ridge*. Follow this briefly, then go right towards *Descent Gully*. Finish up left on snow.
Note: *Tangent* started up the ramp, not the gully as described in the guidebook.

Scarebear   150m   VI,5. Andy Nisbet, Heike Puchan. 12 Jan 2014.
A well defined gully formed between the pillar with *Goldilocks* and a shorter steep wall to the left. Climbed on thin and hollow ice but rarely forms better. Start up snow up and then right (as for *Goldilocks*) to reach the base of the gully (70m). Climb the main section of the gully, with thin ice on the wall right of a blocking overhang being the crux (55m). Finish up the easier upper gully (25m).

Slogra   150m   V,4. Andy Nisbet, Masa Sakano. 14 Jan 2014.
An ice filled groove halfway along the upper wall at the left end of the crag. Start up a parallel break left of *Scarebear*, then trend right to the groove (70m). Climb the groove on thin ice on this occasion to a poor belay in an upper groove (50m). Finish up this, trending right to avoid the cornice (30m).

CARN ETCHACHAN, Lower Tier:

A Momentary Lapse of Reason   120m   E3. Michael Barnard, Liam Brown. 6 Jul 2013.
The main feature of this route is an off-width crack, very obvious from the scree fan below *Castlegates Gully* but not visible from directly below. This gives an excellent piece of wall climbing, though very serious (without a huge cam). Start left of *Crystal Groove*, below slabby grooves leading up to a short undercut wall.
1. 55m 4b Move easily up to climb a short arete immediately left of the overhang.

Traverse right beneath the next overhang, then move up to follow left-trending grooves.

2. 30m 4b Continue up and left, then traverse a grassy ledge system to below the off-width crack. Climb up to the base of the crack.

3. 35m 5b Climb the wall using the crack and the left arete, only moving into the crack near the top. Walk back along the top of the block and go up a short corner, then move left to climb a tricky groove up to easy ground below the terrace.

SHELTER STONE CRAG:
The Spire, Independent Start   120m   E1 **. Michael Barnard, Alan Hill. 21 Jul 2013.

This start could also be used for *Haystack* or *Steeple*. It has a very fine second pitch. Start below the initial corner of *Haystack*.

1. 30m 4b Move up left onto the arete and continue up leftwards to climb a crack immediately right of a grassy fault. Trend up and right to belay near the right end of a grassy ledge (junction with *Haystack*).

2. 50m 5b Climb the right-hand crack up the slab; where this runs out, step right to continue up another crack leading into an obvious short corner. Move left along the ledge and go up a right-slanting corner (as for *Haystack*).

3. 40m Move up and right to gain a fault leading to the terrace (as for *Postern*). Step left to belay below the shallow groove.

Note: On the second ascent of *The Needle* on 2 Jun 1968, Malcolm Rowe & Davy Moy didn't like the look of threading the needle, last pitch, because it was green and slimy, so from the belay set off left up the wall, across to the arete and up that to the top. On reflection a bold bit of climbing. Don't think anyone else has gone that way. Maybe 5b or 5c.

Note: *Stone Bastion*
The upper section is confusingly described in the guidebook. Two recent ascents took the following line, with pitch 7 being possibly new.

7. 15m 5c Go up the groove on the right past loose rock, then move left into a corner. Climb the corner past a dubious flake to a good sloping shelf (original route comes in from the right here).

8. 30m 6a Climb the corner above and swing out right onto a sloping ledge occupied by some blocks (the hold at the top of the corner is best avoided). Climb the crack in the right wall of the next corner until able to bridge into the corner, then continue up the fine wall on horizontal breaks. Belay in a recess.

9. 10m Pull out right and scramble to the top.

HELL'S LUM CRAG:
Diawl Bach   25m   VS 4b. Michael Barnard, Alan Hill. 20 Jul 2013.
Eliminate but enjoyable climbing up the green slabby tower between *Big De'il* and *Wee Devil*. Start below a grassy groove leading into a crack. Go up the groove then step right to climb direct up horizontal breaks and the slab above to gain the final diagonal crack. Move up this to finish up the crack on the right.

Note: *Arc of a Diver* - The first pitch was thought 5b, the third pitch 5a (not vice-versa).

CRAIG RAIBEIRT:
The small compact crag between Stag Rocks and Stac an Fharaidh is cut into three tiers and provides worthwhile mixed climbing.

Hurricane Rib 70m Severe. Tom Prentice, Simon Richardson. 21 Jul 2012.
The well-defined left edge of Craig Raibeirt is comprised of four distinct sections/steps.
1. 30m 4a Start at the foot of the rib and climb the first section up easy angled cracks to a gap. Climb the second step up a short steep crack on the left to reach a large terrace at the top of the second tier.
2. 40m 4a Climb a vertical flake-crack on the left edge (crux) and continue up the final slabby section to the top.

Hurricane Rib 70m III,6. Simon Richardson, Roger Webb. 4 Jan 2014.
As for the summer line.

Meteor Cracks 60m V,6. Simon Richardson, James Edwards. 22 Feb 2014.
A good sustained route taking a line up the left side of the front face.
1. 30m Start just right of the gully separating the front face from *Hurricane Rib* and climb twin turfy cracks to a ledge. Continue up the continuation line and exit onto a second ledge into a small triangular alcove. Step right, and follow a left-trending groove to a broad terrace at the top of the second tier.
2. 30m Move 5m right and climb a narrow chimney through the wall above, before finishing up an easier-angled left-facing corner to the top.

Lightning Corner 60m V,6. Simon Richardson, Roger Webb. 4 Jan 2014.
The right edge of the front face is cut by attractive twin corners.
1. 30m Climb the left-hand corner to a ledge (top of first tier), then move up and right across a steep wall into a hanging groove (and left of the right-hand corner of *Thunderbolt Crack*). Continue up this to a broad terrace at the top of the second tier.
2. 30m Climb through a break near the right end of the terrace and move up to the prominent short V-corner up and right. Climb the initial short step, then break out left near the top and follow easier ground to the top.

Thunderbolt Crack 60m V,7. Simon Richardson, Roger Webb. 22 Mar 2014.
The right-hand of the attractive twin corners.
1. 30m A steep start leads to the right-hand corner which is technical but well protected. Climb this to a broad terrace at the top of the second tier.
2. 30m From the right end of the terrace, step right and climb a gully/slot to the foot of a prominent short V-corner up and right. Climb this in its entirety and short continuation gully to the top.

Whirlwind 55m IV,5. Simon Richardson, Roger Webb, James Edwards. 9 Feb 2014.
A natural line of weakness cutting the cliff from right to left.
1. 25m Start 15m up and right from *Thunderbolt Crack* and climb a short groove and steep wall on the left to exit into a short groove-chimney. This exits on to the broad terrace at the top of the second tier.
2. 30m Climb through a break near the right end of the terrace (as for *Lightning*

Corner) and move left to the left-slanting line left of the V-groove of *Lightning Corner*. Follow this over a steep step to the top.

Typhoon Corners   50m   V,7. Simon Richardson, Roger Webb. 22 Mar 2014.
A line based on a prominent roofed corner at the right end of the crag. A steep entry leads to the corner. Climb this to where it becomes a wide crack, then make a difficult move left to a turfy ledge and continue up to a diagonal break. Climb twin cracks in the line of the break to a good long ledge, and continue up the short headwall above.

Note: Changing around the top pitches of *Lightning Corner* and *Whirlwind* would be more logical (no change in grades).

STAC AN FHARAIDH:
Shielden   100m   II. Susan Jensen, Andy Nisbet. 5 Jan 2014.
Roughly the line of the summer route, but entirely on snow and ice. In peak conditions it disappears under snow.

Deja Vu Left Finish   30m   IV,3. Sandy Allan, Andy Nisbet. 8 Jan 2014.
Where the normal route finishes right, go diagonally left on ice above the left-facing corner of the following route. The grade is for the whole route; this pitch would be Grade III.

Parfait Glacé   100m   III. Andy Nisbet. 10 Jan 2014.
Start up *Apres Moi* to where it reaches the right end of the main lower overlap. Cross this on ice right of the slot which *Apres Moi* climbs, then continue up (*Apres Moi* goes left) into a left-facing corner which curves left and forms a big feature leading to the top.

Spritus Sancti   160m   IV,5. Sandy Allan, Andy Nisbet. 8 Jan 2014.
A chimney line on the right side of Broad Buttress, initially close to *Narrow Gully*. Start on the left side of the bay below *Narrow Gully* and climb a vertical back and knee chimney (20m, crux). Continue up the fault-line above (50m). Keeping to the right edge of the buttress, climb to and up a narrow chimney with a prominent chokestone and walls above (50m). Move right under a steep wall and back left above to finish (40m).

Shallow Rib   80m   II. Andy Nisbet. 24 Feb 2014.
The rib left of *Shallow Gully*, started by going left from some 10m up *Shallow Gully*. The next gully left was Grade I and used in descent.

Hypoglycaemia   80m   III. Andy Nisbet. 24 Feb 2014.
A shallow gully on the right side of the right-hand of the distinct buttresses left of the Western Sector (SMCJ 2012). It led to steep moves left to gain the top not far right of *Wobble Block Chimney*.

Twee Gully   80m   III. Andy Nisbet. 23 Jan 2014.
The gully between the right and central of the distinct buttresses left of the Western Sector (SMCJ 2012). A short steep ice pitch led to a chimney, then an easier finish.

Note: The large gully between the central and left buttresses was Grade I with a short ice pitch which could easily bank out. It has probably been climbed before.

Lookout Buttress 60m III,5. Andy Nisbet. 23 Jan 2014.
A mixed line on the left buttress. Start up a left-facing corner some 8m from the left edge of the buttress. Climb this and a short awkward wall into a continuation corner which led to a distinctive narrow chimney. Squeeze up this and continue until easy to gain the buttress on the right. Finish easily up this.

LURCHERS CRAG:
The Baby Dragon 80m VI,6. Adam Booth, Gustav Mellgren. 27 Jan 2014.
The right edge of the front face of the buttress left of *North Gully*.
1. 20m Follow a crack up the right edge of the steep slab, breaking right onto a steep turfy ramp at 5m. Follow the ramp for 15m (crux) to a large ledge on the left below a short corner.
2. 40m Follow the corner past a difficult move, onto easier mixed ground above, then continue up cracks to a large ledge.
3. 20m Climb a steep corner-crack up the obvious final headwall.

Note from John Lyall: The route described as *K9* but climbing the ice direct is the original line of *Window Gully* and rather than the original Grade III, is thought to be V,5 by the icicle on the left but V,6 by the longer right icicle (which formed in 2010 but not 2014). The route described in the guidebook as *Window Gully* was climbed by Ewan Clark & Andy Nisbet in February 1984 at IV,5; the name *Diamond Gully* is suggested as it was climbed after a retreat (one of many) from *Tiara* in Garbh Choire Mor. The following routes are near the original *Window Gully (K9)*.

Far from the Madding Crowd 220m III,4. Matt Griffin, Adrian Dye. 29 Dec 2013.
The route climbs the rib left of the icefall of *Window Gully*. Start left of *Window Gully* underneath the following two icy lines where a rising ledge leads left to the apparent crest of the rib.
1. 50m Traverse the ledge to the rib and climb the rib up slabby ground to below a steepening.
2. 30m Traverse left from the stance along a slab into a short icy corner. Surmount the block in the corner (awkward) and exit to easier ground. Belay on the easier slope above.
3. etc. Climb up the rocky crest above and follow it to the top by a choice of lines.

Robodog 170m IV,5. Andy Nisbet, Jonathan Preston. 1 Jan 2014.
The left-hand icy line mentioned above and which forms in a corner which forms the right side of the rib. Climb a short step to cross easy ground near the start of the rising ledge (20m). Climb a steep icefall and the subsequent corner (45m). Continue up the corner to easy ground, then trend right (ignoring an easy ice pitch which is more in line with the below) towards a large icefall which breaks out left (50m). The route now joins *K9* which gains (25m) and climbs the icefall (30m).

Ermine   230m   V,4. Sandy Allan, Andy Nisbet. 25 Jan 2014.
Another ice line, often thin, which forms on the slab right of a second corner, the corner right of *Robodog*. Icy runnels lead left to the corner. Step right on to the middle of the slab (thin ice) and climb a thickening ice streak to an easing. Go up this to a belay (65m). Climb easier angled ice above leading to snow (or turfy slopes). Head up to its top, below a smaller icefall right of the *Robodog/K9* upper icefall (70m). Thinner ice runnels gain the main icefall. Continue up a rocky rib (70m). Finish up an optional steep corner and the easier rib (25m).

Tetraidekaphobia   240m   V,6. Susan Jensen, Andy Nisbet. 14 Feb 2014.
The face to the right of *Window Gully*. Start right of *Window Gully* and climb the face (steep snow) to the base of a rock outcrop (30m). Move right and climb to the right end of the roof system down which the icicles of *Window Gully* form. Continue up (40m). A groove above may be possible but this ascent went diagonally left, then round a steep and difficult corner to an easier line leading up right (40m). Continue up the face staying left of the crest (50m). Gain the crest and other routes. Follow the crest (50m, 30m).

Impulse Grooves   240m   VI,7. Roger Everett, Simon Richardson. 16 Feb 2014.
A sustained mixed climb following grooves up the front face of the buttress between *Window Gully* and *Central Gully*. Start just left of the crest of the buttress.
1. 30m Climb slabby ground to a right-facing groove and belay at the top of this at a spike.
2. 35m Climb straight up a series of short corners, then trend left (*Overdraft* crosses here from the right) and back right to a good ledge with a large block.
3. 30m Step back left and climb a short steep groove (crux), then trend slightly left to a small bay. Exit right from this into a short groove, then step right and trend up and right to belay in an open groove with cracks left and right.
4. 30m Climb the groove to a large overhang, then move round this to the right to enter a fine groove on the crest. Climb this to the top of the difficulties.
5. and 6. 115m Move left and climb easier ground to the right of the upper part of *Window Gully* to the top.

Doorway Ridge, Left Start   45m   II. John Lyall. 16 Jan 2013.
An easier start to the ridge, making it Grade II overall. Start on the left side and follow the obvious line slanting up right to the notch on the ridge.

COIRE GARBHLACH, Upper Corrie:
Willow Ridge   110m   IV,4. Susan Jensen, Andy Nisbet, Jonathan Preston. 29 Dec 2013.
The ridge to the left of *Deep Freeze*. Start just inside *Deep Freeze*. Climb a short groove, then move out left to the crest (30m). Climb a big corner system to its top and a pinnacle on the right (35m). Go along a sharp horizontal arete, then up two ridge steps to reach the upper slopes (45m).

Chilled Out   120m   III. Andy Nisbet, Jonathan Preston. 25 Nov 2013.
The buttress to the right of *Deep Freeze*. Start up easy turfy ground right and back left to reach the steeper upper half. Move left until nearly overlooking the gully. Climb steep turf and move back right into the centre. Go left up turfy steps

and up to reach the summit crest from the left. Finish along a narrow easy crest. Slopes lead to the top (not in length).

BRAERIACH, Coire nan Clach:

Umbrella Couloir 70m II. Simon Richardson. 20 Apr 2014.
The well defined couloir defining the left of the buttress containing *Hey Teacher*, leads up to a small ice umbrella.

Moonflower 70m III. Roger Webb, Roger Everett, Simon Richardson. 10 Nov 2013.
The triangular buttress between *Prospector's Rib* and *Alaska Highway* is cut by a short chimney on its front face. Climb up to the chimney from the left, and trend left up grooves to a stance (40m). Finish up the final pitch of *Prospector's Rib* (30m) to the top.

RRS Rib 70m II. Roger Everett, Roger Webb, Simon Richardson, 10 Nov 2013
The rib right of *Alaska Buttress* is well defined early in the season, but will largely bank out under heavy snow.

Coire Domhdail:

The buttress containing *Tempest Rib* (SMCJ 2012) is cut by a series of short grooves and characterised by a horizontal break at one-third height.

Blizzard Grooves 70m II. Simon Richardson. 29 Mar 2014.
The discontinuous series of grooves just right of the left edge of the buttress.

Turmoil Groove 70m III. Simon Richardson. 29 Mar 2014.
Start right of centre to avoid a smooth step wall and climb turf up to a horizontal break. Trend slightly left to gain a short slanting groove that cuts through the headwall. Easy ground leads to the top.

Storm Force Wall 70m III,4. Simon Richardson. 29 Mar 2014.
Start just right of *Turmoil Groove* and climb steep turf to the horizontal break. Move up to a left-slanting ramp under the headwall and climb it via steep turf and sculptured rock in the centre to reach easy ground leading to the top.

Cyclone Edge 70m II. Simon Richardson. 29 Mar 2014.
The tapering narrow buttress between *Tempest* and the Grade I gully to the right. Climb a steep initial section to the horizontal break and continue easily up to the steepening. Spiral round this to the right to gain easy ground.

Coire Bhrochain:

Petzl Buttress 80m III,4. Roger Everett, Simon Richardson. 17 Nov 2013.
The headwall of the buttress left of *Powerpoint* is cut by a shallow square-cut gully-groove.
1. 20m Climb a shallow right-facing corner in the slabs directly in line with the gully-groove.
2. 30m Move left onto more slabs and pull through a steep crack to a ledge. Move right under a bulging nose to belay below the gully-groove
3. 20m Zigzag up the gully-groove, moving from ledge to ledge, to its top.

4. 10m Easy snow on the left leads to the plateau.

CREAGAN A' CHOIRE ETCHACHAN:

Pikestaff, Direct Start   30m   VS 4c. Michael Barnard, Alex Gaastra. 13 Jul 2013.
The obvious lower arete, starting on the left. A pleasant pitch.

BEINN A' BHUIRD, Coire an Dubh Lochain:

Note: Julian Lines & Danny Laing freed the diedre variation of *The Scent* at E2 6a or E3 6b in Jul 2013.

Dividing Buttress:

Note: Dave McGimpsey & Andy Nisbet in Jan 2014 climbed a line up icy grooves just left of *The Fringe*, then trended right to easier ground above the slabs, continuing up short steps to 'the huge boss of rock' near the plateau. Some 250m Grade II, pleasant in icy conditions but no real line.

BEN AVON, East Meur Gorm Craig:

This largely disappointing winter cliff has two well-defined buttress/ridge lines to the left of the summer routes.

Sheep of Destiny   60m   III,4. Simon Richardson, Roger Webb. 24 Nov 2013.
The left-hand ridge-line looks steep and improbable from below.
1. 40m Avoid the lower section by climbing an open gully on the right to left-trending ramp. Follow this to a hidden left-facing corner that leads through the blank section.
2. 20m Continue up the crack-line above, and surmount the final wall on the right.

The Sheep, The Sheep   60m   III,4. Simon Richardson, Roger Webb. 24 Nov 2013.
1. 40m The right crest of the right-hand buttress is gained via an open corner and a zigzag line up a slabby wall. Move left along an easy ramp below the crest to the foot of a steep corner.
2. 20m Climb the corner, pull through steeply on the right at its top, to exit onto easy ground. Scrambling leads to the top.

MOUNT KEEN, Quartz Cliff:

Heliotrope Wall Alternative Start   18m   VS 4c. Greg Strange, Rob Archbold, Brian Findlay. 9 Sep 2012.
There is a scoop of bubbly rock below the larger left-facing corner mentioned in the original description. Climb a short flake feature left of the scoop, continue up for about 4m, then traverse right across base of the corner (above the scoop) and up to join the original at the top of the ramp.

The following two routes climb the clean slab right of *Heliotrope Wall*.

Etnach Way   50m   VS 4c. Rob Archbold, Greg Strange. 26 May 2013.
Step off the large detached block and climb up and slightly left. Cross the ramp and continue up to briefly join *Heliotrope Wall* (runners) before moving right to

base of the right-hand of twin cracks. Follow the crack, then break right to climb the centre of the headwall on good holds. Continue to finish just right of a cracked pale block.

Mystery Train 50m VS 4c. Greg Strange, Rob Archbold. 26 May 2013.
This climbs the right side of the slab, aiming for a prominent right-slanting crack which passes just right of the headwall. Commence as for *Heliotrope Wall* but continue straight up from the start of the ramp. At 18m, move right below a small bulge, then go back up slightly left before trending right to base of a slanting crack. Climb the crack, then move left on to the headwall (where the crack becomes mossy) to finish as for the previous route.

LOCHNAGAR, The Stack:
Nice 'n' Squeezy 50m V,7. Michael Barnard (unsec). 3 Mar 2013.
Climbs the far left-hand side of the short steep buttress overlooking the top section of *Black Spout* (up and right of *The White Spout*). Move up into an obvious overhung niche; from here traverse left to gain a left-slanting squeeze chimney. Struggle up this (crux) then continue more easily to the top.

The Stuic:
Millennium Buttress Direct 90m V,5. Roger Everett, Simon Richardson. 9 Nov 2013.
Good climbing up the series of grooves cutting into the left side of *Millennium Buttress*.
1. 25m Start just left of the buttress crest and climb a steep left-facing corner to a good ledge.
2. 20m Climb the awkward step above to a narrow ledge below a steep wall. Climb this just right of centre (bold), then move left more easily to a good stance by the 'window' of *Millennium Buttress*.
3. 25m From the left side of the 'window', climb up a left-facing corner cutting through the headwall. Follow this to a good stance on the right.
Continue more easily to the top.

CREAG AN DUBH LOCH, Broad Terrace Wall:
Take the Throne 150m VII 6. Uisdean Hawthorn, Callum Johnson.12 Jan 2014.
An independant winter line between *Last Oasis* and *Sword of Damocles*, climbing ice roughly on the line of *Mirage Variations*.
1. 40m Start up a short groove, then up some steps to the base of the slabs.
2. 50m Climb the slabs to the base of a steep corner to the left of *Sword of Damocles*, sustained climbing.
3. 60m Climb the steep corner to easier ground.

Note: *Sword of Damocles* had several ascents on ice at a grade of VII,7.

Defence of the Realm 100m VII,7 ****. Greg Boswell, Guy Robertson. 11 Jan 2014.
A rarely formed but exquisite ice route based on the big square-cut fault between *The Crow* and *Falkenhorst*. Previous attempts in summer have failed due to the compact nature of the rock.
1. 35m Follow the iciest line approximating to the summer line of *Falkenhorst*

CREAG AN DUBH LOCH
Broad Terrace Wall - RH

1. Defence of the Realm . . VII,7
2. The Cure VIII,8
3. Hustle VII,7
4. The Sting VII,6
4a. The Sting, Alt Finish IV,4

Photo: Doug Hawthorn.

until the right end of the obvious ledge system can be gained. This is followed up and left to a spacious belay just right of the main icefall. A bold pitch.
2. 25m Step left and follow steep ice over several overhangs to gain the big upper groove.
3. 40m Climb the groove past a final steepening to easier ground and the top.

The Cure 135m VIII,8 **. Will Sim, Nick Bullock. 11 Jan 2014.
Start up a line of seams and slim corners 5m to the right of *Defence of the Realm*. A hard initial pitch of high quality mixed climbing leads to two pitches of brilliant thin ice.
1. 45m Climb the corner with some tricky moves but good protection to beneath a large capping roof. Make a thin traverse horizontally right for 5m to gain ice and the far left-hand section of *The Sting*. Climb up this for 20m to a hanging belay on rock.
2. 30m Move up and left to cross slabs on thin ice and which lead to a groove and a comfortable belay in the back of an obvious niche/cave.
3. 60m Two awkward mantelshelves are gained in the first 10m. From the higher one a streak of ice is reached and linked with other ice to the top of the crag.

Hustle 120m VII,7. Iain Small, Simon Richardson. 11 Jan 2014.
A steep ice line climbing a thinly iced wall to the left of the main icefall of *The Sting*.
1. 60m Start at the same point as *The Sting* and climb directly up hanging icicles to reach a point at 30m where the icefall splits into a Y shape. Take the left branch up thinly-iced walls and pull over a capping roof (on *Falkenhorst*?) to a hanging stance in a small right-facing corner. A serious pitch on thin ice with spaced ice screw protection.
2. 60m Continue more easily up the well defined left-branch over a series of short steep steps to the plateau.

Central Gully Wall:
The Giant VII,7. Doug & Uisdan Hawthorn. 29 Dec 2013.
A winter ascent on ice.

Vampire Pitch 3 Variation 35m E1 5a **. Michael Barnard, Alan Hill. 22 Jun 2014.
Equally good (though bold) and makes the route E1 overall. After the initial step around the arete onto the slab, go back up leftwards to the arete. Follow this for a few metres before moving right up a line of holds to reach thin cracks (microcams useful). Climb up leftwards to join the normal route at the end of its toe traverse, then continue up this to the stance.
Note: It seems unlikely that this pitch is any easier than the normal route.
It has been suggested that the existing variation (going straight up the main corner at E3) is named *Vampire Direct*.

North-West Gully Buttress:
Icefall of Doom 80m V,5. James Wheater, Steve Addy. 2 Mar 2014.
The obvious blue icefall about halfway up the right side of *North-West Gully*. It should be possible, at a harder grade, to reach the end of the difficulties in one big pitch if the icefall is climbed direct all the way (about 45m). Climb *North-*

Doug Hawthorn, 2nd ascent of Taking the Throne (VII,6), Broad Terrace Wall, Creag an Dubh Loch. Photo: Iain Small.

West Gully to the foot of the icefall (120m).

1. 25m Climb 70 degree ice up to the base of a steep hanging icicle. Climb this icicle direct (crux) to belay (ice screws) behind the upper icicle/icefall in a recess on the right.

2. 25m Step back onto the icefall taking an upwards trending line leftwards over icy steps and ramps, then step back right to finish straight up to easy ground, followed for about 10m. A better but harder line would be to climb the icefall direct from the belay.

3. 30m Climb easy snow to the top.

GLEN DOLL, Maud Buttress:

Rollerwall 150m III. Roger Everett, Simon Richardson. 15 Feb 2014.
A zigzag line up the right side of the crag. A steep entry gains a prominent left-trending ramp that leads to a tree (40m). Continue up the ramp until an awkward step right above a steep wall leads to the prominent right-trending ramp. Follow this to its end (50m). Continue up and left to a bay with a short frieze of icicles. On the first ascent these were too delicate to climb, so a traverse right was made to finish up the easier icefall on the right (30m). Finish straight up the continuation line (30m) to reach the broad terrace at the top of the crag.

GLEN CLOVA, Bassies:

Whitehaugh Buttress Right-Hand 300m II. Simon Richardson, Ben Richardson. 28 Dec 2013.
To the right of *Whitehaugh Gully* is a massive triangular buttress. This route takes the easiest line starting up a snow slope on the right to gain the broad right-hand edge that leads up to the apex of the buttress with a narrower crest to finish.

Whitehaugh Buttress Direct 300m III. Simon Richardson. 29 Dec 2013.
The direct ascent of the buttress takes the prominent curving gully that cuts deep into the left side of the lower barrier wall. Climb easy snow above and then trend right through the next steep tier to a steep exit onto the apex of the buttress. Follow the crest to the summit plateau as for *Whitehaugh Buttress Right-Hand*.

GLEN PROSEN, South Craig:

Spanish Dinner 150m V,6. Tim Chappel, Henning Wackerhage. 4 Jan 2014.
The large open gully in the centre of South Craig is taken by *Summit Gully*. A small bay 10m to the left indicates the start of a series of grooves and left-facing corners which provide three pitches of entertaining mixed climbing, interspersed with easy steep ground. The crux is near the top, a steep rock band with good hooks and protection.

Freebird 120m V,6 *. Tim Chappel, Henning Wackerhage. 8 Feb 2014.
On the right side of South Craig, immediately to the right of a noticeable prow almost at the lowest point of the crag, is a steep left-facing book-corner, 10m high. In good conditions this forms a fine icefall; above it steep moves lead to a second corner, often festooned with giant icicles, above which a groove leads to an iced-up cave (belay). The line of the route follows the best and steepest ice protectable on the day.

GLEN PROSEN, North Craig:

Unforgiven   45m   II. Martin Holland, Ian McIntosh, Sharon Wright. 24 Jan 2014.

A pinnacle like feature can be seen at the top of the crag some 20m right of *White Sun of the Desert*. Easy snow ramps and ledges lead to a steep wall at half-height. This is bypassed on the left by heathery ledges. Finish up a good corner-groove on the left of the pinnacle.

Note: The same team climbed a variation on *White Sun of the Desert*, taking a more direct line on the right up the steep section by an icy corner and groove.

NORTH-EAST OUTCROPS

NIGG BAY TO COVE BAY, The Long Slough Note: *A Momentary Lapse of Reason* (SMCJ 2013) had been done before (editor's mistake including it).

COVE BAY TO CLASHRODNEY, Sickle Row:

Finbar 366   20m   E5/6 6b. Neil McGeachy (ground up). 7 Aug 2013.
Start 4m to right of *Mao*. Climb direct up a thin crack in the middle of the initial wall of an overhanging recess, aiming for a triangular downward spike in the middle of the arch. Now gain a steep pink hanging slab on the left. Exit the slab leftwards via an undercut flake, then climb direct until forced to join *Mao* near the top. A bold start could be avoided by climbing pockets and a corner system on the left of the recess but would obviously lower the grade.

Sesame Snap   20m   E5 6a. Neil McGeachy. 18 Aug 2013.
Climb a corner on the right-hand side of Sesame Cave to undercuts below the right-hand side of the roof. Pull powerfully through the roof until a bridging position above steepness is gained. Traverse with care diagonally left up an obvious slab until undercuts and gear are gained. Finish up steep broken ground to the top. Abseil inspected and cleaned.

New World Order   25m   E6 6b ***. Tim Rankin. Jun 2013.
A superb route taking the stunning diagonal line just left of *Glasnost*. It's probable the line has never been dry enough to climb before! Start up *Glasnost* to just below the roof, then step left to place protection in a crack below a hanging groove. Return right and use twin aretes to move up left to undercuts below the hanging groove (wet on first ascent). Now boldly squirm up the groove to a good hold and welcome protection. Yet more hard climbing leads left to gain the base of a fine quartz crack. Finish with sustained interest up this.

The Mincer Cliff:

Amazing Grace   35m   E4 5c **. Graham Tyldesley, Russell Birkett. 16 Feb 2014.
A line tackling the steep central section of the crag gives a sustained and well protected outing. Start on the central squat buttress on the *Girdle Traverse*. Move up this buttress to its top where a chimney-crack line cuts into the steepness. Climb this for a couple of metres, arrange high gear and then step left out onto the pillar. Climb the pillar to its top.

FINDON CLIFFS, Orchestra Cave:

Virtuoso 40m E6 6b ****. Tim Rankin, Graham Tyldesley. May 2013.
A stunning voyage up the overhanging groove line on the left wall of the cave in one mighty pitch. Start as for *Resinate* below twin cracks right of the short sport routes. Climb an easy groove, then the cracks above to a small ledge. Take the obvious line trending right across red rock to gain a sloping perch below the groove line proper. Climb the groove with committing moves out to the lip of the largest roof (large cam). The crux follows getting over the lip and up to the next roof which is climbed on the right. Return left to finish over the last roof to gain the very lip of the crag and pull over triumphantly! Well protected yet committing. Climbed on-sight with one fall and yoyo from the sloping perch.

Little O Wall:

Swordfish Trombones 25m E6 6b. Neil McGeachy, Graham Tyldesley. 3 Aug 2013.
The corner and stepped roof right of *Treacherous Trombone*. Start as for *Treacherous*, break right at 3m up a ramp and corner. Follow undercut blocks and sidepulls straight up to the left side of the big roof. Enter the hanging corner from the right and fight your way upwards. Finish via rather worrying blocky ledges. Climbed ground up.

Note: *Choir Boy* (SMCJ 2013) has seen several repeats with quality confirmed but E3 5c has been proposed.

Just right of Choir Boy, a fine wall runs right and slants up until it diminishes into easy ledges and grooves. Two obvious crack-lines start from a slanting ledge system.

Dissonace 20m E1 5b *. Tim Rankin, Graham Tyldesley. Spring 2013.
The left-hand crack leading to the easy upper groove provides a fine line. Gain the ledge easily from the right and move left to below the crack. Climb the pleasant crack until a tricky traverse right leads into the easy upper groove. The first ascent climbed an awkward overhanging little groove just right of the obvious seeping groove directly below the crack to gain the ledge (E2 6a) but this is out of character with the rest of the route and usually wet.

Rococo 20m E4 5c *. Tim Rankin, Graham Tyldesley. Spring 2013.
The fine wall left of the crack and just right of *Choir Boy*. Start up the right-hand groove start to *Choir Boy* and follow this until the split block. Arrange a high runner in the crack above (extend well) and swing right on good holds onto the wall. Either arrange dubious protection here (0 tri-cam, small RP's) or more boldly step up to good holds just below a good break. Take the short wall direct above and finish up a flake trending left into the top of *Choir Boy*.

Doo Cove:

At the south end of the Findon Ness headland is a deep narrow inlet which cuts back north into the headland, the Doo Cove. It has an impressive but usually wet west facing wall of dubious looking rock. The routes are found on a hidden set of small crags on the south side of the Doo Cove inlet. There are three separate cliffs which provide a varied spread of both climbing styles and grades mostly on very good rock. All three walls can be viewed from the north end of the Findon Ness headland looking south.

Storm Wall:
Partially Tidal   South-East Facing
The most northerly and best hidden cliff is essentially the south-east entrance to Doo Cove. The rock is sound water-worn mica schist with several impressive quartz dykes. The cliff is characterised by a short, very steep lower wall and easy angled slabs above. The slabs seep and takes a while to dry but as long as the lower wall is not getting wet it is possible to negotiate the seeps at the lip and on the easy slab. Although the left end of the wall is tidal, all the routes should be accessible except during big swells. At low tide it is possible to approach the routes from below Doo Slab, otherwise make a 45m abseil in from anchors in an exposed block in the grass above the easy slab and over looking Doo Cove. The wall catches a fair bit of sun but because of its close proximity to the sea can suffer from lingering dampness. Like most coast venues, the best conditions would be found on a cool breezy day after the sun has been on the wall but the rock provides surprising friction even in less than ideal conditions. Route lengths are given up to belays on the slab from where a further 20m of easy ground leads to the top of the cliff.

G-Force 15m E4 6a **. Graham Tyldesley, Tim Rankin (on-sight). May 2013. At the left end of the wall are two unclimbed short groove lines. This route climbs a longer continuous groove to the right with a line of quartz running up it. Boldly gain a quartz jug on the lip of the roof. Pull onto the wall proper and climb the groove above mostly using the right wall. At the flake roof, move right to pull onto the easy slab at an obvious little pillar as for *White Lightening*. Well protected after a committing start.

White Lightening 15m E6 6c **. Tim Rankin (inspected). May 2013. An appealing line up the most obvious line of quartz through the very steep lower wall and forming a crack higher up. Reach out from a small undercut (usually wet) in the bulge to place protection in the quartz crack. Now swing out on the jug and power through on reasonable holds to gain a good break just over the lip. A further hard move brings better holds in the quartz crack. Climb the fine crack to pull over onto the easy slab at the pillar.

Thunder Struck 15m E5 6a **. Tim Rankin, Graham Tyldesley (on-sight). May 2013. The compelling central line. Climb the flake-crack through the initial roof, then the continually sustained leaning crack above with a sting in the tail. At the flake-roof, move left to pull over as *White Lightening*.

The steepness of the wall now relents with three consecutive short grooves leading on to the easy upper slab being the obvious features.

Derecho 18m E3 5c **. Tim Rankin, Graham Tyldesley (on-sight). May 2013. The arete and first groove is much harder than it looks. Use good holds on the granite arete to move up and right onto a ledge. Return left and climb the steep wall just left of an obvious little box niche to pull right into the base of the groove. Now climb the interesting groove to gain the easy slap.

Squall Line   18m   E1 5b *. Graham Tyldesley, Tim Rankin (on-sight). May 2013.
The next finishing groove line. Climb a short crack to gain the large ledge. Climb the wall above past a quartz protrusion onto the next sloping ledge. Move up left slightly to finish up the steep groove with interest. Several hard moves but not sustained.

Bow Echo   18m   E2 5b. Sam Williams, Tim Rankin. May 2013.
The third finishing groove. Start around to the right and climb a bottomless groove to gain the large ledge. Now climb the obvious wide crack in the arete boldly to pull left onto the sloping ledge. Move up and climb the groove above mainly by its right arete. Poorer rock and protection than the other routes on the wall.

Supercell   20m   E1 5a *. Graham Tyldesley, Tim Rankin (on-sight). May 2013.
The continuous groove line up the right edge of the wall. Start up the bottomless groove as for *Bow Echo* to the ledge. Step right and continue up the groove to pull out left at the top. The rock is much better in the top groove than it would appear.

Doo Slab:
Partially tidal, North-East facing
Just to the south of Storm Wall is Doo Slab, sitting above a slanting platform which drops into the sea. The rock is more reminiscent of granite than schist and the climbing is mostly slabby and delicate rather than steep and strenuous. The wall is approached from the steep slop above and just south of the Storm Wall abseil point. The top of the wall is easily located by an obvious leaning block at a perfect gearing up spot. The block provides a convenient abseil point and belay. It is also possible to descend the easy slab on the north side of the wall below the black wall or down *Doo Chimney*. The routes are described from the seaward end.

Red Doo   16m   VS 5a *. Tim Rankin. May 2013.
A fine wee route at the left end of the wall where there is an obvious flake-crack up a corner. Left again is a small roof just above red rock. Climb to the roof and swing right into a hanging groove. Climb this to the easy slab and move up through a niche to a belay at the block. It is possible to step left at the roof and cross it direct but it is a bit contrived (HVS 5b).

Just Doo It   15m   H.Severe. Tim Rankin. May 2013.
The corner flake-line is steep to start it then relents onto the easy slab. Finish through the niche to the block belay.

Deep Doo Doo   15m   E3 6a **. Tim Rankin. May 2013.
The steep wall right of the corner. Climb to below the roof and use a side-pull to reach left and place a cam in a good slot. Use the slot to gain a small handrail up and right and make hard moves up the crack to better holds. Now continue up the surprisingly challenging crack in the slab above. It is possible to bypass the crux

by leaning in from the corner on the left and reaching up to the undercut flake (E2 5c).

Howdoo　10m　E2 5b. Tim Rankin. May 2013.
Right again the wall slants up right ending at an easy chimney. Start up easy slanting shelves to below a hanging alcove. Pull over the roof into the alcove, then step up left into a deep short groove. Climb this to finish straight up the wall above.

Whodoo　10m　E2 5b *. Tim Rankin. May 2013.
Climb into the alcove as for *How Doo*, then step out right to climb the faint shallow groove and shield feature above to the top. A fine delicate route which requires RPs to protect.

Doo Chimney　10m　Mod *. Tim Rankin. May 2013.
The short chimney provides a pleasant climb and an easy descent. It can be gained from continuing along the shelves or better from a lower ledge up a steep groove for the next route (Diff.).

Doo Arete　15m　V.Diff *. Tim Rankin. May 2013.
Right of the chimney is an undercut arete. Start from a lower ledge and climb a steep groove past an obvious bird perch to pull left onto a ledge below the *Doo Chimney*. Swing right on a good break and use quartz holds above to pull over the roof. Continue boldly in a fine position to gain and finish up a juggy crack.

Don't Doo It　15m　Severe. Tim Rankin. May 2013.
A hanging groove and right-slanting ramp-line starting from the lower ledge up the black wall. Crossing the roof into the groove is well protected but the ramp is quite serious but straightforward. Perhaps better to finish up *Doo Arete's* top crack at V.Diff.

The Black Streak Wall:
The smaller black streaked wall sitting behind Doo Slab. The rock is inferior to the other walls and needs to be handled with more care. The routes are described from right to left with the most obvious features being two right-slanting cracks on the right side of the wall.

Splitter Crack　6m　VS 4c. Tim Rankin. May 2013.
The short rightmost crack is steep but well protected.

Turtle's Head　7m　E2 5b. Tim Rankin. May 2013.
A worthwhile but serious little wall climb between the two cracks. Make an easy start up good holds to the last protection at a break, from where thin moves lead up past the turtle's head protrusion to better holds and the top.

Hawkeye　8m　HVS 5a *. Tim Rankin. May 2013.
The left-hand slanting crack provides a pleasant short route.

Break Up　10m　VS 4b. Tim Rankin. May 2013.
A line of weakness up breaks and cracks 5m left of *Hawkeye*, finishing just to the

right of the highest part of the wall.

Ayespy 12m H.Severe *. Tim Rankin. May 2013.
A complete surprise find! Start just left of *Break Up* and climb the line of a thin crack up amazing jugs and breaks aiming for a small notch in the final headwall. Finish direct past this at the highest part of the wall. Excellent rock and protection.

Raven Face 10m VS 4c. Tim Rankin. May 2013.
The short crack in the upper wall is gained by good breaks. Finish direct up the short upper wall or pull out left.

Beak Slab 10m Severe. Tim Rankin. May 2013.
Left again is a hanging ramp high on the wall. Climb slanting ledges and breaks to gain the ramp. Finish up this or the wall to its left.

DOWNIES, The Knaps, Gorilla's Head:
Monster 15m E6 6a *. Tim Rankin, Russell Birkett. Apr 2013.
The steep wall right of *Animosity* requires double medium cams to protect. Excellent steep, sustained climbing with adequate protection. Start at the very base of the wall at the left edge of the cave. Climb breaks to a good ledge, then take the thin crack in black rock above to the next break and surprising good holds on the right. Move up to another break in black rock and place critical protection. The crux follows; step left and make a big move up to the good hold on the lip of the bulge and junction with *Animosity*. Continue boldly up *Animosity* taking in its crux to the top flake where it moves left. Make an airy step right to swing right around the arete to finish up the slab in a fine position.

NEWTONHILL CLIFFS, Cranhill Crag:
Two lines added on a cliff with fairly adventurous rock. Both lines were climbed ground up on-sight. Although some cleaning took place during the ascents, some flaky rock may still remain in places.

Jaffa 20m E5 6a *. Russell Birkett, Graham Tyldesley. 16 Feb 2014.
A route aiming for but in the end avoiding the thin crack-line left of *In the Pipeline*. Start at the base of that route. Climb up the groove then left to the base of the crack. Arrange some dubious gear. Head right and make tricky moves up to a good break and gear underneath the roof. Traverse left underneath the roof to regain the crack, and follow this to break through the roof on good holds to follow the obvious line to the top.

In the Pipeline 20m E3 5c *. Graham Tyldesley, Russell Birkett. 16 Feb 2014.
At the north end of the crag is a smooth wall. This line takes a stepped corner in the centre. Start up the initial corner. Step out right onto its rib and climb up to the base of the next corner. Climb this and continue up. Escape left along a ledge a couple of metres from the top. Well protected after an initial bold start.

Peedie Inlet:
Three worthwhile DWS are possible on the right end of the south-east facing wall. At high tide they can all be started by traversing in from the south end as low as possible until a sloping ledge is encountered on the lip of the overhang

which bars easy progress any further (this ledge is foot traversed by the route *Peedie Traverse*). At medium tide it is possible to make a more direct start through the lower overhang from the barnacle ledge assessed by descending a slab from the north side. The rock is excellent and the top outs are never more than 8m above deep water at medium to high tide. Route lengths include the traverse in. All Tim Rankin, May 2013.

Peerie Corner   12m   5 * S1.
Above the left end of the ledge is a small right facing corner. Pull onto the ledge and climb the corner and wall above.

Nert Wa   12m   6a * S1.
Pull over the ledge rightwards to climb the overhanging wall just left of the overhanging arete on the right.

Muckle Span   14m   6b+ ** S2.
This route attempts to climb the right arete of the wall from as low as possible and provides a surprising amount of hard climbing. Hand-traverse the ledge right making a difficult move to gain a jug at the top of an overhanging groove (crux). Now launch direct up the fine overhanging arete above to finish. The crux is above deep water but with height the arete leads over the right wall of the inlet but the climbing is much easier here and a short jump left would give deep water.

Two low starts are possible form the barnacle ledge at medium tide.

Slykees and Weet Feeties   4m   6b * S1.
Just left of the obvious overhanging groove is a little hanging corner in an arete. Start just left of this. Take a line of holds out over the overhang to gain breaks just down left of the sloping ledge mentioned above. Pull up to rest and finish up one of the other routes, or much better continuing straight into *Muckle Span* without pulling out left to rest (7a ** S1).

A Bit Nippit   4m   6a S1.
From as far left as possible on the barnacle ledge, traverse the overhang out left over the water to pull up to good breaks on the traverse line. Traverse right to finish up one of the upper routes.

WHINNYFOLD, Tangerine Point:
Tangerine Scream   15m   E6 6b **. Russ Birkett. 17 Sep 2013.
The left side of the steep prow. From the short roofed corner and ledge, move up right to the arete and up to a square-cut notch in the roof. Pull direct to gain a horizontal break, make technical moves directly up the wall to gain the lip and swing left to easy ground.

Berkley Menthol   15m   E5 6a *. Neil McGeek, Russ Birkett. 17 Sep 2013.
Climb the pocketed wall left of *Nyama* direct to below the large roof at the flat hold shared with *Nyama*. Climb direct through the roof and move up till a step right gains an obvious large quartz hold. Finish direct up the arete.

Nyama   15m   E4 6a *. Phil Jack, Neil McGeek , Russ Birkett. 17 Sep 2013.

This climbs the groove on the right side of the prow to the left of *Bamboo* and swings right under the big roof. Steep moves into and up the groove lead to a large flat hold below the roof, move up and crimp rightward below the roof to gain the arete and easer ground above where it joins *Bamboo* final moves.

Kenyan Cowboy 15m E1 5c **. Phil Jack, Russ Birkett, Neil McGeek. 17 Sep 2013.
The roofed corner left of the main prow has a tricky exit. Great line.

Easy Peel 12m HVS 5a *. Russ Birkett, Neil McGeek. 17 Sep 2013.
The leftmost line on the crag taking the fine undercut crack and corner system.

Carriage Crag:

The following routes have been climbed on the steep buttress 15m right of the obvious corner of *The Fat Controller*. They give steep positive and well protected climbing. The rock is generally sound although it should be noted the ascents were made ground up on-sight so loose rock may remain and due care will be required. The crag will be birded through the summer months and an abseil may be required to clean off remaining nests in the autumn. Good cam belays are available on the ledge just below the top.

Coming Round the Bend 20m E3 5c **. Phil Jack, Russ Birkett. 12 Mar 2014.
The steep wall 15m right of *The Fat Controller*. Starting at a shallow groove gain an obvious quartz recess via steep moves on good holds. Continue direct through the bulge above to easier ground.

Steam 20m E3 5c **. Russ Birkett, Phil Jack. 12 Mar 2014.
Starting in the initial groove of *Coming Round...*, traverse up and right to below a steep bulge directly underneath twin hairline cracks in the steep wall above. Pull through and follow this line to a step right at the top.

Diesel Power 20m E4 5c **. Russ Birkett, Phil Jack. 12 Mar 2014.
Pumpy climbing through the roof right of *Steam*. Follow *Steam* to below the steep bulge stepping right to move directly to a big jug on the lip (crucial small cam in break above). Pull direct in a wild position to gain the groove on the right and an easier finish.

Loco-Motion 30m E4 *. Graham Tyldesley, Russ Birkett. 20 Sep 2013.
Another adventurous route climbing the bulging wall and thin crack below the left end of the long girdle ledge. Start at an overhung recess 10m to the left of *The Night Train* starting chimney.
1. 20m 5c Move up into the recess and swing right to then move directly up the steep wall to below the roof and thin crack. Climb this direct to make a long reach to the ledge and belay. Well protected and pumpy.
2. 10m 5b Traverse a short way right along the belay ledge to step right onto the impending headwall and climb direct to the top.

The Night Train 30m E3 *. Russell Birkett, Graham Tyldesley. 20 Sep 2013.
This takes an adventurous line up the Embankment Wall starting 30m east of the Wagon Wall routes.

1. 10m 4c Climb a left-facing chimney stepping left leading to the centre of the long ledge below the impending headwall.
2. 20m 5b Climb directly up the central crack-line in the steep headwall which gives well protected sustained pumpy climbing.

CRUDEN BAY TO NORTH HAVEN, The Hellgate Cliff:
These lines are what remain after the substantial rock fall described in the current guide. All climbed ground up on-sight on good rock.

The Griffin   20m   E3 5c **. Russell Birkett, Graham Tyldesley. 22 Mar 2014.
This climb follows the rib between *The Phoenix* and the first chimney line to the right. Start at the foot of *The Phoenix*. Climb up into a groove on the right, and follow this to emerge on the front of the rib. Climb the thin flake-crack direct to the mantelshelf at a junction with *The Phoenix*. Finish directly over the bulge.

The Phoenix   20m   E2 5c **. Graham Tyldesley, Russell Birkett. 22 Feb 2014.
This climb follows the corner-line at the right-hand side of the square-cut inlet – perhaps this is the altered line of *Pretty Vacant*? Follow the corner-line. At the steepening at the top, make an awkward mantelshelf onto a shelf on the right before stepping back into the main line to finish.

Note: After the rock fall described in the current guide, *The Beast* is still feasible and E4 6a **.

Crockadillo Wall:
Caiman   18m   E2 5b **. Russell Birkett, Graham Tyldesley. 22 Feb 2014.
The north end of Crockadillo Wall is bounded by a headland. Facing out to sea on the end of this headland is a fine granite wall. The wall is split by a crack towards its right-hand side. This route climbs the crack with an excursion out left to a flake before re-joining the crack-line a couple of metres further up.

LONGHAVEN, The Red Tower:
Akela   E7 7a or F8a S2. Julian Lines. 4 Dec 2013.
Climb *Bagheera* to the flake, step right and levitate up the blank wall to a chunky undercut and pocket on the original line. Finish up the left-diagonal flake.

COVESEA:
Zugzwang   12m   E3 5c. John Hall, Dave Monteith. 7 Jun 2013.
The arete to the right of *Sandanista*. Gain a sloping ledge 3m up the arete either from the right or left. Runners were placed in the crack of *Private Dancer* on the first ascent to help protect the moves from the right. A cam 000 can be placed from the ledge. Then go straight up the arete with a good cam 00 at half-height. An excellent line. Top-rope practice.

CULLEN AREA, Unnamed Crags:
(NJ 542 672) Non-tidal
Approach: Park at the Findlater Castle car park which is signposted approximately 2.5km east of Cullen. From the car park, follow the signs for the castle and turn right at the view point. Follow the path for 1km until the fence on your left turns down towards the sea. Follow the fence until it is possible to cross

it and drop down to a flat rocky area. The top of the main buttress is on the left. Descend to the right (looking out), 15mins.

The main buttress is small and steep but clean with three obvious cracks running top to bottom. Although the climbing is fairly easy, it is a very pleasant venue and an excellent crag for beginners and those wishing to learn how to place gear, as most of the routes are very well protected. All routes climbed on 15 Jun or 7 Jul 2013.

Eeny 10m V.Diff. Pete Amphlett, Tom Sharp
Climb the slab at the left end of the crag to an obvious thread in the steep arete. Move left onto the steep wall and up to the top.

Meeny 10m Severe. Pete Amphlett, Tom Sharp.
Climb the first crack to the right of *Eeny*, with steep moves through the overhang.

Lettuce 10m H.Severe 4b. Pete Amphlett.
Right of *Meeny* an obvious fault runs up from left to right. Climb the fault with a hard move through the overhang and finish as for *Miney*.

Miney 10m V.Diff. Pete Amphlett, Tom Sharp.
The next vertical crack to the right.

Mo 10m V.Diff. Tom Sharp, Pete Amphlett.
The final crack to the right of *Miney*.

Gremlin 10m Severe. Pete Amphlett, Tom Sharp.
The slab to the right of *Mo* is an eliminate but good climbing nonetheless. It is cheating to use the holds in *Mo*.

Polly 10m V.Diff. Tom Sharp, Pete Amphlett.
The corner-crack to the right of *Gremlin* leads to a steep chimney.

Cookycat 10m V.Diff. Tom Sharp, Pete Amphlett.
Right of the start of *Polly* is a small overhung bay. A boulder move out of the bay leads to the slab, and easily to the top.

Corky 10m. Severe. Tom Sharp, Pete Amphlett.
Right of *Cookycat* is a small left facing corner on the slab above the overhang.. Start below this and make a hard move up to the corner. Climb cracks to the top.

A clean grey slab lies 20m to the right of the main buttress. Cross a boulder filled gully to the base of the slab. There are three routes presently recorded here. The rock at the top requires some care, but the slab itself is clean and sound.

Lentils 12m V.Diff. Pete Amphlett, Tom Sharp.
Starting from the pointed block, climb the left edge of the slab to the top.

Cullen Skink 12m V.Diff. Pete Amphlett, Tom Sharp.
Right of *Lentils* is an obvious clean crack-line. Follow this with excellent protection.

Split Pea   12m   VS 4c. Tom Sharp, Pete Amphlett.
There is a right-facing overlap to the right of *Cullen Skink*, where the crag changes colour to yellow. Climb the edge of the overlap until it splits, and then follow the crack going straight up to the top.

CLACH NA BEINN:

Owl's Crack   25m   HVS 5b ***. Michael Barnard (unsec). 31 Jul 2013.
An excellent climb, sustained with the crux at the top. Climb the lower section of *Bogendreip Buttress* to an obvious big jug on the left, make a tricky move left into the *Crack o' the Mearns* corner, then move up to finish up the hanging crack immediately to its left.
Note: The tricky move left previously climbed by Julian Lines (SMCJ 2004).

Silver Wings   20m   E1 5b *. Michael Barnard, Alex Gaastra. 10 Aug 2013.
Variations on *Silver Rib*. Start down from that route's initial crack, 1m above the base of the rib. Step onto a foothold and move up the rib to protection (Direct Start). Instead of moving left into the groove, step right to climb using the arete and the crack to its right.

Snake Bite   12m   VS 5a. Michael Barnard. 4 Aug 2013.
An eliminate line with some good moves. After the direct start to *Python Cracks*, climb the left arete (crux) to rejoin that route. Finish up the arete on the right.

Note: *Rough Rider* should perhaps be VS 4c.

PASS OF BALLATER:

Fear and Loathing   20m   E6 6b. Iain Small. 11 Mar 2012.
The steep right wall of *Anger and Lust* corner, with weird and bold stemming from the corner into the overhanging wall and exposed arete finish to right of *Anger and Lust* direct finish.

DEESIDE, VAT BURN:

Many new lines have been climbed here, including an E8 by Julian Lines. An on-line guide is planned.

GLEN CLOVA, Red Craigs, Central Crag:

Burning Bright   30m   E6/7 6b. Iain Small, Adam Russell. 18 Sep 2013.
Follow *Burning Lands* over the roof and instead of traversing right into *Sunset Song Direct*, climb directly up the very blind technical wall. Run out and maybe low E7 if you don't trust a shallow tricam placement.

HIGHLAND OUTCROPS

With the new guide in production and many new routes, they have not been recorded here.

BEN NEVIS, AONACHS, CREAG MEAGAIDH

North-East Buttress:
Orient Express IX,8. Dave MacLeod, Adam Hughes. 18 Feb 2014.
Follow the summer line with tenuous and poorly protected climbing on the first pitch.

Douglas Boulder:
East Ridge 60m IV,5. Simon Richardson, Rose Pearson. 29 Jan 2014.
A winter ascent of the summer line. A good route for a poor day. Surprisingly, there appears to be no record of a previous winter ascent.

Tower Ridge, East Flank:
Alaskan Highway 110m IV,4. Simon Richardson, Stefan Jacobsen. 30 Jan 2014.
A route up the left side of the buttress right of *Lower East Wall Route*.
1. 60m Start about 50m down and right of *Lower East Wall Route* and climb icy grooves up and left to gain a snow slope and a steep groove trending up and right. Climb this to its top and belay below a steep wall.
2. 50m Climb the wall by a break on it right side, move left up a short ramp and continue up the easier mixed ground above to gain the crest of *Tower Ridge* (just below the finish of *Lower East Wall Route*) above the first steep section above Douglas Gap.

Secondary Tower Ridge:
Breaking Good 150m II. Adrian Clifford, Mark Lambert. 11 Mar 2014.
Start at a groove some 10m left of *1934 Route*. Climb this (20m) to join *1934 Route* for its easy snow section. Where that route bends right, go straight up to reach *Tower Ridge* (this has probably been climbed before).

Creag Coire na Ciste:
Note: A new Alternative Start to *Avenging Angel Direct* was made by Iain Small & Tony Stone on 6 Dec 2013. It followed a parallel corner line to the left of *Angels with Dirty Faces* (2011).

South Trident Buttress:
Restoration 75m E2 *. Michael Barnard, Alan Hill. 8 Jun 2013.
Climbs the true line of the *Strident Edge*. The crux section is short but intimidating and a little faith is required, but holds and protection do appear. Start 5m left of *Sidewinder* (as for *Strident Edge*).
1. 15m Climb up to belay in the corner of *Sidewinder*.
2. 35m 5b Follow the crack of *Strident Edge* for a few metres before hand-railing out right to the blunt arete. Easy but bold climbing leads to the first bulge, where a tricky move gains a good hold and protection. Continue up the arete until forced into thin cracks on the right. Move up these to a good hold, before making thin moves to easier ground (crux). Step right up a flake-crack, then back left up the arete to reach the *Strident Edge* belay.
3. 25m 4b Follow the left edge of the arete to the top.
Note: Inspected on abseil.

Salvation   75m   E1 *. Michael Barnard, Alan Hill. 8 Jun 2013.
1. 40m 5a Climb the initial corner of *Devastation*, but continue directly up the obvious hanging corner-crack above to join the *Slab Climb* crack. Follow this for 5m, then traverse right to a flat mossy ledge directly below an overhanging bulge split by a crack.
2. 35m 5b Move boldly up the wall to gain protection below the overhanging crack. Launch up the crack (crux), then continue more easily to the top.

The Clanger   Severe. Michael Barnard. 25 May 2012.
The winter line is worth a star or two in summer. The big flake is an excellent feature and the through route is equally entertaining.

1944 Route   VII,7. Ian Bryant, Pawel Wojdyga. 28 Jan 2014.
A complete ascent. The first two pitches of are part of *Eastern Block* and the final groove is a finish to *Under Fire* (VII,7).

North Trident Buttress:
Scoop Wall   60m   E2 **. Michael Barnard, Alan Hill. 8 Jun 2013.
The main feature of the lower tier is a large slabby scoop with an overhung wall below and a short steep headwall above. This fine bold route gains the scoop from the obvious corner on the left, then traverses it to finish up a short corner on the far right.
1. 30m 5a Start up a crack (*Geotactic*), then step right to climb the corner until it is possible to move right onto the slab. Tip-toe down this then traverse the easy section of the scoop to belay in the centre of the wall.
2. 30m 5b Traverse 2m right (protection), then move rightwards up the scoop with a delicate and runout section before good cracks are reached. Continue more easily up and right to the obvious top corner. Surmount this, then move back left to finish.

Gallifrey Groove   60m   IV,5. Simon Yearsley, Malcolm Bass. 20 Jan 2014.
A short but pleasant climb which takes the icy groove system between *Nereid Gully* and *Day of The Doctor*. Start at the foot of the groove system.
1. 35m Climb the groove with an awkward step back left after 20m to the base of the upper groove.
2. 25m Continue up the groove, moving left up a V-groove near the top and finish leftwards to the horizontal ridge crest.
Thirty metres rightwards down the horizontal ridge crest is a large block with an in-situ sling and krab. A 60m abseil from here leads back to the base of the route.
Note: On the first ascent the groove system was climbed mostly on ice. It would be possible, but probably harder, in less icy conditions.

Day of the Doctor   170m   IV,5 *. Simon Yearsley, Helen Rennard. 23 Nov 2013.
A pleasant climb which takes the very obvious left-trending ramp-line at the right side of the buttress between *Nereid Gully* and *Left-Hand Ridge*.
Start at the foot of the ramp.
1. 30m Climb the ramp; the lower section is trickier than it looks.
2. 30m Continue up the ramp, finishing direct at the top to join *Left-Hand Ridge* above its crux.

3. 60m Follow *Left-Hand Ridge* up the ridge crest, then along the horizontal arete.

4. 50m Climb the straightforward turfy grooves immediately right of the crest of the buttress between *Jubilee Climb* and *Nereid Gully*.

Number Five Gully Buttress:

Turkish 180m VII,7 *. Malcolm Bass, Simon Yearsley, Helen Rennard. 4 Jan 2014.

Follow the summer line for the first two pitches and possibly the third. Surmount a short wall at the very base of the corner, trending left across delicate slabs to below a vertical, clean right-facing corner (3m left of another corner with some blocks). From the base of the vertical corner, descend an obvious slab diagonally down and left for 3m. The crux moves were getting round the bulging wall at the base of the slab to pull into a steep groove with blocks/flakes at its top. Climb directly up a steep corner to a platform and belay. It was assumed that the 'large loose blocks' in the summer ascent were the blocks/flakes mentioned above. On the winter ascent, these were safely frozen in place, enabling the peg tension to be dispensed with. On pitch five, continue up the fine corner system to the top rather than bearing hard right as per summer.

Note: The final two final pitches are common to *Free Range* (Feb 2011).

Carn Dearg Buttress:

Antonine's Wall 50m E6 6b. Iain Small, Tony Stone (both led). 30 Jul 2011.
A good long pitch up the right wall of the *Sassenach* corner.

Note from Ian Taylor: The description of *The Bat* says that from the terrace after pitch 6, it is possible to traverse right and abseil down *Titan's Wall*. Actually it is necessary to traverse right and down climb 30m from the terrace to reach the first abb point. This is hard to identify from above and it is probably less hassle to continue to the top of the buttress.

North Wall of Carn Dearg:

From the Jaws of Defeat 220m VIII,8. Iain Small, Simon Richardson. 23 Mar 2014.

A steep mixed climb through the triangular headwall right of *Waterfall Gully*. Start as for *Staircase Climb*.

1. 40m Following the initial section of *Staircase Climb*, climb up to the foot of the *Straight Chimney Variation* and take a slanting slot leading up left to a good ledge with a massive triangular block. Step left and climb a steep right-facing corner to a small ledge below a spectacular overhanging fin. Pull onto the overhung wall on the left and climb a corner on the left side of the fin to its top. Good flake belay.

2. and 3. 100m Continue up the central depression (snow and easy mixed) to below the impressive triangular headwall.

4. 30m From a point 5m up and left of the right toe of the headwall, move up and right across a short slab and climb a steep vertical crack to easier ground. Move up, then left, and gain a good stance in a shallow cave below the central groove line cutting straight up the centre of the headwall.

5. 50m Climb the groove, steady at first, but with two difficult sections and an awkward slabby finish to reach the apex of the wall. The route finishes here.

The Castle, Ben Nevis. Photo: Hon. Ed.

Three ropelengths lead up and left to the upper crest of *Ledge Route*.

MAMORES, MULLACH NAN COIREAN, Coire Dearg:
(NN 13071 66105 – base of route)   Alt 600m   NE facing
An impressive-looking crag tumbles from the summit slopes of a small top between the main summit of Mullach nan Coirean and its SE top at NN 12937 65845. It is split by a long couloir system which encompasses well defined gully sections and broader snowfields.

Solitude Gully   300m   II. Colin Wells. 28 Mar 2014.
Start at the base of a shallow snowfield/gully system splitting the middle of the crag and follow it to a narrows on the right with a 10m ice step. Climb this to a small snowfield and trend right to another icy narrowing. Surmount this to gain a broad upper snowfield. Go straight up to a break in the rocks on steep snow and thence to the upper summit slopes and the ridge.

AM BODACH:
Sonsie Face   350m   II. Andy Nisbet, Jonathan Preston. 25 Jan 2014.
The next bay right and some 100m lower than the bay below *Redbreast Gully* (SMCJ 2013) holds the icefall routes like *Hemulen* (SMCJ 2012). This route climbs a shallow gully which leads out from the top left side of the bay. Towards its top, a left branch leads on to the rib on the left. Follow this bending right and passing right of a bay with overhangs to reach a rib high on the face. Follow this to the top, finishing at the same place as the following route.

South Buttress   350m   II. Ricardo Guerra, Andy Nisbet. 30 Jan 2014.
There are two (not three) main full height buttresses come ridges on the face. Central Buttress should be renamed North Buttress and this is the other. The area with the icefall routes like *Hemulen* is on its left flank. Start up a gully at its base (left of a wider easy gully). Climb this through a narrowing on the left (50m), then slant up right to where the crest of the buttress becomes defined (50m). Follow the easier buttress to the top.

AONACH BEAG, Lower West Face:
The following two routes climb the buttresses either side of the gully named as *Torquing Nonsense* in the current guide. These are very likely to be the buttresses taken by the summer routes *Crevassed Rib* and *North Buttress*, although easier lines were taken in winter.

Crevassed Rib   100m   IV,5. McGimpsey, Andy Nisbet. 6 Dec 2013.
Start some 15m right of the gully, where a big icy ramp slants up right. This right side of the buttress holds several huge blocks and crevasses. Take the first easy line up left into a bay. Climb a flakey groove on the left, then step back right and jump into a capped trough. Go up the trough until near the cap, then pull out left and climb blocky ground to the crest. Move left (escape into the gully possible here) and back right up a turfy line to below the 'final slab'. Climb a right-slanting crack-line on the right side of the slab to reach easy ground.

North Buttress   120m   III. Dave McGimpsey, Andy Nisbet. 6 Dec 2013.
A zigzag winter line up the buttress. Start about 20m left of the gully base.

Follow a groove slanting right and containing a flat 1m chockstone. Turn left and climb an easy ramp to the buttress crest (50m). Climb a short slabby section into another right-slanting ramp, then turn left again and climb to the crest (50m). Easier ground leads to the top (20m).

North Groove 80m V,5. Susan Jensen, Andy Nisbet. 26 Dec 2013.
A big groove on the left side of *North Buttress* has a steep section at 20m and which gave 10m of unprotected climbing, but the rest is much easier. VI,5 on the day but could be easier with more or less ice. Finish at the same point as *North Buttress*.

North Gully 100m I. Susan Jensen, Andy Nisbet. 26 Dec 2013.
A gully which bounds *North Buttress* on its left. It hold ice in lean conditions but banks out.

Pugilist 80m III,4. Susan Jensen, Andy Nisbet. 26 Dec 2013.
The buttress left of *North Gully* holds a narrow left-slanting gully joined by a deep chimney which starts to its left. Climb the left-slanting gully over a step to a larger step which was climbed direct by SJ but avoided on the left by AN. This leads to a slabby step climbed on its left side and leading to easy ground.

Pacifist 100m I. Susan Jensen, Andy Nisbet. 26 Dec 2013.
The gully left of *Pugilist*.

BINNEIN SHUAS, North-West Buttresses:
Approach: Start as for the main climbing on Binnein Shuas, but follow the left-hand folk at the junction in the forest track, eventually going to the right to reach the bottom of the buttress. The foot of the lowest buttresses is at altitude 560m. Near the summit, there are two tiers of Summit North-West Buttresses.
Descent: From the summit, walk NW to the forest track.

Location, Location, Location 55m III,4. Masa Sakano, Yuki Sakano. 16 Feb 2014.
Start at a recess at the foot of the lowest buttress, a few metres left of a cave. Climb a turfy and icy groove, then follow steep grooves.

Laggan Fantasy 28m IV,5 *. Masa Sakano, Yuki Sakano. 16 Feb 2014.
Start at the rock below the centre of the lower tier of the summit north-west buttress. Negotiate rocky steps for a few metres, then climb the steep thinly iced groove in the centre of the buttress to the top.

Summit North-West Buttress 40m II. Masa Sakano, Yuki Sakano. 16 Feb 2014.
Climb the most obvious zigzag snow line at the centre of the buttress. Straight up first, then diagonally left, then diagonally right to top out on the summit ridge some 80m west of the summit.

BEN ALDER, Maiden Crag:
Gold Diggers 250m II. Dave McGimpsey, Andy Nisbet. 9 Nov 2013.
The buttress containing *Wingeing Sassenach* has a continuous crest on its left edge. Gain this by a rib below its start, then follow the crest to the top of the

Long Leacas. Climbed in very deep snow.

Peleton   250m   III. Dave McGimpsey, Andy Nisbet, Jonathan Preston. 22 Nov 2013.
A mountaineering route based on the crest left of *Tour d'Alder*. Zigzag up ramps mostly left of the crest, the crest being slabbier and at times too close to the gully. Low in the grade despite its steep appearance.

Enigmatic Buttress:
Hirondelle   220m   IV,5. Dave McGimpsey, Andy Nisbet. 24 Nov 2013.
An intermittent groove line left of the crest and existing routes. It runs the full height of the cliff and was climbed fairly direct. Start just up from the left end of the cliff base.

BEINN BHEÒIL, Sròn Coire na h-Iolaire:
(NN 515 706)   Alt 790   North-East facing
This small broken cliff is located 250m north-east of the top of Sròn Coire na h-Iolaire and can be seen in profile when descending south from the Munro. An obvious gully (40m, I) at the right side of the cliff has a more interesting shallow rock ridges on either side, both about Grade II (50m). About 20m to the left is a shallow groove with a steeper step at mid-height (40m, II). All were climbed under very good snow cover by Brian Davison on 7 Feb 2014.

GEAL CHARN, Loch Coire Cheap Crag:
Cheap Shot   120m   II. Andy Nisbet. 10 Mar 2014.
The buttress which forms the left end of the crag. There was a very large build-up, especially at the base. The buttress was climbed by starting left of the base and linking snow patches on its left side.
Note: All the routes in the current guide were largely banked out, but this is unusual.

Sron Gharbh   150m   II. Andy Nisbet. 10 Mar 2014.
A ridge further right (NW) in the corrie and starting higher than the top of the main crag. It is named in exactly the correct place on the 1:25000 map. A fine feature, climbed by grooves filled with neve, the crux being a steep step high up and passed by a groove on the right.

CREAG MEAGAIDH, Post Face:
Note: Doug Lang & Neil Quinn had previously climbed *Centre Post Right-Hand* (SMCJ 2013).

Inner Corrie:
Fairy Godmother, Direct Start   110m   IV,4. Scott Frazer, John Lyall, Mick Twomey. 19 Feb 2013.
A good direct start up the lower buttress. Starting at the same point, go straight up the icy right-facing corner and continue to the top of the terrace to belay. Climb thin ice past the right end of a long, low roof, then slant up left on icy vegetation to a belay overlooking the gully of *The Sash*. A steep wall then leads to easier slopes and a snow crest, before joining the original line.

CARN LIATH, Coire nan Gall:

Note: Graeme Hunter & Doug Lang climbed three summer routes here in June 1969 at 'sporting VS'. They were not recorded at the time mainly due to the disappointing quality of the rock. It looked quite impressive on the approach but the rock structure was flakey and the main slab a bit hollow and unstable. From a topo provided, the central line of *Gallic Corner* 120m VS climbed the corner which *The Mighty Willow* (Ben Nevis guide p314) is based on. *Gallic Rib* 120m VS starts at the same point but near a subsidiary corner on the left. *Gallic Slab* 110m VS starts on the right edge of a large slab right of *Gallic Corner*, goes left up an obvious fault, then back right.

GLEN COE

BUACHAILLE ETIVE MOR, Creag na Tulaich:

Glory Hole   45m   E3 5c. Alasdair Fulton, Alastair Robertson. 24 May 2014.
Start 2m left of *Too Cold for Comfort*. Climb up to the first break. Move upwards and leftwards to a prominent hole on the face at about 5m. Climb upwards with possible escape to the left into the ramp of *Dwindle Wall* after about 10m. Continue directly to the top of the crag. The route is poorly protected, a bit eliminate and dirty.

STOB COIRE NAN LOCHAIN:

Shadhavar   100m   E3 6a ***. Ian Taylor, Tess Fryer. 21 Jul 2013.
The finely-positioned crack on the right wall of the upper section of the *Unicorn* corner. More amenable than appearances would suggest.
1. 35m 5b Climb *Unicorn* until level with the triangular roof on the right arete.
2. 35m 6a Traverse out right to the thin crack and follow it directly with excellent protection. Near the top swing round the right arete for a few moves, then go hard left (to avoid some loose blocks) into *Unicorn*, which is followed to the ledge.
3. 30m 5a Follow *Unicorn* to the top.

Note from Ian Taylor: Pitches 2 and 3 of *Unicorn* have a combined length of 60m in the guidebook, but can be climbed in a single 35m pitch! Also the rating in the guidebook of *Scansor* as being overrated is overrated. Any loose bits are generally easy and though it appears mossy from below, the holds are clean. Worth **.

Gecko Wall   60m   E6 6b,6a. Iain Small, Tony Stone, Blair Fyffe. 25 Aug 2013.
A direct line up the Chandelle like buttress left of *SC Gully*. Wild bridging and hard wall climbing.

Eggäschpili   50m   IX,9. Olov Isaksson, Karin Zgraggen. 28 Feb 2014.
Climbs the left wall of *SC Gully*, opposite the following route.
1. 20m Start in a left-facing corner. Technical and sustained climbing with limited protection leads to a system of cracks. Climb these to a ledge and move right into another left-facing corner.
2. 15m Climb the corner, which is still sustained but with better protection, to a small slanting ledge.

The west face of E Buttress, Aonach Dubh, Glen Coe. Photo: Hon. Ed.

3. 15m Climb 5m of steep terrain followed by 10m of easier climbing, to reach a big slanting ledge.
4. etc. Either follow easy ground to the top or add a short pitch probably on an existing route, or abseil off.

Slenderhead 100m   VIII,8. Nick Bullock, Guy Robertson. 13 Jan 2014.
1. 30m A corner left of *East Face Route* on the right wall of *SC Gully*.
2. The ice line and wide crack above the corner until a line of flakes leads right to the arete. Follow the arete direct and belay beneath a slim tower to the left of the final corner pitch of *East Face Route Direct*.
3. Climb directly up the front face of the tower, difficult to start, to overhanging cracks. A difficult move left leads to a wide crack on the left side of the tower which is climbed. From behind the tower, finish direct.

Year of the Horse   100m   IX,9. Iain Small, Blair Fyffe. 31 Jan 2014.
1. 40m Climb the large groove between *Slenderhead* and *East Face Route* up and left through ever steepening ground to a niche below an overhang. Pull strenuously over this and climb crack to a ledge above.
2. 30m Move up and right to another ledge. Climb up a steep wall above to another groove. Follow this back up left to join *Slenderhead* and follow this to belay below the final corner of *East Face Route Direct*.
3. 30m Step down and right and into a groove. Climb this and a corner to below the obvious rectangular overhang. Traverse right under this and make an awkward move right around the arete into a groove. Follow this back up and left to the top.

Note: *Central Grooves*. On the original summer ascent, Ken Bryan and Roger Robb traversed out right in a spectacular position from a high overhang (SMCJ 1961). Winter ascents went left at this overhang and this has been incorporated into the summer description despite being much less good in summer. The summer route by the original line is recommended.

Scansor   IX,9 ***. Iain Small, Tony Stone. 17 Jan 2014.
By the summer route, giving technical climbing with a bold section on both pitches. The second pitch provided the technical crux, reaching and then traversing the break just above the thin ledge that is traversed in summer.

AONACH DUBH, North Face:
Note: Ian Taylor thought *Bungee* (SMCJ 2009) to be E3 5c 6a. Well protected and ***.

BIDEAN NAM BIAN, Church Door Buttress:
Angels   VIII,9. Donald King, Mike Pescod, Andy Nelson. 13 Jan 2014.
A mixed route on the front face of the buttress. Start to the right of *Flake Route*. Climb the front face of the flake by thin cracks in the first half, then a small right-facing corner in the second half. Make a small link pitch down *Flake Route* for 2m, then go left to a small bay. Finish up a groove on the right, possibly coinciding with *Flaked Out* (2010).

Note from Ian Taylor: *The Fundamentalists*. Pitch 2 is now very overgrown and probably unclimbable without cleaning, but the upper section of the route is still accessible by climbing the excellent pitch 2 of *Lost Arrow*. Pitch 3: The 'undercut left and pull round the roof' section can be easily avoided by going straight up from the belay and moving left to the same point, while the section described as 'continue steeply on good holds' is actually a difficult crack. Pitch 4: Many variations exist on this pitch.

ETIVE SLABS:
Swastika, Variation Pitch 7 25m HVS 5a. Michael Barnard, Neil Redgrave. 29 May 2014.
An alternative for folk struggling on the 5c pitch. Traverse the slab to reach the next corner on the left. Reach up for holds on the left wall and pull onto the arete. Move rightwards up this, then go straight up to gain the tree belay below the final corner.

GARBH BHEINN, South Face Lower Tier:
Note: An alternative first pitch to *Scimitar*, by Adrian Camm, Elsie Riley, 14 Jun 2014, which may be dry if the steep crack is wet. It takes the wall between *The Gralloch/The Gay Blade* and *Scimitar*, passing the obvious triangular niche. HVS 5a **. Climb the curving shattered ledge for 8m as for *Scimitar*. Below *Scimitar's* steep crack, move left along a slanting ledge for 3m, then climb flakes which lead up to the left of a triangular niche. Move slightly left, then back right up easier ground to the foot of *Scimitar's* easy groove.

SGURR NA BA GLAISE (MOIDART), North Face:
Note: *Summit Gully* (SMCJ 2013) has been done before as *The Serpent* (SMCJ 2001).

SOUTHERN HIGHLANDS

THE COBBLER, North Peak, South Face:
Little Rammer 30m VS 5a **. Andy Bain, Jake Thackrey. 14 Jul 2013.
This route starts at the deep cleft of *Ramshead Gully* on the upper left just at the start of *Silence of the Rams* (SMCJ 2013). Climb up the toe, staying on the left crack and head up and over the scoop. Take the arete directly, with the small recess on the right, to the large terrace.

South Peak, South-East Face:
Ardgartan Blended 120m V,6 *. Andy Bain, Jake Thackrey, Dougie Beck. 31 Jan 2014.
This enjoyable route starts 15m up from the toe of the buttress where an obvious shallow groove slants up left to join the arete.
1. 30m Follow the groove with little protection over the bulge at 5m, then continue up grooves in the arete to belay at the end of the terrace which slants up the corners of *Gladiator's Groove* and *Ithuriel's Wall*.
2. 30m Keeping to the right of the cracks of *Ardgartan Arete*, climb the wall above to a ledge, then go up a second wall. Bear right 4m and climb the wall

direct to a ledge. Traverse 3m left back to the final cracks on the *Ardgartan Arete* to the terrace

3. 60m Climb easily leftwards up the terrace overlooking the South Face.

STOB GHABHAR, North-East Corrie:

Morrowind 55m II. Steve Kennedy, Andy Macdonald. 11 Jan 2014.
On the upper left side of the corrie, as the summit crags peter out, is a broad easy angled ridge. Climb the ridge, moving leftwards at the top to finish.

Bloodmoon 55m III *. Andy MacDonald, Steve Kennedy. 11 Jan 2014.
Start up the broad easy gully right of *Morrowind*. Take the right-curving branch near the top, via a steep icy step, to a corniced finish.

BEINN AN DOTHAIDH, North-East Corrie, West Buttress:

Best of a Bad Bunch VI,7. Willis Morris, Euan Ryan. 20 Jan 2014.
A direct version of *Stormbringer* (III) and its *Direct Start* (V,6). Start some way to the right of *Stormbringer*, but left of its *Direct Start*.
1.   Climb an obvious groove to a tricky overhang. Go over this (joining *Stormbringer Direct Start*) to below a steep ice ramp.
2.   *Stormbringer* continues up the icy gully. Start up this but then follow the buttress on the right up a groove with thin ice.
3.   Move left up into the entrance of the gully and climb it for 5m, then follow the crack system on the left wall of the gully that leads up and over a roof (crux, short but maybe tech 8). Continue up this to a ledge.
4.   Finish the route up a mixed crack system to the top just left of where *Stormbringer* finishes.

MEALL DHAMH (near Cruach Ardain)

Note: Correction to note in SMCJ 2913. The Grade I gully at NN 3982 1720, climbed by Anne Craig, Andy Willie & Willlie Jeffrey in 2011, is situated 20m right of *Meall Damh Ramp* (not *Stollen Grooves*).

LOWLAND OUTCROPS

GLASGOW AREA, Auchinstarry Quarry:

Fool's Gold 25m E3 5b *. Brendan Croft. 27 Sep 2013.
Climb directly up the slab between *Trundle* and *Walk on the Wild Side* past thin cracks at 5m (micro wires). Reach right and place wires in the twin cracks of *WOTWS*. Gain a prominent hold in the centre of the slab and climb on to this. A long move (crux) to a left-facing flake gains the midway ledge.
Note: The route has been top-roped before but no lead recorded.

Tardis 15m Severe 4a. Oliver Heyes, Samantha Black. 16 Mar 2014.
Start to right of *Tar*. Climb up to a sentry box and overcome the overhang to join the line of *Tar*.

GALLOWAY HILLS, WOLF SLOCK:

Connoisseurs' Choice (SMCJ 2012) climbed free at E2 5c by S.Reid, C.King, 22 Jun 2014.

YELLOW TOMACH, Russet Wall:

A Tale of the Tomach 8m VS 4b. Ian Magill, Stephen Reid. 7 Jun 2013.
The right-hand crack system to the ledge. Finish more easily above or traverse off left.

The Main Slab Area:

The New Covenant 55m HVS *. Stephen Reid, Ian Magill (alt). 7 Jun 2013.
The route started and overcame the main overlap via *The Auld Alliance*. Direct variations added by Stephen Reid, Graeme Barr (alt), 15 Jun 2014.
A splendid route when dry. Start directly under the main slab, 2m left of a clean left-facing corner.
1. 25m 5a Climb up to a small spike, then make a bold move up and right across the slab to gain a hold and wire at the top of the corner. From a ledge, make a difficult move to overcome a small overlap. Continue up until stopped by a larger overlap and ascend this via a stepped corner. Traverse right along the lip of the overlap and belay on the lip using wires in a crack high in the slab.
2. 30m 5a Climb the slab to the thin crack in its centre and move up left to the foot of a slab on the left. Traverse left along a shelf and make a tricky move onto the slab to gain a shallow rock niche. Exit right from this and make delicate moves directly up the centre of the slab to a grass niche. Gain the crack above and follow it to a character building finish on oozing sods.

THE TAUCHERS, The Giant's Stairway:

Tow Line 100m VS *. Stephen Reid, Graeme Barr. 29 Sep 2013; Pitch 3 added by Graeme Barr, Stephen Reid, 13 Oct 2013.
Start at the left-hand rib which is quite blocky.
1. 30m 4c Gain the rib and follow it until it becomes too steep and make a tricky traverse right into a corner which leads to a heather terrace. Belay on top of a large block on the left.
2. 35m 4c Climb a quartzy patch in the wall above the block to gain a rib and follow it to a grassy bay. A ledge at the back of the bay gives access to a short corner and a crack which is climbed to just below its top. Make an airy step left onto a steep slab and traverse this diagonally down and left (bold) until easier rock can be climbed to a small stance just below a terrace.
3. 5m 4a Evade the steep headwall by moving left underneath it and belay immediately at the base of a groove.
4. 30m 4c Climb the groove via a reverberating flake, following it leftwards and up to grass. Gain more grass by climbing a short wall just right of a very short chimney and climb a corner just right of a slightly longer chimney.

The Tiers:

It'll End in Tiers 85m HVS *. Stephen Reid, Graeme Barr (alt). 13 Oct 2013.
A good route despite the grassy sections. At the right end of the barrel shaped wall are some large blocks.
1. 25m 4a Step off the left-hand block into a capped groove and gain a footledge on the right. Traverse right and then go up the cleanest rock to grass and short rock steps to a spike a short way below inverted Y cracks in the smooth slab above.
2. 20m 5a Climb the cracks and the short crack directly above. Scramble up to a smooth wall with insipient disjointed cracks.

3. 15m 5a Starting from a small rectangular flake top under the right-hand crack, hand-traverse left and move up the left-hand crack before bearing up rightwards to a terrace.

4. 15m 4b Climb a shallow right-facing corner and the short off-width above and so reach another terrace.

5. 10m 5a The curving off-width on the right side of the final buttress is what gives the climb its name!

DUNGEON OF BUCHAN, Silver Slab:

Stairway to Heather, Square Chimney Finish VS 4c. Stephen Reid, Paul Wood. 5 Sep 2013.

An entertaining alternative. From the square grass ledge, make one move up, then step right under a hanging fang of rock and climb the eponymous chimney.

MEMORIAL CRAG:

Reach for the Sky 8m VS 4c. Stephen Reid, Jonathan Hughes. 11 Jul 2013.

Cracks just right of *Mij's Chimney* lead to ledge and a bulging groove which leads to the top.

Ground Control 8m E2 5b. Jonathan Hughes, Stephen Reid. 11 Jul 2013.

In the centre of the short wall is a curious long horizontal jug which is probably just out of reach. From the jug gain a horizontal break, which is poorer than it looks, and use this to traverse left and finish up a shallow square-cut scoop. All rather sustained.

Boot Hill 22m E4 6a ***. Jonathan Hughes, Stephen Reid. 11 Jul 2013.

The soaring crack-line that bisects the traverse of *General Dynamics* gives a very sustained but well protected climb. Make hard moves to gain and the crack which leads to a welcome semi-rest at the break. Even harder moves are necessary to follow the upper crack to a second break. Only the final moves are easy.

CRAIGDEWS:

There is a new stile located on the right side of the car park behind some bushes.

White Slab:

Traverse of the Goats 25m Severe 4b. Stephen Reid, Ian Magill. 10 Oct 2013.

An enjoyable right to left girdle. Start from a flat boulder come flake at the right end of the Long Ledge just up and right from the bottom of the crag. Step off the boulder onto the slab and gain a break. Foot-traverse this leftwards to the triangular ledge of *Three Men in a Goat*, then hand-traverse left to the short chimney on *One Man, One Goat*. From the top of the chimney, teeter left to the arete of *Just Kidding* and finish up this.

Central Section:

A number of route descriptions have been unearthed that describe climbs done by George Fraser in the 1950s. George Fraser, who was also involved in early explorations on Carnmore, disappeared on Ama Dablam in 1959. It is notable, that despite the rudimentary equipment of the time, all his routes are given a grade easier than they would be today.

Kid's Buttress (NX 49961 72336):
Located a long way to the right of the other climbs and almost the rightmost area of rock visible on the hillside. Although only 14m high at the most, the rock is superb. The routes and a topo are in the descriptions on the SMC website.

WATERSIDE HILL CRAG:
(NX 6120 8225) Alt 160m South facing
This 8m high metamorphic crag lies in a fine position on Waterside Hill above Allangibbon Bridge on the A713 half a mile or so north of Dalry. The routes and a topo are in the descriptions on the SMC website.

THE BORDERS & DUMFRIES, CLIFTON, Hollowstones Wall:
Bonny Lass 15m HVS 5a *. Stephen Reid, James Kinnaird. 8 Aug 2013.
Follow the very left edge of *Sideshoot's* slab to the ledge, then climb the wall left of *Sideshoot's* final groove by a tricky layaway move (protected by runners in *Sideshoot*).

Little Clifton:
Who Forgot the Rope? 11m H.Severe. Stephen Reid, James Kinnaird (alt). 8 Aug 2013.
Start 3m down and right of *Gorillar Warfare* at a juggy off-width crack.
1. 3m 4b Climb the crack to a good ledge and huge flake.
2. 8m 4a Scramble up heather and climb the wall to exit to the left of the hanging block overhang.

EDINBURGH AREA, Traprain Law:
Hexagon Edge 25m H.Severe 4a. Fiona Reid, Michael Watson. 6 May 2014.
Follow the extreme right edge of the grey wall to the left of the black slab with a thin move to join *Dangle*. An eliminate, where any deviation leftwards is much easier.

FAST CASTLE HEAD AREA:
The following three climbs breach the overhanging north face of The Wedge, the small southernmost fin in the immediate vicinity of The Souter.

Prawn Slippy 12m E5 6a. Stuart Green. 5 Oct 2013.
From slightly left of the centre of the face, climb direct to the obvious diagonal weakness and make a short rising traverse up this, almost to where it meets the seaward arete. Continue up the face above on surprisingly good holds among the veins until they lead onto the arete at about 8m. Pull round and finish up *Edge of the Wedge*.

Puffer Daddy 20m E3 6a. Stuart Green. 11 Oct 2013.
From 1m left of a boulder at the landward end of The Wedge, climb direct to the obvious diagonal weakness and make a rising traverse up this to where it meets the seaward arete. Pull around and finish up *Edge of the Wedge*.

Skate Bush 12m E7 6b. Dominic Jeff. 5 Oct 2013.
Start as for *Puffer Daddy*. Climb directly through jugs and crimp up the wall to a notch on the fuzzy arete at 8m, which takes a Camalot 3 with relief. Commit

back left and upwards to a triangular pocket which gives access to a series of veins and a jug on the arete a few feet below the summit tat.

SPORT CLIMBS

CENTRAL LOWLANDS, Dumbarton Rock:
Unfinished Symphony   22m   8b+. Alan Cassidy. 25 Aug 2013.
The bottom half of the '9b project', climbed as far as the obvious big undercut at the top of the black streak. Follow *Persistence of Vision* to its belay. Crimp and side pull your way to the big ledge which is followed rightwards to a big move into *Requiem*. Exit this immediately (crux) to rejoin the bolt line at the frustratingly slopey ramp. More hard moves on positive holds lead to the undercut. Lower from here, unless you are part of the next generation!

Dunbar Crag:
It has been noted on UKC but not confirmed that many of the rusty bolts have been replaced by staples.

Balgone Heughs:
(NT 563 823)   Alt 40m   North to North-West facing
Approach: In order to maintain good relations with the landowner (whose house is just above the crag!), don't take cars into the estate but park as for North Berwick Law and follow the John Muir way south until a kinked road is reached. At this point take the track signposted Balgone Barns south through the farm and into the hidden valley behind. The crag is on the far side of the valley but may be hidden by the trees, 25mins.
The climbing is crimpy and technical and provides a pleasant contrast to the reachiness of the nearby North Berwick Law. There is the occasional bit of crumbly rock and a helmet is recommended, at least until the routes have bedded in. The listed routes have been equipped with stainless steel glue-ins and double bolt lowers in autumn 2013.
Note: A climbing ban for the pheasant shooting season between 1 Oct and 1 Feb has been agreed.

Balgone Heughs, Left Buttress:
Heuthanasia   13m   7a+ **. Jamie Sparkes. 25 Feb 2014.
The leftmost line on the crag, taking the bouldery wall above a short right-facing corner.

Heugh know nothing (Jon Snow)   15m   6c **. Jamie Sparkes. 11 Jun 2014.
The hanging ramp is gained from the left. Leaving it is tricky to say the least.

The Entheughsiast   17m   7a *. Jamie Sparkes. 11 Jun 2014.
Break out left from beneath the roof on *Statement of Heuth* on undercuts into smeary layaways up the flake to a well earned rest before swinging out left again to the *Heuthanasia* lower-off. Pumpy

Statement of Heuth 15m 7a+ ***. Gordon Bisset.
The central line up the left-hand buttress. Pull with difficulty into the hanging corner and leave it rightwards with further difficulty! A new bolt line and cleaned in 2013.

Heugh and Cry 15m 7a **. Jamie Sparkes. 22 Feb 2014.
Climb the short corner to an overlap, pull through this to a ledge. From here, climb the intricate wall above on pockets, crimps and sidepulls to a pumpy finish.

Balgone Heughs, Hinge Buttress:
The Wanderer 17m 6b+ **. Seb Rider. 9 Nov 2013.
A fun meandering route through the overlaps. Start up the rib and groove on the left, exit this rightwards, step right, and climb up towards the overhang. Pull through this to reach a slab on the right to finish more easily on the left side of the nice arete.

Ivy Wall 15m 5+ *. Seb Rider. 9 Nov 2013.
The left route on the slab. A tricky start, then climb straight up to the lower-off.

The Curling Pond 15m 6a **. Seb Rider. 30 Nov 2013.
Start to the right of *Ivy Wall*. Climb 4 bolts, then join *Ivy Wall* clipping its last bolt.

Balgone Heughs, Right Buttress:
The Wasp 15m 6c **. Seb Rider. 29 Oct 2013.
Furthest left route on the right buttress. Climb through the overhang at its weakness (ancient peg) and follow the groove more easily to the head wall. Climb directly up the bulge left of the obvious protruding block on small holds to a breather below the tricky final roof, which is tackled direct. The central bulge can be avoided by weaklings by slinking rightwards into *Pheasant Corner* at 6b but there is no avoiding the top move!

Pheasant Corner 15m 6a **. Seb Rider. 29 Oct 2013.
Nice climbing through the overhang to the obvious corner above. Tackle the overhang with gymnastic moves (good holds to the right of the bolts) to gain the corner which is climbed to its top.

To the right are several old lines with spaced, poor quality fixed gear. Grades unknown.

Mr. Fox 15m 7a **. Seb Rider. 17 Dec 2013.
Bridge up the groove to the left of *Heughvenile Antics* to a good hold. Then make precarious moves right above the 3rd bolt to join *Heughvenile Antics* below its crux.

Heughvenile Antics 16m 6c+ ***. Gordon Bisset.
The obvious rib up the centre of the right-hand buttress leads to a hanging corner. A good sustained and technical route. A new bolt line and cleaned in 2013.

Bullrush   15m   6c **. Seb Rider. 9 Nov 2013.
Currently the furthest right route on the crag. Take a rib via a flake to an overhang. Surmount this onto a slab, which leads to a second overhang. Pull through this (crux) and climb the slab above. An undercling allows for an exit to the right more easily to the lower-off.

Ratho Quarry:
Buzooka   20m   7b+ **. Neill Busby. 9 May 2013.
New bolted line left of *Pettifer's Wall.*

Kamikaze   7a **. Neill Busby. 16 May 2013.
A bolted line right of *Pettifer's Wall.*

Slow Strain   6b+. Neill Busby. 25 May 2013.
The retro-bolted version of the *Slow Strain* arete.

John McCain   12m   6b **. Neill Busby. 28 Jun 2013.
Start from the left edge of the upper ledge, just left of *Panzer.* Climb up on well-cleaned incut holds, which are well-spaced requiring a couple of balancy moves.

Panzer   10m   6a+ *. Neill Busby. 28 Jun 2013.
Third line right of *Pettifer's Wall.* Nice moves to a balancy finish

The Corrieman   15m   6c **. Neill Busby. 7 Jul 2013.
A good sport addition in between the two *Wallys* and independent of both. Climb the slim groove with an ugly mantle to start then elegant climbing up and onto the final ledge.

Pea Shooter   5.
Pillar right of *Sedge Warbler.*

Impure Allure   6b+. Neill Busby. 10 Jul 2014.
Left of *Shear Fear.*

ARGYLL, Innellan Quarry:
The quarry has been developed so the routes probably no longer exist, but can't be accessed anyway (info Yann Gautherin).

PERTHSHIRE, Dunira:
The estate have started objecting to the parking place, so please park at the houses (NN 734 238) which the guidebook suggests as an alternative.
A hold would seem to have come off the top section of Dunira or Die, as it is now much harder than 7a.

Lower Lednock:
Harry Snotter is now 6c+ or 7a, as the snotter fell off during rebolting.

ARBROATH SEA-CLIFFS:
(NO 66962 42204)   Tidal
A new wall left of an arch which is beyond the Deil's Heid area. Continue on the

path beyond Deil's Heid and when the path goes down some steps to the beach, turn right at the end of the steps to get to the arch. The left route is *Avertical* (5). The middle route, which goes to the same lower-off, is *Alex Corner* (4) and the right route starts up *Alex Corner* and goes right, *Short Leap* (4+). A continuation of this gives *Follow the White Rabbit* (6b). The grades are all provisional (Ron Shoenberg, 14 Apr 2014).

ABERDEEN SEA-CLIFFS, Orchestra Cave:
The following three routes have been added to the left side of the cave all finishing at the *Mad Cows'* lower-off.

Time Will Tell   12m   7a. Tim Rankin. Sep 2013.
A worthwhile eliminate up the wall and overhang left of *Mad Cows*. Use a long draw on the 3rd bolt to avoid splatting on the ledge.

Start a Revolution   10m   6b *. Tim Rankin. Sep 2013.
The arete right of *Mad Cows*. Clip the first bolt of *Mad Cows*, then move right to the arete. Not much new climbing but a surprisingly good little warm-up.

Moonlight Sonata   10m   6c *. Tim Rankin. Sep 2013.
A fine wee route and the best of the bunch. Climb the roof and shield feature right of *Mad Cows*.

Violent Concerto   12m   7c **. Tim Rankin. Sep 2013.
More superb moves through the roof between *Underland* and *Bitter Sweet Symphony* including a photogenic double kneebar on the lip. Joins and finishes up *Bitter Sweat* from its 4th bolt.

Birth of the Coull   20m   7c+ ****. Tim Rankin. Sep 2013.
Yet another stunning route taking the eye catching overhanging arete on the left edge of the granite wall. Climb easy ground to gain the bolts, then launch out up the roof crack and along the lip to the arete proper. Superb moves on equally superb holds lead up the very edge, then right to the lower-off. Difficult to get in good condition but not to be missed when it is.

What the Funk   18m   8a/8a+ ***. Tim Rankin. Apr 2014.
Climb *Blobstrop* until after its crux past the 4th bolt, clip a high bolt on the right, then make a hard move right to below the hanging groove. Now turn up the funk and climb into the groove and an outrageous bridging rest. The lower-off awaits above the next roof. Some of the best climbing in the cave.

Longhaven, North Glash (NEO p289):
The sport crag in this quarry features one east facing slab and one west facing slab. The top half of the latter catches the afternoon / evening sun. Routes by Danny Laing (jnr), 2014.
Approach: Park at the Scottish Wildlife Trust car park (NEO p282) or alternatively if it is quiet, then park at the fork in the road, making sure not to block access. Then follow the road left and drop into the field to follow a faint landrover track directly to the crag. A cairn marks the descent into the quarry which is non-tidal but slightly boggy at the base. The lower-offs on the Revision

Slab should be visible from the top of the cliffs.

Revision Slab:
AWOL   16m   6c.
Leftmost line of bolts, trending leftwards from the 3rd bolt to thin moves to the chains.

A Little Bit Irish   16m   6a+.
Take the leftmost line of bolts until the 3rd bolt, then trend up and right to join the next route.

Resit   16m   6a.
Middle line of bolts. Thin initial moves lead to better holds and an easier second half.

In the Army Now   16m   5.
Right-hand line of bolts. Thin moves lead to a glorious jug fest!

Broke Back Wall:
Brace Yersel   10m   6c+.
Left-most line of bolts trending rightwards on the break at the top to reach the chain.

Up n Aboot   10m   6a.
Middle line of bolts. Thin slab climbing with a spicy finish.

Roon the Bend   10m   6b.
Stay left of the right-hand line of bolts (until the overlap) and avoid using the crack of the next route. Lovely rock-overs between positive holds.

Crack n Up   10m   5+.
Furthest right line, fun climbing up the obvious crack.

HIGHLANDS EAST, Brin Rock, Zed Buttress:
14 new routes, see topo opposite. A 40m rope should do. The routes generally are fingery with hard cruxes.

The Camel:
Over the Hills and Farr Away   22m   7a+. Neil Shepherd. Aug 2013.
This climbs the steep wall to the right of *Two Humps*. Nice steep climbing on generally good holds.

Moy Rock:
Eldorado   24m   6a **. Andy Nisbet. 4 Sep 2013.
A route at the far left end of the crag, in the next bay left of *Holly Tree Groove*. Here is a water runnel forming a groove high up and the route climbs the wall to its right to join it at the very top. Start next to a ramp on the right but try not to touch the ramp. Climb the wall to move right under an earthy scoop. Climb a ramp leading right to another scoop where another ramp leads right. Go briefly up the ramp before moving on to the wall. At its top, traverse left into the main

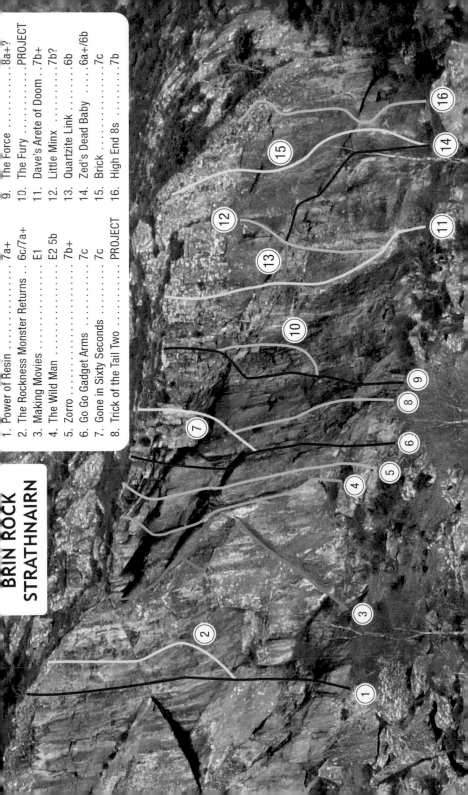

BRIN ROCK
STRATHNAIRN

1. Power of Resin . . . . 7a+
2. The Rockness Monster Returns . . 6c/7a+
3. Making Movies E1
4. The Wild Man E2 5b
5. Zorro . . . . 7b+
6. Go Go Gadget Arms 7c
7. Gone in Sixty Seconds 7c
8. Trick of the Tail Two . . . . PROJECT

9. The Force . . . . 8a+?
10. The Fury . . . . PROJECT
11. Dave's Arete of Doom . . 7b+
12. Little Minx . . . . 7b?
13. Quartzite Link 6b
14. Zed's Dead Baby . . . . . 6a+/6b
15. Brick 7c
16. High End 8s 7b

lower-off is above a heather ledge. Two abseils using a 60m rope; three abseils using a 50m rope (there are abseil points).

Teuchter   10m   6a *. Gregor Callum. Jan 2013.
Sixty metres right of *Jenny*, just right of a huge overhang. Climb delicately up a slab, eases with height.

Incomer   10m   6a. Seb Rider. Jan 2013.
To the left of the slab. Start trickily at the bottom of a hanging corner. Climb the corner and slab.

Little Torboll:
The following routes are on the steeper left side of the crag.

Riding the Rainbow   12m   6b **. Gregor Callum. 20 Jul 2013.
The furthest left route, offering good sustained climbing to the end. Climb straight to the embedded boulder continuing to the break and up through the bulge and lower-off above.

Mr Happy   12m   6b+ **. Seb Rider. 20 Jul 2013.
Climb up through the overlap and continue with tricky moves to gain the break. Climb the bulge above trending left to gain the lower-off.

Sport Secrets   13m   6a+. Seb Rider. 20 Jul 2013.
Climb the left side/arete of the small slab to gain a right-trending groove. Follow this to its end, then climb the arete on the left to finish. Watch for potential loose pebbles in the upper section. A more direct version, following the arete all the way, can be climbed with added difficulty.

Barny's Wall (Wick):
Seb Rider climbed the project just right of *Da Ma Wick* at 6b in May 2014. He also thought *At Ma Wick's End* was too close to other routes to be worth doing, but would be 6a if done as described (it would share a slopey finish).

HIGHLANDS WEST, Creag nan Cadhag:
Ronald Raygun Direct   7c **. Andy Wilby. 2013.
Where Ronald Raygun moves right at the 6th bolt, go straight up.

Nuclear Nightmare has been climbed by Alan Cassidy at 8a+ ** on 20 Apr 2014.

Note: There is now a new lower-off at the 6th bolt of *Nuclear Nightmare*. Finishing here gives *Nuclear Litemare* 7a **.

Am Fasgadh:
Bat Day   6a+. Ian Taylor. 2013.
A short route on the left side of the crag

Super Warm-Up   7b+ *. Ian Taylor. 2013.
From the normal lower-off, gain the undercuts above, move right to a flake and go up steeply to a lower-off. This supersedes the original poor extension.

The Pillar was climbed by Alan Cassidy at 8a on 19 Apr 2014 (previously a project).

Bogtalla Left-Hand 7c **. Lawrence Hughes. 2013.
From the 5th bolt on *Bogtalla*, go straight up to a lower-off under the quartz band. Strenuous clipping the chain. If energy remains and dryness allows there is a further extension to another lower-off above the quartz band, 7c+.

Goat Crag:
Gap Toothed Gypsy 7b+ *. Lawrence Hughes. 2014.
Climb the start of *The Prow* to the sloping ledge, then head straight up, following three new bolts, before pulling left into *Mac Talla*. Finish up *Mac Talla*.

Note: *The Fun Prow* is 8a.

Goat in the Woods:
(NG 966 915)   West facing
Marked as Carn na Gaoithe on the OS 1:25000 Map. If coming from Dundonnell, drive past Jetty Crag, then about 200m past the Gruinard estate buildings, and park on the verge on the left (at a right-hand bend in the road). The crag can be seen above the trees to the east. Walk along a path beside a fence into the trees, then continue spookily until 50m past a fallen tree. Slant slightly leftwards uphill until the crag can be seen through trees, then zigzag upwards crossing a broken fence. Stay on the left side of the slope to gain the crag. The routes have about 5 bolts.

From the left:

Evil Eye 15m 6c ***. Andy Wilby. 2013.
Tricky start, then pumpy.

Boltaholic 15m 6c+ *. Andy Wilby. 2013.
Hard and blind at the bulge.

Death by 1000 bites 15m 7a+ *. Andy Wilby. 2013
Hard moves to gain the corner, then a steep headwall.

Drillbit Taylor 15m 7b+ ***. Ian Taylor. 2013.
Bouldery section, then pumpy at the top.

Jungle Gym 15m 7b **. Ian Taylor. 2013.
Seeps a bit, but still climbable. Look out for the knee bar.

Pink it and Shrink it 15m 7a+ *. Ian Taylor. 2013.
Crux at the bulge, but it's not all over after that.

Cote d'Or 15m 7a ***. Ian Taylor. 2013.
Easy enough through the roof, then lovely rock with a sting in the tail.

Project – Right-hand finish to *Cote d'Or*.

Lemon & Co   15m   6c+. Paul Tattersall. 2014.
From the ledge, start up the steep arete, then the wall above to finish at the *Midgens'* lower-off.

Midgens   15m   6a+ *. Ian Taylor. 2013.
An awkward start onto the ledge, then steady to the top.

MULL:

Several sport routes have been climbed here, but since some crags have a mixture of sport and trad routes, they are listed in the Inner Hebrides section.

*****

Blàbheinn: Alastair Matthewson has submitted the extended notes below.

The crag known as *Eastern Slabs* in Skye Scrambles (2011) is called *South-East Buttress* in the Cuillin Climbers' Guide (2011). The crag is dismissed in the latter as offering an infinite number of scrambling routes. There is no denying its laid back angle, major half-way ledge and rambling nature of the upper section as it fades into screes under the summit. However, the rock is by no means 'climb-anywhere', and the routes described below are defined lines.
   The crag was first climbed on in 1907, but the original description is much too vague for the route to be identified with certainty. A note appeared at the time in the Sligachan Climbers' Book:

> <u>Blaven</u>   Climbed buttress on East face nearest great Central Gully over slabby rocks 2½ hours. This buttress starts somewhat higher than the more northerly ones but finishes just short of summit.
>
> R. A. Brown
W. A. Morrison
H. MacRobert   June 1907

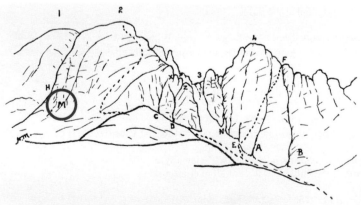

FIG. 17.—Blaven and Clach Glas from the East

1. Blaven, S. top.   2. Blaven, N. top.   3. Clach Glas Bealach.   4. Clach Glas.
The dotted lines show the easiest route to Blaven and an easy scramble up Clach Glas.

It then appeared in the 1923 SMC Skye Guide (Steeple, Barlow, MacRobert & Bell). See the diagram at the foot of the previous page.

> *South-Eastern Buttress.*—This is the buttress (M in fig. 17) on the north side of the great scree-filled gully referred to above which separates the two tops of Blaven. It was climbed in 1907 by H. MacRobert, R. A. Brown and W. A. Morrison. The route, which was rather indefinite, lay over easy slabby rocks and up trap dykes.

In the most recent Cuillin Climbers' Guide (2011), a scramble is described up the left-hand side of the buttress and is also named South-East Buttress, though this may not be the same as the original route.

> South-East Buttress   300m   Grade 3 ***   (1907)
> The best and longest line stays on the left edge of the buttress. Start left of the small pool, cross the obvious left-slanting chimney line then pass three broad terraces with slabs gradually easing in angle to the summit slopes. Superb!

Since this route is described as crossing the obvious left-slanting chimney line (K Route) it is a little misleading to say that it stays on the left edge of the buttress. Also, the date and party details need amending in the first ascent list:
S   1907 June   South-East Buttress   II. MacRobert, R. A. Brown and W. A. Morrison.

The following lines have been climbed on the crag in the last few years by AM. The routes are described from L to R. (The Hon Ed also did a variation finish to the first route on this year's Skye Meet.)

1. **Original Route (?)**   Grade 3
Probably the same as the scramble called South-East Buttress in the recent Cuillin Climbers' Guide. AM soloed this route on 21/07/2011 (first visit to crag – I chose the natural line, unaware of any routes other than Dyke Route).

This route climbs the left edge of the lower slabs, left of the diagonal chimney/gully, before moving rightwards to climb the upper slabs by the easiest line.

Start a few metres left of a pool at the base of the cliff. Slabs lead straight up to a scree-covered ledge at the base of the cliff proper. Climb the slabby narrowing buttress above – a bulge above a cone sheet providing the short crux.

The upper tier is easier. Take the wide scree ledge rightwards, crossing the diagonal gully. Aim to pass just left of an obvious large square block/overhang low down (right of two offset gullies). Much higher up, after a section of easy scree, there is an optional but highly entertaining subterranean excursion.

Enter a wide slot with a huge chockstone which is passed under. A number of possibilities unfold. The daylight option is to move right and continue up the wide horizontal fissure above, leading to screes. Alternatively, descend leftwards into a cave. A vertical chimney with chockstones looms above. Ignore this and keep crawling leftwards towards a daylight hole. This leads into a gully overlooking Great Scree Gully. Climb the slabby left wall to easier ground. *NB: This fissured section of cliff is a potentially active area of landslip. The objective dangers from rockfall or catastrophic cliff collapse are high.*

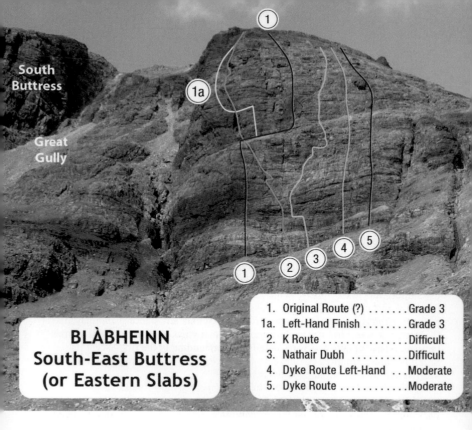

South
Buttress

Great
Gully

1. Original Route (?) . . . . Grade 3
1a. Left-Hand Finish . . . . Grade 3
2. K Route . . . . Difficult
3. Nathair Dubh . . . . Difficult
4. Dyke Route Left-Hand . . . Moderate
5. Dyke Route . . . . Moderate

BLÀBHEINN
South-East Buttress
(or Eastern Slabs)

1a. **Left-hand Finish**   Grade 3

At the main terrace, instead of traversing a long way right, climb good rock midway between the gully of *K Route* and a left-facing corner further right. Before the wall becomes too steep, traverse left along a cone sheet. Cross the gully of *K Route* and scramble up a pleasant buttress parallel to the gully. Eventually curve rightwards to finish as for K Route. *Climbed by DNW on 6/6/2014.*

2. **K Route**   Difficult

The left-slanting chimney/gully line seems to have been expunged from the 2011 Cuillin Climbers' Guide. It was first described in the MacInnes guidebook (Constable, 1971): 'A route of Diff/V Diff standard up chimney and face to top.' It is assumed that MacInnes probably climbed this himself, possibly *circa* 1967? *Climbed by AM solo on 22/03/2012.*

Climb slabs straight up into the narrow slanting gully which is wet and easy at the start. At the first steepening move 3m right on a cone sheet then delicately back left on an impeccable slab (crux). The second steep section is avoided by a groove in the left wall and an awkward step down back right into the gully. Continue up to terrace.

The upper gully is easier – chockstones are taken on left or right (drier). Where the gully runs out, climb the upper of two left-slanting corners to an orange cone sheet ledge. Follow this for a few metres, then climb up to an overhanging prow on the left (with a steep corner on the right). Move left under the prow, and slant round left, overlooking big gully to easier ground at another cone sheet ledge. Climb this rightwards to where the angle relents.

3. Nathair Dubh   Difficult
This route finds a wandering but natural way up the lower tier between *K Route* and *Dyke Route Left-hand*, then ascends the upper cliff more directly by way of a sinuous crack. *Ascent by AM solo: Lower tier 19/10/2011 (Moderate); Upper tier 15/10/2013 (Difficult).*

Start down and left of *Dyke Route Left-hand*, below the lower tier of slab, some 20m up and right of the small pool at a thin dyke. Slabs lead straight up to a scree-covered ledge at the base of the steeper cliff. Climb the shallower right-hand of two gully lines containing a 1m-wide dyke (the left-hand gully is *K Route*). Higher up, pass an obvious rock boss and keep following the dyke up clean slabs to a heather alcove below a steepening of darker wetter rock. Ignore the ledge leading right – instead, scramble up and right on pale rock aiming for a block on a rib. At the block, step right round the rib and traverse hard right to the base of a short grassy gully. Easier rocks right of the gully lead to less steep ground and the wide scree-covered ledge below the upper tier. Above, a thin recessed black dyke snakes up the face. Climb this – the crux is a steep section at the start, but above the angle soon relents. Move right onto a buttress of rough rock to join the upper section of *Dyke Route Left-hand*.

4. Dyke Route Left-hand   Moderate
Ascent by AM solo: Lower Tier 15/10/2013; Upper Tier 19/10/2011.

This fine route climbs a thinner dyke left of *Dyke Route*. In the lower tier its very upper part looks like twin right-slanting cracks; the lower section is black with lichen. Follow the dyke with a minor deviation on the right to avoid a steepening above a cone sheet. Higher up, the twin cracks are taken direct on clean rough black rock. Above the terrace the dyke continues up the easier slab staying left of the scab-like overlap of *Dyke Route*, eventually joining this route below the small tower.

5. Dyke Route   Moderate
See *Skye Scrambles* for description.

MISCELLANEOUS NOTES

THE W.H. MURRAY LITERARY PRIZE

As a tribute to the late Bill Murray, whose mountain and environment writings have been an inspiration to many a budding mountaineer, the SMC have set up a modest writing prize, to be run through the pages of the Journal. The basic rules are set out below, and will be reprinted each year. The prize is run with a deadline of 1 May each year.

The Rules:
1. There shall be a competition for the best entry on Scottish Mountaineering published in the *Scottish Mountaineering Club Journal*. The competition shall be called the 'W.H. Murray Literary Prize', hereafter called the 'Prize'.
2. The judging panel shall consist of, in the first instance, the following: The current Editor of the *SMC Journal*; The current President of the SMC; and two or three lay members, who may be drawn from the membership of the SMC. The lay members of the panel will sit for three years after which they will be replaced.
3. If, in the view of the panel, there is in any year no entry suitable for the Prize, then there shall be no award that year.
4. Entries shall be writing on the general theme of 'Scottish Mountaineering', and may be prose articles of up to approximately 5000 words in length, or shorter verse. Entries may be fictional.
5. Panel members may not enter for the competition during the period of their membership.
6. Entries must be of original, previously unpublished material. Entries should be submitted to the Editor of the *SMC Journal* by 1 May for consideration that year. Electronic contributions are preferred and should be submitted via e-mail, although double-spaced typewritten hard copies will also be accepted by post. (See Office Bearers page at end of this Journal for address etc.) Any contributor to the SMC Journal is entitled to exclude their material from consideration for the Prize and should so notify the Editor of this wish in advance.
7. The prize will be a cheque for the amount £250.
8. Contributors may make different submissions in different years.
9. The decision of the panel is final.
10. Any winning entry will be announced in the *SMC Journal,* and will be published in the *SMC Journal* and on the SMC Website. Thereafter, authors retain copyright.

THE W.H. MURRAY LITERARY PRIZE 2014

It was another difficult year for the judges. The prize is awarded for articles about 'Scottish Mountaineering', so the view was taken that articles about mountain running and skiing would not be considered even though there is no denying that these activities can involve mountaineering skills. The prize this year goes to Ian Taylor for *Opening the Church Door* his overview of the history of climbing on Church Door Buttress in Glen Coe. His well researched and clearly written article is the first review of the climbing on this rather enigmatic crag. One of the judges enthused 'a move away from cosy, comfortable sports routes and back to the uncomfortable, dangerous and exploratory.' It's good to know that climbers have not lost interest in the high mountain crags. When the Hon. Ed. went up to photograph the crag one evening this summer, he saw a party just starting to climb the west face. They were still only half way up their route when he left the corrie at nine o'clock. Ian's article should inspire other climbers to pay a visit to this crag which was first explored by Collie 120 years ago.

There were several other worthy contenders. *Fogies Unlit* is 'written in a modest, almost self effacing, style. It describes a challenging and difficult route undertaken by two outstanding mountaineers. The description of the action is gripping and the background information about the area and the circumstances of the expedition add greatly to the quality of the article.'

How The Day Turned Out was also well regarded. 'Journal articles serve different purposes. Some tell us of adventures and places with which we are not familiar and although we may find ourselves fascinated and inspired they will, sadly, mostly remain beyond our own experience. Others take us back to places we know well and they frequently remind us of our own small triumphs and disasters. They allow us, in a way, to revisit and enjoy once again some of these wonderful mountain days. This article is certainly in the second category. I enjoyed it immensely not least because it was written in such an engaging and unpretentious style.'

The judges also enjoyed *Why?* 'Conveys very well the sensations of being alone in dangerous, stressful circumstances with primitive fear nibbling at the edges of rational thought, resulting in what may have been irrational perceptions.' '... the author made an excellent job of describing the threatening atmosphere and the deteriorating weather conditions at the start. Consequently the reader's interest and anticipation increase and heighten as the article proceeds to its conclusion. References to mountain tragedies can sometimes be made in a clumsy and insensitive manner but I felt that in this case it was done in a compassionate, almost affectionate, manner.'

A number of other aricles made the short list. Indeed most of the articles this year appeared on one or other of the judges' long leets. Contributors are thanked for their interesting and wide ranging submissions.

Please start early for next year. The official deadline for submissions is 1 May 2015.

SCOTTISH WINTER NOTES 2013–14

THE 2014 WINTER SEASON was an unusual one. Higher than average temperatures and almost continuous south-easterly gales led to huge depths of snow across the Highlands, but a lack of freeze-thaw meant that ice formation was limited. The last months of 2013 brought an almost continuous series of storms and calm days were few and far between. The atrocious weather peaked over the Christmas and New Year period, but during January and February the strong winds continued. Huge cornices were formed from vast amounts of wind-blow plateau snow, and dangerous full depth avalanches occurred in many corries. The result was that few cliffs came into good climbing condition, but those that did – namely Creag an Dubh Loch, Stob Coire nan Lochan in Glen Coe, Coire Mhic Fearchair on Beinn Eighe, and the Minus Face on Ben Nevis – yielded a rich series of routes for those fortunate enough to be in position at the right time.

The BMC International Meet, which fortuitously was held in the last week in January (one of the coldest spells of the winter) was the most productive period of the season. Throw together 44 talented international climbers from 26 countries with an equal number of highly motivated and experienced Scottish climbers, feed and water them at Glenmore Lodge, and let them loose in the Highlands for a week, and you have a recipe for success regardless of weather. Despite continuous gale force easterly winds, the 2014 Meet was the finest ever, with over a dozen new routes and a significant number of repeats.

Creag an Dubh Loch

The early winter storms were not all bad news because at an altitude of 750m or so, the rapid temperature fluctuations were perfect for ice formation. The finest example was on the great cliff of Creag an Dubh Loch in the Eastern Cairngorms, which came into the best ice climbing condition in living memory.

The 300m-high Dubh Loch cliffs have the highest concentration of summer E-grade mountain climbs in the country, however it is notoriously difficult to find the crag in good winter condition. The smooth fine-grained granite needs a very specific weather pattern to create a coating of ice to render it climbable. In late December however, continuous gale force southerlies transported snow on the plateau to the more northerly aspects of the cliff, and a rapid series of freeze-thaws around Christmas time allowed ice to ooze down the main drainage lines.

The first indication that the cliff was in condition came when news broke of the first winter ascent of *The Giant* (VII,7). This 200m-high summer E3 had been admired as a futuristic possibility by winter climbers for over three decades, but ice had never formed down the full length of the corner. Incredibly, the father and son team of Doug and Uisdean Hawthorn were in the right place at the right time to make the coveted first winter ascent on 29 December. Photos of their ascent on the Internet attracted several strong teams to Central Gully Wall at the next weather window a few days later. Unfortunately, an overnight thaw softened the ice, and none were successful, except for Team Hawthorn who bided their time and then made a matter-of-fact second winter ascent of *Sword of Damocles* (VIII,9) the following day when the temperatures dropped again. The Giant collapsed a few days later as the freezing level rose, but this was the perfect ice-making scenario for the higher altitude routes on the neighbouring Broad Terrace Wall.

Callum Johnson teetering up the bold second pitch on the first ascent of Take the Throne (VII,6) on Creag an Dubh Loch's Broad Terrace Wall. Photo: Doug Hawthorn.

Guy Robertson, Nick Bullock, Greg Boswell, Will Sim, Uisdean Hawthorn, Iain Small and Callum Johnson after making first ascents of Defence of the Realm (VII,7), The Cure (VIII,8), Hustle (VII,7) and Take the Throne (VII,6) on Creag an Dubh Loch's Broad Terrace Wall. Photo: Simon Richardson.

The 120m-high upper tier of Broad Terrace wall is the steepest mountain cliff in the Cairngorms. Its summer climbs are highly prized, but rarely climbed because they are almost always wet. In winter, the wall had only been climbed five times by four separate routes, but all this changed on 11 January when four new winter routes were added. The crack team of Guy Robertson and Greg Boswell were first to arrive and climb the plum line of *Defence of the Realm* (VII,7) which continues straight up a spectacular inverted staircase of hanging ice smears above the first pitch of the summer E1 *Falkenhorst*. A little to the right, Iain Small and I climbed *Hustle*, a thinly iced VII,7 to the left of *The Sting* (VII,6), the only existing route on this part of the wall, and first climbed by Doug Hawthorn and Dougie Dinwoodie way back in January 1993. Between these two routes, Will Sim and Nick Bullock scooped *The Cure* (VIII,8), the most difficult new route of trio. The sight of three of the finest Scottish winter climbers (namely Robertson, Sim and Small) leading new routes in parallel on one of the most revered cliffs in the Highlands was an extraordinary sight, and the uniqueness of the day was emphasised by the young pair of Uisdean Hawthorn and Callum Johnson making the first ascent of *Take the Throne* (VII,6), the thinly iced rib left of *Sword of Damocles*.

The weather remained cold and stable over the next three days. *Defence of the Realm* and *Take the Throne* both saw repeats, and Robin Clothier and Richard Bentley made an ascent of *The Last Oasis* (VI,6), which was first climbed in 1980 by Andy Nisbet and Neil Spinks and had only been repeated once in the following 30 years. Alongside this spectacular run of successes, there were also failures on *The Giant*, *Sword of Damocles* and *The Sting*, which highlighted both the difficulty of these routes, and the exacting conditions required for success. In light of this, the record of the Hawthorn team (two major new routes, and three second ascents) was remarkable. Their ability to predict conditions and be in the right place at the right time (a key Scottish winter skill) was particularly impressive.

From afar it appeared that the Hawthorns had a pact with the Devil, but the reality was as impressive as it was ordinary. Doug Hawthorn, one of the unheralded stars of the vibrant 1980s scene, only resumed climbing recently when his sons became teenagers. Although he now lives on the West Coast, Doug has always been fascinated by the winter possibilities on Creag an Dubh Loch, and set a winter ascent of *The Giant* as his prime target. He had made several winter trips into Dubh Loch to check on conditions in recent years, and after climbing *Savage Slit* with Uisdean on Boxing Day, he had a sense that *The Giant* may be icing up. A reconnaissance two days later confirmed his suspicions, and a quick phone call to Uisdean, who was in the CIC Hut at the time, saw the duo leaving the Glen Muick at 6 a.m. next morning. Their round trip time of just over 11 hours car to car for the route illustrates their speed and extreme mountain competence. All in all, the first winter ascent of *The Giant* reads like a Scottish winter climbing fairy story, where intelligence, mountain fitness and absolute focus came to the fore.

Stob Coire nan Lochan

The week after the Dubh Loch Broad Terrace Wall ascents, the focus turned to the other side of the country and Glen Coe. Will Sim and Greg Boswell set the ball rolling with the second and third on sight ascents of *The Tempest* in Stob Coire nan Lochan. This touchstone route was first climbed by Neil Gresham in

Iain Small climbing the crucial second pitch on the first winter ascent of Scansor (IX,9) on Stob Coire nan Lochan in Glen Coe. Photo: Tony Stone.

Olov Isaksson making the first ascent of Eggäschpili (IX,9) in Stob Coire nan Lochan in Glen Coe. Photo: Karin Zgraggen.

2001 as an M9 winter sports route by pre-placing the gear. Also that day, Guy Robertson and Nick Bullock climbed the icy groove left of *East Face Route* before continuing up the series of icy corners above. It is likely that *Slenderhead* (VIII,8) shares its first pitch with a route called *Boomshanka* that was first climbed by the late Mark Miller in the 1980s, but was left unreported at the time. Unfortunately, it is not known whether Mark finished his route and continued to the top of the crag, but Guy was quick to point out that the first pitch is the crux, so full credit to Mark for leading a modern Grade VIII pitch over 25 years ago using Chacals and Foot Fangs. Dave Almond and Helen Rennard also made the second ascent of *Twisted*, a three-pitch VII,7 to the left of *Chimney Route* put up in March 2013 by Simon Yearsley and Malcolm Bass.

The next big event in Stob Coire nan Lochan took place a few days later when Iain Small and Tony Stone made the first winter ascent of *Scansor* (IX,9). This summer E2 takes the prominent pillar to the right of *Unicorn* and had seen at least four attempts in recent seasons including one by Iain and Tony. All parties had ground to a halt on the thin and exposed second pitch, but this time Iain found a devious line to gain the crucial traverse ledge.

At the end of January during the BMC International Meet, Greg Boswell and Mirko Breckner and Andy Inglis and Martin Zumer (Slovenia) made early repeats of *Central Buttress* with the *Starting Blocks Start* (VII,8), and *Slenderhead* (VIII,8) saw second and third ascents by Will Sim and Michelle Kadatz (Canada) and Ian Parnell and Olov Isaksson (Sweden). The finest performance came from Harry Holmes and Polish climber Piotr Sulowski who made an ascent of *Unicorn* (VIII,8).

In late January, Iain Small followed up on his Scansor ascent with the equally demanding *Year of the Horse* (IX,9). Climbed with Blair Fyffe, this steep technical mixed route takes the soaring V-groove capped with a double overhang on the imposing wall to the left of *East Face Route*. A month later, Olov Isaksson from Sweden and Karin Zgraggen made an enterprising weekend trip from Switzerland to add *Eggäschpili* (IX,9). This outstanding mixed line takes a series of slim corners on the left wall of *SC Gully*, and is one of the most difficult Scottish winter first ascents ever climbed by an overseas team. It was spotted by Olov when he climbed *Slenderhead* during the BMC International Meet.

Coire Mhic Fearchair

The south-easterly gales during January and February prompted many teams to visit the high north-facing cliffs of Coire Mhic Fearchair on Beinn Eighe. On the third day of the BMC International Meet, Will Sim and Michelle Kadatz (Canada) made the fourth ascent of the fabled *West Central Gully* (VII,8), arguably the most difficult gully climb in Scotland. Andy Inglis and Martin Zumer (Slovenia) made the third ascent of *Hydroconicum* (VIII,8), and Dave Almond and Michal

Guy Robertson following the vertical ice section on the bold second pitch of One Step Beyond (IX,9) on Beinn Eighe during the first ascent.

Photo: Pete Macpherson.

Sabovcik (Slovakia) climbed the now classic *Blood, Sweat and Frozen Tears* (VIII,8).

The following day, the pace stepped up a notch when Nick Bullock, Jon Walsh and Greg Boswell made the first ascent of *Making the Cut* (VIII,8), a major new line taking the soaring crack-line left of *West Central Gully*. Will Sim and Olov Isaksson (Sweden) also added *Crazy Eyes* (VII,9), the left-facing corner, roof crack and offwidth corner above *Hydroponicum*, and Andy Inglis made a return visit with Piotr Sulowski (Poland) to climb the brilliant *Sundance* (VIII,8). The last day of the Meet saw a grand finale with ascents of *Central Buttress*, *Shang High* and *Kami-kaze* and another ascent of *Sundance* by Dave Almond and Gustav Mellgren (Sweden).

The undoubted highlight of the exceptionally busy season on Beinn Eighe, was the first ascent of *One Step Beyond* (IX,9) by Pete Macpherson and Guy Robertson on the Far East Wall. The route is based on an unusual hanging ice smear that oozes from a seep half way up the wall left of King of the Swingers, and is a contender for the hardest new route of the season. The first winter ascent of the very steep summer E2 *The Root of All Evil* (IX,8) by Murdoch Jamieson and John Orr was another challenging addition, as was Nick Bullock and Tim Neill's *Creme de Violette* (IX,9) on West Central Wall. The latter was an attempt to repeat Ian Parnell's *Bruised Violet*, however a route finding error meant they followed a largely independent line. Also of note was the second ascent of *Vishnu* (VII,7) on the Far East Wall by Small and Jamieson – a Nisbet-Cunningham creation that had waited over 25 years for a repeat!

The Minus Face, Ben Nevis

With a huge amount of snow lying on the Minus Face for most of the season, Ben Nevis regulars knew that when it consolidated then conditions would be exceptional. A swift thaw in early March followed by a brief high pressure was the perfect recipe to transform the mountain into a Christmas cake of rock hard frozen snow. Iain Small and Uisdean Hawthorn were quickly on the scene to add *Dark Star* (VI,5), the much-eyed line of grooves on the left side of *Astronomy*, and the following day they joined up with Murdoch Jamieson to climb *Minus One Superdirect* (VII,6). This archetypical Nevis thin face climb links together the 1977 and 2010 routes and is the first winter route to climb the very crest of the much sought-after Minus One Buttress. The star performers however were French guide Remi Thivel and Laurence Girard who had an outstanding two days when they climbed four routes including the second ascent of *Shooting Star* (VI,6) – the longest route on the Orion Face, and an early repeat of *Point Blank* (VII,6). Their highlights were the first ascent of *Total Kheops* (VI,6), the impressive hanging groove cutting into the left flank on Minus One Buttress, and Remi's solo of *Urban Spaceman* (VII,7) in a mind-boggling 40 minutes.

A deep thaw meant that these once in a lifetime conditions only lasted three days, but a heavy snowfall two weeks later brought the mixed routes on Càrn Dearg Buttress into condition. Guy Robertson and Nick Bullock nipped in for a new VIII,7 direct finish to *The Shield Direct*, and Iain Small and I climbed *From The Jaws of Defeat* (VIII,8), a direct line up to, and through, the triangular headwall on the adjacent North Wall of Càrn Dearg. Soon afterwards a slow thaw set in, and by early April, the pristine white snows of Ben Nevis were rapidly disappearing into the raging Allt a' Mhuilinn en route to Loch Linnhe and the sea.

Murdoch Jamieson nearing the top of Minus One Superdirect (VII,6) on Ben Nevis.
Photo: Iain Small.

Ben Nevis and the Central Highlands

Ben Nevis is taking over from the Northern Corries as the venue of choice for high standard early season mixed. Harry Holmes and Dan Tait set the tone on 21 November with an ascent of the steep corner-line of *Cornucopia* (VII,8) on the left flank of Creag Coire na Ciste. This route has become something of a modern test-piece, but it can be even more challenging early in the season when the tricky entry pitch is not banked out by metres of snow in Number Three Gully. The following day was forecast to be a little warmer, but Iain Small and Tony

Stone decided to take a chance and came away with the second ascent of *Storm Trooper* (VIII,8) by the original start up the flake-crack and finished up the final chimney of *Cornucopia*.

On Saturday 23 November there were plenty of strong teams in action on the high cliffs of Coire na Ciste. Andy Inglis and Neil Adams climbed *The Secret* (VIII,9), whilst nearby, Blair Fyffe, Richard Bentley and Robin Clothier made an early repeat of *Archangel* (VII,7). Across on Number Three Gully Buttress, Iain Small and Tony Stone made the third ascent of *Arthur* (VIII,8). This steep and rarely climbed summer HVS was first climbed in winter by Bruce Poll and Tony Shepherd in January 2004, and was repeated by Ian Parnell and North American ace Kelly Cordes during the 2005 BMC International Meet. The following day, Pete Macpherson and Erick Baillot visited the Archangel area and made the second ascent of *Avenging Angel Direct* (VIII,8). Direct, steep and uncompromising, this is one of the finest mixed lines on the mountain and was only first climbed in its entirety by Neil Adams and Jim Higgins the previous February. Neil Adams and Andy Inglis made it a memorable weekend with an early repeat of *Apache* (VIII,9), the steep crack-line to the right of Sioux Wall on Number Three Gully Buttress, and next door, Harry Holmes and Helen Rennard made a smooth ascent of the modern classic *Sioux Wall* (VIII,8).

Although December proved to be unusually mild, there was a brief burst of cold air early in the month that produced a flurry of activity on Ben Nevis. Three notable ascents took place on 6 December – an early repeat of *The Knuckleduster* (VIII,9) on Number Three Gully Buttress by the powerhouse team of Martin Moran and Pete Macpherson, a possible second ascent of *The Sorcerer* (VII,8) on Creag Coire na Ciste by Keith Ball, Kenny Grant and Guy Stephen, and a new start to *Avenging Angel Direct*.

The Sorcerer takes an unlikely line through the steep wall below the exit gully of *Lost the Place*, and to the best of my knowledge, it had not been repeated. Steve Ashworth and Nils Nielsen from Norway made the first ascent during a memorable day on the 2007 International Winter Meet. They climbed *Darth Vader* (VII,8) in the morning, followed by *The Sorcerer*, before racing up *Thompson's Route* to warm down! The new *Alternative Start* to *Avenging Angel Direct* (VIII,8) on Creag Coire na Ciste was added by Iain Small and Tony Stone. The sustained Tech 7+ pitch follows a parallel corner line to the left of *Angels with Dirty Faces* (VIII,8) – a Small-Stone addition from February 2011.

Neil Adams and Andy Inglis pulled off an important second ascent on Ben Nevis on 1 January when they repeated *The Brass Monkey* (VII,8) on the east side of Tower Ridge. This imposing corner which bounds the right side of Echo Wall is a rarely climbed summer HVS, and was first climbed in winter by Pete Davies and Tim Marsh in December 2008. A few weeks later on the International Meet, Greg Boswell and Mirko Breckner from Germany made the second ascent of *Heidbanger* (VIII,8) on Central Trident Buttress. This challenging winter climb is graded E1 in summer and was first climbed by Rich Cross and Andy Benson in 2007.

Overall, new route activity was remarkably quiet, although the first winter ascent of *Turkish* (VII,7) on Number Five Gully Buttress on Ben Nevis in early January was a notable coup by Malcolm Bass, Simon Yearsley and Helen Rennard. Also in January, Donald King, Mike Pescod and Andy Nelson made the first ascent of *Angels* (VIII,9). This excellent new mixed route on the front face of Church Door Buttress on Bidean nam Bian in Glen Coe was climbed on a rare

Iain Small moving through a bulge on From The Jaws of Defeat, a new VIII,8 on the North Wall of Càrn Dearg, Ben Nevis. Photo: Simon Richardson.

day of good conditions and light winds, with well rimed rock and usable ice. On Ben Nevis, Dave MacLeod made the first winter ascent of *Orient Express* (IX,9) in February with Adam Hughes. This tenuous looking winter line follows the line of the summer E2 on the First Platform of North-East Buttress – a good venue for very snowy conditions.

Nick Bullock and Canadian climber Jon Walsh set the pace on the second day of the International Meet with the third ascent of *Extasy* (VIII,8) on Creag Meagaidh. Nick and Jon encountered difficult thin ice conditions on this long, serious and poorly protected route, which was first climbed during the 2005 International Meet by Bruno Sourzac and Dave Hesleden, and had only been repeated once before.

Northern Highlands

In general, it was too warm for good conditions in the Northern Highlands away from the high cliffs of Beinn Eighe, however on the last day of the International Meet the centre of the activity transferred to Beinn Bhan where there were four teams in action on the stupendous Giant's Wall of Coire nan Fhamair. *Gully of the Gods* (VI,6) and *Great Overhanging Gully* had early repeats, *Genesis* (VII,7) saw its fourth ascent in the hands of Andy Inglis and Piotr Solowski (Poland), and Will Sim and Olov Isaksson (Sweden) made the fourth ascent of *The Godfather* (VIII,8). Nearby in Coire na Poite, Neil Silver and Kenshi (Japan) pulled off the long-awaited second ascent of the 370m-long *Realisation* (VI,6). The most impressive achievement of the day however, was the first ascent of the magnificent groove-line of *Last Orders* (VII,8) on An Teallach by Neil Adams and Kenro Nakajima (Japan).

New route activity elsewhere in the Northern Highlands was limited, although John Mackenzie and Andrew James applied some deep cunning to succeed on *Hogwarts Express* (IV,4) on Sgùrr na Muice in Strathfarrar, and Andy Nisbet, Jonathan Preston and Sandy Allan braved big cornices in early March on Ben Wyvis to succeed on *Risk of Ice* (V,4) in Coire na Feola.

Cairngorms

Away from Creag an Dubh Loch, the major event in the Cairngorms was Greg Boswell's first winter ascent of *The Demon* (IX,9) in Coire an Lochain in the Northern Corries. Greg followed the E2 summer line, as opposed to the alternative line of *Demon Direct* first climbed by Alan Mullin and Steve Paget in 2001. Of particular note was the style of Greg's ascent and *The Demon* joins a very select group of Grade IX routes that have had on sight first ascents. Elsewhere in the massif, Andy Nisbet took advantage of the unique conditions of heavy snow to make the first ascent of *Scarebear* (VI,5) with Heike Puchan on Stacan Dubha in the Loch Avon Basin. This prominent line, with a pronounced overhang at half-height, was one of the last unclimbed gully lines in the Cairngorms. Also of note was the addition of two new gully lines to South Craig in Glen Prosen by Henning Wackerhage and Tim Chappell – *Spanish Dinner* (V,6) and the fine looking *Freebird* (V,6).

In the Northern Cairngorms, Lurcher's Crag was a good choice in the heavy snow conditions. Arguably the key event here was John Lyall's detective work (shades of Robin Campbell) that showed that the initial icefall of the popular route *K9* is, in fact, *Window Gully* (V,5), an impressive first ascent and undergrading at Grade III by Bill March, John Cleare and J. Bradshaw in March

1972. Above the shared icefall start, *K9* continues up a prominent second icefall up and left of the main gully line, and this area saw three new additions. Matt Griffin, Adrian Dye were first on the scene with *Far from the Madding Crowd* (III,4), which climbs the rib left of the initial icefall of *Window Gully*. This was accessed by traversing underneath two icy lines that subsequently resulted in *Robodog* (IV,5) by Andy Nisbet, Jonathan Preston, and Ermine (V,4) by Sandy Allan and Nisbet. Just to the right on the Arctic Monkeys buttress, Susan Jensen joined Andy Nisbet for *Tetradecaphobia* (V,5), which takes the right end of the roof system down which the icicles of K9 form, before climbing the grooves and corners to gain the crest of the upper buttress. A few days later, Roger Everett and I climbed *Impulse Grooves* (VI,7) that follows a direct line of grooves up the front face of the buttress. Also of note in the Northern Cairngorms was the development of Craig Raebert by Roger Webb, James Edwards and myself. This compact crag on the south side of Cairn Gorm overlooks the Loch Avon Basin and provided six mixed routes in the Grade IV to V category.

There were also a number of significant repeats. On 17 December Will Sim and Greg Boswell made the second winter ascent of *Babes in the Wood* (VIII,8) in Coire an t-Sneachda. This 30m-long summer E2 follows a slanting crack-line on the left flank of Aladdin's Buttress and provides a very sustained winter pitch with a thin crux at the top. The route was first climbed in winter by Dave MacLeod and Scott Muir in December 2004. Pete Macpherson and Martin Moran added to their long list of cutting edge ascents with an ascent of *Diedre of the Sorrows* (VIII,8) on Lochnagar's Tough-Brown Face on January. This much-celebrated route was first climbed by Dougie Dinwoodie and Andy Nisbet in March 1986, and has only seen two other repeats. Will Sim and Adam Booth visited Coire an Lochain in the Northern Corries in late February, and made the probable third ascent of *Open Heart* (VIII,9). This very steep test-piece, which takes a direct line up to the crux of *Ventriloquist*, was first climbed by Ian Parnell and Guy Robertson in April 2006. It saw a second ascent by Dave Almond and Simon Frost in December 2011.

Although it is tempting to focus reports such as these purely on high standard climbs, winter exploration in Scotland continues to take place at all levels. This is best illustrated by the development of Creag na h-Iolaire on Cairn Gorm during the International Meet, which saw the addition of six new routes from II to IV by teams including climbers from New Zealand, Portugal, Bulgaria, Israel, Mongolia and the Czech Republic. Despite the wild Cairngorm weather, and having to crawl onto the plateau at the top, everyone returned to the Lodge with big smiles across their faces, happy to have had the 'full Scottish experience'!

Simon Richardson

100 YEARS AGO: THE CLUB IN 1914

THE 25TH ANNUAL MEETING and Dinner took place on Friday 5 December 1913 in the St Enoch Station Hotel, Glasgow, with Godfrey Solly presiding. Treasurer Nelson announced a balance of £179 4s. 8d., which together with the Life Membership Fund of £282 1s. 4d., and the still-unused legacy of £100 from the Gaiter Club, brought the Club's total funds to £561 6s. The Rules were tinkered with, increasing ordinary Committee Members to 9, but limiting office to three consecutive years. The Librarian invited borrowing of the several pairs of ski belonging to the Club.

At the Dinner, Geoffrey Young, representing the Alpine Club delivered the following impressive doggerel:

> To think that they can eat, and drink, and talk as us
> These Alexanders of remote Caucasus!
> To think that rocks Circassian have rung
> Beneath the boot nails of a worthier Young!
> To think that other virgin peaks still ring
> With echoes from the hallowed heels of Ling!
> To think, as morn to eve, and night to day turns,
> The torch they kindled with a brighter Ra(y)e burns
> > On seven vanquished peaks
> > In scarce as many weeks!
> To think that they *still* climb, and rest, and talk as us—
> These fellows who have conquered half the Caucasus.

Club Meets

The New Year Meet, which extended for 13 days, including Christmas as well as New Year (*Oh, how I wish!*), was held at Crianlarich with 43 members and 8 guests attending. The weather was, as usual, mixed, with little snow – bad news for the many would-be ski-ers. The Hogmanay Dinner was enlivened by a display of conjuring by Percy Hillhouse. The usual avuncular visits were made to the Ladies Club Meet at Killin. The only climb of any sort was an ascent of Ben Lui's *South Rib* by the Arthur brothers, Backhouse, Raeburn and Goggs on 3rd January. This was the first meet of William Inglis Clark's long Presidency.

The Easter Meet, attended by a stupendous 52 members and 14 guests, was held at Fort William, in the Alexandra and Caledonian Hotels. According to the recorder, the weather, was 'of the worst description' during Easter weekend (9–12 April) but improved for those who lingered until the 17th. There was so much snow on Ben Nevis that the Observatory, now converted to a Hotel, remained hidden below it. Despite this, there were several ascents of *Castle Ridge*, and Raeburn and Tyndale climbed the *North-East Buttress* on the 13th. Several parties traversed the Devil's Ridge in the Mamores. Ling, Sang and Tyndale had an exciting day in *No. 3 Gully* on the 9th. They proceeded unroped to below the cornice, which Tyndale attempted to breach. 'He had only about three feet to go when suddenly the whole top of the gully peeled off, to the depth of two or three feet, and we were all swept down with it. Our axes were torn from us, and we were covered and blinded by the snow. At a steep place where the gully narrows, we were off the ground, then went on in all about 600 feet before we came to rest where the angle eased. We were none of us any worse; we had to grind up again for our axes …' (*Ling's Diary*, Book 11, pp. 48–9).

Easter Meet 1914, Alexandra Hotel, Fort William.
H. MacRobert, Arnold Brown, James C. Thomson, D.A. Clapperton, R.C. Paterson (guest), ?, Robert E. Workman (smoking). Photo: A.K. Reid (Club Image Archive).

The experiment of a Whitsun Meet continued with a visit to Achiltibuie and Inchnadamph Hotels, attended by President Clark, Arthur, Goggs, Johnston, Ling, Menzies, Russell, Sang and Young. A good deal of climbing was done, on Stac Polly, Cul Beag and Mor, Suilven and Quinag. But the most audacious exploit was Ling and Sang's ascent of the *Nose of Sgurr an Fhidleir* on 31 May. From the description in the record of the Meet (presumed to be by Sang), they appear to have climbed up to the Pale Slab, where they were repulsed, and continued, after a right traverse, by vegetatious ledges and a gully on the northern flank of the Nose. On Cul Beag's western cliffs (30 May), Ling, Sang and Goggs climbed 'a well-defined chimney … to the right of [and above – according to Ling] a gully culminating in a prominent green patch' by means of a surprising through route, while Clark and Russell climbed the rocks to its left. It should be possible to locate this, but it doesn't feature in present guides.

Spring

In February, President Clark gave a well-attended lecture about a holiday to the Dolomites, illustrated throughout by his own coloured lantern slides (*J.*, 13, 113, which boasts that 'No such fine series of natural colour slides has been seen in Scotland before').

In early April Goggs organized a five-day traverse of the Knoydart, Glen Dessary and Glenfinnan hills along with Charles Deards and H.M.D. Watson. The journey began by boat to Inverie, and continued on foot to Glenfinnan, bagging Meall Buidhe and Luinne Bheinn, Sgòr na Cìche and Sgòr na Coireachan, and the Streaps along the way. The tour was described in entertaining fashion by Deards ('Knoydart and Glen Dessarry', *J.*, 13, 90–98).

Naismith enjoyed a ski tour in the Alps in late April, where he climbed the Zermatt Breithorn (without the assistance of uplift, naturally!) and the Mettelhorn, before moving to Kandersteg to climb the Wildstrubel. There were several other perhaps less interesting ski tours by members. Indeed, the Journal devoted three pages to these efforts (*J.*, 13, 116–8)

Parker and James Crombie explored the huge vegetatious buttress of Craig Maskeldie on 19 April. Parker also described The Barns of Bynac in detail (*J.*, 13, 177–8) after a visit at the end of June.

Ling began his annual campaign in the Lake District with an ascent of Pillar's Very Severe *North-West Climb* with Raymond Bicknell (who led throughout) and Mabel Capper (*Diary*, Book 11, pp. 53–4). Capper – not related to the well-known namesake suffragette – was an able LAC member who was plainly more than comfortable on Lakeland rock too.

James C. Thomson and J. R. Young spent a productive two days on Skye in early June. From a base in Broadford they climbed *C-D Buttress* on the East Face of Blaven; on the following day they climbed *South-East Route* on the Bealach Tower Buttress of Clach Glas. These were the first efforts here since the explorations of Sydney Williams and the Clarks around 1900. Also in early June, Skye was visited by two gritstone climbers, Henry Bishop & Douglas Yeomans, who climbed *North Gully* in Coire a' Mhadaidh and an extension to Window Buttress known as *Bishop's Climb*, and by Liverpool climbers James B. Burrell & C.N. Cross, who found *Trap Face Route* on Sròn na Cìche.

The Club Abroad

Just as in 1913, the highlight of the summer season was a successful expedition to the Caucasus by Raeburn. Ling and Young were unavailable, and his companions in 1914 were R.C. Richards (C.C. & S.A.C.), H. Scott Tucker (A.C.) and Rembert Martinson, the young Danish-Russian who had performed so well in the 1913 expedition. There is a brief report in *J.*, 13, p. 227 and a lengthy account in *AJ*, 29, 142–58. Raeburn's two diaries of the expedition are in our Archives (items 128 and 129). The party first visited the Tsaya (Zea, Zeh) Valley in the Adai Group, occupying the same camp as in 1913 on 12 July. From a high camp below Uilpata, following a suggestion of Freshfield's, they forced a difficult route to the Uilpata-Songuta col (13,300ft.), easy on the Karagom side. This was one of Raeburn's goals, since no pass between the Tsaya and Karagom glaciers existed. They had hoped to continue to Songuta (14,629ft.), but worsening weather prevented this. The next venture was to reach the North Tsaya Glacier. This glacier – the key to many of the Adai peaks including Uilpata, the highest – is cut off from the lower glacier by a daunting ice-fall which had repelled many attempts, including Raeburn's in 1913. However, Raeburn had corresponded with Vittorio Ronchetti, another Caucasus pioneer of the period, and learned from him of a 'back door' into the North Tsaya reached from the South Tsaya by a gully passing behind Woolley's Rock. Taking this route to the North Tsaya, the glacier was traversed and the southern, higher, of the two Bubis Peaks (14,876ft.) was reached by a couloir.

The expedition then moved valleys westwards to a new base camp on the right moraine of the Karagom glacier, above Dsinago. A high camp at 9000ft. was established on July 28th. From there they climbed a rock peak, Vologata c. 13,700ft., and Karagom East 14,805ft., third highest of the Tsaya-Karagom peaks. They then descended and shifted base west again *via* the Stir-Digor valley to the moraine of the Tana Glacier, arriving at camp on the 31st. From there they climbed Laboda 14,169ft. by its East Buttress. Descending the Stir-Digor valley on 2 August, they got the first news of the impending War. Their convoluted

Stob Ban and Mullach nan Coirean from Sgùrr a' Mhaim, 16-4-1914.
Photo: James R. Young (slightly different from the image in J., 13, op 146).

month-long journey home has been recently described by John Mitchell in 'Harold Raeburn's Journey Home' (*J.* 37, 298–309).

In the Alps, the weather hindered climbing in the first part of July. Later in the month a strong party of Arnold Brown, Ling, MacRobert and Sang visited Cogne, from which they climbed the Grivola, the Herbetet and traversed the Gran Paradiso, all in fairly desperate weather and conditions. Most members' seasons were curtailed by bad weather at the start and War at the end. Young spent almost the whole month of August in the Canadian Rockies and Selkirks. Making use of guides, he climbed The Mitre, Mts Victoria (both peaks), Deltaform and Hungabee, Sir Donald, Tupper, Tomatin and Findhorn. The trials and tribulations of those mentioned and others effecting a return to Britain were described in a lengthy series of Journal notes (*J.*, 13, 228–48). Many were reduced to using a Consulate-provided charter ship, the S.S. Cretic of 13,900 tons 'lying dismantled in Genoa', an emigrant ship with steerage accommodation for 2,000 and an abundant population of rats: most of the passengers slept on deck.

The Journal

Besides those mentioned above or in last year's review, there were several interesting articles in the Journals of the year. In the February number Walter Galbraith introduced the members to the wonders of the Tricouni bootnail (*J.*, 13, 62–3). The October number featured a learned discussion of mountain form ' Hills and Mountains: the Highlands and the Alps' by Marion Newbigin, Editor of the Scottish Geographical Magazine (1902–1934), and a pioneer of modern geography. This was followed by *two* articles competing to praise the virtues of Kinlochleven, 'Kinlochleven and its Surroundings' by Wm. Inglis Clark (illustrated with three of Clark's autochromes, and J.R. Young's very fine portrait of Stob Ban), and 'Notes on the Kinlochleven District' by James C. Thomson.

Robin N Campbell

SCOTTISH MOUNTAINEERING TRUST – 2013
Scottish Charity Number SCO 09117

The Trustees met on 19 April and 18 October 2013. During the course of these meetings, support was given to:
Scottish Council for National Parks; M Gilmour – BSES; Mountaineering Council of Scotland – Mountain Safety Events; Lochaber Mountaineering Club – Steall Hut; R Crawford – Dundee Mountain Film Festival; Mountaineering Council of Scotland – Visually Impaired Course; Beryl Leatherhead – Campaign for Planning Permission for Hill Tracks; John Milne – Scottish Wild Land Group, Scottish Mountaineering Club – Journal; Jonathan Conville Mountaineering Trust – Scottish Winter Courses 2013/14; Mountaineering Council of Scotland – Winter Course; Mike Dixon Research – Tom Patey; T Davenport – Fort William Festival.

For the year to the Club AGM in December 2013 the Trustees were AD Nisbet (Chairman) (Ex Officio Immediate Past President of the SMC), R Aitken, R Anderson (Ex Officio Convener of the Publications Sub-Committee), PJ Biggar, WH Duncan, CM Jones, JRG Mackenzie (Ex Officio President of the SMC), CR Ravey, DN Williams (Ex Officio Editor of the SMC Journal), and D Whalley. With effect from the Club AGM in December 2013 there were the following changes: R Aitken has retired from the Trust by rotation. AF Fyffe is a new Trustee.

The present Directors of the Publications Company are RK Bott (Chairman), BM Whitworth, SL Jenson, CR Ravey and T Prentice (Publications Manager). CR Ravey (who is both a Director of the Publications Company and a Trustee) provides valuable liaison between the Publications Company and the Trust as does R Anderson in his capacity as Convener of the Publications Sub-Committee.

The following grants were committed by the Trustees during 2013:

Scottish Council for National Parks	£ 500
M Gilmour – BSES	£ 250
Mountaineering Council of Scotland – Mountain Safety Events	£4,500
Lochaber Mountaineering Club – Steall Hut Grant	£2,000
Loan	£2,000
R Crawford – Dundee Mountain Film Festival	£1,500
Mountaineering Council of Scotland – Visually Impaired Course	£2,400
Beryl Leatherhead – Campaign for Planning Permission for Hill Tracks	£2,000
John Milne – Scottish Wild Land Group	£1,000
Scottish Mountaineering Club – Journal (p.a. for 3 years) up to	£4,500
Jonathan Conville Memorial Trust – Scottish Winter Courses 2013/14	£1,000
Mountaineering Council of Scotland – Winter Course	£ 920
Mike Dixon – Research – Tom Patey	£ 500
T Davenport – Fort William Festival	£ 500

The Trustees record their gratitude to Bob Aitken (who retired by rotation) for his services to the Trust over a period of the last 7 years. Bob's expertise and guidance have been invaluable.

J.D. Hotchkis

MUNRO MATTERS

By Dave Broadhead (Clerk of the List)

This report covers 1 January to 31 December 2013. The five columns below give number, name and year of Compleation of Munros, Tops and Furths as appropriate. *SMC member, **LSCC member.

No.	Name	Munros	Tops	Furths
5201	Ian W. Desbottes	2012		
5202	Linda Connell	2012		
5203	John O'Brien	2012		
5204	Jos Mahon	2012		
5205	Bob Mahon	2012		
5206	Calum M. McPhee	2013		
5207	Isobel Freeman	2008		
5208	Glenn Evans	2012		
5209	Anna M. Feist	2012		
5210	Ali Welsh	2012		
5211	Catherine Ford	2013		
5212	Alexander D. Bryce	2013		
5213	R. G. Stephenson	2012		
5214	Jesper Jorgensen	2012		
5215	Dave Fussell	2013		
5216	Daniel M. Smith	2013		
5217	Mark J. Smith	2013		
5218	Hugh McNeilage	2002	2005	2005
5219	Frank W. Starkey	2012		
5220	Alex Dalrymple	2013		
5221	Deborah Jane Hall	2013		
5222	James Hall	2013		
5223	David Hughes	2013		
5224	James B. Hoyle	2013		
5225	Sandy Reid	2013	2013	
5226	Drew Lamont	2013		
5227	Malcolm Smith	2013		
5228	Andrew Henderson	2013		
5229	Elaine Edwards	2012		
5230	Carol Fitton	2013		
5231	Les Fitton	2013		
5232	Roger Cook	2013		
5233	Chris Miles	2013		
5234	Stephen Ralph	2012		
5235	Helen Dunford	2013		
5236	Stephen Thomson	2012		
5237	Craig Hull	2013		
5238	Neil W. E. Potter	2013		
5239	David Nisbet	2013		
5240	Andrew D. Hogg	2012		
5241	Valerie Dyer	2012		
5242	Stephen Sears	2013		
5243	David W. Heath	2013		
5244	David Shinn	2013		2013
5245	Tony Thornley	2013		
5246	John K. Kennedy	2013		
5247	David Furness	2013		
5248	Peter Arnold	2013		
5249	Ian Winterflood	2013		
5250	Jonathan Hanson	2013		
5251	Ian Mitchell	2013		
5252	Michael J. Harris	2013		
5253	William N. Lemon	2013		
5254	Susan Watts	2013		
5255	Thomas Mundell	2008		
5256	Sarah Mundell	2013		
5257	Iain Beedie	2013		
5258	Gordon Eccleston	2013		
5259	David Pettit	2013		
5260	Heather Kerr	2004		
5261	Mitch Kerr	2004		
5262	Chris Lodge	2013		
5263	Andy Clifford	2013		
5264	Steve Langton	2013		
5265	Andrew Khaliq	2013		
5266	Jim Robertson	2013		
5267	Margaret Young	2013		
5268	Tim Taylor	2013		
5269	Bronwen Currie	2013		
5270	Lindsay Hemmings	2013		
5271	Bob Hemmings	2013		
5272	John Lyle	2013		
5273	Michael J. Dennis	2013		2013
5274	Neil Young	2013		
5275	Mairie Hughes	2013		
5276	Martin Pippard	2013		
5277	Alistair Ballantine	2013		
5278	Vera Wealleans	1995		
5279	Richard Baker	2013	2013	2013
5280	Stephen Oliver	2013		
5281	R. Mark Tocknell	2013		
5282	Mark Robson	2013		
5283	David Henson	2013		
5284	Justin St. J. Wilkes	2013		
5285	Allan McConnochie	2013		
5286	Ewan Mearns	2013		
5287	Ian J. Young	2013		
5288	Jamie Dobson	2013		
5289	Michael Nash	2013		
5290	Steve Taylor	2013		
5291	Derek Matheson-MacIver	2013		
5292	David A. Scott	2013		
5293	Terence Johnstone	2013		
5294	Andrew Dogett	2013		
5295	Anne Marie McMorrin	2013		

5296	Richard Jones	2013
5297	Richard A. Hynd	2013
5298	Adrian Bergin	2011
5299	Robert Murning	2013
5300	Peter Garner	2013
5301	Mark Bannan	2013
5302	Kathleen Monteverde	2013
5303	Hugh Findlay	2013
5304	Ian M. Shaw	2013
5305	Alasdair Macpherson	2013
5306	Fiona Macpherson	2013
5307	Eileen McLaren	2013
5308	John McLaren	2013
5309	Colin Ross	2013
5310	Nicole Morschett	2013
5211	Godfrey Bancroft	2013
5312	Muriel Abbott	2013
5313	Theo J. M. Beanen	2013
5314	Patrick Revell	2013
5315	Michael H. Chmiel	2013
5316	Alastair Ewen	2013
5317	Alan J. Stewart	2013 2013
5318	Margaret Clair Bale	2010
5319	Andrew R. Anderson	2013
5320	John Sheridan	2013
5321	Jessica E. Crowder	2013
5322	Ian Struthers	2013
5323	Christian Walker	2013
5324	Forbes Manson	2013
5325	Lorraine Shepherd	2013
5326	Kevin Wallace	2013 2013 2013
5327	Gerald Cruickshanks	2013
5328	Carolyn Winter	2013
5329	Andy Green	2013
5330	Richard H. Thomas	2013
5331	Jonathan Orchard	2013
5332	Alex Tuff	2013
5333	Elizabeth J. Taylor	2013
5334	Derek J. Goffin	2013
5335	Geoff Donnelly	2013
5336	Simon Barrett	2013
5337	Leigh-Ann Plenderleith	2013
5338	Graham Slater	2013
5339	Jenifer Dunn	2013
5340	Andy Dunn	2013
5341	Judy Semple	2013
5342	Justin Livesey	2013
5343	David P. Bell	2013
5344	Roger Boston	2013
5345	Margaret Hart	2013
5346	Michael Hart	2013
5347	Arthur Dobson	2013
5348	Peter Dixon	2013
5349	David Cumming	2013
5350	Gordon Picken	2013
5351	Chris Warwick	2013
5352	Anita Laidlaw	2013
5353	Susan Hodgkinson	2013
5354	David Martin	2013

5355	Brian Heaton	2013
5356	Christine Potts	2013
5357	Eric Carruthers	2013
5358	Alistair Ewing	2013
5359	Ross McEwan	2013
5360	Alan S. Hardie	2013
5361	Fiona Priestley	2013
5362	Stuart Clark	2013
5363	Ian Campbell	2013
5364	Patrick Salisbury	2013
5365	George Johnson	2013
5366	Larry Watson	2013
5367	Alistair Dickson	2013
5368	Ian A. Young	2013
5369	Michael Robertson	2013
5370	Dennis Reed	2013
5371	Richard Scroop	2013 2013
5372	Barry Cross	2013
5373	Audrey Latto	2013
5374	Joan Walsh	2013
5375	Sarah Atkinson	2013
5376	Euan Ballantyne	2013
5377	David Spence	2013
5378	Jim Martin	2013
5379	Andrew Jackson	2013
5380	George Swanson	2013
5381	Colin Cowie	2013
5382	Neil Macgillivray	2013
5383	Jack Cooper	2013
5384	Jacqueline Payne	2013
5385	Keith Gaines	2013
5386	Harry Eastman	2013
5387	Ade Kearns	2013
5388	Michael J. Ellery	2013
5389	Elspeth Colburn	2013
5390	Duncan Colburn	2013
5391	John C. T. Rigby	2013
5392	Ian G. Hargreaves	2013
5393	Beverly Bain	2009
5394	Pavel Hubacek	2013
5395	Richard Thornely`	2013
5396	Pete Monk	2013
5397	Amy Ottway	2013
5398	Alastair D. Wood	2013
5399	Daniel Hernon	2013
5400	Robin Forrest	2013
5401	Phil Jolliff	2013
5402	*Alastair Mathewson	2013
5403	Graham Bell	2013
5404	Alexander Edgar	2013
5405	Harry Bach	2013
5406	Caroline Shaw	2013
5407	Ann White	2013
5408	John King	2013
5409	Ray Aiken	2013
5410	Edwin J. Ludlow	2013
5411	David McLennan	2013
5412	Robert Council	2013

5413	Sue Kirkpatrick	2012	5424	Peter G. Ford	2013
5414	David Kirkpatrick	2012	5425	Sandy Taylor	2013
5415	Frank Schyvens	2013	5426	Alison Shepherd	2013
5416	Pete Hamilton	2013	5427	Andrew Shepherd	2013
5417	David Cash	2013	5428	*Gordon Macnair	2013
5418	David F. R. Williamson	2013	5429	Brent Craig	2013
5419	Stephen B. Bell	2013	5430	Thomas L. Wilson	2013
5420	Phil Wilson	2013	5431	Stephen Nussey	2013
5421	Graham Rebecca	2013	5432	Glyn Nussey	2013
5422	Scott Campbell	2013	5433	Kenneth Humphreys	2013
5423	Alan Dow	2013			

Before dipping into the correspondence I always like to do a simple analysis, comparing last years figures (in brackets) as follows: number of new Munroists 233 (248); male 81% (79%); resident in Scotland 60% (63%); couples 11% (18%); average age 54 (52); size of Compleation party 12 (11); time taken 25 (25); *Golden Munroists* 7 (9). This helps to build up a picture of the average Munroist, if such a being were to exist. Looking back in my jotters containing an old fashioned hard copy record, of the 1583 Munroists I have registered since August 2007, 935 reside in Scotland i.e. 59%. I also record the place of residence of Munroists, using the old counties abolished in 1975, which divided Scotland into a convenient 33 shires as follows:

County/shire	Number of Munroists	% Scottish total
Mid Lothian (incl. Edinburgh)	156	17
Lanark (incl.Glasgow)	153	16
Aberdeen	104	11
Fife	68	7
Inverness (incl. Harris)	68	7
Perth	64	7
Angus (incl.Dundee)	41	4
Stirling	33	4
Renfrew	31	3
Ross (incl. Lewis)	30	3
Ayr	28	3
West Lothian	26	3
Argyll	19	2
Dunbarton, Moray	17	2
East Lothian	16	2
Dumfries	7	1
Peebles	7	1
Roxburgh	6	1
Selkirk	6	1
Nairn	5	1
Kincardine, Kinross	4	<1
Caithness, Kirkudbright	3	<1
Banff, Berwick, Bute	2	<1
Sutherland, Wigton	1	<1

No Munroists registered by me from Galloway, Orkney or Shetland but otherwise a good spread across the whole of Scotland. This is a suitable opportunity to mention a small oversight from last year's report. Elizabeth Smith (5048) modestly omitted to mention that she is Conservative List MSP for Mid Scotland & Fife. The first Munroist MSP was of course Murray Tosh (2788) and it is always reassuring that we have some small representation in the corridors of power. Using this geographical theme for a review of the year's most interesting letters, I would also like to highlight the part played by the many local clubs around the country which have helped introduce many of us to the hills and supported hill-goers through their Rounds.

ABERDEEN   Sandy Reid (5225) climbed many of his Munros with *Deeside Hillwalking Club*, Compleating on Beinn Sgritheall accompanied by six registered Munroists plus one unregistered. Jack Cooper's (5383) Compleation on the Inn Pinn 'aided by some young lads from Portree' was made even more exciting when 'I had the pleasure of seeing Finlay Wild running up the east ridge and virtually stepping off the top and free climbing the west ridge – he made it look so easy – on his way to breaking the 3 hour barrier for the whole Cuillin Ridge.' Kevin Wallace (5326) finished his Munros, Tops and Furths in the same year and reflected 'I consider An Teallach and Liathach to be pre-eminent in the List. Being an Aberdonian I have a soft spot for the Queen of Deeside – Lochnagar. A good hill is a fine day out, irrespective of its height. Suilven for instance beats most Munros hands down!'

ANGUS   Michael J. Ellery (5388), having promised to write an article for his club journal, sent me a list of questions but no mention of the name of his club!

AYRSHIRE   *Golden Munroist* Ian A Young (5368) (51 years) finished musing over his Round thus: 'The Munro journey has been a long one, punctuated by periods when I could not easily get to the hills or was tempted away from walking by the excitements of climbing, skiing and other outdoor pursuits. I was asked if I had finished: I think I have actually just started. I don't know a mountain when I have just reached its summit. As Eliot put it; 'in my end is my beginning'.

BUTE   Caroline Shaw (5406) 'decided to climb all the Munros within 3 years to raise funds for Multiple Sclerosis Scotland and raised approximately £5,300.' A fantastic achievement, living on an island with a full time job.

DUMFRIES   John C. T. Rigby (5391) is 'now hoping my grandsons will follow in my footsteps as I have started taking them ages 5 & 6 up some of our local hills and hope to encourage them further and higher.'

EAST LOTHIAN   Stephen Ralph (5234) started with the *Scottish Life Hillwalking Club* and gave an interesting analysis of his Round which is probably fairly typical:

Munros by year	Munros by month		Munros per day
2001 = 1	Jan = 4	Jul = 25	7 = 1 (S. Glen Shiel ridge)
2007 = 8	Feb = 6	Aug = 22	6 = 2 (Fisherfield & Grey Corries)
2008 = 24	Mar = 9	Sept = 40	5 = 7

2009 = 94	Apr = 45 Oct = 8	4 = 18
2010 = 102	May = 58 Nov = 4	3 = 11
2011 = 42	Jun = 59 Dec = 3	2 = 38
2012 = 12		1 = 48

David A. Scott (5292) reported a very windy Compleation on Mount Keen, accompanied by 9 Munroists in the summit party of 36, with 60 family and friends attending the Ceilidh in Edzell afterwards!

FIFE   Ten years ago, recovering from breast cancer, Linda Connell (5202) 'decided to swap pub crawling for Munro bagging' and joined the *Ancrum Hillwalking Club*. Andrew Jackson (5379) with family and friends from the *8 Miles High Mountaineering Club* had a nasty surprise while Compleating on Am Faochagach. 'Unfortunately we were called upon to alert the rescue services as we found a walker who had passed away on the hill due to a heart attack. Although a tragic event, our group consensus was that he had died doing the thing he enjoyed.' Neil Young (5274) started as a sixth-former at Bell Baxter High School, joining *Glenrothes Hillwalkers Club* later in life.

INVERNESS   Nicole Morschett (5310) 'climbed my first Munro while on holiday. One year later I moved from Germany to Inverness and soon got into hillwalking and backpacking.' She is now on a second Round, including Tops, concluding 'it will certainly never get boring and I will never get enough of the Scottish hills!' It is always interesting for me to hear from old friends and former colleagues who I have not seen for many years such as Jenifer (5339) and Golden Munroist Andy Dunn (5340) (50 years) from Kingussie High School and Sarah Atkinson (5375) from the *Inverness Mountaineering Club*. Ross McEwan (5359) remembered re-upholstering my wife's chaise-longue, a family heirloom which still gives good service!

KINCARDINE   Alasdair MacPherson (5305) became another *Amazing Octogenerian*, Compleating on Ben Hope with his daughter Fiona MacPherson (5306) after a 17 year Round together. This feat justified an informative feature in The Press and Journal (2 Oct 2013) which revealed that although born at the foot of the Cuillin, Alasdair did not climb the Inaccessible Pinnacle until he was aged 79. Louis Skinner (2710), Robert Waterston (3210) and Pamela E. Wigston (4408) also Compleated in their eightieth year and all share the distinction of *Munrosis Venerabilis* (oldest Munroists). As well as an easy to remember number, Robert is also *Munrosis Longus* with the record for the longest Round of 69 years. Alasdair wrote to tell me that he and Robert worked together as vets and that Robert 'was my inspiration as I was only half way through them when he Compleated. He will be 90 in April 2014.'

KINROSS   Ian Campbell (5363) just missed out on *Golden Munroist* having climbed his first in 1964 'during a month's 'Outward Bound' course at the Moray Sea School, Burghead.'

LANARK   A very wee weegie, Daniel M. Smith (5216) took over the mantle of Youngest Munroist at the age of 9, having climbed his first Munro aged 6. He

Daniel with his father Mark Smith (5216 & 5217) in the Cuillin, Skye.
They both compleated in Glen Lyon on Meall Buidhe and Stuchd an Lochain.

now has his sights set on Kilimanjaro, no doubt leaving the Corbetts for his old age, when he becomes a teenager! Isobel Freeman (5207) did most of her Munros with the *Glasgow Glenmore Club* and Compleated on Liathach's Mullach an Rathain, 'climbing the final few steps in the Rev. Robertson's boots which a friend had lent me for the occasion.' Glenn Evans (5208) reported a remarkable *Contiguous Compleation* on Ben More (Mull) having 'also completed my final Wainwright and final Welsh 3000s on the same long day, during a solo effort and a bit of fast sleep deprived driving! Starting at 1.30 am in Snowdonia with Elidir Fawr, then on to Black Fell in the Lake District, then to Mull to finish.' *Golden Munroist* David McLennan (5411) (52 years) 'abandoned cycling in favour of climbing in 1963 and Compleated in the company of a dozen fellow members of the *Strathaven Mountaineering Club*.'

MID LOTHIAN Summiting Beinn Fhionnlaidh from Loch Mullardoch with the help of Angus the boatman, David Alexander (508) finished his third Round and is not far off his 1000th Munro. Accompanied by Ian Mackintosh (2937), finishing his second Round and Steve Langton (5264) his first, this is possibly the first 1-2-3 *Simultaneous Compleation*. Terence Johnstone (5293) started his Munros with *Heriot Watt University Mountaineering Club*. Three years ago, with 50 still left to climb, he was diagnosed with early onset Parkinson's Disease and wrote that 'the discipline of continuing with them has had a huge boost to both my morale and my health.' Leigh-Ann Plenderleith (5337) explained her late start on Munros, aged 28, because 'I grew up on a hill farm and was a competitive highland dancer so I was occupied with other hills and highlands until then'.
Euan Ballantyne (5376) finished an interesting summary of his Round with a

rather dubious claim. 'I lived for 7 years in Australia and am a full citizen – do you think I can claim to be the first Aussie to Compleat?' Harry Bach (5405) climbed his last Munro 'in the company of good friends from the *Edinburgh Mountaineering Club.*'

MORAY Gordon Eccleston (5258) of the *Moray Mountaineering Club* is relieved 'to be able to start going on the monthly bus meets without the burden of looking for a Munro to do.' Roger Boston (5344) reported 'all have been climbed solo, including the In Pin on a beautiful summer evening that I had to reverse, as I had no rope. The last 51 were climbed after having both knees replaced in 2010.'

PERTH Fiona Priestley (5361) and Stuart Clark (5362) 'topped out together on Stob Dearg after climbing up Curved Ridge and standing on top of Crowberry Tower. We met through the *Walkhighlands* website on a group walk in Glenshee and were living together 6 months later. On our final Munro summit, surrounded by friends from this website, Stuart surprised Fiona by proposing on bended knee at the summit cairn!' Back in 2009, Beverly Bain (5393) did not think her Compleation on Mullach Fraoch-choire with friends from *Perth JMCS* was important. Unfortunately 'a full hip replacement followed 2 years later & following a problematic recovery, I find myself back out on my beloved hills and now feel I would like to mark the occasion.'

RENFREW Alastair Ewen (5316) Completed on Beinn Sgritheall 'a great day with family and friends. My brother played the pipes for me at the summit. My first Munro was Schiehallion, aged 15, with my brother who was 11 at the time – it was just the two of us, no adults!' Alistair Dickson (5367) was part of a well coordinated *Coincident Compleation* on Beinn na Lap along with Larry Watson (5366), George Johnson (5365) and Patrick Salisbury (5364). Like myself, they had all recently qualified for their bus passes and 'were piped to the summit to the cheers and applause of our families and friends. The celebrations continued that evening with a fine dinner, singsong and telling of tales at the excellent restaurant at Corrour station.' Alistair reminded me we had last met at the renovation of Ollisdale bothy in Skye in 1985!

ROSS Margaret Clair Bale (5318) 'had been encouraged by someone to 'keep an eye' on Corbetts while Munroing' so was able to report Compleation of both in the same year, with less than 20 Grahams still to climb. Another of my neighbours, Lorraine Shepherd (5325) Compleated on Ben Sgulaird which makes me think that we must have one of the highest resident densities of Munroist? Our member Alastair Mathewson (5402) reported views from the summit on 78% of his hill days. He also remembered his best day as 'a winter Cuillin traverse achieved in 1994. Blue skies, perfect conditions, the ridge smothered in névé and a bivi under the Inaccessible Pinnacle; two days spent in a dreamlike trance. Munro bagging never felt more Alpine.'

STIRLING Hugh McNeilage (5218) 'took up walking as a hobby to try and get fit after standing at a bar for many a year.' When he finally got around to writing he reported 4 Munro Rounds plus Tops and Furths. He is presently 'trying to do another Round in memory of my son who we lost in September 2012.'

SUTHERLAND Chris Warwick (5351) Completed with fellow members of the *Oban Mountaineering Club.*

WEST LOTHIAN Margaret Young (5267) Compleated on Ben Klibreck accompanied by a party of 20 ranging in age from 13 to 82 and reported that 'we all stayed at the Altnaharra Hotel who provided us with a magnificent celebratory meal afterwards.' Alexander Edgar (5404) described how he 'put a pound in a piggy bank every time I bagged a Munro so at the end I had £284 and bought all my friends and some family some drinks.'

ENGLAND & WALES County of residence information will have to wait for a future report. Jacqueline Payne (5384) started her Round with 'Slioch closely followed by Beinn Alligin and An Teallach. Definitely a baptism of fire for a beginner.' Her Compleation on Ben Lomond sounded no less dramatic. 'Accompanied by my family and 24 other walkers – 13 of whom are also Compleatists. We started in low cloud and drizzle and summited in sunshine, with a cloud inversion and several Brocken Spectres. It was magnificent.' Ali Welsh (5210) 'had walked up about 70 when I decided to run up the remaining Munros, taking advantage of early retirement....I Compleated on Slioch during the Slioch Horseshoe hill race.' He is now running round the Corbetts, 'finding them much harder than the Munros.' R. G. Stephenson (5213) 'made the annual pilgrimage to Scotland with *Keswick Athletic Club*' until aged 67, deciding not to waste any more time, he used a campervan to make 'a concentrated attack' on his remaining 167 summits. Now he is busy on Bill Birkett's *Lakeland Fell Almanac* of 541 tops over 1,000 feet and the Nuttalls 335 *Tarns of Lakeland*. James B. Hoyle (5224) notes that 'with respect to plans for the future, my wife is currently devising my next challenge – 282 things which need attention around

Tim Taylor (5268) sits on his final summit – Meall Buidhe, Knoydart – 16 March 2013.

the home.' Tony Thornley (5245) 'managed to wear the same anorak for the first and last mountains which may be a record for 45 years (double ventile – still windproof and highly absorbent).' He was accompanied by *Golden Munroist* David Furness (5247) (56 years) who noted that he had 'accompanied my father Eric L. Furness (340) on a significant portion of his Munros'. Not all sons are so dutiful – Jonathan Hanson (5250) was joined by his wife and daughter but reported 'my 16 year old son preferred to stay at home under the guise of revising for his GCSEs. It became clear he had organized a party when we were phoned by our next door neighbour!' Peter Arnold (5248) was accompanied by 'thirteen other members of the *Christian Walking Club*', Susan Watts (5254) by twenty six other members of the *Ibex Mountain and Hillwalking Club* and Ian G. Hargreaves (5392) by 18 family, friends and members of the *Gritstone Club*. Patrick Revell (5314) reported 'over the course of 9 years I made 14 backpacking expeditions, each concentrating on Munros in different parts of the Highlands, using public transport to travel up from Southampton and get around Scotland.' For more details see <www.munros.patrickrevell.me.uk>. Vera Wealleans (5278) explained the 17 year delay in reporting her Compleation thus 'I decided to register after having had a job interview. The interviewer said the panel were all intrigued and wanted to know what Munro and Corbett bashing was! I spent a good part of the allotted time explaining the finer points of this pastime and got the job.' I often receive copies of hill logs, diaries, spread-sheets etc all of which go into the National Library of Scotland archive along with the letters. There is a PhD there for someone, sometime. Richard H. Thomas (5330) condensed details of his entire 38 year Round, including hills and companions on to a handwritten card including a striking summit silhouette on the cover entitled "THE MUNROS This is my round". Fantastic draftsmanship and a real work of art. Andy Clifford (5263) gave a very neat summary of the appeal of the Munros, explaining 'my mountaineering and canoeing expeditions have taken me all over the globe several times, with the exception of Antarctica. There is nowhere else on the planet that equals the Scottish Highlands for beauty, impact, geology, geography, history, culture and…. Fun! It has been a privilege to enjoy the Highlands, share them with family and friends and meet so many great people.' Graham Bell (5403) explained that he gives 'an illustrated talk on 'Munro bagging' which I call 'Eyes to the Hills', so far on more than 20 occasions and any fee I receive I donate to the John Muir Trust.' Edwin J. Ludlow (5410) reported something of an epic while Compleating with a winter traverse of the Aonach Eagach when both his companions broke their crampons and he dropped his ice axe. Clearly not lacking in experience, he mentioned also having climbed Island Peak, Pumori, Mustagh Ata and had reached 7900m on the North side of Everest. Godfrey Bancroft (5311) became another *Golden Munroist* (50 years) and similarly Gordon Macnair (5428), to my knowledge the first club member to become a *Golden Munroist*, having stretched his Round to 50 years. Many of his companions on the way were able to join him to celebrate Compleation on Ben More (Mull) for which a former President composed *A Ballad*, including the stanza *'Others have been here before/Gordon is number 5 thousand one hundred and 74'*. Gordon was a bit slow in writing in, so I had to change this to *'Others have been here, so by fate/Gordon is number 5 thousand 4 hundred and 28'*.

IRELAND Kathleen Monteverde (5302) reported requiring 'exactly 40 trips from Northern Ireland' explaining 'in 2001 I climbed Kilimanjaro where I met my future husband, Mervyn Picken (4570) who had 60 Munros done. I had heard of them but needed someone to do them with so Munros brought us together and we married in 2006.' David Spence (5377) from County Down originated from Kilmarnock. A former member of the *Glasgow JMCS*, he was joined for his Compleation on Liathach's Mullach an Rathain by number of old friends who have progressed into the senior Club. Jim Martin (5378) from County Dublin is also 'currently walking the Camino de Santiago over three stages.'

OVERSEAS   Jesper Jorgensen (5214) is the first Danish national Munroist, though he lives and works in Britain. Theo J. M. Beunen (5313), a Dutchman from The Hague, Compleated on An Teallach with Graham Rebecca (5421) and five friends from *Deeside Hillwalking Club*. Having climbed 223 Munros alone, Theo wrote that 'this party was very special for me with champagne and whisky at the top.' Also living in Holland for the past 16 years, Alan J. Stewart (5317) started his Munros while working in Dulnain Bridge. Pavel Hubacek (5394) from the Czech Republic lives in Glasgow and became the first Czech Munroist when he Compleated on Sgurr na Banachdich. He wrote 'I have already started my second Round. Nowadays I walk sometime with some Czechs and Slovaks living in Scotland that I found on Facebook. My special thanks belong to Steve Fallon. I followed most of his routes as he described them on his website.' Now living in France, *Golden Munroist* Alastair D. Wood (5398) (54 years) explained his long Round because 'I have been living and working outside Scotland since 1967 when I had only 18 Munros left to climb. My next was climbed in 2010 when I was informed that due to revisions in the Tables I still had 28 to do, not the 18 I had anticipated!' Although living in Clackmannanshire, Frank Schyvens (5415) is the first Belgian Munroist. His Round got off to a poor start on the Aonach Eagach when he and another Belgian friend had to be rescued by the Glencoe Mountain Rescue Team.

AMENDMENTS

The eight columns give number, name and year of each Compleation of Munros, Tops, Furths, Corbetts, Grahams and Donalds.

Num	Name	M	T	F	C	G	D
1933	Dave Irons	1998	2005	2005	2010		
997	Lindsay D. Munro	1991			2005		
		2000					
		2012					
998	Roderick C. Munro	1991			2005		
		2000					
		2012					
2463	Martin Likeman	2000	2012	2008	2004		
		2010					
4923	Paul Keen	2011		2012			
3873	Catherine B. Waddell	2007			2012		
1432	Karl Nelson	1995	1995	1996	2009	2009	2009
		2009	2009	2010			

Num	Name	M	T	F	C	G	D
4625	Jim Bull	2010					2013
3535	David Jeffery	1999	1999		2013		
2761	Pamela Black	2002			2013		
1807	Alan J. Black	1997			2013		
1564	David Spencer	1996		1994	2004	2012	
1911	Martin J. Almond	1997 2006	1997		2012		2013
2956	Roger Reeves	1993	2003		2013		
2475	Alan Sewell	2000		2002	2013		
147	Ron Davie	1976 1982			1994	2013	2012
2414	Chris Crocker	2000	2000	1992	2013		
1529	Richard R. Cooper	1994			2011	2005	
508	David Alexander	1986 2000 2013					
2937	Ian McIntosh	2003 2013					
358	Michael B. Slater	1984 1988 1990 1993 1996 1999 2003 2008	1987	1987 2009 2011 2013			
1757	Tony Baker	1997 2013	2008				
2669	Brian Mucci	2001	2005		2013		
2670	Alison Claxton	2001	2005		2013		
3217	Ian K. Ratcliffe	2004 2011			2013		
3783	Alan Taylor	2006			2009	2013	
3112	Bert Barnett	2001 2001 2009 2012	2002 2009	2002 2007	1998 2007 2013	2000 2009	2012 2013
225	Alan L. Brook	1980 2002	1980 2002	1978	2004	2013	2010
3139	Alan J. Winchester	2004	2013				
4305	Michael Earnshaw	2009	2013	2010	2011	2012	2011
3423	Trefor Beese	2005	2013	2008			
2531	Katherine Heal	2001	2000		2013		
2532	Mathew Heal	2001	2000		2013		
399	Ian T. Stalker	1985 2013					
707	Robert F. Gibson	1989	1996		2013		
62	*Hamish M. Brown	1965 1969	1965	1967 1969	1976	2013	1982

Num	Name	M	T	F	C	G	D
		1970		1971			
		1974		1978			
		1975		1979			
		1979					
		1984					
3438	Hazel Strachan	2005					2011
		2008					2012
		2010					2012
		2012					
		2013					
1169	Garth B. Fenton	1993		1994	2010		2013
2918	Martin D. Knott	2003			2013		
4476	Valerie Inglis	2009					
		2012					
1806	Ross Gervis	1997	2012	2011	2010		2011
		2013					
1915	John S. Dickson	1997		1989	2013		
2556	Dave Liddle	2001			2013		
2641	Alan G. Duncan	2001		2005	2013		
3054	Geoff Sutton	2003		2013			
2959	Roger Squires	2003			2010	2013	
4120	Frank Johnstone	2003			2011		
		2013					
2795	Maria R. Hybszer	2002		2013	2006	2012	2012
		2010					
3460	Bob Stewart	2005			2013		
2943	Donald R. Sutherland	2003		2013	2006	2011	2010
1258	Michael Hanlin	1993	1998	2013			2008
5287	Ian J. Young	2013	2013				
2183	Murdo McEwan	1999		2013	2012		
1318	Catherine S. Gray	1994			2004	2013	
1319	Robert P. Gray	1994			2004	2013	
		2010					
1621	Mhairi Ross	1996			2013		
1622	James Ross	1996			2013		
4396	Mark Gibson	2009	2013				
2624	**Lisa Silver	2001			2013		
2890	John Wright	2003			2013		
2494	**Rhona B. I. Fraser	1984	1995	1997	1990	2003	2000
		1994	2013		1998		
		2000			2006		
		2013					
941	Wal Clarke	1990			2012		
3987	Colin Lees	2004	2012	2013			
		2007					
		2011					
1568	Richard Bryan	1996			2006		
		2013					
3141	Peter D. Cottam	2004	2002		2013		

Num	Name	M	T	F	C	G	D
2261	Martin Cole	1993 1999			2010		2013
3211	Margaret Squires	2004			2010	2013	
1951	Margaret Prentice	1998			2013		
2147	Neville Cohen	1992	1992		2013		
256	Hugh F. Barron	1981 2006	1997	1988	2002	2013	2010
5057	Robert Phillips	2012			2013		
3833	Murray Papworth	2001	2001	2001	2013		
3885	David S. Batty	1994 2011	2011	2013			
3786	Douglas Stuart	2007			2013		
5009	Max Landsberg	2012	2013				
1933	Dave Irons	1998	2005	2005	2010	2013	
4006	Chris Pine	2007			2012	2013	
5320	John Sheridan	2013					2013
382	Roger Stonebridge	1985	2013				
3785	Jim Robertson	2007	2013				
455	A. Laurence Rudkin	1986 1996 2006 2013	1991	1989	1995	2005	

This year I received 82 amendments, compared with 89 in 2012. One interesting issue carried over from last year concerns a letter from John Farrow (1526) reporting his Corbett Compleation. He also commented 'I am currently Secretary of the *Rucksac Club* of which J. Rooke Corbett was an active founder member. We work on the assumption that he completed the Round in 1939.' The years of Corbett's first Corbett Round Compleation has always been uncertain, with 1943 being favoured by some authorities, so I immediately emailed asking for evidence to back up this interesting claim. My query was passed on to Gordon Adshead (590) and Roger Booth (462) who have a detailed knowledge of the achievements of *Rucksac Club* members. Unfortunately neither has been able to shed any more light on the matter, so the mystery continues.

Five couples reported together, compared with six in 2012. Brother and sister Lindsay D. Munro (997) and Roderick C. Munro (998) reported finishing a third Munro Round together, all ending on Ben Wyvis. On Compleation of his second Munro Round on Mount Keen, Ian T. Stalker (399) was presented with a belated Compleation Certificate by his daughter Kirstin, 28 years after finishing his first Round. I do not issue certificates in advance or for subsequent Rounds, but am always happy to register rounds or issue a first Munro or Corbett certificate no matter how long after the event. Tony Baker (1757) reported during his second Munro Round 'whilst staying at the Camas Lunie bunkhouse in Glen Elchaig I had the pleasure and privilege of staying for two nights with Miles Hutchinson (23) who at 87 is the earliest and eldest living Munroist. He is currently working his way through the Marilyns and was an absolute inspiration.' Regular correspondent Hazel Strachan (3438) Compleated a 5th Munro Round on Glas Maol and wrote 'I think this Round has been my favorite Round. Lots of great days out, especially in winter. Highlight was a two day traverse of the Cuillin in June when the cloudy weather cleared to expansive views.'

Roger Stonebridge (382) added the Tops finishing on Little Pap, Lochnagar, and sent me a photocopy of a personal handwritten letter from the then Clerk of the List, Bill Brooker, acknowledging his original Munro Round in 1985. Changed days with the advent of word processing! Max Landsberg (5009) added the Furths when he climbed Galtymore. He also included an interesting analysis of our completion data available on his blog at <www.callofthemountains. blogspot.co.uk> where I learned that he has also written a book *Call of the Mountains* describing his Munro Round and launched at Watersons in London in October. Colin Lees (3987) finished his Furths on Scafell with *Dunfermline Walking Club*. Michael B. Slater (358) celebrated his new hip with a fourth Round of Furths, finishing on Knocknapeasta.

Corbetteer Catherine B. Waddell (3873) started hill-walking with *Paisley Ramblers Association*. Robert F. Gibson (707) reported his last Corbett, Ben Lair and noted he had lived near Muir of Ord many years before, recounting 'I once went out with the *Inverness Mountaineering Club* but I find club types keep stopping all the time.' John S. Dickson (1915) finished his Corbetts on Beinn Tarsuinn on Arran and remembered his first was Ben Ledi, climbed in 1962 by steam train to Callender on the Edinburgh-Oban Line. Dave Liddle (2556) finished his Corbetts on Creag nan Gabhar accompanied by a number of friends from *Turriff Hillwalking Club*, while Alan Duncan (2641) did likewise on Streap on a *Moray Mountaineering Club* week-end. Peter D. Cotham (3141) finished his Corbetts with The Cobbler, accompanied by 17 others, including 9 Corbetteers and 8 Grahamists who managed to get through a bottle and a half of Oban Malt on the summit! Springbank was the celebratory dram enjoyed by Martin Cole (2261) and party of 8 plus dog finishing his Donalds on Molls Cleuch Dod. 'Yes, the dog does like whisky! Margaret Squires (3211) finished her Grahams on Stac Pollaidh and let slip that her Marilyn total currently stands at an impressive 1258.

Full House is achieved by completing all six of the lists recorded on the website. Bert Barnett (3112) reported a second Round of Donalds, finishing on King's Seat, making him only the second person, after Ken P. Whyte (319) to achieve an amazing second *Full House*. Meanwhile the indefatigable Hamish M. Brown (62) became only the second SMC *Full House* after Mike Dixon (959). He wrote, on a characteristic postcard of Jbel Toubkal, 4167m, summit of the Atlas, 'At long last I can record completing the Grahams on Beinn Mhor (Loch Eck). Not an easy doing once they resurfaced as a possibility (I'm into my 80th year) but it helps to be a bloody minded Fifer!' Also achieving *Full House*, Alan L. Brook (225) finished his Grahams on Carn nan Tri-tighearnan, followed a few days later by Michael Earnshaw (4305) who finished his Tops on Sron na Lairige. The last one in 2013 and the 28th recorded so far was achieved by Hugh F. Barron (256) who finished his Grahams on Beinn na Muice, accompanied by his mother, aged 80 and his youngest son, aged 12. SMCJ Editor Noel Williams was also present but apparently 'had to dash off to Glen Coe to attend an SMC meeting at Lagangarbh.'

Showing similar dedication to my Club duties I am always very pleased to hear from anyone who would like their achievements added to our six lists. Please write to Dave Broadhead, Cul Mor, Drynie Park North, Muir of Ord, IV6 7RP. For a Munro or Corbett Compleation Certificate, please enclose an A4 sae

Hugh Barron (256) – in red – compleats his Grahams and a Full House on the summit of Beinn na Muice, 20 October 2013.

(with the correct postage please). Check <smc.org.uk> for further details and to view the picture gallery of Munroists and Corbetteers celebrating on their final summit.

Enjoy your hills.

Dave Broadhead
Clerk of the List

*****

CLIMBING THE KERRY 'FURTHS'

By Gordon Jarvie

A brief background note to this 2002 expedition is perhaps relevant. My climbing partner and I were both Munro-baggers of sorts, and both of us needed to compleat the five 'furths' in Co Kerry in order finally to get Ireland ticked off and under our belts. We had both (separately) climbed Lugnaquilla in Co Wicklow and the Galtee Mountain in Co Tipperary many years earlier, myself as long ago as the early 1960s and Steven in the 1990s. So, all we had left to achieve was the cream of the Irish crop. Readers will probably know these comprise three walks, covering the stand-alone Brandon Mountain halfway down the Dingle Peninsula; plus two walks for the four furths that make up the two horseshoe ridges of Macgillycuddy's Reeks. These horseshoes converge at the summit of Carrauntoohil, Ireland's highest hill.

The trick is, of course, as with all mountaineering expeditions in the British Isles, to catch some favourable weather. That is no easier to orchestrate for three back-to-back walks in Co Kerry than for any other area. In fact it seems harder to guarantee, because the Kerry hills are so far away from Scotland. If you're only nipping down the road from Limerick, say, you can wait for a good forecast and then make your lightning strike to Kerry and take full advantage of any favourable weather that's going. Whereas, if you're taking two and a bit full days (car and ferry) merely to get to your base camp, there's no saying what kind of weather conditions will be awaiting you when you eventually arrive to start Walk 1 far less Walk 3 several days later. But our arrival on a sunny evening was promising. Fingers were crossed for good weather, and we found a good B&B beside the main road from Moll's Gap to Kenmare town.

In the event, we were extremely lucky with the weather. Day 1 on Brandon Mountain was good after the early-morning cloud cleared, with visibility perfect by midday. Day 2 was a bit iffy, although it had cleared by the time we got off a cloudy Carrauntoohil onto the col (top of Hag's Glen) at the start of the eastern ridge to Cnoc na Peiste – so we were lucky enough to do the ridge in reasonable visibility. We took it easy and had a non-climbing day for doing the tourist bit on Day 3. Day 4 was the best of the lot for hilltop weather conditions.

How many 'baggers' regard expeditions to faraway places like the hills of Kerry as a chore or a nuisance? Quite a few probably. That is a shame. Do them when it suits you, or when you're good and ready. Take enough time properly to enjoy them. Do them as a special treat and a delight, even if you wait forty years to do them. We allotted them a full week, enjoying brief forays among the Twelve Bens of Connemara as well as a climb of Ben Bulben (Co Sligo) on our return journey to Scotland. The poem below tries to capture some of the pleasure of the expedition.

'We', by the way, are Gordon Jarvie (Munroist 2647) and Steven Fallon (Munroist 1045, and currently the person who has compleated most Munro rounds). Gordon's Climber's Calendar (Loose Scree, 2007) is a record in poetry of some of his Munro climbs. Steven's Classic Hill Runs and Races in Scotland (Pocket Mountains, 2009) is a well-illustrated and comprehensive practical guide suitable for novices and experienced hill runners.

FOUR DAYS IN KERRY

I Brandon Mountain (13 July 2002)

Exceptional weather. An Aegean blue
from Smerwick harbour hurts the eye. The Dingle Way
jinks in and out of view around the bay.

The old cart-track of the Saint's Road climbs steadily.
Marked out with moist cairns and white crosses,
it guides us through the mosses and a cloud inversion

to emerge on the rocky lump called Brandon Mountain.
Views of the long curve of Brandon Bay stretch beyond

and an open moor slants up toward Brandon Peak.

The Pilgrim's Route looks an interesting scramble,
and tomorrow two questing souls may clamber
past dewy fuchsia hedges to do a close appraisal.

II Macgillycuddy's Reeks, Part 1 (14 July 2002)

Today is misty so instead we tackle Carrauntoohil
from the east, leaving the car at Kate Kearney's cottage.
A parking fee is charged: nice little earner.

The route follows Hag's Glen and the Devil's Ladder:
an eerie coincidence of spooky names in slapping fog,
as all the way a wet wind taunts with wreaths of mist,
and right to the summit of Ireland's highest hill
there's hardly any view, boo-hoo.

The cloud lifts here and there. We begin to see
bits of where we've been, bits of the horseshoe
we're headed to. Stacks on a knife-edge ridge
to Knocknapeesta look like a good scramble
and then we see our route along the scree.

Too soon we're on our final rocky top
complete with holy niche and grotto to guide us
safely off the hill, back down and into the glen.

III Interval (15 July 2002)

A day off, easy
to slip into tourist mode
along the long arm
of the Beara Peninsula,
across the Destitution Road
and down to little villages
with great big names
like Castletown Berehaven,
complete with gift shops
and harbour coffee bar.

Later, at Beara's end
we gaze across the water
at fields on Dursey Island

with its swinging cable car
slung across a choppy strait.
We're tempted to go over
but we're here for the hills,
so we decide against,
and leave Dursey for another day:
Dursey unvisited.

IV Macgillycuddy's Reeks, Part 2 (16 July 2002)

The western horseshoe of the famous Reeks
is a fine arc linking tops and three main peaks.
Dame Fortune smiles upon a flawless Kerry day
of sun and breeze. From Skregmore to Caher,
scrambling Beenkeragh's boulders and jagged arête
we take life easy-peasy, and enjoy it all the way.

For the second time in three days
we clamber onto Carrauntoohil's peak,
still rejoicing at the day's clement weather
and the peerless views we have in all directions.

I got the first of my Irish 'Munros' in 1962
and today on Caher I climb my last.
In a sense, this is a long-awaited day –
forty years a-questing, but why hurry.

Other gems shine down the years along the way:
not one but two Slieve Snaghts in Donegal,
forby the fine twin peaks of Muckish and Errigal;
the Tyrone sisters called Bessy Bell and Mary Gray;
Sligo's bold Ben Bulben on another fine and windy day.

Concentrating, I contemplate a roll-call of Irish hills.
They stretch across a life. I mind them all.

PROCEEDINGS OF THE CLUB

The following mountaineers were admitted as members of the Club at the Committee Meeting of October 2013. We welcome:

DANIEL BAILEY (39), Journalist, Aberdour, Fife.
MARK W GORIN (36), Architect, Glasgow.
KAREN LATTER (48), Company Secretary, Alyth, Perthshire.
STUART MCFARLANE (31), Postman, Stevenston, Ayrshire.
HELEN RENNARD (35), Social Worker, Fort William.
SIMON YEARSLEY (50), Company Director, Bankfoot, Perthshire.

And at the Committee Meeting of April 2014:

ROBERT M ADAMS (30), Telecomms Manager, North Shields, Tyne & Wear.
KAREN A CAMERON (32), Research Scientist, Montrave, Fife.
P ROSS COWIE (36), Environmental Protection Officer, Almondbank, Perth.
PETER W MAYHEW (54), Conservation Manager RSPB, Inverness.
FIONA J L REID (40), Consultant, Edinburgh.
GUY N STEVEN (27), Mountaineering Instructor, Fort William.

The One-Hundred-and Twenty-Fifth AGM and Dinner
7 December 2013

A combination of wet weather in the hills and the prospect of a memorable talk swelled the numbers at the afternoon presentation. Needless to say we were not disappointed as Sandy Allan showed slides and short videos of his traverse of Nanga Parbat starting up the Mazeno Ridge and descending by the Normal Route of the north flank. This was completed with fellow member Rick Allen in 2012 and in recognition of this achievement they were awarded the Piolets d'Or. Sandy was too modest and seemed to refer to the traverse as just an 18 day multiple Munro-bagging trip. However the audience knew and were amazed at the commitment needed to undertake such a climb.

To bring us back the sea level, the club then held the 125th AGM. First significant information was that the printing of the journal had been completed overseas at a substantial cost saving, but now the full consignment of journals were delayed in the docks of Mumbai by a strike! Members were assured they should be delivered in the next few weeks. Mention was also made of a possible Alpine meeting in 2014, probably combined with the Alpine Club and the Fell & Rock CC. Finally the Northern District of the club has been able to restart with a series of winter talks.

At times members may think little changes when it comes to Dinners. We struggle to find a venue that can take the number of diners required and that is able to provide sufficient accommodation. This year we were back at the Ben Nevis Hotel in Fort William but a pleasing change was that our guest speaker was able to accept his invitation. Twice Peter Gillman has been billed to appear and twice he's been unable to join us, once due to being snow bound in London and last year due to a broken leg. However this year he made it. Peter has a long history of links with members of the Club including Tom Patey and Dougal Haston. However the main theme of his speech was information that has recently come to light concerning George Mallory's first climbing experiences on Ben Nevis in April 1906 at the age of 19. Diaries and minutes from Winchester School's 'Ice Club' showed that Mallory took part in numerous winter climbs on the Ben over a period of 10 days all done without prior knowledge of any earlier ascents. And all were undertaken from their accommodation in Fort William. These climbs included an ascent of North-East Buttress and Ledge Route.

Sunday was another wet day. The President delegated the responsibility for the President's Walk to the Vice-President and a small number of members, one guest and one dog made their way along the Steall Gorge, snacked at the Steall ruin in Glen Nevis and then returned. Many more congregated at the indoor climbing option in Kinlochleven. Even Mallory might have made the same indoor choice.

Chris Huntley

Lakes Meet, Robertson Lamb Hut, Langdale
6–8 September 2013

The early arrivals gathered from mid-afternoon on the Friday but the weather was poor and walking to and from Sticklebarn for an enjoyable group pub meal was about the extent of activity.

Saturday brought more poor weather with wild wet and windy conditions interspersed with short spells of utterly vile though some clearances in the afternoon produced fine rainbows to lift sodden spirits. A variety of lower level fells and walks were completed including: Lingmoor Fell complete with an entertaining squeeze through a narrow rock cleft, a traverse of Rossett Pike, a combined walk and steamer trip at Ulswater and even some open water swimming in Lake Coniston by two hardy CC guests.

As always, the Saturday night dinner was a triumph cooked and served with great panache by Dick and his brigade of commis chefs.

Sunday finally brought an improvement in the weather and despite the pervious rain, the preceding period of drought meant that some of the lower crags were dry enough to climb in the morning though some drizzle and showers returned early afternoon. Ascents included some of the finely positioned routes of Upper Scout Crag and the polished horrors of Lower Scout Crag. Two parties visited Gouther Crag in remote and wild Swindale and both ascended the excellent Fang (MVS). Impressively, the second group were the ones who spend the morning on Upper Scout Crag.

Most of the remaining attendees headed for Jack's Rake on Pavey Ark with three reaching this by Crescent Climb and others scrambling up the Rake and on to Harrison Stickle. A couple of this group visited some prospective crags with new routes and were in time to see the second ascent of a new HVS – a good effort in the conditions!

Another group visited the two Scout crags to view and photograph the action and then took a trip up White Ghyll.

Stuart Murdoch on Cub's Crack (HS,4b), Lower Scout Crag, Langdale.
Lakes Meet, Sept 2013. Photo: Dick Allen.

Lakes Meet 2013

Back row (on benches) L–R: Ian Crofton; Mark Hudson; Bob Appleyard (guest); Peter Sterling (guest); David Jenkins; Maureen Suess (guest); Colin Stead; Des Rubens.
Middle row (standing): Pete Betess (guest); John Wood; Cam Forrest; Pippa Cocker; Laetitia Sterling (guest); Jane Murdoch; Mike Cocker; David Broadhead; Stuart Murdoch.
Front row (sitting): Dick Allen; David Stone; Ian Gray (guest); Max Biden (guest) Photo: David Stone. Not included: Hamish Brown.

Members: David Stone, Hamish Brown, Stuart Murdoch, Jane Murdoch, Des Rubens, David Broadhead, John Wood, Colin Stead, Dave Jenkins, Cam Forrest, Mike Cocker, Pippa Cocker, Mark Hudson, Ian Crofton, Dick Allen.
Guests: Bob Appleyard , Pete Bettess , Max Biden, Ian Gray , Laetitia Sterling, Pete Sterling , Maureen Suess.

Ski Mountaineering Meet, The Raeburn Hut, Laggan
8–9 March 2014

Friday night saw club members and guests gradually arrive at the Scottish Mountaineering Club Raeburn hut on the A889 between Dalwhinnie and Laggan (G.R. NN 6360). They came from the south and west of the country. Discussion then centred on the prospects of skiing at all, given the weather forecast and in anticipation of poor conditions continued, well-oiled, long into the night.

On Saturday morning Ann, Colwyn Dave and Niel found, to their collective relief, that the Cairngorm ski road was closed owing to storm force winds in the ski car park. Now free from the tyranny of crossing the 4000m contour, they eventually headed north of the village of Carrbridge and from the west of the B9007, set off walking through Aucherteang farm, an intervening bothy and climbed to the springy, lichen covered summit of Carn Glas-choire (659m, grid ref NH892292). The ascent was simple enough but the increasing altitude was accompanied by substantially higher wind speeds which made standing by the triangulation pillar for any length of time, something of a trial. They headed east along the ridge to Creag na h-Iolaire (552m) and continued their wind assisted descent enjoying a refreshing drink in Carrbridge and a trip to the local general store to buy bulk supplies of domestic matches, prior to their return to the hut.

Team Peden (including Paul from Bavaria), Thomson, Walker, Shackleton and Ravey decided to use maximum height advantage gained through mechanical means from the A9 and attack Geal-charn (917m) from Balsporran Cottages through a curtain of driving rain. Skis were donned at the snow line at approximately 731m (apart from Anthony who continued walking upwards apparently in search of drier snow…) and height was gained in true SMC style with individuals fanning out in all directions and disappearing into the ever increasing wind and clag. Debate over whether they were at the summit was confused by those with global positioning satellite equipment, which meant that they spent longer than needed in the blasting wind and rain having to explore alternative indeterminate high points. The true summit eventually attained was similarly bleak. The ensuing joy of descending resulted in loss of navigational concentration which was only rectified when they emerged from the mist. Lunch in what felt like relatively sub-tropical temperatures, and lower altitude delayed their return until 14:00 hours. The attraction of a second Munro in the afternoon was insufficient to overcome the lure of the fleshpots and they retreated to the luxury of rehydrating in a local coffee shop.

Sunday dawned brighter and perhaps less windy with most of the attendees heading back down to the nearby western Drumochter hills. We heard later that the access road to the Cairngorm mountain ski area was again closed owing to high winds. With a selection of cars at either end of the hills allowing good access, and skis on at 503m, there followed a traverse of Sgairneach Mhor

(991m), Beinn Udlamain (1010m) and A' Mharconaich (975m) with a fine descent back down to the 470m contour and a short bogtrot back to a car.

Messers Craig and Eaton reported a great if short day out on Geal-charn (917m). They enjoyed a good ski up the ridge, as pioneered the previous day, followed by a lovely run back down in the better visibility and softer snow; Sunday was without doubt the better day!

The Drumochter hills feature yet again in an SMC ski mountaineering meet report. The result was another successful ski meet, despite the weather and snow conditions, rather than because of them.

Members: Chris Cartwright, Dave Eaton, Colwyn Jones, Ann MacDonald, John Peden, Chris Ravey, Jim Thomson, Brian Shackleton, Anthony Walker.
Guests: Paul Bueching, Niel Craig, Jamie Peden, Mandy Peden.

Colwyn M Jones

Easter Meet, Kinlochewe Hotel, Torridon
24–27 April 2014

Members and guests returned to a favourite watering-hole, the Kinlochewe Hotel, for the traditional Easter gathering of the Club where exclusive occupation of the premises ensured the best of service from our hosts, Andrew and Gail Staddon. Unfortunately, the weather was not so kind to begin with; cool temperatures, showers and low cloud resulting in fewer visits to the higher crags. Conviviality was thus the order of the day and a splendid Friday evening was hosted by John Hay in his charming house at Annat on the shores of Loch Torridon. But the steeps were not forgotten altogether and hills ascended included Sgùrr Choinnich, Sgùrr a' Chaorachain, Slioch, Liathach by the Northern Pinnacles, Beinn Alligin, A' Ghlas Bheinn in Kintail and the rocky little peak of An Sgùrr at Kishorn. Many single-pitch routes were also climbed on the low level crags at Moy, Diabaig, the Inveralligin sea-cliffs, Stone Valley, Loch Tollaidh, the Tollaidh Crags and the exotically named Aztec Tower near Gairloch.

And so to dinner on Saturday evening. Recalling their pre-selected choices was a trial for some members but the Secretary's computer print-out was on hand and one of the best Easter meals in memory was served. The Malcolm Slesser Memorial Whisky Fund has unsurprisingly long been exhausted but nevertheless bottles of malt appeared as if by magic and the President toasted the Club and absent friends. One member missed the dinner to appear on stage in Inverness but dutifully reappeared on Sunday morning in good spirits if a little hoarse.

Those attending the meet were the President, John R G Mackenzie, R Aitken, P J Biggar, P V Brian, D J Broadhead, H M Brown, R D M Chalmers, G Cohen, Helen G S Forde, C Forrest, J R R Fowler, P W F Gribbon, J Y L Hay, A M James, P F Macdonald, W S McKerrow, G Macnair, P R Moffat, S R Perry, R T Richardson, R J C Robb, D W Rubens, G R Simpson, I H M Smart, A C Stead, D Stone, D J Temple, M L Watson and J A Wood.
Guests: Cath Fryett, Katie Long and Eve Mackenzie.

JRRF

***Easter Meet 2014**: Standing (L to R): Cath Fryett, PWF Gribbon, ML Watson, JRR Fowler, Marion Moffat, PR Moffat, DJ Temple, DJ Broadhead, C Forrest, RJC Robb, DW Rubens, RT Richardson, AC Stead, PV Brian, HM Brown, R Aitken, G Macnair, JA Wood, HM Smart, D Stone, GR Simpson, JYL Hay, G Cohen, WS McKerrow, Katie Long. Sitting/Kneeling (L to R): Margot Gribbon, AM James, Eve Mackenzie, JRG Mackenzie (Club President), Helen GS Forde, RDM Chalmers, SR Perry.*

Skye Spring Meet, Allt Dearg Cottage, Sligachan
31 May – 7 June 2014

On the whole we had a rather poor week of weather, but a couple of very good days made the meet. John and Helen did the Loch Lochy Munros on their way to Skye, and Peter and Alan climbed the Great Prow on Blàbheinn before ariving at the cottage.

Sunday was not so good, but Tom, Mike and Pippa went up Sgùrr Beag, crossed Lota Corrie and ascended Bruach na Frithe. Noel walked out to the delightful sandy bay at Camas Daraich, and explored around the Point of Sleat. The crags south-west of the 74m spot height are not worth bothering with, but a tiny crag overlooking the aforementioned bay looks better.

Monday was also dreich but Peter and Tom did the circuit of the Beinn Deargs and Glamaig, while Mike and Pippa walked up Ben Tianavaig.

On Tuesday, Tom, Alan, Peter and Noel did Raeburn's Buttress on Sgùrr nan Each in the wet, but things improved and they continued over Garbh-bheinn and Belig. Mike and Pippa climbed Jamie Jampot and Fertility Right at Suidhe Biorach.

Skye Spring Meet 2014
(L–R): Paul Brian, Tom Prentice, Robin Campbell, Peter Macdonald and James Hotchkis.
Photo: Noel Williams.

The Hon. Ed. leads the 3rd pitch of Golden Calf (VS,4c), Coire nan Laogh, on the first ascent.
Photo: John Mackenzie.

Wednesday was the best day of the meeet. Peter, Alan and Tom did White Slab Direct in Coire a' Ghrunnda. They found it an enjoyable route, though Tom remarked that there is a paucity of protection. Meanwhile Noel and The President found a surprisingly good new route on the slabs in Coire nan Laogh.

On the Thursday Paul, Robin, James and Peter walked from Allt Dearg to Peinachorran, and the last two also returned over Ben Lee. The President organised a mineralogical outing to the huge basalt sea-cliffs of Sgùrr nam Boc, south of Loch Eynort. However, in the damp conditions he couldn't convince Eve and Noel that it was simple matter to descend all the way to the shore.

Friday was better again. James and Peter did Amphitheatre Arête, while Paul, Robin and Noel did routes on the Eastern Slabs of Blàbheinn. Tom travelled to Applecross and climbed with Simon Richardson.

Members present: Paul Brian, Robin Campbell, Mike Cocker, Pippa Cocker Helen Forde, John Fowler, James Hotchkis, Peter Macdonald, Eve Mackenzie (Guest), John Mackenzie, Tom Prentice, Alan Smith, Peter Wilson and Noel Williams.

Noel Williams

JMCS REPORTS

Edinburgh Section: In 2013/14 club members have been as active as ever in mountains and on crags all round the UK and abroad, summer and winter, seeking any opportunity to leave behind work, domesticity and whatever else people want to leave behind in order to join the queue across the Forth Bridge or the queue at the airport check-in desk, en route to (we hope) no queue at the foot of a route or a mechanised uplift facility.

Three aspects of the Club's affairs strike me as worthy of comment this year.

The first is the number of folk from outside the UK who have done us the honour of joining. On our list of members there are or have been North and South Americans, Antipodeans, citizens of several EU states and (to the extent not included in the former category) Scandinavians. The down side of this is that we often have to say good bye to them all too soon as they finish their degrees or their visas expire, but they make a notable contribution to the Club while they are with us and in this age of the internet and social media it is easy to keep in touch with them even when they are on the other side of the world.

The second – talking of social media – is the opening of an Edinburgh JMCS Facebook page. I do believe that this has been A Good Thing but it has also been a reminder that people of different ages or stages communicate in different ways, so that the longest and most intense interchange on Facebook, illustrated by the most brilliant photographs, can be entirely lost on those who only e-mails know, and vice versa. This reflects the nature of a Club; it is a scarcely defined bundle of activity, of which the Annual Newsletter is no more accurate a reflection than the Climbs book in the CIC hut is of what happens on the Ben. In either case, some of the truth finds its way into some of the accounts that some people read, but no single source or readership captures it all.

Club members help our previous President celebrate his last Munro!

The third concerns Melancholy Occurrences. After many injury free years, at different times during the summer of 2013 two members hit the ground from high enough up to sustain leg injuries which kept them housebound for months on end. And one August night the Club was at Aberdour when a member of a kindred Edinburgh club sustained fatal head injuries in a fall at the end of the evening, just as rucksacks were being packed and a pint thirsted for. The apparently random nature of these events leaves us shocked and concerned, but not even the limping survivors seem any more inclined to give up climbing than they were before. Who knows the source of our addiction to this habit?

If, despite those gloomy thoughts, you are interested in joining the Edinburgh JMCS, we always welcome new faces. Please come along to our Monday or Wednesday night activities and meet and climb with some of the existing members. We go to Ratho on winter Wednesdays and Alien Rock on winter Mondays. During the summer we will be inside or out, depending on the weather; you can see where we are going by looking at our website which also lists our forthcoming weekend meets. Just Google 'Edinburgh JMCS'. It is probably best to contact Bruce Macrosson, the Membership Secretary, beforehand to make sure there has been no last minute change of venue.

Our huts are available for booking by kindred Clubs; please contact the Custodians whose names are shown below. We have 'the Cabin' in Balgowan, between Laggan and Newtonmore, and 'the Smiddy' at Dundonnell in the North West.

The present committee includes: *Honorary President*: John Fowler; *President*: Terry Lansdown; *Vice President* and *Smiddy Custodian*: Helen Forde (30 Reid Terrace, Edinburgh, EH3 5JH, 0131 332 0071); *Secretary*: David Small (5 Afton Place, Edinburgh, EH5 3RB, <secretary@edinburghjmcs.org.uk>); *Treasurer*: Bryan Rynne; *The Cabin Custodian*: Ali Borthwick (01383 732 232, before 9pm please); *Membership Secretary*: Bruce Macrosson <bmacrosson@outlook.com>.

David Small, Secretary.

Glasgow Section: The Glasgow Section of the JMCS provided their members with another very successful and busy year in the hills. Currently club membership stands at 95 members; 70 of whom are affiliated to the Mountaineering Council of Scotland. There are 54 ordinary members and 41 life members. Four new members joined in 2013 and 5 existing members had survived long enough (25 years of continuous membership) to become life members.

Reflecting the general enthusiasm within the club, throughout 2013 there were 23 official weekend meets including the annual work meet to the fine club hut at Coruisk over the late May bank holiday. Coruisk, on the Isle of Skye provides simple, cheap and ferry accessible accommodation in a beautiful setting; see the website for details <http://www.glasgowjmcs.org.uk/coruisk.php> or to book the hut e-mail Coruisk Hut Bookings – Iain Sneddon <coruisk@glasgowjmcs.org. uk>.

Throughout the year JMCS weekend meets were held across Scotland, the Lake District and visited all of the SMC huts; the CIC, Lagangarbh, Raeburn, Ling and Naismith huts. Additionally a 'cappuccino night' is held in the Balcony

Dee Gaffney on the Forbes Arête. Photo: Roger Everett.

Café at the indoor wall of the Glasgow Climbing Centre every fortnight on Thursdays, where both new and established members can meet and train together on the indoor wall.

The annual general meeting and club dinner, where we had 45 diners, were again convened at the ever popular Kingshouse Hotel in Glen Coe on Saturday the 9 November 2013. Two weeks later the retiring president; Matthew Dent held his retiral bothy meet in the fine Allt Sheicheachan bothy behind Blair Atholl below Beinn Dearg on a fresh, cold frosty weekend.

The long cold winter allowed members to bag a number of classic winter routes, including Recess Route, Crowberry Gully, Smith's Route (Creag Meagaidh), Emerald Gully, Boomer's Requiem, Sickle, Slav Route, Stringfellows and Shelf Route.

Despite the fine weather only four members were present at the regular midsummer evening bivouac meet on the summit of The Cobbler. Three of them made an ascent of Gladiator's Groove Direct, and joined the fourth at dusk on the North Peak for beer and biscuits, before a comfortable midge-free bivvy and the typical early morning dash back to work. The dry spring and hot summer also provided good mountain climbing conditions; e.g. Torro, Haystacks, Yoyo, Pincer, Long Reach.

Overseas trips started early with members off piste skiing in Chamonix, where conditions were better than expected in early January. Members went Nordic backcountry skiing in the Fjallabak in Iceland. There was a ski trip to the Dolomites in Corvara. Hillwalking in Southern Ireland was reported as superb during the July heatwave. In August peaks included, in central Switzerland (Galenstock 3560m and Mount Titlis 3238 m), Germany (KG-weg, Alpspitze,

2628m and Nordkante (north ridge) on Hollentorkopf 2150m), Austria and an ascent even recorded in Lichtenstein (Ochsenkopf, 2286m). The fine ascent of Galenstock, the second highest peak in central Switzerland was up the fantastic airy south-west rib to reach the summit snow field in glorious sunshine. The descent back to the excellent Sidelen hut included a relay of three 50m abseils down a cliff using artificial stations comprising chains and gratings bolted to the vertical face as intermediate stations; quite exciting! Other routes climbed by JMCS members included Mont Blanc by the Pope Route, Forbes Arête on the Aiguille de Chardonnet, the north face of The Tour Ronde, the east ridge of Mutkogel in the Otztal (AD), and the North Face West Spur (D-) of the Mittaghorn near Saas Fee was described as very enjoyable.

Autumn rock climbing trips included the islands of Gozo and Malta.

The present committee includes: *President*: P. D. Smith; *Secretary*: Charlie Craig <secretary@glasgowjmcs.org.uk>; *New Members Secretary*: Simon Taylor. To go on a meet or find out more about the club individuals should contact Simon <newmembers@glasgowjmcs.org.uk>. New members are welcome to come along to any of the club meets.

Colwyn Jones

Lochaber Section: 2013 ushered in some big changes for the club, not least with the former secretary, Kenny Foggo standing down after some 16 years arranging all the weekend meets, taking the club minutes and informing the club members of the up-coming events, all with his usual good wit and humour. Some had even indicated to Kenny that standing down was not possible until his last breath had been gasped. Thankfully Kenny is still entertaining us with his musings. Many thanks Kenny for all your hard work over many years.

The club continues to use the extensive network of huts around Scotland and also put in a camping meet to Loch Morlich this year, as well as a meet to Steall Hut at the head of Glen Nevis. During the summer of 2013 we carried out many improvements to Steall Hut, including installing new bunk beds in the ground floor 'Prince's Room', which coincided with the purchase of 16 new PVC covered mattresses which will make it easier and more comfortable for those using the hut. The kitchen fitments were spruced up and new cookers installed along with the replacement of the gas powered generator to provide lighting throughout the hut. There would appear to be an increase in bookings of the hut since these improvements were made, with many positive comments being received. The hut is ideally positioned to access an extensive variety of mountain and wild land terrain at any time of year. Further information and contact details for Steall Hut can be found at <www.steallhut.co.uk>.

The club resurrected the winter evening slide show events with excellent talks on trips to the Himalaya and the Grand Canyon which have proved very popular, with former club members putting in appearances and often leading to the discussions and reminiscing continuing for some time afterwards. The year came to a close with the club dinner being held at the Ledgowan Lodge Hotel in Achnasheen, where we also held the club AGM prior to the dinner. This has been a very successful format, allowing members from outwith the Lochaber area to attend the AGM and contribute to the issues of the club, which had previously been held in Fort William on a winter evening.

Frenchie Cameron (in kilt) compleats his Munros on Beinn na Lap, 21 September 2013. Photo: Iain MacLeod.

The present committee includes: *President*: Phil Stevenson; *Secretary*: Iain MacLeod <ia.macleod@btintemet.com>; *Treasurer*: George Bruce; *Hut Bookings*: Ewen Kay; *Hut Custodian*: John Matheson.

Iain MacLeod

London Section: This was another year of mixed activity with most of our meets being held at our cottage in Bethesda, North Wales. A number of 'away' meets were however especially successful. In February, we were based for a week in the excellent Blackrock Cottage in Glen Coe and enjoyed sunshine and good winter conditions. In April, we had our first meet in the fine Robertson Lamb hut in Langdale. Again the weather was good, with several routes being completed on the Langdale crags, walks around the valley and mountain biking. In June, a flotilla of three yachts circumnavigated Skye via the Shiant Islands with stops in Loch Scavaig and Loch Scresort on Rum. Our thanks go to Chris Bashforth for organizing this sailing trip. Meets were also held in the Peak District and a successful club dinner took place in the Brecons, another 'first' for the section.

Work has continued to improve the comfort and ambience of our cottage in Bethesda, which is available for use by other clubs and offers a perfect base for exploring the hills and crags of Snowdonia. 2014 will mark the 50th anniversary of the purchase of the property, which will be celebrated accordingly.

More recently, on a sad note, we lost our former Treasurer and Secretary Dave Edmonds, who contributed vastly to our Section over the years. Our thoughts are with Dawn, Bob, Katy and the rest of Dave's family.

At the end of 2013 membership stood at 41 with five additional life members.

London JMCS Members on the Coruisk Meet, June 2014. Photos. Trevor Burrows.

The present committee includes: *President*: Chris Comerie; *Secretary*: John Firmin (telephone 0208 291 2141); *Treasurer*: David Hughes; *Glanafon Hut Bookings*: Rod Kleckham (telephone 01252 721049).

John Firmin

SMC ABROAD

SKIING THE FRENDO SPUR

The Frendo Spur, a route on every apprentice Alpinist's wish list, 1100m high consisting of a beautiful rock spur topped by that elegant spine and crowned with the upper buttress. It is the most aesthetic route on the North Face of the 3841m Aiguille du Midi. The alpine route was opened on 11 July 1941 by Edouard Frendo and René Rionda. The spine was first skied by Jean-Marc Boivin and Laurent Giacomini on 2 July 1977 before they abseiled over the buttress to join another slope which led to the bottom. That day Giacomini was in the zone and on his 2.10m 60mm wide skis made big turns that for many people marked the start of freeriding. It should be remembered that in this era jump turns were the norm, since the long stiff skis were difficult to control. Since then the route had seen only a few repeats due to fickle conditions and the changing nature of the hanging glacier.

May 2013 was characterised by few sunny days, cool temperatures and reasonable precipitation. The line was looking good but a few attempts we made got off to false starts due to wind, slabby snow and rain runnels on the lower face. These days were stressful, as you never know if your partners will read the conditions the same way or want to go regardless and I wanted to ski the line in primo conditions. Eventually I decided to take a break from the Chamonix valley and went to Finale rock climbing for a few days. This gave me the chance to relax, forget about the mountains and recharge the psyche. On my return to Chamonix I randomly met Bird Early, Minna Rihiimaki and Camille Jaccoux at the Midi and we skied the Cosmiques together. The snow was perfect for steep skiing and I suggested to Bird we pair up and go for Frendo the following day.

Luca Pandolfi and Ben Briggs were also keen to go and in the morning Minna Rihiimaki also joined us so after a quick discussion we decided to ski as a team of five so as not to endanger each other with sluff. Up the Midi my psyche was high, there was no niggling doubts about the slabs or hard snow and it felt like it was the day to go. There was 30–40cm of perfect cold well-bonded powder allowing some big turns down the initial 45° slopes. Everyone was smiling and happy as we got to the first abseil point. There is a couloir that runs down the side of the upper buttress that is usually glacial ice and an Abolokov anchor is required for the diagonal abseil to cross it. I went last since I had been shooting, pulled the back-up ice screw and started off down the ropes on skis. Near the end of the diagonal rap it was nearly impossible to hold an edge on the black ice and I started to wish I had left the ice screw in at the anchor in case I took an uncontrolled pendulum. By the time I'd pulled the ropes and joined the others the stress levels were high. A short exposed traverse right on 55° led under the upper buttress and delivered us to the arête. Here I had the challenge of getting stable enough to look through the viewfinder and shoot without loosing my balance!

Ben skied first releasing sluff that poured down the face from the arête building into a spectacularly full-bore avalanche off the end of the serac and sweeping the face for 1000m towards the Plan de l'Aiguille below. Seeing that the snow was great enabled us to relax and enjoy those incredibly special turns in an amazing situation. When I climbed this route in 1997 it never occurred to me that I might ski it one day but I now felt more secure on skis than I did on crampons all those

The author on the upper section of the Frendo. Photo: Luca Pandolphi

years ago. At the tower we rapped down the mixed route Boulevard Haussman and leapfrogged two sets of 60m ropes to speed up the rope work. Being a sunny day at the end of May it was due to get hot and the mountain would eventually purge all the excess snow.

The lower 500m also held good snow and with no further technicalities each turn was relaxed and super smooth in the sloughy 50° powder. A few minutes later we were skiing out the bottom of the face, ecstatic and with big smiles and putting some distance behind us en route to the bar at Plan de l'Aiguille where the party started and continued into town!

I got to ski this fine line with my good friends, Bird Early, Minna Rihiimaki, Luca Pandolfi, Tom Grant and Ben Briggs. Bird followed in the tradition set by Giacomini and put in big turns down the skier's right side of the spine unleashing a spectacular slough that went the distance providing suitable entertainment to the onlookers at Plan de l'Aiguille.

The memories from this day will last a lifetime and I was very lucky to be able to shoot with my SLR in those situations.

Ross Hewitt

MONT BLANC RANGE 2013

Following on from our 2012 visit, Tom Prentice and I visited the Mont Blanc Range in August 2013 to look around some more new corners.

Our first objective was the great slanting groove cutting through the vertical East Face of Petit Mont Greuvetta on the Italian side of the massif. We'd noticed this prominent feature when climbing on Mont Vert de Greuvetta the year before, but from from afar, it was impossible to judge the steepness of the groove. After a long approach involving a bivouac we started up the route (with some trepidation) on 12 August. We climbed four pitches up a subsidiary groove to the left until we were sucked into the main groove-line. Here, horror of horrors, we found an old abseil sling. Clearly someone had been there before us, but we continued for another seven pitches up the upper part of the groove followed by a ramp that lead to the summit ridge. We descended our line by abseil, making another bivouac on the way. Back in the valley we discovered that the route had first been climbed by the legendary Italian climber Gian Carlo Grassi with Lang and Meneghin in 1982. We were aware that Grassi had climbed a route in the vicinity, but thought his route was further right on the east face of the main peak.

Our next objective was a prominent rock pillar on the south side of the Aiguille du Chardonnet. Countless skiers must have passed underneath this attractive feature on their way to the Col du Chardonnet when doing the Haute Route, but as far as we knew it was unclimbed. Our approach to the col in summer conditions of unstable moraine and receding glaciers was a long and gruelling affair (which involved yet another bivouac), but we managed to squeeze in our 350m-long TD route before the weather broke. Nine varied pitches led to the summit crest of Pointe Alphonse Couttet, and once again we abseiled our line of ascent, just making the glacier by nightfall and reaching our bivouac site at midnight.

By the time the bad weather had cleared there was time for just one more route. It was now late August and the glaciers were beginning to break up, so we decided to return to the Greuvetta and attempt the line that we thought Grassi had originally climbed. This provided us the best route of the trip; an excellent eleven-pitch TD+ involving bivouacs on both the approach and descent. We were completely alone in a remote cirque on the Italian side of the range for three days only accompanied by choughs, so Casa Dei Gracchi (House of the Choughs) seemed an appropriate name to capture the savage location. Once again, the descent was a race against time and we arrived on the Greuvetta glacier to crashes of thunder and bolts of lightning with flash floods in the valleys below.

It had been another successful trip, but it was now time to go home.

Simon Richardson

Too Old for Mont Blanc?

Tom Patey taught us the art of climbing down gracefully. What about the art of growing old disgracefully? Jenny Joseph showed one way to do it in her poem 'When I grow old I shall wear Purple', but she isn't a mountaineer. Des Rubens and I like to think we belong to that strange clan. Des had a fixation with the Peuterey Ridge. I had dismissed it as unrealistic when I can barely cycle up the Edinburgh Mound. It was 45 years since I had done the south ridge of the Aiguille Noire; was this really the right time to try and complete the route to Mont Blanc? From the Monzino Hut it looked an awfully long way. I had forgotten that the Dames Anglaises col is a full 1000m above the hut, and that's just the start of the ridge. Our acclimatisation programme had involved barely an hour above 3500m since our arrival in the Alps, so perhaps it was just my usual unrealistic optimism that had imagined us bivvying on the col Peuterey (3900m) and storming over the top the next day. It seemed better to plan a bivvy at the Craveri Hut (Dames Anglaises) and hope to reach the Vallot from there.

For many climbers of my generation the geography of the south face of Mont

Blanc is engraved on our minds through reading Bonatti's account of the 1961 tragedy on the retreat from the Freney Pillar. On the hellish descent down the Rochers Grubers and Freney glacier the wilting French and Italian climbers dropped off one by one. Through the night Bonatti urged them on: 'We must reach the col d'Innominata by dawn.' This col marks the boundary between the Freney and the easier slopes leading down to the Monzino hut.

I almost came to grief even before we reached the col Innominata: in an inexplicable 'senior moment' I found myself sliding down easy scree-covered ground, only to stop, equally inexplicably, a few feet above a vertical and life-terminating drop. At the col, the size of the task ahead became a little more apparent. Across the narrow Freney glacier – hideously contorted higher up but quite benign on our path – rose the Point Gugliermina, which we had each climbed in different seasons about thirty years ago. In the col between it and the towering north side of the Aiguille Noire stood the two English ladies – angular and most difficult of access – who guarded the tiny bivouac hut somewhere around their ankles. Rising above the Gugliermina the ridge reached the snowy Aiguille Blanche, reputedly the most difficult Alpine four thousander, and hidden beyond was col Peuterey and much of the final 1000 metres of ridge. Left of the ridge the pillars of Freney frowned down remotely.

Despite memories of scrambling down with Ian Dalley thirty years ago, the tottering rock below the Innominata suggested an abseil down to the Freney glacier would be a more attractive and life-preserving option. The sudden appearance of a rock falling from nowhere enlivened the abseil preparations, and then, as I fumbled with my large gloves to get onto the rope, the sticht-plate sprang out of my hands and clanged off to oblivion. A karabiner brake was the obvious alternative, but what if I dropped a clutch of our very small set of krabs? To preclude further ignominy I abseiled 1970's style, using a sling round the crotch and a rope over the shoulder.

Fortuitously the glacier crossing was the easiest part of the whole expedition. Instead of proceeding direct to the Dames Anglaises col up a couloir known for its stonefall, we embarked on the recommended Schneider couloir, the normal descent from the Gugliermina. At this stage, though Des was, as usual, brimming with strength and enthusiasm, I was labouring – something to do with very light Alpine boots and crampons with a dubious fit. We reached a small rocky neck on the right of the couloir, where the description indicated we should traverse into the col to reach the hut. However a traverse would have led only onto a very steep flanking wall, so we mistakenly continued up the couloir. By a strange coincidence we had each independently misconstrued the statement that the hut was on the Brenva side of the col. Without any discussion it seemed both of us had got it into our heads that we would descend to the hut from above the col on the Brenva side. Alas, having puffed our way up two more trying pitches it was immediately apparent that we had it quite wrong. Leaving gear we retreated to the neck and tried again to make sense of the description. A descending traverse led me to a place where I could peer down towards a chimney adorned with a fine capstone and a nest of old ropes, but the ground was horribly loose and offered no safe anchorage at all. After a retreat from this descent and a rejection of Des's suggestion of a long descent to the Dames Anglaises couloir, we slowly found another way around to the nest of ropes. Here Des, with commendable imagination, crawled through the capstone window and discovered on the far side a line of ledges leading to our long-sought bivvy hut.

Craveri Bivouac Hut, Dames Anglaises. Photos: Des Rubens.

We had expected to reach there around midday and get a good rest before setting off early next morning, but it was now about 4 p.m. and it seemed appropriate to draw some conclusions from the day's halting progress. I suggested a rest day! Admittedly this is not a very common practice on Alpine routes, but we were veterans of many a long fester in the Greater Ranges. In any case we had an excellent weather forecast and an unnecessarily large amount of food. The hut was very cosy for two, wood-lined and even equipped with some stores of its own. Provided no large party of super-confident young climbers suddenly appeared from the direction of the Noire we would have to ourselves this isolated perch with its stunning views across to the Dent du Geant and the Jorasses massif. My unimpeachable logic won the day and we settled to enjoy a site almost as grand as the Garbh Coire howff below Cairn Toul.

So the next 36 hours were spent very pleasantly sleeping, eating, reading and briefly sallying out to recce the best way to regain our ridge. The hut book contained only meagre tales of derring-do. Doubtless most of those who pass this way are serious alpinists, intent on a fast and competent ascent. There seemed to be only about ten parties per year. While few seemed to have been overly harrowed by the mighty abseils down from the Noire summit, quite a number told of route-finding difficulties bypassing the Dames. A noteworthy entry was by Paul Ramsden, frequent companion on Mick Fowler's more outrageous exploits; he seemed to have soloed the Integrale late in October one year.

All good things come to an end: at about 5 a.m. on Bastille Day we abandoned our comfortable staging post and re-embarked on the route. In glorious sun we soloed across the broken eastern flanks of the Gugliermina and climbed easily up towards the Blanche. Des, though voluntarily carrying the rope, forged ahead on the final snowslopes. The two summits of the Blanche are connected by a beautiful curving snow arete, with plunging depths on both sides. Without waiting for a discussion my fearless companion flew along the edge leaving me to follow trepidatiously in his wake. Finally, after five or six hours we were on the highest summit and could look down on col Peuterey and the challenges beyond.

The view from the Blanche was like a superb tour of Alpine history: the great sweep of the Brenva face on one side, the Freney straight ahead and the fine Innominata face beyond on the left. Below, to our left, the putative escape route over col Eccles looked highly forbidding – steep snow marked with occasional streaks of stonefall. Directly below us, the flat col would obviously make a delightful stopping place. It abutted against a surprisingly rocky Peuterey ridge. I had been mistakenly seduced into thinking the upper part was a pure snow climb, but we were going to have about 400m of rock and mixed to reach the summit of the Grand Pilier d'Angle. At first glance the rock ridge starting at the col didn't look too steep, but a slightly more careful look suggested it would be awkwardly holdless. The guidebook recommended advancing from the col for a short distance up snow on the Freney side and then cutting diagonally back to join the ridge above its steepest part.

First we had to get down to the col. A few abseils on a grotty face of loose rock and ice took us to a point a few hundred feet above the col. Having pulled through the ropes from the last abseil Des started front-pointing down the snow as fast as he could go. I tied myself onto the end of an old rope (point of attachment unknown) and started to gather his rope, shouting to him that I wanted to put him on belay. But my lusty companion had failed to remember his

Summit of Aiguille Blanche in front of Freney face.

Ecclesiastes: the race is not always to the swift. He suddenly accelerated downwards while I still held in my arms a bundle of rope that at one end was, fortunately, attached to him. While I was pulled off my steps but held by the mysterious old rope end, he hurtled over the rimaye and came to rest unharmed a little lower down. Continuing more cautiously the flat col was reached, and then he was able to direct me to front-point well over to one side to outflank the treacherous ice that had undone him.

Thus we foregathered at lunchtime in this blazing snow bowl without much appetite for the swimming stage to follow. Sinking well above the knees and advancing at the pace of a very weary snail I made my way under the edge of the rocks, till at the first half likely break, we tried to escape from the porridge. I fixed myself a belay on a small pedestal, but then, examining the line above, began to think it might be a bit too hard for an old snail. Des the accelerator had no such misgivings; leaving his sack behind he launched bravely up the overhanging crack and swiftly demolished it. No sooner had I left my stance to assist the two sacks on their ascent of the pitch than a sack-sized lump of ice flew down and smashed into the platform where I had been attached minutes earlier – yet another mercy from the gods. Another VS pitch followed Des's tour de force, and then we just had pitch after pitch of grade II/III mixed ground. The afternoon wore on and even the accelerating snail was getting a little low on juice. Finally we crested the ridge above the Pilier d'Angle, only to find ourselves in the teeth of a biting evening wind. The view was noble indeed, but the position felt a little too exposed. It was high time we found a bivouac spot. The guide had mentioned such a place beneath a large gendarme, and thither we hastened, via a slight descent on the sheltered side of the ridge. Oh, joy! A fine flat snowy ledge at the gendarme's base, well away from the keen north wind.

Boots off, rack tied up, mats and pits out, stove on. Soon we were lying comfortably, admiring the Chandelle of the Freney pillar directly across from us, and the great swoop of glacier below leading out to the hazy peaks of Italy in the gloaming.

Day four: the weather is still settled, and today we will reach the top. First we have to regain the ridge and cross a little more mixed ground; then it's out onto open snowy slopes and just a steady cramponing upwards, with the eye always drawn to the magnificent Pear and Major routes on the Brenva, the Maudit cirque, the Aiguilles de Diable, and beyond the Geant and Rochefort, the Verte and Dru – so many old friends, almost as good as naming peaks from the top of the Buachaille. The sinuous aretes became a little icy in places and we gave ourselves the comfort of a rope and even (believe it or not) belays. We also, somewhat unexpectedly, found ourselves in a line of steps for the first time since starting.

Finally, around midday we breasted the ridge at Mont Blanc de Courmayeur. After four days alone on the face I found emotion welling up, old snail's tears behind the glasses. With infinite slowness I plodded up to the true summit of Europe to join the crowds. Suddenly we were among the dozens of happy parties who had worked up the steady groove of the Bosses Arete. There was even a young man in trainers, though the snow was quite hard!!

After our hugs, handshakes and photos it was a quick and worry-free descent to the Vallot, which despite its squalor provided some welcome escape from the sun. Our original plan, inspired by a tale of Allan Pettit's, had been to traverse to the Aiguille de Bionnassay. We certainly intended to return on the Italian side. The traverse of the Dome de Gouter was less of an exhaustion than I had feared, and soon we were following tracks along the elegant snow ridge that leads towards the Bionnassay. We had not been this way before and were greatly enjoying the unaccustomed views, to say nothing of the relatively untesting ground. But the Bionnassay itself would undoubtedly require care and some extra energy, even in fine conditions such as this. Without much reluctance I gave up the idea and we decided to take the standard descent to the Miage glacier.

From the Piton des Italiens the route goes down an easy ridge to a small col and then down a straightforward snowslope to the glacier. Did I say straightforward? Well, yes, provided there are no avalanches. Fresh signs of such ill-mannered mountain behaviour were all too evident, and the afternoon sun was rapidly making the porridge worse. Taking a diagonal line all seemed to be going well until Des lept a little too unenergetically over the bergschrund and found himself with his upper body wedged in some soft snow of unknown solidity and his legs waving in space over a great chasm.

'Don't pull, you're pulling me into the bergschrund,' he shouted.

'What do you want me to do?'

'Can you go round below me?'

'I'll have to stop belaying you then.'

To my surprise he thought he was stable enough where he was, so I made as long a detour as I dared, keeping the rope on, and at a point where the 'schrund looked narrowest leaped as far as I could.

I was over, but there was a problem! The snow was so soft that I had gone in up to my waist. I could move one foot but the other felt completely stuck.

Summit arête of Grand Pilier d'Angle, with Grandes Jorasses & Matterhorn in distance.

Summit arete of Peuterey Ridge, Mont Blanc, 15 July 2013.

Beginning to panic I frantically tried to scoop away the snow around my legs with my bare hands. After about five or ten minutes the gods relented and my poor foot was released. I rapidly traversed back to my no longer accelerating companion.

Our mighty ex-president was beginning to look a little grey around the gills. He didn't want me to approach too closely in case I fell in too. So standing about fifteen feet below him I threw him a loop in the hope that he could pull himself out. Those who know us will not be surprised to hear that we are not well versed in the techniques of crevasse rescue, despite many years spent on glaciers of varying degrees of trickery. With no purchase for his feet, and snow too soft to mantelshelf on it was difficult for Des to haul himself out, while his faithful but puny companion stood absolutely no chance of pulling this very large fish. As I watched his grimaces become more and more extreme he somehow managed to slowly extricate himself.

The whole episode had probably taken less than half an hour, but Des was very cold and wet. Fortunately there were no more difficulties and he soon warmed up as we completed the descent to the Gonella Hut. We found a beautifully modern building, above a filthy tottering bit of glacier, and were given a warm welcome despite arriving with no warning on the dot of dinner-time. It was of course gratifying to get a few pats on the back from a superbly strong guide who had soloed the Peuterey Integrale some years earlier.

Our adventures were not quite over. At the Gonella you are still in the heart of the mountains, a long way up the Miage Glacier. The descent was delightfully varied and quite reminiscent of the Himalaya. We followed grassy rock buttresses and terraces down to the snow then had several miles of flattish walking where we could look across and speculate on the exact line of the recent Richardson-Tunstall route, a proud SMC addition to the climbs of the range. Once on the moraines we eschewed the normal path and made our way over to the true left where we were suddenly rewarded by an enchantingly green ablation valley that led back through woods to our starting point.

We had no doubt been quite lucky, both with the weather and the few contretemps. We both felt we had enjoyed our finest ever Alpine route.

REVIEWS

Boundless – An adventure beyond limits: Karen Darke. (Akreative, 2012, pbk, 288pp, ISBN 978-1-904207-66-5, £12.99.)

Karen Darke is likely to be known already to most SMC readers. A keen runner and mountaineer, she had a bad accident on the Aberdeen sea-cliffs, and at the age of 21 found herself paralysed from the chest down. She recounts the story of that episode in her life, together with her earlier returns into the world of adventuring, in her book *If You Fall*. Her second book, *Boundless*, tells the tale of three of her more recent adventures over a two year period between 2006 and 2007.

The first, and the main focus of the book, is her incredible 600km month-long sit-ski crossing of the Greenland ice-cap as part of a team of six. This was a hugely committing undertaking, and makes an engrossing read. The second is a short recounting of an ultimately unsuccessful attempt to canoe round Corsica in rough February conditions. The third is the story of her preparation for and subsequent ascent of Zodiac on El Capitan with amongst others Andy Kirkpatrick, a multi-day jumaring epic. Of these, the Greenland trip is by far the best read, the sheer demands of the undertaking being so thought-provoking. The Corsica trip is told in a mere 9 pages, which seems unsatisfyingly brief, as there must have been much more to say about the island and the attempt, though the author's point in including it in the book is to show that she has finally learnt when to stop of her own volition. And the El Cap climb seems so nuts at times it is hard to treat it on the same level as the Greenland section – undoubtedly a feat of teamwork and pull-ups, however one is always conscious that the climbers are only ever a series of abseils from the ground.

Karen carefully blends the telling of the stories into the background of her personal and emotional life, the result being an extremely engaging and honest account of what she did, the particular challenges she faced in her circumstances, and what they meant to her in the overall scheme of her life. Clearly she is a hugely driven person, and in the book Karen tries to explain what makes her push herself to such extraordinary limits – successfully, as the reader is left willing Karen on, and at the same time sensing that her motivations in seeking adventure remain the same as our motivations, paralysis or no paralysis. Except that for Karen the simple things that the rest of us take for granted are themselves potential stoppers, which must be overcome as a preliminary to taking on the challenge.

The book's strengths are its characterisations, its exploration of the personalities who play the key roles, Karen's examination of her own motivations, and her descriptions of the personal challenges she faces and overcomes. While the nature of each expedition is well explained too, there is less attention given to the actions of skiing/kayaking/climbing, probably because there is a limit to the number of ways the author can say what it was like and just how hard the basic motions were. We respect and marvel at her ability to rise to her particular challenges and to embrace these on the basis that there truly should be 'no limits'. With a hugely successful ongoing paralympic career and such an inspirational personality, another volume of Karen's memoirs cannot be far away.

Alec Keith

Mammals in North East Scotland: Adam Watson. (Paragon Publishing 2013, 155pp, ISBN 978-1-78222-147-0, £14.99.)
This book is one of a series of publications recently produced by club member and ecologist Adam Watson. The book is the result of many decades of research and observations undertaken by Adam in Deeside, Angus, Perthshire and the Cairngorms into the mammals, fish and reptiles that inhabit the area. These in the main are Red Deer, Mountain Hare, Wildcat, and also a great variety of smaller mammals and fish.

Whilst the main objective of the book is to produce a scientific and analytical account of the area, there is never the less, much of interest to us mere mortals with regard to the multitude of animals that we may be fortunate enough to observe on our days out on the hill. There is plenty of anecdotal evidence and comments from inhabitants of the area including 'good keepers' such as John Robertson who used to be at The Spittal of Glen Muick; he gives great accounts of animals he used to see on a regular basis and how over the years these have declined. Incidentally (not covered in this book) John Robertson was probably only the second pilot to fly over Mount Everest, this was during his service in the Second World War.

The sad fact that comes across is the continuing persecution and the destruction of habitat of numerous species including Wildcat, Mountain Hare, and Raptors by so called sporting estates, who seem to be immune from criticism and above the law, surely a situation that cannot be tolerated any longer.

Adam has donated a copy of his book to the club library and it is well worth a read.

Brian Findlay

Tears of the Dawn: Julian Lines. (Shelterstone, 2013, hbk, 288pp, ISBN 978-0-9576817-0-5, £20.)
Surely one of the greater challenges in writing any kind of climbing autobiography is to on the one hand impress and inspire the reader, while on the other securing and retaining their empathy. We are all of us ensnared by both darkness and light. Without some kind of emotional connection between the author and the reader, the latter will feel alienated and – in the worst case scenario – will ultimately become disinterested. We all like to hear tales that make our jaws drop and our palms sweat, but the best ones are those that we can in some way connect with and understand. For someone as unique in British climbing as Julian Lines, achieving this empathy must have been an extraordinarily challenging task. But with his first book *Tears of the Dawn* he achieves it convincingly.

Of the many notable features of this fascinating book, this is perhaps one of the most striking – that a climber who usually climbs solo, often in the mountains, and sometimes ground-up into unchartered Extreme rock, can come across as so human, so vulnerable; far from the super-calm Zen Master personality that the soloist stereotypes might have us believe. Very far from it, in fact. Even on what might be considered as 'easy' solos within the context of his wider achievements, Lines often becomes frightened – terrified even – at the crux section of his chosen climb, which has the extraordinary effect of transposing the reader quite literally 'into his shoes'. (Terrified is, of course, just exactly how the great majority of us would feel in these most precarious of climbing predicaments).

But despite the fear, there were many occasions when *Tears of the Dawn* made me want to run for my chalk bag and boots, jump in the car and just get out on rock as far as possible from the madding crowds. A long and silent Cairngorm classic, a mystical Northumbrian fluting, or a high and windswept Gritstone slab – all unencumbered by the tangle of relationships, and the fiddle and faff of ropes and ironmongery. Perhaps this book should have been released with a public health warning?

There were also times however when I could barely read on, so appalling was the abrupt reality of the extreme soloist's fate, and so brutal was the honesty and candidness of the author's presentation of it. I suspect some readers may struggle with these elements of the book – the author's repeated transformation from Commander to crash victim. For me, however, this is simply Lines telling it from his own perspective exactly how it is. It's not always pleasant reading, but it's certainly not pretentious.

Despite the at times quite wearing effects of this trickle-fed trauma, there is a tremendous sense of liberation about this book. This is particularly so in those passages where the author explores the landscape and his abilities as a young climber amongst the great stones of the Cairngorms. There are other tales perhaps more gripping – such as a terrifying solo of an out of condition ice gully – where the author seems less attuned to his surroundings, and an almost tangible sense of angst and urgency makes for most uncomfortable reading. But it is surely in describing his early explorations on Cairngorm granite, Northumbrian sandstone and the infamous Gritstone edges that Lines truly finds freedom of expression – both in his actions on the crags and in the words used to recount them.

There is a brutal honesty in the book that is perhaps unusual in climbing literature. The author, for example, readily admits that solo climbing – the very thing that drives him forward and gives him core passion in life – is also the very same thing that often wakens him with fear in the middle of the night. And there is a near-constant internal battle in the run up to each hard solo where the 'conscious' and 'sub-conscious' minds duel it out for control of his actions. Whether he actually states it explicitly or not, these passages are effectively an admission of irrational, careless and on occasion flagrantly uncalculated behaviour that flies in the face of the 'calculated' risks most mountaineers apparently subscribe to. Nowhere in the book is this admission more raw than in the description of the author's carefree gambling with stocks and shares – at times it almost seems as if his climbing fulfils the same function. Once again, Lines achieves the impossible here – making recklessness seem not only acceptable, but somehow desirable.

There are of course aspects of the book which some readers might find a little frustrating. The recurrent suggestion, for example, that 'normal' or 'family' life is somehow inherently mundane, or prevents us all from living life to the full, may serve to disconnect some readers. A more shrewd approach would perhaps have been to draw parallels between the propensity of life to throw up unexpectedly brutal challenges with the rude awakening of the soloist who suddenly finds himself out of his depth. But one can't help feeling that these at times slightly dismissive glances at the mainstream of society are in some way representative of an inner resentment or alienation within the author himself. Lines most certainly carries some 'baggage' – not least in relation to his father. Unfortunately, however, although there are countless occasions when this is mentioned in passing, we are not given any meaningful insight as to what it was that actually went on in Lines' childhood. For me, personally, this was a missed opportunity – to give the reader a genuine insight into the *why* as well as the *what, where and when* of this unique and colourful character. How was it, for example, that he ended up at times, as he says, with 'nothing' despite having been given so many wonderful opportunities for exploration and adventure? Perhaps if these aspects weren't up for discussion then they should not have been mentioned it at all. On the other hand, maybe these deeper reflections will provide substance for his future writing.

But these areas don't detract from the impulsive thrust of the book and the quality of Lines' writing. He has perhaps the richest and most emotive turn of phrase of any writer of his generation. With a subject as inherently engaging and exciting as solo climbing and mountaineering it isn't always necessary to craft one's prose so finely to grip the reader. Events themselves can often be enough. Lines, however, produces a narrative so wonderfully vivid that his words seem to come alive from the page and fill the senses with images, textures, emotions and – above all – a most striking sense of place. There were times when I felt I was, quite literally, taking a walk through the pages of this book.

I suspect *Tears of the Dawn* will make you smile and grimace in equal measure. Smile with anticipation on a crisp Autumnal morning as you squeak your boots and chalk your fingers at the base of the crag and 'a wedge of dense fog nuzzles into the valley like an imaginary glacier'. But grimace soon after as the author succumbs to his 'Satanic power of commitment' only to find he had once more pushed the boat out just a little too far. Whether it's light or dark you're after, this is undoubtedly a fascinating, lucid and at times uneasy account of some of the most arresting and poignant moments in the life of Britain's most accomplished solo climber.

Guy Robertson

Place names in much of north-east Scotland: hill, glen, lowland, coast, sea, folk: Adam Watson. (Paragon Publishing, 2013, pbk, 403pp, ill., ISBN 978-1-78222-069-5, £19.99.)

This is a compendium of place names derived from the people who live, or have lived in the area rather than an academic exercise in which names are picked off a map and puzzled over by erudite scholars. The grid references are given where applicable and the present and past pronunciations are noted in the international phonetic alphabet with a special section relating IPA to the local Scots pronunciation. The entries are terse. The area covered is roughly East of Glenshee to the sea, south to the Mearns and as far north as Speyside. The boundaries are not exactly defined hence the word 'much' in the title. There are sections devoted to names contributed by Donnie Smith the last fluent speaker of Speyside Gaelic. There is even, surprisingly, a section on the Gaelic names of Kinlochbervie by Bobbie Macleod which is about as far North-West as you can get from the North-East.

This gives the character of the work; it is a compendium of the information gained by Adam and his friends over the course of many years. Beneath the careful scholarship there is a feeling for the humanity of the community and culture that generated the names. The section on the place names around Turriff is especially rich as it is Adam's homeland. There are photographic portraits of Adam's informants – the people who were brought up with the names and actually spoke them. Also some good landscape photographs. There are 8

Chapters with some 30 sub-sections devoted to separate glens, Dee fishing pools, coastal names and offshore fishing names.

As a consequence the book is difficult to use. You have to know exactly where the names you are interested in are in relation to the boundaries of Adam's subdivisions. All in all a fascinating collection of place name lore valuable to the scholar and non-specialist. Anyone who knows the area covered will find it interesting to spend a happy hour wandering from name to name.

Iain Smart

Scottish Explorers: Anthony Kamm. (National Museums Scotland Enterprises, 2013, pbk, 48pp, ISBN 9781905267439, £5.99.)

Scottish Explorers is a book about explorers who travelled into unknown parts of the world. The book is divided into different sections – the Arctic, Antarctica, Africa, Canada and Australia and there are also chapters on scientists, mountaineers and aviators. It is full of interesting facts and pictures, diagrams and maps. At the end there is also an activity section.

The book tells you a lot about where, when and how people explored. They all started off their journeys by boat and then continued by horse, dog and canoe or on foot. They did not have the same equipment and technology that we have now so it was harder to keep in touch and many of them got lost. Many lost their lives when exploring coastlines, rivers and large areas covered by deserts or ice. The explorers also discovered new types of plants and animals.

The booklet doesn't go into great detail about any individual explorers but if you wanted to to find out more you could go onto the internet. My favourite section of the book is the chapter about Australia because I liked reading about the things that the explorers did there.

Georgia Miller
(P6, Crown Primary School, Inverness)

Nature's Peace – A Celebration of Scotland's Watershed: Peter Wright. (Luath Press Ltd, 2013, pbk with flaps, 191pp, ISBN 978-1908373830, £16.99.)

I first came across the concept of the Scottish watershed back in 1996 when I read the excellent *Walking the Watershed* by Dave Hewitt (TACit Press). A diary note at the time records 'a strangely appealing account of a 12 week hike through Scotland – a psychological as much as a physical challenge.' Hewitt is clearly no slouch on the hill, but his solo trek from the English Border to Cape Wrath stretched him close to his limit and makes an absorbing story.

Jumping forward to 2012 I came across *Ribbon of Wildness* by Peter Wright (Luath Press 2010), earning a terse 'great topography' in the diary. Not such a gripping story as Dave Hewitt's, Peter Wright took a total of 64 days over several trips in 2005 to cover the whole 12,00km (745 miles), finishing at Duncansby Head. His subsequent account was very well researched and packed with geographical information on land use, conservation designations and a lot of interesting stuff of which those of us who enjoy the Scottish outdoors should be more aware.

I was surprised to find out that *Nature's Peace* is now Peter Wright's third book on the subject along with *Ribbon of Wildness* and *Walking with Wildness (a detailed guide to twenty-six beautiful day or weekend walks along Scotland's Watershed).* There is also a *Ribbon of Wildness News* (Issue 3, February 2014), a website and a Facebook page, giving the impression that Wright's promotion of Scotland's watershed has become something of a cottage industry.

This latest volume is intended more for coffee table than rucksack, published to tie in with the centenary of John Muir's passing in 2014, *Nature's Peace* is a slightly larger than usual paperback but fits nicely in the hand. I noticed colour photos on almost every page, but out popped an ERRATA slip, advising me to *please read page 55 before page 53.* Oh dear. Looking more closely at the photographs I soon spotted another mistake on pages 24–25 where *Quinag from Glas Bheinn* has been mixed up with *Ben Hee.* Dear oh dear. For £16·99 we should expect better from the otherwise excellent Luath Press. The photo captions are very informative, concisely naming the subject then giving a brief description of other features in each picture and the name of the photographer. I was initially puzzled by the letters and numbers in the tiniest of print below each caption, until I realised this was the grid reference of the camera location. Doh!

Sadly, the photographs are a big disappointment overall. Photographers were invited to submit suitable images and the work of over fifty has been chosen for inclusion. By a wry coincidence, as I was reading the book, Peter Wright organised a promotional talk in Inverness and I was able to gain a full appreciation of the pictures, striking when projected onto a big screen, which have lost their impact in print. Sacrificing quality for quantity, too many images have been squeezed in, some reduced literally to postage stamp size.This is a pity when there are so many fine photographers now working in Scotland. Another couple of small niggles about the images – when there are photos on every page, it is helpful if text and pictures match up as closely as possible – not much evidence of that here. I also counted an inauspicious thirteen pages devoted to Peter Wright's pretty flower snaps but no helpful captions, no names, no locations, nothing! Having had the good fortune to attend a presentation by wildlife photographer Laurie Campbell featuring his work for the Harris Trust, there is just no comparison.

Nature's Peace is of course one of John Muir's many inspirational phrases and Stuart Brooks, Chief Executive of the John Muir Trust, contributes an enthusiastic Foreword, urging us as ever to 'do something for wildness and make the mountains glad.' Next comes a short poem by the author which I enjoyed very much and two of my favourite pictures: *Great Glen Sunset* shows the backs of two young children looking north-east towards Loch Ness, bathed in the red glow of the setting sun while *Carrifran Fencewalkers* features two warmly clad walkers looking down into a wild looking Borders corrie in bright sunshine with a wintry dusting of snow. Both images capture a moment in what this reviewer imagines was a memorable adventure for the subjects.

Unfortunately, Wright's almost evangelical tone in promoting Scotland's watershed makes me feel a little uncomfortable, especially when I read at the end of this first chapter that 'for many, it has all the promise of offering an eco-spiritual experience.' As in *Ribbon of Wildness* the author divides his route into a series of Marches (pertaining to 'the traditional name for a boundary' – nothing to do with soldiers or pipe bands) and adding, for good measure, the *Viking March* to include Orkney and Shetland. The Marches conveniently form the next six chapters. With an average elevation of some 470m it is not surprising that, apart from Cumbernauld, the watershed avoids all but a small number of human habitations and structures. Regular hill-goers, especially baggers like myself, will recognise plenty of familiar ground. The frequent use of the dreaded term 'bog' discourages me from aspiring to repeat the route, though others have, including Colin Meek who ran the whole way in 2012.

The author's prose is functional but his generous use of local names helps bring the descriptions to life. Randomly opening at page 157 and reading about *Eday, Flaughton Hill, Greeny Brae, Sanday, Tofts Ness* and *Point of Burrian* makes me want to head up to Orkney at the first opportunity! Names are of course one impact humans have had on the landscape, enriching our cultural experience but I empathised with the author's scathing comments on more recent human intrusions – blanket forestry plantations, the proliferation of wind-farms and the threat of a huge pump-storage hydro scheme in the Great Glen.

The penultimate chapter *Threats and Conservation* tackles these issues head on and suggests 'the designation and creation of a chain of UNESCO Biosphere Reserves centred upon the Watershed of Scotland.' A concluding chapter tries to tie in John Muir again, but I think it a bit cheeky to make up a quote. A couple of blank pages follow, then finally a Glossary comprising a measly eight words including 'Mountains – There are many different forms referred to in this book, including: Fell, Pike, Law, Beinn, Sgur, Carn… These denote a variety of meanings such as elevation, character, local derivation and shape.' Left wondering who may find this information useful, I would suggest that if you want to know more about Scotland's watershed, read *Ribbon of Wildness* or *Walking the Watershed* and if you want to celebrate John Muir, read the great man for yourself.

Dave Broadhead

Everest; The First Ascent. The untold story of Griffith Pugh, the man who made it possible: Harriet Tuckey. (Rider Books, 2013, hbk, 400pp, ISBN 9781846043482, £20.)

Harriet Tuckey is the daughter of Griffith Pugh, the physiologist who accompanied the successful 1953 Everest expedition. In this entertaining and informative book, which deservedly won the 2013 Boardman Tasker prize, she tells the story of his life and work. Along the way she sheds a good deal of light (often unflattering light) on aspects of twentieth century British and Commonwealth mountaineering culture and the personalities of some of its leading figures.

Ms Tuckey's thesis, which has been thoroughly researched and referenced, is that without her father's work on high altitude physiology the 1953 expedition would have been yet another gallant failure. Whether or not one accepts this view – that Everest would not have been climbed in 1953 without the adoption of at least some of Pugh's recommendations – there can be no doubt that for the originality of his work and the soundness of his advice on acclimatisation, oxygen use, hygiene, diet and equipment Pugh deserves a far greater share of the limelight than he has usually been accorded.

Interwoven with her praise of Pugh's scientific achievements, which went far beyond his input to the 1953 expedition, Ms Tuckey paints a painfully frank portrait of her father's personal characteristics. Although a brilliant, clear-sighted scientist, he characteristically looked no further than himself in his personal and emotional life, especially where his family was concerned. His failure to have consideration for others could sometimes be excused as the scientist's single-minded desire for the truth, but Ms Tuckey is not afraid to recognise that it went deeper than that. Pugh behaved badly to his wife and children and, although capable of charm, he often acted like a complete shit. After a long rift between them, Ms Tuckey deserves considerable credit for having been able to come to terms with all aspects of the man that her father was. She attributes his unpleasantness and his originality alike to his ungoverned childhood years spent in a Welsh wilderness, where he got used to pleasing himself and paying no heed to others. To be honest, that struck me as a convenient excuse, rather than a convincing explanation, but she is better placed to judge than I am and I would like to believe her.

With its strong story line, fascinating central character and background cast of well known mountaineers – including W H Murray – this book held my interest from start to finish. There are many fascinating nuggets of information along the way, especially illustrations of the uneasy relationship between mountaineers and science, which seems to have arisen from the tenacity with which mountaineers clung to fallacies founded on the reasoning that suffering is good for you, climbing mountains involves suffering and therefore climbing mountains is good for you. My favourite titbit is Geoffrey Winthrop Young's assertion that drinking water on a climbing expedition was indicative of weakness and that the leader should set a corrective example by sucking a prune stone instead.

If I may be allowed a Pugh-like moment of objectivity to mention a couple of aspects of the book which I don't particularly like, they would be as follows. Firstly, Ms Tuckey's style is sometimes too close for comfort to that of a Sunday supplement. So, for example, she tells us that Sandy Irvine was 'handsome' and George Mallory 'formidably handsome' while Michael Ward was both tall and handsome and walked 'with a graceful, easy stride' and Eric Shipton stood out as 'famously attractive with a lithe figure and penetrating blue eyes'. He would presumably have been a good match for Rebecca Stephens, who is 'a renowned beauty'. Secondly, the main episodes of the book are not described in chronological order – there are a number of zigzags in time – and this did make me pause every so often to check quite where we were in the order of events.

But those are minor complaints. I've read this book twice and will read it again. It provoked in me all the reactions that a good biography should – sympathy, exasperation, laughter, incredulity, sorrow – and left me with a better understanding of the human condition. I strongly recommend it.

David Small

The K2 Man (and his molluscs). The extraordinary life of Haversham Godwin-Austen: Catherine Moorehead. (The In Pinn (Neil Wilson Publishing), 2013, hbk, 279pp, ISBN 978-1-906000-58-5, £24.99.)
Haversham Godwin-Austen (1834 – 1923) was the first person to survey not only large parts of the Karakoram, but also considerable areas of Kashmir, Ladakh, Zanskar, Bhutan, Assam, Manipur and northern Burma. Between 1858 and 1874 he accomplished a phenomenal amount of exploration in these Himalayan regions, often covering extremely difficult terrain, both at high altitude in the north-west of British India and in the humid jungles of the north-east. This minutely detailed book is the fruit of prodigious research into

Godwin-Austen's life and times, showing him to have been a scientist of first rank and an accomplished artist in addition to his outstanding achievements as a surveyor.

Catherine Moorehead, who has herself travelled and climbed in Ladakh, Zanskar and Bhutan, has taken enormous pains to ferret out the origins and history of the Godwin-Austen family, even following them up to the present day. We are first given a vivid picture and potted history of the wealthy Surrey 'squirearchy' from which Godwin-Austen originated, then his life in India is followed, with many original diary extracts, and much fascinating background description of life in mid-Victorian India. The latter half of the book covers the late Victorian and Edwardian period which Godwin-Austen, a dedicated natural historian and taxonomist, devoted to his collections of Indian molluscs and other fauna.

For mountaineers the most interesting part may be his explorations of the Karakoram. In the early 1860s he explored the mountains around Skardu, penetrating among others the Hushe valley, the Chogolungma and Panmah glaciers and most famously, the lower Baltoro. He was the first person to get a moderately close view of K2. Among the many excellent plates in this book is a watercolour he made from his first sighting of K2, some thousands of feet above Urdukas (an essential camping stage about two days trek from the snout of the Baltoro). John Cleare has contributed a photo of the slopes above Urdukas, but it is a pity that the author did not obtain a photograph corresponding more or less precisely to the view that Godwin-Austen sketched. Instead she has included a photo looking back down the Baltoro from Concordia towards Urdukas and Masherbrum. I suspect that some readers may end up a little confused. However she has included a plate of Godwin-Austen's map of the K2 area; how he ascertained the details of his eponymous glacier (which leads from Concordia to K2) and the terrain at the east end of the Baltoro given that he appears to have proceeded no further than Urdukas is something of a puzzle to me.

The story is told with many lively extracts from Godwin-Austen's diaries to embellish the straightforward chronological account. He was a true Victorian polymath measuring, and recording careful observations on, not only the topography and geology of the country he was exploring and the flora and fauna to be found, but also the nature of the agriculture, the types of housing and the clothes, customs and languages of the people he encountered. In 1861 he spent nearly three months in the field, the only westerner with a party of 66 coolies, *shikharis* and an interpreter, and during this time, as we find from the book's detailed appendices, he climbed upwards of twenty passes and peaks ranging up to 5500m, and surveyed parts of about twenty glaciers, including such as the Biafo, Panmah, Choktoi, Chogolungma,and Kerolungma.

The above was only one of his many expeditions. In 1862 he explored Zanskar and Rupshu and climbed a peak of about 6250m in the process, and in 1863 he crossed from Ladakh into western Tibet, but was turned back by the Tibetans. Perhaps more impressive (though less well recorded) were his six seasons of surveying in north-east India, where he had to cope not only with very difficult jungle terrain and an extremely wet climate, but also with hostile headhunting tribes, some of whom used poisoned arrows and laid traps with poisoned stakes.

The book is valuable too for its overall picture of upper-class life in mid-Victorian India and in early twentieth century England, though Godwin-Austen may not have been typical, particularly with his early 'muslim' marriage to a young woman of good birth from the Poonch area of Kashmir. He had two further marriages which are described with sensitivity and depth, his last being the longest and happiest, with a wife who shared his interests in natural history.

While crammed with interesting detail, for my taste this book has not been sufficiently edited. The flow is too often interrupted, and much of the detail seems to stray too far from the main theme. The author's personal experiences are sometimes interlaced into the narrative, in a way that may enliven the narrative for some, but for me felt like an unnecessary distraction. As a teacher of English the author sometimes gives her pedagogical instincts too much sway. Having described the survey team's river crossing in '*zuks*, a native raft made of inflated goatskins to which poplar stakes are lashed and which is propelled by the current and the power of *insh'allah*' we are treated to the following footnote: 'This term, meaning, "If Allah wills it", I first learnt in 1989, after an odyssey of terror being driven in the dark down the Karakoram Highway by two Afghans in a rickety lorry, thousands of feet directly above the murky Indus.'

Though the footnotes appear over-zealous, the appendices are a formidable tribute both to Godwin-Austen's industry and to Catherine Moorehead's tenacity. Her bibliography details eight books by Godwin-Austen; seventeen papers on mountain exploration and surveying; twenty-nine on geology, glaciology and physical geography; ninety-three on malacology and conchology; twenty on ornithology and lepidopterology; thirteen on ethnology and anthropology; and sixteen miscellaneous other publications. Her own sources of books, maps, unpublished papers and websites consulted are all meticulously documented, making the whole a valuable scholarly enterprise. It is only a shame that having delved so deeply she was unable to include more detailed maps of the areas described. The maps provided are only just adequate for the reader to follow the main expeditions.

Geoff Cohen

A Snow Goose and other utopian fictions: Jim Perrin. (Cinnamon Press, 2013, pbk, 228pp, ISBN 978-1-907090-92-9, £8.99.)

> '*The Scots have their whisky, the Welsh have their speech,*
> *Their poets are paid about ten pence a week,*
> *Provided no hard word on England they speak,*
> *Oh Lord! What a price for devotion.*' (Dominic Behan)

How short should a short story be? The question is unanswerable. Conrad's *Secret Sharer* is fifty-three and a half pages long, even in a small print edition. Chekhov's *Misfortune* is a mere twelve and a half. Perhaps length or brevity is not really the point, but rather what makes a tale a short-story is something to do with its form; something to do with the author's ability to create a world or a situation or a relationship in a concise, uncluttered way. You can't waste any words and yet short-story writing is not poetry. What it certainly is, is difficult. Even Anthony Trollope wasn't at his best here – his tales tend to be mini-novels: a common trap. One time in a hundred the Goddess smiles on the struggling writer. She really smiled on Peter Lars Sandberg when he wrote *The Devil's Thumb*, barely 13 pages long, taut and spare; not a word out of place: one of the best climbing stories I've ever read. He'd been at it for a while when he wrote that and it shows.

This is Jim Perrin's first big effort at writing fiction. There are only five stories in this collection which runs to 195 pages (not counting notes). E.M. Forster's *Collected Short Stories*, including *The Machine Stops*, contains 12 stories in 212 pages, so we can certainly say that some of Perrin's tales are long short-stories.

I'll focus on two of them, perhaps the most important ones. *After the Fall* (65 pages) is loosely based on H.G. Wells's *The Country of the Blind* (26 pages). Briefly to summarise: two climbers, one nice and one nasty, fall from a Himalayan peak and find themselves in the country of the Yetis, a race of people having unusual psychic powers, living virtuous, agrarian lives roughly according to Buddhist principles. The nasty climber (Rigby) cannot adapt to life in this rarefied atmosphere, tries to escape and is drowned. The nice climber (Moss) stays on, marries a local girl and eventually, as foretold, their son becomes the new Rinpoche of the monastery at Kartaphu.

Frankly, I found the introductory part of this story tedious and far too long: a couple of paragraphs would have sufficed. (When writing a short story it is a good idea to throw away the first few pages; one usually finds that anything requiring explanation can be done retrospectively). However, the second part is much better. Here Perrin uses his description of the life of the valley in order to criticise western values. All sorts of things come under inspection: egoism, materialism, drunkenness, sex and the way we treat our children. There is wisdom here, perhaps the fruit of long and bitter experience. Moss's spiritual guide, Nunez (himself a refugee from our world), says:

'We do not worship our children, as they do in the countries we left.... Nor do we abuse them. Are not these polarities most telling?' (p78)

The critique of western sexuality is fascinating. The Yetis pair off for life but only make love until the woman is pregnant. Thereafter they become each other's *Dear One*: a little like the couple suggested by the Beatle's wonderful song, but without waiting to reach the age of 64. They are thus freed from the terrible insistence of mechanical desire which seems to plague us and which has spawned the sex industry. Moss remembers a former girlfriend called Lyn peeing on his face in a back garden and Perrin contrasts this nasty image with the innocent but expert love-making which goes to create the future Rinpoche.

Many years pass and, at the conclusion of the tale, Lyn appears again, at Kartaphu, metamorphosed into a 'western Buddhist' but really just the same as she was under this veneer. Moss, now an old man, has travelled there to collect sacred bowls – a spiritual present to the country of the Yetis – from his son. She looks at him:

'There was something familiar about his features, his self-containment... "Are these for sale?" she asked.' It is the perfect comment. The story could have ended there.

Whereas, *After the Fall* is critical of modern sexual attitudes, *The Burning* describes the start of a passionate relationship between two young students in Wales. This was my favourite story and I felt Perrin was really at home here: castigating stuffy Anglo-Saxon attitudes, indulging in a bit of Home Counties bashing and celebrating his beloved Wales. The plot is a simple girl meets boy. They travel through Wales having mini-adventures, fall in love, meet the boy's relations (Auntie Angharad, look you!) who receive them warmly and they end up outside the chemist's shop arguing about who will go in to purchase the condoms (I seem to remember a lanky youth sitting in a battered mini in Ullapool High Street having a similar conversation with a very irritable girlfriend, but at least he eventually did the deed; Perrin's youth lets the girl do it: one up for Scotland, so to speak...).

Summarised like this it seems corny, but it isn't, it's touching and very well done. By contrast with all the warped, western sexuality which Perrin criticises in *After the Fall*, this story reminds us of the possibility of innocent, young love which shines the more brightly for being compared with other relationships glanced at in the tale. It is a nice, ironic touch that the rather Lawrentian description of lovemaking actually occurs in *After the Fall* which, after all, is partly about sexual abnegation. In *The Burning* Perrin only hints at the sexual delight of the young pair, and this is wise. The tale has a dramatic conclusion too which I won't spoil.

In terms of style I think Perrin is too keen to display his learning in these stories: this is a form of self-indulgence. I found the various passages in Welsh intrusive. After all one would hardly include passages in Gaelic in a story about the North West, not, at least, without explaining them for the unenlightened. Learning has to be used sparsely when telling a story: best to let the tale speak for itself.

Perrin shouldn't have quoted directly from H.G. Wells in *After the Fall* – the reader is stopped in his tracks and left wondering why there is this italicised passage and why the style has changed all of a sudden. You really can't quote in fiction, as you may in essay writing, and the use of italics makes the clang all the louder. One could, of course, echo Wells's writing, but the parallel is obvious anyway. The other tales in the collection all have something valuable to say and the reader can discover it for him or her self.

Lloyd-George was the Welsh Wizard, some unkind people called Neil Kinnock a Welsh Windbag, and perhaps there's a little of both qualities in a very good first attempt at the short-story by a justly celebrated master of other forms. Mind you, it's a pity the Welsh are so backward politically. There's no need to burn the Sassenachs' cottages, there are other less messy ways of getting rid of them. Maybe R.S. Thomas had a point when he said:

'You cannot live in the present,
At least, not in Wales...'

By the time this review appears, Scotland may be an independent country. Ireland managed it ages ago, but that was really messy.

Pete Biggar

Ralph's Secret North: Wildest Caithness and Sutherland: Ralph MacGregor. (Curlew Cottage Books, 2013, 206pp, ISBN 978-0-9538703-3-2, £15.99.)

Ralph MacGregor has published two previous books to the 'Far North' – *Ralph's Far North* (2000) and *Hills of the North, Rejoice!* (2004). These two volumes are based on articles which originally appeared in the *Caithness Courier* over many years. They describe Ralph's many solo outings on foot and on bike in, what for many is, a little known part of the country. These earlier volumes were not reviewed in the Journal, but they should have been. I can strongly recommend them. The word 'evocative' succinctly describes Ralph's writings. He clearly has a real feeling for the special landscape in the north of the country. Although some of the chapters describe outings in other mountain areas such as the Cuillin, it is the tales of Ralph's solo adventures in the desolate parts Caithness and Sutherland

that work best. If you wonder if it's possible to have real adventures in that part
of the world, Ralph will certainly enlighten you. The text in both books is also
complemented by delightful line drawings by Moira Webster.

Ralph's Secret North is a rather different sort of book. The emphasis is much
more on colour photographs rather than text. The photographs are generally
excellent and they certainly highlight how wild and beautiful the coastline and
countryside are in the far north. The text, however, is still of great interest. Many
of the outings describe sea-kayaking trips rather than walks.

Many of the photographs in the book may give climbers ideas for new climbs,
though it has to be said the rock is not always the best. The last chapter is about
a sea-kayaking trip to the Island of Stroma north of John o' Groats. There seem
to be opportunities for some impressively long traverse lines on the sea-cliffs on
the west side of the island, including one through a spectacular feature called The
Gloup – not to be confused with a feature of the same name on Deerness, Orkney.

On some of his more serious trips Ralph sought out the company of fellow
paddlers. He must be getting old!

                                                          Noel Williams

The Sunlit Summit: the Life of W.H. Murray: Robin Lloyd-Jones.
(Sandstone Press, 2013, 386pp, ISBN 978-1-908737-38-0, £19.99.)
W.H. Murray, for the benefit of those few readers who may not know of him, was
a strong Glasgow-based climber who became our President 1962–4, our
Honorary President 1989–96, and who wrote two books, – *Mountaineering in
Scotland* (1947, Dent) and *Undiscovered Scotland* (1951, Dent) – which defined
the spirit of traditional mountaineering here for many years.

Robin Lloyd-Jones has put together a biography of Bill Murray which
describes his life and work in a manner liable to appeal strongly to most readers.
There are 34 short and well-focused chapters, 50 excellent photographs, five
appendices, a bibliography (but of books only – I have partly remedied this
below), and a good index. So it is a book that you can dip into, and easily find
whatever might interest you about Murray. There is a certain amount of repetition
across the chapters, but since this assists the virtue just mentioned. There are a few
errors, but since the initial print run was short there will be a second revised
edition before this review appears, so it seems pointless to enumerate them.
There is also an 'Online Appendix' – that is to say, a collection of further
appendices accessed through the Sandstone Press website. This amounts to 274
pages, almost as many as the book itself, which has 358, and the bulk of it is
taken up by a very thorough 'Chronology of Murray's Climbs up to 1945', with
extensive commentary, by Mike Cocker.

The Murray aficionado will complain that there is not much new material in
The Sunlit Summit. We already have a well-reviewed autobiography[1,2,3,4,5],
many obituaries[6], and several useful articles about Murray from our own Journal
and others[7,8,9,10]: naturally, much of the book draws on these sources. And
Lloyd-Jones had no access to Murray's diaries or incoming correspondence,
while publishing outgoing correspondence was prevented by copyright
restriction. So it is not surprising that there are few novelties. One interesting
new claim is that Murray had a 'fairly long-term relationship' in the 1950s with
Fiona Graham (of 'The Grahams'), which eventually came to an end some years

before his marriage to Anne Clark (Chapter 32). Unfortunately, Lloyd-Jones does not tell us how he came by this information. Fiona Graham had the misfortune to see her List of Highland Hills between 2000 and 2500 feet[11] anticipated by Alan Dawson's Highland Marilyns in the same height range[12] in 1992; then, as Helen Fiona Torbet, she was brutally murdered in 1993 by Donald McMillan, the son of her hostess, at a guest house in Inverinate (not Bridge of Orchy as stated by Lloyd-Jones). The other principal novelties are what might be described as extended essays about Murray's interest in mystical theology and meditation (Chapters 12, 13 and 14), and about his methods of writing (Chapters 18, 29 & 30).

So far as the first essay is concerned, was it really true that 'the quest to find self-fulfilment through union with the Divine Essence, with absolute Beauty and Truth, was the most central and important thing in [Murray's] life (p. 97)'? It seems unlikely. The autobiography is about mountaineering, conservation, and writing, but has little to say about mystical theology or meditation beyond an indication of continued interest and practice (p. 286). Certainly there is ample evidence that Murray was a confirmed realist where Beauty was concerned: like the Romantic painters Caspar David Friedrich and Joseph Turner he sought the Sublime in Nature, and endeavoured to portray it. But his attitude to Truth seemed more flexible. Lloyd-Jones recounts how Murray insisted on the retention of the mystical and philosophical passages in *Mountaineering in Scotland* against the advice of Dent's editor, Graham Irving (p. 125, Autobiography p. 129), yet when he came to write his autobiography he spurned the opportunity to write from his heart, if that was what was in it. I prefer to suppose that by then he had realized that an author's first duty was to write what people would want to buy and read, and also that metaphysical and ontological questions were a battleground on which he was not best equipped to fight (see Young's essay[9]).

Turning to Lloyd-Jones' second essay, Chapter 18 'From Coleridge to Changabang' identifies literary influences – largely following Jim Perrin's analysis[13], and Chapter 29 'A Supreme Craftsman at Work' puts a finger on some of the trademark devices used by Murray in his writing. Chapter 30 'At Play in the Fields of Fact' endorses Mike Cocker's view that Murray sometimes mixed fiction with fact in his two best-known books[10]. But Cocker notes two climbs certainly done by Murray which don't appear on his Application Form – Douglas Boulder with Lister, and The Chasm with Laidlaw and Redman, both climbed in 1940 – so it is strange that he should conclude that two other expeditions missing from the Form ('Cairngorm Blizzard' and 'Castle Buttress' from the books) are fictional. Here I am disposed to believe that the two books are truthful accounts of real expeditions. Deception was not one of Murray's devices.

Although there is little in them that is new, Chapters 23 'Highland Landscape' and 24 'Saving the Wild Lands' do a very effective job of describing Murray's valiant work in the '60s and '70s for NTS and the old Countryside Commission (now subsumed by SNH). His book *Highland Landscape*[14] must have given him much satisfaction. Murray's writing and argument are of the highest quality, and the presentation of the book – with superb design by George Mackie and beautiful maps drawn by Robert Anderson – could not be bettered. It deserves all the praise heaped on it by Lloyd-Jones and others. It would doubtless pull a wry grin from the shade of Murray to learn that despite being offered to our members

at a knock-down price on several occasions by the present Librarian, there has
been only one taker. If the modern mountaineer seeks the Sublime, he does not
seek it in Nature.

Robin N Campbell

1. W. H. Murray, *The Evidence of Things Not Seen* (Baton Wicks, 2002).
2. Mike Jacob, 'Review of (1)', *SMCJ,* 38/194 (2003), 502–5.
3. Dave Hewitt, 'Review of (1)', *The Angry Corrie,* 58 (September 2003).
4. Michael Ward, 'Review of (1)', *Alpine Journal,* 108/352 (2003), 343–5.
5. Jonathan Waterman, 'Review of (1)', *American Alpine Journal,* 45/77 (2003), 434–6.
6. Obituaries by Donald McIntyre, Douglas Scott, W.M. Mackenzie & Robert Aitken, *SMCJ,* 36/187 (1996), 149–58.
7. Gordon Smith, 'Sron na Ciche without Cliché', *The Angry Corrie,* 35 (January 1998).
8. Des Rubens, 'W.H. Murray Revisited', *SMCJ,* 37/191 (2000), 253–9.
9. Andrew Young, 'On Faith as the Substance of Things Hoped for', *SMCJ,* 37/191 (2000), 260–70.
10. Mike Cocker, 'Notes on W.H. Murray's Climbing and Writing', *SMCJ,* 42/203 (2012), 119–29.
11. Fiona Graham, 'And now The Grahams', *The Great Outdoors,* (November 1992), 10–13.
12. Alan Dawson, *The Relative Hills of Britain* (Cicerone, (April) 1992).
13. Jim Perrin, 'The Ice Climbers', *Climber & Rambler,* (October 1982), 26–8.
14. W.H. Murray, *Highland Landscape* (Aberdeen U.P. for NTS, 1962).

— · —

Tom Weir: An Anthology: Ed. Hamish Brown. (Sandstone Press, 2013, pbk, 250pp, ISBN 978908737281, £14.99. eBook ISBNe 9781908737298, £14.99, not available for Macs.)
Tom's eyebrows would have risen if he knew his writings as published here were available in electronic form; not that he was switched on digitally, far from it. One day I received a telephone call I could have happily missed – it was Tom wanting advice on word processing. Being very much his own man he ignored my approach and instead followed the preachings of a meenister of the kirk (probably the only time he did), buying some dedicated word processor I had not even heard of. His brave foray into the world of bytes did not last long, but I suspect that one reason was not technical but that he preferred the slightly slower pace of a typewriter, along with the enforced discipline that this needed in order to avoid the white blotches of Tipp-Ex.

I enjoyed reading most of this anthology. The so-far unpublished early pieces from Tom's life are interesting, though marred by typos. I cannot believe that the original manuscripts, now securely held in the blessed NLS, contained these; Tom would have sweated blood in producing them, so I assume they arose during some scanning or typesetting process. The courage of the man, in chucking his job in the Co-op store and starting a new career in the always uncertain world of writing, is to be admired. It could only be taken once his older brother qualified as an engineer and could then be the main breadwinner for the family (Tom's father had been killed in what was then Mesopotamia, and Tom never knew him.)

Hamish Brown, another writer of an earlier generation who disdains the new-fangled computer, has had the thankless task of choosing the writings. I enjoyed the earlier pieces the most, where each and every outing by Tom which gave rise to prose was obviously a new adventure which made an impact on him and so made the words flow that bit easier. The articles on the Scottish islands and Highlands in particular I often found to include some of his best word pictures. In 'Across Sutherland Hills', taken from his book 'Highland Days', Tom sets out alone on his embarkation leave of one week, to explore the wilds of Sutherland with food but sans tent.

'All this land was new to me and my heart rejoiced to recognize Beinn Klibreck and see Ben Loyal leap from the moor in rocky spires. The vastness of these moors made a profound impression: warm-coloured by the sun and threaded by blue streams and dotted by little gems of lochs.'

One of these lochs, approached over the shoulder of Ben Loyal, became a destination, if only for its position in the heart of the mountains.

'What an evening that was! An evening of blue-washed hills and bluer lochs, lochs the colour of blue dye that had seeped into the very burns. For contrast there was the near mass of Klibreck, a great sweep of russet patched with shadow. Shadows in Sutherland, this bare land, assume the significance of physical features, like the vasty sky that domes this edge of Scotland where it fringes the northern seas.'

I even enjoyed his Himalayan expedition writing, something which normally leaves me a bit cold. The sense of youthful excitement and wonder at the scenery he succeeds in transferring to words, a skill which is harder than one might think. Following on from an enjoyable 1952 expedition to the Himalaya, Tom and his companions found that they were left with £50 each of unspent funds. After some calculation of travel costs they realised this would enable a trip to Norway, and so it was! 'They' were Tom, Adam Watson Jnr, and Douglas Scott. Brown had to edit down considerably to fit his available space, but on occasions it would have been good to know more details, especially their names.

In essence however, this anthology should encourage more readers to look up Tom Weir's writings, particularly the available classic books which are in print at a reasonable price. Which takes us neatly to a final point, which is charging the same price for the ebook version as the paperback (in itself a basic production and a shade pricy). Unless the publication has a complex design with many illustrations, there is no excuse for this.

Ken Crocket

My Father, Frank – Unresting Spirit of Everest: Tony Smythe. (Baton Wicks, 2013, hardback, 324pp, ISBN 978-1-898573-87-6, £20.)
Frank Smythe(FS), born in 1900, was arguably Britain's foremost mountaineer during the interwar years, renowned not only for his Alpine and Himalayan exploits but also for his prodigious output as an author, photographer and lecturer. His numerous books, describing stirring adventures in a reflective, lyrical style made him a household name. As a lad, I remember seeing *The Mountain Vision* on the family bookshelf and looking with awe at the black-and-

white photographs of men balancing near huge cornices over dreadful precipices. Eventually, his achievements led to membership of three British expeditions to Everest during the 1930s, although he was not selected for the trip of 1924 (Mallory & Irvine) on the basis of a moot report[1] by Howard Somervell who described the go-getting FS as 'an intolerable companion'. Here's a clue, then, as to why this biography might offer more than just a tribute by a loyal son to a legendary parent. The promise of a whiff of contention always adds spice to a story, presuming that the author is honest with his findings and impartial in his judgements. So, whilst objectivity might be a potential stumbling block for Tony Smythe(TS) the advantage is that he has unique access to the facts of his father's somewhat turbulent upbringing and home life, and these details might help to clarify FS's character. I looked forward to reading this book and I was not disappointed.

The chapters of FS's relatively-short life are described in vivid style with the author adding imaginative descriptions and sensible analyses here and there to give colour to routine facts. TS is an accomplished mountaineer and well placed to make these calls. He adds his own experiences too, at times, and they complement the story rather than intruding upon it. However, it's risky to try to interpret the body language and facial expressions of subjects in photographs as in the photo taken by Graham Macphee of FS and T. Graham Brown at Montenvers in 1927. The author sees (p86) self-consciousness and the imposition of one man's will upon another, whilst I feel that this is an over-interpretation – an example, perhaps, of wishful thinking given what was to eventually happen to the relationship between the two men?

FS had an inauspicious start in life. His father died when he was a baby and his mother became over-protective and stifling. His schooling was a failure and attempts to find a rewarding career ended in disappointment and frustration. However, he felt fulfilled amongst the mountains and decided to try to earn a living by writing about his exploits, a bold venture into unexplored territory. He had followed the traditional route from home hills – including participation in the pivotal first ascent of Longland's Climb on Clogwyn d'ur Arddu – to the Alps, with the obligatory epics and near-misses. There is SMC interest in that he was friends and climbed with J.H.B. Bell and G. Macphee. Then in 1928 came a fateful event that had a double-edged impact upon his life, the first ascent with Brown of Route Major on the Brenva Face of Mont Blanc. This ground-breaking climb opened the expedition and publicity doors for FS but unfortunately a disagreement between the two men over a relatively trivial matter became a bitter quarrel. TS deals with this episode with impartiality and maturity, examining the existing archival material and speaking to those who knew them and leaves it up to the reader to draw his/her own conclusion. Mine, for what it's worth, is that FS allowed his ambition to exacerbate the friction between them but that Brown didn't have the strength of character to accept FS's attempts at reconciliation, preferring instead to carry on a vitriolic campaign of disparagement.

Whilst Brown festered with resentment for the rest of his life, FS moved on and concentrated his energy on his burgeoning writing/lecturing career and on

1   In an ironic role reversal, FS was given the unenviable task of vetting aspirants for the 1936 Everest attempt and his eventual choice excluded Colin Kirkus, the candidate with by far the best climbing record.

expeditions to Kangchenjunga, Kamet and, in 1933, Everest. Aficionados will not need to be reminded that all the early British attempts were upon the north side of the mountain and the description of FS's solo attempt, after his companion Eric Shipton became too tired to continue above camp 6, is gripping. TS writes that the printed words on the page vanished ...I was there with him, willing him to succeed. I too panted in the thin air and felt the powdery snow and icy rock freezing in my hands. I sensed the terrifying void underneath and you have to marvel at FS's resolve, on ground that had turned from being more dangerous than difficult to being both dangerous and difficult, kept warm only with multiple layers of woollen vests and pullovers and with no supplementary oxygen. He reached 28,200 feet, less than a thousand feet to go but a thousand feet, no, a thousand weary miles...

You can taste the anti-climax upon returning to suburbia, the mundane necessities of domestic life and the time-consuming demands of writing/ lecturing. There were two further expeditions to Everest and another trip to the Indian Garhwal where he made several more first ascents including the tricky Mana Peak, an exceptional solo achievement which illustrated his determination and sound judgement. Passages from FS's books/diaries are used to good effect; for example, to contrast the sense of peace of his unexplored Valley of Flowers and its status as a tourist attraction now. But all was not well within his marriage and never really had been. You sense that it was doomed from the outset, especially given FS's long absences and driven nature. TS admits that he faced the prospect of writing about the failed relationship and broken home with trepidation but he handles it with openness and consideration. Then WW2 intervened and FS's mountaineering expertise was put to use, not very successfully in reality, with a spell in the Cairngorms training commandos in mountain/snow warfare about which he knew nothing. Luckily, John Hunt was at hand as his chief instructor. A similar role waited in the Canadian Rockies but it was ended by illness, a transfer to Italy, further medical problems and the end of the war.

FS was never happier than when in a mountain setting, either on his own or with a few close friends or companions, among whom he numbered his native porters. He wrote (in The Spirit of the Hills) that climbing Everest had almost become a national duty far removed from pleasurable mountaineering, so it comes as no surprise that he organised small post-war trips to Switzerland, Canada and India again. Throughout, TS weaves details of FS's personal life and his short time as a young son within it, and it makes for somewhat despairing if unsurprising reading to learn that FS was incapable of showing the paternal love and guidance that had been missing in his own life. Tragically, he succumbed to cerebral malaria in 1949 and it is with frustration that we are told that his second wife later destroyed most of his papers including some 50,000 photo negatives, an act of wanton misjudgement whatever her reasons.

I spotted a few errors. The author is unaware (p39) that the founding of the SMC (1889) predates that of the Yorkshire Ramblers (1892). Bernard, Frank's half-brother, is described (pic.18) as his brother-in-law. The men referred to on p204 as being on the 1921 expedition were actually 1922 members. My pet gripe is the irritating overuse of the comma in the modern idiom. However, these are all minor hiccups and could easily be corrected in a second edition of this excellent, well-researched book in which the author has unearthed some fascinating new material; for example, improbity at the Alpine Club and the spotting in 1936 by Smythe of Mallory's body through a high-powered telescope. There are nearly 100 illustrations with 57 previously unpublished photos although there are no maps so you need to know, for example, the locations of many Alpine huts and peaks. In summary, Tony Smythe has succeeded in producing a thoughtful, candid and poignant portrait of his father; it's interesting, engrossing at times and well worth its cost.

Michael Jacob

More days from a hill diary – Scotland, Norway, Newfoundland, 1951–80: Adam Watson. (Paragon Publishing, 2014, 170pp, IBSN 978-1-78222-176-0, £14.99.)
This delightful little book is a follow-on from an earlier book, *Some days from a hill diary*. Most of the diary excerpts describe winter days on skis throughout Scotland – many with SMC stalwarts, including Glaswegians Tom Weir, Douglas Scott, Allan McNicol, and North-easters, Mike Taylor and David Grieve. Judging by the excellent black-and-white photos, in the 1950s the snow seemed to lie in great quantities and at low altitude for a long time, enabling the author and his friends to don skis at the road or bothy – eliminating a long carry to reach the snow.

Modern ski-mountaineers would shudder at the thought of traversing the Cairngorm high tops with the primitive gear available in the early days. Climbing boots rammed into cable bindings with no toe or heel release; long wooden skis with no metal edges; an old raincoat cut short into something that vaguely resembled an anorak, and old trousers turned into breeches.

July 5, 1952: 'Getting off the bus at Braemar Castle, I took a swede from a field as my food for the weekend.'

One can only hope he had something more nourishing in his pack to keep it company!
And we talk about austerity!
Most of his contemporaries made the annual pilgrimage to the Alps, but Adam saw his natural environment in the north – Iceland, Norway, Canada and Baffin Island – where he took part in some pioneering expeditions and, of course, there was an abundance of his beloved snaa!

I particularly enjoyed reading about his days out with Luibeg keeper, Bob Scott. Bob occasionally shot a hind for his own pot – not the laird's – and was wary of anyone around witnessing the deed. On one occasion, since there were a few walkers in Glen Derry, Adam told Bob to hide the hind and he would carry it back, later in the day, to Luibeg, as Bob found difficulty walking in deep snow.

So, after a ski tour over Beinn Mheadhoin and back down Glen Derry, Adam, with great difficulty hoisted the hind onto his back and skied back the two miles to Luibeg.
And we talk about modern fit mountaineers!
In the 1950s–1960s an enjoyable feature of climbing in the Cairngorms from Luibeg Bothy was the abundance of red deer. Walking up to Luibeg from the Black Bridge in the dark nights of October with the rutting stags roaring, their

eyes shining bright and keeping pace with you in the trees was scary, but it was part of the Cairngorm experience.

February 9, 1954. 'I counted 530 stags, 60 hinds in Glen Lui between Luibeg and the Black Bridge, and about 30 hinds and followers in the woods on the east side of Glen Derry.'

Nowadays, you will be lucky to see any in Glen Lui or the Derry. They have shot most of them.

And we talk about wild life conservation!

Derek Pyper

Far, Far the Distant Peak – The Life of Wilfrid Noyce, Mountaineer, Scholar, Poet: Stewart Hawkins. (Curbans Books, 2014, hardback, 334pp, 42 photographs & 15 maps, ISBN 978-0-9574043-0-4, £25.)

Having been born in 1917, Wilfrid Noyce was roughly a contemporary of Bill Murray, and similarities are readily discerned between these two distinguished mountaineers. Both grew to adulthood largely without a father, Murray's having died at Gallipoli and Noyce's being absent in India; both held army commissions in the Second World War, Murray fighting in North Africa and Noyce cracking Japanese codes in India; and both subsequently abandoned staid occupations (Murray as banker and Noyce as schoolmaster) for the precarious life of the writer. Moreover they shared traits of character, not least a spiritual or indeed mystical response to mountains and in consequence a sometimes discomfiting abstractedness: 'He saw angels on every pitch' (Murray), and 'He's just not with it' (Noyce).

By coincidence this absorbing account of Noyce's life has appeared shortly after Robin Lloyd Jones's biography of Murray, which is reviewed elsewhere in the Journal; and if both books have a weakness it is the author's tendency to eulogise his subject. Stewart Hawkins was a pupil of Noyce when he taught modern languages at Charterhouse in the 1950s, and to his late master he owes his love of climbing and his distinguished service in the Scout movement. Hawkins went on to become a friend of the Noyce family, so his partiality is understandable and in truth readily forgiven.

While still at school, where he was an outstanding scholar and all-round athlete, Wilfrid Noyce had begun to climb on British rock with his older cousin, Colin Kirkus. By the age of nineteen he had put up a dozen hard routes in North Wales, often with the equally talented John Menlove Edwards. Then, as a student at Cambridge, he enjoyed the patronage of A C Pigou which enabled him to climb in the Alps with the prominent guides Armand Charlet (1937) and Hans Brantschen (1938). His natural flair, complemented by fearlessness and superb balance, was thus developed through much early practice with exceptional companions.

Young Wilfrid remained remarkably fresh-faced and scatheless amidst an exotic coterie that included an increasingly troubled Edwards, the dandified G Winthrop Young, and that falsetto-voiced misogynist Arthur Pigou. On Mickledore Grooves however he took a serious fall in 1937 that smashed his jaw and resulted in plastic surgery; and at Easter 1939, having climbed Gardyloo Gully with a CUMC party, he had his leg broken by a dislodged boulder after '…

they had reached the top of Raeburn's Arête.' Hawkins does not explain this puzzling conjunction of routes, but credits Jackson Murray of the SMC with Noyce's evacuation to Fort William the following morning.

In 1942, having been graded 'C' by an army medical board – one wonders why, for he was an exceptionally fit man – Noyce was judged unsuited to active soldiering and was instead hastily taught Japanese and posted to a signals intelligence unit in Delhi. His time in India, which included spells of leave and some months in Kashmir, gave him the opportunity to mount several short expeditions to the Himalaya. These the author relates in some detail, drawing not only on Noyce's diaries but also on archived correspondence with his fellow intelligence officer Ian Grimble, who went on to have a distinguished career as a Scottish historian and broadcaster.

For some years after the war, Noyce's freedom to climb was somewhat constrained by commitments to teaching, to family (he had two young sons), and increasingly to writing. Of this period Hawkins writes that '... in recent years he had done more modest climbs and his activities had been largely confined to taking boys climbing. "I have done little more than being led up Very Severes."' Nevertheless in 1952 he accepted John Hunt's invitation to join the following year's Everest expedition. Although he knew none of the other members except Hunt, and at thirty-four would be one of its oldest members, Wilfrid Noyce had been carefully chosen for his temperament, physique and Himalayan experience. Hawkins quotes Edmund Hillary: 'In many respects I considered Noyce the most competent British climber I had met.'

In later days the tale of the 1953 ascent was widely retold in fund-raising lectures and in several expedition books, not the least being Noyce's own *South Col*, which I can remember being set as a home-reader in the late '60s – for a teenage lad, a well-chosen and congenial alternative to *Pride & Prejudice* or *Hard Times*. Noyce's main contribution on the mountain, as Hawkins explains, was his forcing of the Geneva Spur with the Sherpa Anullu, which opened the route to the South Col and restored the expedition's momentum 'on one of those critical days in the second part of May.' More generally, his ability to rub along with all manner of men was evidently valued, and this indeed was a virtue that surfaced in many places and with diverse companions throughout his climbing career.

In the later 1950s Noyce resumed his climbing in the Alps and greater ranges, often in the company of such Alpine Club luminaries as John Hunt, David Cox and Michael Ward. While some of Noyce's circle (and in particular Hunt) are familiar to the wider public, I suspect that a good few of those mentioned *en passant* by Hawkins will be unknown outside the hallowed halls of the AC and the Climbers' Club. The occasional footnote or thumbnail sketch would therefore have been welcome, not least to describe that unflappable, pipe-smoking history don, David Cox, whose death in 1994 must have deprived Savory's, the Oxford tobacconist, of a sizeable portion of its income; he had at least one route in the Cairngorms to his credit.

Perhaps the high point (for 'summit' is not the *mot juste*) of this later period was the attempt on Machapuchare (22,958ft) in 1957, when Noyce's companions were Cox, Charles Wylie, Roger Chorley and the legendary Jimmy Roberts. Hawkins tells us that this marvellous mountain, an outlier of the Annapurna Range, was in Noyce's estimation the loveliest of all: 'No mountain scene has ever awed me with a greater sense of the beautiful and inaccessible.' After a determined assault with birch-runged rope ladders, Cox and Noyce at last approached that inaccessible summit: 'I rounded a rib, very near the top of everything as I thought, and saw four or five columns of blue ice, like the claws of some great dragon, thrusting up each to its place on the summit ridge: it was the summit itself, perhaps a little under 150 feet above our heads. .... With that we must be content. .... We made our decision almost without speaking, and David turned imperturbably to the important ritual of lighting a pipe.' The summit itself remains unvisited to this day.

During the Machapuchare expedition Roger Chorley caught polio, and the same fate befell Cox in the Alps in 1958 and Don Whillans when he accompanied Noyce to Trivor in 1960. In an interesting appendix, Hawkins considers but eventually dismisses the possibility that Noyce might have transmitted the disease to his companions, of whom only Whillans recovered without permanent disability.

Besides *South Col* and his account of Machapuchare entitled *Climbing the Fish's Tail*, Noyce wrote several other books with a montane flavour, including *Scholar Mountaineers*, which after an erudite introduction goes on to examine the response to mountains of a dozen literary figures, ranging from Dante and Petrarch to Rousseau, Wordsworth and even Nietzsche. His theme (anticipating Robert Macfarlane by half a century) is man's evolving appreciation of the natural world. Though long out of print, it deserves a fuller endorsement than the sentence or two accorded by Hawkins. On the other hand posterity may not look so kindly upon Noyce's poems, which are occasionally quoted in *Far, Far the Distant Peak* and included a lengthy verse biography of Michelangelo. The dictum 'Les poètes ne pensent pas' can be carried too far.

Readers within our own Club will turn with heightened interest to Hawkins's last chapter, which deals with the British-Soviet Pamirs expedition of 1962. This has already been covered in *Red Peak* by Malcolm Slesser, and more recently in *High Endeavours* by Jimmy Cruickshank, whose research and assistance are generously acknowledged by the author. In describing the accident in which Robin Smith and Wilfrid Noyce fell 4,000ft to their deaths while descending Pik Garmo, Hawkins now feels able to divulge which of the two roped men fell first, whereas previous writers have withheld this information. (My understanding is that John Hunt, who led the expedition and was doubtless acting from the best of motives, immediately swore to secrecy those who had witnessed the event. Decades later this pact was broken by one of the English climbers, who spoke freely to Cruickshank; but he in turn remained silent, at the request of Smith's sister and sister-in-law, so long as Noyce's widow was alive.)

Unlike the Russians Sevastianov and Ovchinnikov, whose view of the slip was partly obscured, Derek Bull observed the accident from start to finish; but he saw it from a tent sited fully 2000ft below the point of slippage. Surely the last word should come from Slesser, the deputy leader, whose verdict Hawkins recalls: 'The question of who slipped was not the question of who was to blame.'

Be that as it may, even Noyce's close friends conceded that he could at times be careless. Though not, I believe, quoted in Hawkins's book, there is a passage in John Hunt and David Cox's obituary of him that addressed this: 'But security was a matter to which he appeared to attach too little importance.' Furthermore, Hawkins towards the end of his book includes the following sentence from Slesser's *Red Peak*: 'We wore crampons and there was Wilf, pipe in mouth, axe under one arm, nonchalantly walking down the slope as if it were his garden path.' Was Slesser admiring or censorious? Perhaps we should have been given the later version, from *With Friends in High Places*, which reads as follows.

'I had watched him crampon down the steep slope that falls from the summit of Càrn Mòr Dearg to the CIC Hut, pipe in mouth, one hand in his pocket, his ice axe cradled under his other arm, supremely confident. I was surprised. It would have taken only a tiny off-balance jerk to send him slithering.'

There are some minor mistakes in this book. Hawkins writes Charles Inglis Clark in full, but misspells the name. Sedbergh, that stern nurse of several SMC worthies, should be so spelled. In his index the author credits our member Graeme Nicol, who was medical officer on the Pamirs expedition, with an ascent of the NW Ridge of the Charmoz, which in fact was done by Hamish Nicol of the OUMC. And (perhaps pardonably) he has trouble spelling the name of that admirable Russian Yevgeniy B Gippenreiter, the anglophile descendant of a Tsarist physician, who was an emollient presence on the Pamirs expedition and was later elected to the Alpine Club. Lastly, Hawkins's punctuation is sometimes chaotic and would have attracted a red 'See me!' from his old teacher. Top marks are due, nonetheless, for a thoroughly researched and enthralling biography that reminds us how much was lost through Noyce's untimely death.

Like Murray, Wilfrid Noyce seldom finished a climb without continuing to the summit, there to experience 'that wonderful oblivion which all mountaineers have before the best of views.' Oblivion is now his lot, but through his writings he lives on. It occurs to me that a librarian arranging the Mountaineering shelf will place Noyce's books just right of Murray's. Perhaps only Nietzsche, that admirer of the superman, will sit contentedly between them.

Graeme Morrison

The John Muir Way: a Scottish coast-to-coast route: Sandra Bardwell and Jacquetta Megarry. (Rucksack Readers, 2014, 72pp plus maps, ISBN 978-1-898481-59-1, £11.99.)

It's probably true to say that the SMC's attitude to formal long distance routes in Scotland has always been ambivalent at best. I recall a meeting with the Mountaineering Council back in the early 1980s, when the then MCofS President, the pawky Alex Small, welcomed me with the comment that he didn't know whether I belonged with the enemy (because I'd recently written the official guide to the brand-new West Highland Way) or with the good guys (because I was representing the worthy Scottish Countryside Activities Council). Similarly, my good friend the late and much missed Peter Hodgkiss managed to compile his authoritative and enthusiastic SMC guide to the *Central Highlands* of 1984 without, as I recall, at any point acknowledging the existence of the recently opened West Highland Way (though he did allow me to feature on the jacket photograph, with my very contemporary shaggy hair and scarlet Crimplene shirt: *O tempora! O mores!*).

So I have to declare an interest in this particular form of packaging and commodification of the experience of the Scottish countryside; unfortunately it's not a pecuniary interest, since I sold the copyright of the WHW guide in 1980 for what I quickly but belatedly recognised was a pittance. But then the SMC itself has been in the packaging and commodification business since it published Sir Hugh's Tables in 1891.

The publication of this guide to the new John Muir Way, opened to mark the centenary of John Muir's death, causes me to reflect ruefully on the evolution of Scottish long distance routes since the power to create them was enshrined in the Countryside (Scotland) Act of 1967, and since the West Highland Way was opened on a day of memorable monsoon at Balmaha in October 1980. It isn't hard to see that evolution as an epitome of much wider political and economic processes over the same period: the WHW and its early successor routes were agency-led ventures with 100% national government funding, partly to ensure that they were carefully designed and developed with appropriate infrastructure, to offer high-quality walking routes with evident entity and attractive landscape character. Since that time, as shown by a map in this new guide portraying only the dozen more formally recognised current routes, LDRs have been progressively allowed to proliferate through the operation of individual initiative and the free market to provide Wider Choice for the Consumer, economic benefit for local communities, and a modicum of profit for the writers and publishers of guidebooks. Increasingly implausible thematic justifications have been advanced to provide a spurious basis for routes of very indifferent quality. As a child of the Atlee dispensation, regarding recent larger political and economic processes as deeply retrograde, I can only view the more modest parallel change in LDRs as a sad debasement of the original currency.

For me the John Muir Way, a 134-mile coast-to-coast route from Helensburgh to Muir's natal town of Dunbar, represents a new low. It's a cobbling-together of very varied bits of pre-existing paths and minor roads with long stretches of canal towpath, largely through the 'countryside around towns' and indeed through several towns of Central Scotland, not to mention Auld Embro itself. To attach the name of the Bearded Patriarch of the American Wilderness to this pedestrian assemblage is an egregious absurdity. To their eternal credit, the authors of this efficient and eminently practical guidebook acknowledge that Muir 'probably wouldn't have been interested in this Scottish route, and might have been baffled by its use of his name'.

Rucksack Readers have established a reputation for crisp, user-friendly guides; Sandra Bardwell and Jacquetta Megarry are a formidably experienced partnership. They have assembled a remarkably effective step-by-step notebook-format guide to the John Muir Way, nimbly negotiating the complications that some of the route was not yet final when they went to press, that lengths of it provide alternative routes for walkers and for cyclists, and that they themselves offer preferred variants in several places. I do regret the narrow focus of their guidance: they most assuredly know their market, but producing an intensely practical guide for use in the hand means that background information, other than a couple of brief but useful preliminary chapters on the Canal Heritage and Habitats & Wildlife, is limited to small gobbets in text boxes. A great opportunity has been passed over to explore and explain, for Scots as well as for visitors, the huge significance of Central Scotland, a historical frontier zone and cockpit from AD140 to 1746, and a key centre of the British Industrial Revolution, among much else.

Ironically, for me the best thing in the guide is an admirably lucid succinct three page note on Muir's life and work, perhaps from the pen of Dr Bardwell, who has a laudable history of concern for conservation of wild land, not least in her native Australia. Perhaps the main omission is any detectable hint of humour to leaven the minute instructions on where to turn left or right and the frequent injunctions to apply due care and attention to crossing busy roads. The essential absurdity of the Way's concept and naming surely required a touch of levity here and there.

SMC members, for reasons of the ambivalence mentioned at the outset as well as for the lack of mountain interest in the route, would seem unlikely to want to engage with the John Muir Way except possibly in short accessible sections for mild exercise. Those who've succumbed to cycling may find it an entertaining if sometimes pernicketingly indirect mode of crossing the central isthmus.

Bob Aitken

Iceman: the making of a glaciologist: Stan Paterson. (Papyngay Press, 2014, pbk, 214pp, ISBN 978-0975574935, £7.91 available from Amazon.)
This story tells how Stan Paterson, a native of Joppa, Edinburgh became a glaciologist and the author of a standard text book on the subject and, almost as a sideline, an adventurous mountaineer – or maybe it was the other way around. His accounts of the 1952 traverse of the Greenland ice cap and surveying in South Georgia with Duncan Carse record the last stages of the primitive heroic age of scientific exploration. His career thus spanned an interesting period. When he began in the fifties of last century the arctic regions were difficult and expensive to visit only possible by government sponsored expeditions – now they are a popular holiday destination. There were equal changes in technology.

Stan's career in glaciology began with the 1952 British North Greenland Expedition which made a traverse of the ice cap determining its depth by bouncing sound waves off the bottom. Results were worked out with log tables and hand-cranked mechanical computers. Nowadays research is well supported and a range of modern techniques are available. Ice cores can be taken through hundreds of metres of ice, new techniques for analysing different layers are available and computers make the treatment of numerical data quick and easy. At the beginning of Stan's career Continental Drift and global warming were almost disreputable speculations; now they are accepted facts. His subject has expanded in many directions and Stan's work has been useful in the interpretation of the icecaps on Mars and the ice shelves on that Jovian planet Europa.

His mountaineering exploits were considerable and are briefly and refreshingly described. He climbed in his native Scotland, Greenland, the Alps, the BC Coast Range and the Canadian Arctic. These would make a book in themselves.

His style is low-key and matter-of-fact with a counterpoint of quiet humour which makes his story delightfully readable.

I H M S

— . —

ERRATA

There was a mistake in a photo caption in the 2013 Journal.
Page 637. The date was 'Sunday 7 April 2013'.

ORDERING THE SMC JOURNAL

Members should automatically receive a copy of the Journal when it is published. Members wishing to order extra copies or non-members wishing to place a regular order should contact the Distribution Manager, Roger Robb, by e-mail <journal.distribution@smc.org.uk>.

SMC JOURNAL BACK NUMBERS

Back numbers of the Journal may be obtained from Clifford Smith, 16 House o' Hill Gardens, Edinburgh, EH4 2AR.

e-mail: <journal.archive@smc.org.uk>
tel: 0131-332 3414   mob: 07748 703 515

The following years are available:

	Year			Year
£5.00	1972		**£12.95**	2000
	1977			2001
	1978			2002
	1979			2003
	1980			2004
	1983			
			£13.95	2005
£5.50	1985			2006
				2007
£5.70	1986			
	1987		**£13.95**	2005
	1989			2006
	1990			2007
	1991			2008
	1992			
			£14.95	2009
£6.95	1993			2010
	1994			2011
	1995			2012
				2013
£8.95	1996			
	1997			
	1998			
£11.95	1999			

Post & Packaging is extra.

SCOTTISH MOUNTAINEERING CLUB HUTS

Bookings can be made to stay at any of the five Club Huts by contacting the relevant Custodian.

CHARLES INGLIS CLARK MEMORIAL HUT, BEN NEVIS
Location: (NN 167 722) On the north side of Ben Nevis by the Allt a' Mhuilinn. This hut was erected by Dr and Mrs Inglis Clark in memory of their son Charles who was killed in action in the 1914–18 War.
Custodian: Robin Clothier, 35 Broompark Drive, Newton Mearns, Glasgow, G77 5DZ.
e-mail <cic@smc.org.uk>

LAGANGARBH HUT, GLEN COE
Location: (NN 221 559) North of Buachaille Etive Mor near the River Coupall.
Custodian: Bernard Swan, 16 Knowes View, Faifley, Clydebank, G81 5AT.
e-mail <lagangarbh@smc.org.uk>.

LING HUT, GLEN TORRIDON
Location: (NG 958 562) On the south side of Glen Torridon.
Custodian: John T Orr, 8 Fleurs Place, Elgin, Morayshire, IV30 1ST.
e-mail <ling@smc.org.uk>.

NAISMITH HUT, ELPHIN
Location: (NC 216 118) In the community of Elphin on the east side of the A835.
Custodian: Andrew Tibbs, Crown Cottage, 4 Crown Circus, Inverness, IV2 3NQ.
e-mail <naismith@smc.org.uk>.

RAEBURN HUT, LAGGAN
Location: (NN 636 909) On the north side of the A889 between Dalwhinnie and Laggan.
Custodian: Clive Rowland, Inverene, Links Place, Nairn, IV12 4NH.
e-mail <raeburn@smc.org.uk>.

SCOTTISH MOUNTAINEERING CLUB GUIDEBOOKS

Published by THE SCOTTISH MOUNTAINEERING TRUST

HILLWALKERS' GUIDES
The Munros
Munros GPS data sets – from SMC website
The Corbetts and other Scottish hills
The Cairngorms
Central Highlands
Islands of Scotland including Skye
North-West Highlands
Southern Highlands

SCRAMBERS' GUIDES
Highland Scrambles North
Skye Scrambles

CLIMBERS' GUIDES
Scottish Rock Climbs
Scottish Winter Climbs
Scottish Sports Climbs
Inner Hebrides & Arran
Ben Nevis
The Cairngorms
Glen Coe
Highland Outcrops
Lowland Outcrops
North-East Outcrops
Northern Highlands North
Northern Highlands Central
Northern Highlands South
Skye The Cuillin
Skye Sea-Cliffs & Outcrops

OTHER PUBLICATIONS
Ben Nevis – Britain's Highest Mountain
The Cairngorms – 100 Years of Mountaineering
A Chance in a Million? – Scottish Avalanches
Hostile Habitats
The Munroist's Companion
Scottish Hill Names – Their origin and meaning

e-BOOKS
Cairngorms Scene and Unseen
A Century of Scottish Mountaineering
A History of Glenmore Lodge

APPLYING FOR MEMBERSHIP OF
THE SCOTTISH MOUNTAINEERING CLUB

The following notes are provided outlining the principles by which climbers may be admitted to membership of the Club.

The Committee does not lay down any hard and fast rules when considering applications but considers each case on its own merits. Candidates must be over 18 and have experience of mountaineering in Scotland in both summer and winter. This experience should have extended over a period of at least four years immediately prior to application and should not be confined to just a single climbing district.

The normally expected climbing standards include:

- Experience of winter climbing including several routes of around Grade IV standard and the ability to lead climbs of this level of difficulty.
- Rock climbing experience including climbs of Very Severe (4c) standard and the ability to lead routes of this level of difficulty. In considering applications, emphasis will be placed on multi-pitch climbs in mountain locations.
- The ascent of at least 50 Munros of which at least one third should have been climbed in snow conditions.

In short, the candidate should be able to show – by producing a detailed list of climbs – that they are competent to lead a variety of outings in the mountains of Scotland in both summer and winter. The technical standards specified refer to applicants currently active and may be varied at the discretion of the Committee for older candidates provided that the applicant's routes reflect a reasonable standard for their time. Climbing in the Alps and elsewhere is taken into consideration. Candidates who do not fulfil the normal qualifications listed above but who have made special contributions to Scottish mountaineering in the fields of art, literature or science may receive special consideration.

It is essential that each candidate, before applying, should have climbed with the member proposing the application. It is also desirable that a candidate should be introduced to a member of the Committee before the application is considered. Application forms must be obtained on behalf of candidates by members of the Club who may not propose or support candidates for election during their own first two years of membership. The annual membership fee is £40.00 (£30.00 for those aged 65 and over) which includes the Club Journal.

A fuller version of these notes for members wishing to propose candidates is available from the Club Secretary who is happy to advise candidates and members on any aspect of the application process. Please contact John R R Fowler, Honorary Secretary at:
        e-mail: <jrrfowler@tiscali.co.uk>
        tel: 0131 226 4055.

OFFICE BEARERS 20013–14

Honorary President: Iain H.M. Smart
Honorary Vice-Presidents: Neil Quinn and Bill Skidmore
President: John R.G. Mackenzie
Vice-Presidents: Stephen D. Kennedy and Roger J.C. Robb

Honorary Secretary: John R.R. Fowler, 4 Doune Terrace, Edinburgh, EH3 6DY. **Honorary Treasurer:** John A. Wood, Spout Close, Millbeck, Keswick, CA12 4PS. **Honarary Membership Secretary:** Geoff Cohen, 198/1 Grange Loan, Edinburgh, EH9 2DZ. **Honorary Meets Secretary:** John R.R. Fowler. **Honorary Editor of Journal:** D. Noel Williams, Solus Na Beinne, Happy Valley, Torlundy, Fort William, PH33 6SN. **Honorary Librarian & Honorary Archivist:** Robin N. Campbell, Glynside, Kippen Road, Fintry, Glasgow, G63 0LW. **Honorary Custodian of Slides:** David Stone, 30 Summerside Street, Edinburgh, EH6 4NU. **Honorary Reporter on Accounts:** David Small, 5 Afton Place, Edinburgh, EH5 3RB. **SMC Webmaster:** Tony Stone, 36 Huntingtower Road, Sheffield, S11 7GR. **Convener of Publications Sub-Committee:** Rab Anderson, 24 Paties Road, Edinburgh, EH14 1EE. **Convener of Huts Sub-Committee:** Andrew M. James, 41 Urquhart Road, Dingwall, IV15 9PE. **Representative to the MCofS:** Brian R. Shackleton, 4A Campbell Road, Edinburgh, EH12 6DT. **Committee:** Robert Durran, James Edwards, Helen G S Forde, Adrian Hart, Graeme N. Hunter and Ruth Love.

Journal Information

Editor: Noel Williams, Solus Na Beinne, Happy Valley, Torlundy, Fort William, PH33 6SN. **e-mail** <journal@smc.org.uk>

New Routes Editor: Andy Nisbet, 20 Craigie Avenue, Boat of Garten, PH24 3BL. **e-mail** <newroutes@smc.org.uk>

Photos Editor: (Vacant)

Distribution: Roger Robb, Blaven, Upper Knockbain Road, Dingwall, IV15 9NR. **e-mail** <journal.distribution@smc.org.uk>

Back Numbers: Cliff Smith. **e-mail** <journal.archive@smc.org.uk>

INSTRUCTIONS TO CONTRIBUTORS

The Editor welcomes contributions from members and non-members alike. Priority will be given to articles relating to Scottish mountaineering. Articles should be submitted by 1 May if they are to be considered for inclusion in the Journal of the same year. Material is preferred in electronic form and should be sent by e-mail direct to the Editor. Most common file formats are acceptable – PDF, Open Document Format (odt), Rich Text Format (rtf), Plain Text (txt) or MS Word (doc/docx).

LibreOffice is an open-source, multi-platform productivity suite which is free for individuals to download from <www.libreoffice.org/download/>.

Those without access to e-mail can send hard copy (typewritten and double-spaced) by post to the Editor's home address. Illustrations not relating to an article should be sent to the Photos Editor.